CHALLENGES TO THE
HUMAN RIGHTS
OF PEOPLE WITH
INTELLECTUAL
DISABILITIES

CHALLENGES TO THE
HUMAN RIGHTS
OF PEOPLE WITH
INTELLECTUAL
DISABILITIES

EDITED BY
FRANCES OWEN
AND DOROTHY GRIFFITHS

Foreword by Orville Endicott

Jessica Kingsley *Publishers*
London and Philadelphia

First published in 2009
by Jessica Kingsley Publishers
116 Pentonville Road
London N1 9JB, UK
and
400 Market Street, Suite 400
Philadelphia, PA 19106, USA

www.jkp.com

Library of Congress Cataloging in Publication Data
Challenges to the human rights of people with intellectual disabilities / edited by Frances Owen and Dorothy Griffiths, foreword by Orville Endicott.
   p. cm.
Includes bibliographical references and index.
ISBN 978-1-84310-590-9 (pb : alk. paper) 1. Mental health laws. 2. People with mental disabilities--Civil rights. I. Owen, Frances Ann, 1952- II. Griffiths, Dorothy M., 1950-
K640.C448 2009
342.08'7--dc22

                           2008028262

British Library Cataloguing in Publication Data
A CIP catalogue record for this book is available from the British Library

ISBN 978 1 84310 590 9
eISBN 978 1 84310 590 9

Dedication

This book is dedicated to the memory of Kathy Tweedy
who was a personal and professional inspiration
for the original 3Rs Team,

To the members of the 3Rs Actors Advisory Group
for their patience and generosity of spirit,

and

To the memory of our friend, Peter Pascoe,
who brightened our lives

Acknowledgements

Completion of this project has required the cooperation of many people. The chapters in this book have emerged from frustration, anger, anguish, inspiration, dedication and the plain hard work of self-advocates and people who strive to support them as researchers, care providers, friends and family members. We hope that these profound feelings are clear in the pages that follow. We owe a particular debt of gratitude to all the contributors to this book who believe in the critical importance of a global commitment to furthering the human rights of people who have been identified as having intellectual disabilities.

The 3Rs: Rights, Respect and Responsibility project that inspired this book has been evolving since 2000 thanks to the hard work and creativity of many undergraduate, graduate and doctoral students, research assistants and community agency staff who continue to build it. Some of these are chapter contributors.

The members of the 3Rs: Rights, Respect and Responsibility project team are indebted to the Social Sciences and Humanities Research Council of Canada, the Canadian Institutes of Health Research, the Ontario Trillium Foundation, Human Resources and Skills Development Canada, Employment Ontario, Community Living Welland Pelham, and Brock University for providing funds to support our research.

Working with Jessica Kingsley Publishers has been an utter delight. We wish to thank Stephen Jones, Lucy Mitchell and Melanie Wilson for their kind and skilful guidance. We have been unfailingly impressed by their patience and good humour.

Personally, we would like to thank our families, who supported us during this project.

Contents

FOREWORD BY ORVILLE ENDICOTT   11

Introduction: The Rights Education Project that Inspired this Book.
Frances Owen, Brock University, Ontario and Dorothy Griffiths, Brock University, Ontario.   15

1. **Historical and Theoretical Foundations of the Rights of Persons with Intellectual Disabilities: Setting the Stage.**
    Frances Owen; Dorothy Griffiths; Donato Tarulli, Brock University, Ontario and Jacqueline Murphy, Niagara University, New York.   23

2. **The Emergence of the Human Rights of Persons with Intellectual Disabilities in International Law: The Cases of the Montreal Declaration on International Disabilities and the United Nations Convention on the Rights of Persons with Disabilities.**
    Jocelin Lecomte, West Montreal and Lisette-Dupras Readaption Centers, Quebec and Céline Mercier, University of Montreal, Quebec.   43

3. **Right to Life.**
    Shelley L. Watson, Laurentian University, Ontario and Dorothy Griffiths.   76

4. **Self-Determination and the Emerging Role of Person-Centred Planning: A Dialogical Framework.**
    Donato Tarulli and Carol Sales, Brock University, Ontario.   102

5. **Legal Rights and Persons with Intellectual Disabilities.**
    Voula Marinos, Brock University, Ontario; Dorothy Griffiths; Leanne Gosse, Brock University, Ontario; Jennifer Robinson, University of Waterloo, Ontario; J. Gregory Olley, University of North Carolina, North Carolina and William Lindsay, University of Abertay, Dundee.   124

6. **Medical Rights for People with Intellectual Disabilities.**
    *Yona Lunsky, University of Toronto, Ontario; Paul Fedoroff, University of
    Ottawa, Ontario; Kajsa Klassen, Brock University, Ontario; Carolyn Gracey,
    Centre for Addiction and Mental Health, Ontario; Susan Havercamp, University
    of South Florida, Florida; Beverly Fedoroff, Athabasca University, Alberta and
    Nicholas Lennox, The University of Queensland, Queensland.*   155

7. **Sexuality and Human Rights of Persons with
    Intellectual Disabilities.**
    *Deborah Richards, Community Living Welland Pelham, Ontario; Nancy
    Miodrag, McGill University, Quebec; Shelley L. Watson, Laurentian University,
    Ontario; Maurice Feldman, Brock University, Ontario, Marjorie Aunos, West
    Montreal and Lisette-Dupras Readaption Centers, Quebec; Diane
    Cox-Lindenbaum, Private Clinician, Connecticut and Dorothy Griffiths.* .   184

8. **Right to Evidence-Based Treatment for Individuals
    with Developmental Disabilities: Issues of the Use of
    Therapeutic Punishment.**
    *Tricia Vause, Brock University, Ontario; Kaleigh Regehr, Brock University,
    Ontario; Maurice Feldman, Brock University, Ontario; Dorothy Griffiths
    and Frances Owen.*   219

9. **Rights and Education.**
    *Christine Y. Tardif-Williams, Brock University, Ontario; Marion Trent-Kratz,
    Brock University, Ontario; Krystine Donato, Brock University, Ontario.* . .   240

10. **Ensuring Rights: Systemic and Educational
    Approaches.**
    *Frances Owen; Mark Julien, Brock University, Ontario; Carol Sales; Christine Y.
    Tardif-Williams; Barbara Vyrostko, Community Living Welland Pelham,
    Ontario and Karen Stoner, Autism Ontario, Ontario.*   263

    CONTRIBUTORS   280

    SUBJECT INDEX   282

    AUTHOR INDEX   285

List of Figures and Tables

Table 5.1 Abilities related to the notion of competency   139
Table 5.2 Strengths and challenges when questioning persons with
intellectual disabilities   145
Table 6.1 The role of the triad in the process of health promotion   165
Figure 7.1 Multifaceted systems approach   209
Figure 8.1 Frequency of all punishment procedures used in JABA treatment
studies from 1985 through 2005   239
Figure 8.2 Frequency of individual punishment procedures used in JABA
treatment studies from 1985 through 2005   239

Foreword

In most parts of the world and in the community of nations, the second half of the 20th century witnessed the emergence of specifically articulated human rights in the face of blatant discrimination against women and minority groups. Driving these domestic and international declarations was a growing acceptance of the obligations of states and international bodies to proclaim and enforce those rights. The Universal Declaration of Human Rights, adopted by the United Nations General Assembly in 1948, was the foundation upon which the structure of rights began to take shape. The Declaration was specific about certain groups whose human rights were to be protected: those who were identifiable by 'race, colour, sex, language, religion, political or other opinion, national or social origin, property, birth', concluding with the catch-all category of 'other status' (Article 2). If anyone of influence in the drafting process was talking about disability as a possible named ground of prohibited discrimination, their suggestions obviously were not compelling enough for the representatives of the nations to include such a ground in the Universal Declaration of Human Rights.

Thirty years ago the Canadian Association for the Mentally Retarded (then the name of what is now the Canadian Association for Community Living) hired a lawyer to establish a National Legal Resource Service. This new service was housed in an office in the Kinsmen Building on the York University campus in Toronto – a building that had been constructed a decade or so earlier as a research centre, complete with one-way glass windows to enable researchers to observe subjects and record data about their behaviour.

An outspoken person in Alberta who published a private newsletter on topics related to intellectual disability covered the story. She obviously agreed that it was high time for the national Association committed to enhancing the quality of life of Canadians who had such disabilities to change its focus from the study of their limitations to promoting changes in the behaviour of the Canadian society that had imposed its own set of limitations upon them. She wrote, 'The retarded need more psychologists like Custer needed more Indians'.

While that observation was crude and provocative, it spoke volumes. The Association that is now known at the national, provincial and territorial levels, and in hundreds of Canadian towns and cities as Community Living, had been formed, beginning in the early 1950s, expressly to advocate for the right of children with intellectual disabilities to be educated (a right that had been almost universally denied until then), and not simply to explore ways in which their education could be carried out more effectively.

Education was the initial focus of what was to become the community living movement, but definitely not the only activity that had been historically off-limits to people with intellectual disabilities. Employment, health services, income support, justice for victims of crime and for those charged with criminal offences, protection from abuse and neglect, the dignity of acquiring control of one's own behaviour without recourse to restraints and aversive interventions, voting in elections, freedom to make decisions for oneself, and opportunities to live in ordinary human relationships in ordinary communities – all of these were experiences consistently and significantly diminished or totally denied to those with intellectual disability labels, and most of them are addressed in this anthology.

One of the most fascinating things about this volume is that only one of its 32 contributors is a lawyer. The rest are teachers and practitioners in various clinical or educational fields, but all of them have a clear understanding of, and commitment to, the principle that every person is entitled to be treated on equal terms with their fellow citizens. The selection of authors demonstrates and affirms a theme that keeps recurring in virtually every chapter, namely that there is an emerging 'culture of rights' that is embedding itself in people's thinking, and particularly in the thinking of the members of professions that have historically been primarily focused on 'fixing' people, rather than fixing the policies, practices, laws and other structures of the society of which they are a part. Here we have ample evidence that leaders in such disciplines are well on the way to realizing that persons who have intellectual disabilities can only really flourish when the supports they need in their personal lives are undergirded by a full recognition of the inherent and equal value of their lives permeating the societal contexts in which those lives are lived. Put more simply, no one can achieve optimal personal development without inclusion and participation in all aspects of life in the community.

It took nearly a quarter of a century before the United Nations (UN) began to adopt new declarations specifically focused on the rights of persons with disabilities, beginning, interestingly enough, with the Declaration on the Rights of Mentally Retarded Persons in 1971 – four years earlier than the more general Declaration on the Rights of Disabled Persons. The latest and most significant milestone at the international level was the adoption by the UN General Assembly of the Convention on the Rights of Persons with Disabilities in December 2006. That Convention is described in detail in Chapter 2 of this book. Since it was opened for ratification by individual countries as of September 25, 2008, 41 countries have ratified the UN Convention on the Rights of Persons with Disabilities, meaning that the critical number of 20 ratifications has been attained, making the observance of the provisions of the Convention a binding treaty obligation on the part of those who have ratified it. Because Canada is a federation in which the provinces and territories are charged with the obligation to provide most public services required by persons with disabilities, ratification of the UN Convention will probably take more time. This volume ought to be a useful contributor to hastening that process, in that it sets out the rationale for recognizing rights entitlements, as well as examples of how those entitlements are already guaranteed in our existing statutes, judicial decisions and government policies.

In this country, federal, provincial and territorial human rights legislation followed a similar incremental path to that which unfolded at the United Nations. The principle that persons with disabilities are entitled to the same rights as the rest of the population began to make its way into our statutes and common law in the 1970s and 1980s, two or three decades after the first human rights statutes were enacted. This developmental period culminated in the adoption in 1982 of the Canadian Charter of Rights and Freedoms, which enshrines 'mental or physical disability' in the section 15 equality guarantee. Canada became the first country in the world specifically to guarantee the rights of persons with disabilities in its Constitution. The second and third countries to do so, as a matter of interest, were Germany and South Africa – the two countries that had been among the most egregious violators of human rights in the 20th century.

The United Nations website speaks of the Convention on the Rights of Persons with Disabilities this way:

> The Convention marks a 'paradigm shift' in attitudes and approaches to persons with disabilities. It takes to a new height the movement from viewing persons with disabilities as 'objects' of charity, medical treatment and social protection towards viewing persons with disabilities as 'subjects' with rights, who are capable of claiming those rights and making decisions for their lives based on their free and informed consent as well as being active members of society. (United Nations n.d.)

I commend this collection of essays for its elucidation of how that paradigm shift has informed the thinking of the authors, as representatives of the support service professions, and how it can and should be expressed in practical terms to welcome and empower individuals. The fact that the book's title begins with the word 'Challenges' conveys the reality that the full entitlement of persons who have intellectual disabilities to be treated as equals has yet to be universally achieved. A book such as this both demonstrates the progress that has been made over recent years, and will also serve to enhance respect for the human rights of persons with intellectual disabilities in the years to come.

Orville Endicott
Community Living Ontario
September 2008

REFERENCE

United Nations (n.d.) 'Convention on the Rights of Persons with Disabilities.' Available at www.un.org/disabilities/default.asp?id=150. Accessed on 28 November 2008.

Introduction:
the Rights Education Project
that Inspired This Book

Frances Owen and Dorothy Griffiths

For those who have been associated with people who have intellectual disabilities as family members, friends, neighbours, co-workers, support professionals or consultants, the experience of witnessing or hearing about rights violations of people with disabilities is all too familiar. As illustrated in the chapters that follow, from the beginning of recorded history people with disabilities have been enslaved, abused, and neglected. This book was inspired by the courage of people with intellectual disabilities who have survived challenges and have worked to make changes in their lives and those of others, including the clinicians and researchers who have contributed to the chapters that follow. It focuses on human rights as liberation, a belief that prompted the development of the 3Rs: Rights, Respect and Responsibility community–university research alliance that has been working to develop and test methods of providing rights education for people who have intellectual disabilities, their care providers and family members.

A critical first step in protecting human rights is informing people about the nature of their rights. 'People who do not know their rights are more vulnerable to having them abused and often lack the language and conceptual framework to effectively advocate for them' (Flowers 1998). The libratory function of education for oppressed peoples has been described compellingly by Paulo Freire (1983) as by those labouring in the American civil rights movement (Herbers 1998). Ramdas (1997) went so far as to suggest that 'we need to redefine Adult Education as Human Rights Education on a global scale' (p.38). Some rights education curricula do exist (cf. Amnesty International 1997; Buckingham 1998; Pike and Selby 1997); however, the specific focus on rights education in the context of the lives of people with identified intellectual disabilities has not been prevalent in the research literature despite the development of local programs (Middlesex Community Living 2000a, b, c, d). Navigating rights issues in the complex context of everyday life requires a broad-based understanding of rights principles and the manner in which they can be applied both responsibly and respectfully. For this reason, rights education must be contextually grounded (Brabeck and Rogers 2000; Owen *et al.* 2003), especially to avoid putting people who are vulnerable at even greater risk as they challenge the status quo.

The development of such a contextually grounded and systematically evaluated rights education program for adults with intellectual disability has been undertaken by a group of researchers and community service providers in Canada. Inspired by a desire to reduce the well-documented elevated risk of abuse for people with intellectual disability (Mazzucchelli 2001; Sobsey 1994) the 3Rs: Rights, Respect and Responsibility research team began in 2000 by assisting a community agency to develop a human rights statement that would guide its functioning. The existence of a statement, developed based on national and international codes, begged the question of which of those principles to which the agency had committed itself were being violated in everyday practice. An extensive survey was conducted that examined the perceptions of both people with intellectual disabilities and their care providers (Griffiths *et al.* 2003). Rights concerns were identified by all groups of respondents, although none was of a seriously and imminently threatening nature. The existence of rights violations, in turn, necessitated the development of rights education for managers, staff and people supported by the agency.

The title of the project 3Rs: Rights, Respect and Responsibility reflects the team's commitment to providing rights information in a socially contextualized manner. Since rights exist for all people equally, there is a high probability that, for people living in shared settings such as group homes, personal rights may conflict in specific daily activities. For example, if a group home has only one television and there is a conflict over which program to watch, since all house members have equal rights to television access, some compromise is required. The 3Rs team has characterized this negotiation as honouring social respect and taking responsibility for one's actions. We see these as inextricably linked to the enactment of rights in a social context.

From the start, the 3Rs project has been committed to a systemic approach to rights education, recognizing that informing people with disabilities about their rights without the prior existence of a responsive infrastructure was, at worst, potentially abusive and at best irresponsible. For this reason, the team has committed itself to training staff prior to training the people they support in order to insure that expressed rights violations will be received in a supportive manner. For staff, rights training can provide a challenge to the way in which they conceive of their job responsibilities. Staff in community services may view their role as largely protective. While this is certainly not carried to the extent that it was in the days of closed institutions, protection in this case refers to the challenge of balancing Perske's (1972) 'dignity of risk' with the need to insure that people they are supporting are not put in the way of obvious harm. The definition of serious harm is, of course, contentious and open to situational interpretation. To assist in negotiating this difficult balance the project includes a requirement that all participating agencies have in place a rights adjudication committee to receive concerns from both people supported by the agency and from staff (Owen *et al.* 2003).

The 3Rs educational package includes three formats. All formats have as their central goal, facilitation of participants' ability to differentiate between rights violations and nonviolations, to describe the nature of violations and to describe or enact appropriate remedial actions to address the rights problem.

The first version of our training program is an adult-education class-room-based format that introduces the key concepts of rights, respect and responsibility and allows for discussion of the relevance of these principles to the everyday life of training participants (Owen *et al.* 2003; Tardif-Williams *et al.* 2007; Tarulli *et al.* 2004). The second version of the program includes an interactive CD-ROM that presents videotaped scenarios of everyday rights dilemmas with built-in choice points that allow participants to select between two options that are then played out to their logical conclusion. A narrator guides participants through this process. Evaluation of this program showed significant pre–post improvement in participants' ability to identify, describe and suggest remedial action for rights violations (Tardif-Williams *et al.* 2007). Currently, the 3Rs team is testing a game-based version of the training.

The growth in the international focus on human rights awareness is promoting changing social attitudes and methods of providing support for people with disabilities. Fortunately, the increasing focus on the rights of people with intellectual disabilities has, to some extent, resulted in the loss of cheap labour for exploitive employers and a challenge to the hegemony of the professions. As people with disabilities are educated about their rights and make decisions about their own lives, their relationships, where they work and live, their medical care and their consumer behaviour, those who care about them are facing the challenge of redefining their role to living with what Robert Perske (1972) called the 'dignity of risk'. The historic pull between the protection of the individual and the protection of the community at large has, to some extent, given way to a different dichotomy: the tension between protection of the individual and the promotion of the individual's right to self-determination. This poses a vast range of questions for families and for care providers. If my family member chooses to stay out late at a party how do I know he will come home safely when he cannot read street signs? Will I be responsible as a group home carer if a person whom I support chooses to eat a poor diet? Should I restrict a person's access to sugar if she is diabetic? I thought my job was to support people but how can I do that if I am accused of infringing on rights when I try to keep them safe?

While a theoretical commitment to human rights would likely receive general support from most care providers, the enactment of this commitment is considerably more complex, as illustrated by these questions. The nature of choice, whether for a person with a disability, a family member or a person providing care, always includes an element of social risk. Group living demands compromise whether in a family context or in the context of a group home.

As Flowers (1998) has suggested, people who are not aware of their rights cannot exercise them effectively. The goal of the 3Rs rights education program is to provide information about rights to both individuals who have intellectual disabilities and to the people who support them. To do this effectively requires a total commitment on the part of the agency and, in many ways, reflects the aspects of the evolving rights movement reviewed here. The process started with what amounted to the articulation of agency manifesto rights. As discussed above, these could not be enacted effectively without the existence of a supportive infrastructure provided, in this case, by the existence of a rights facilitation committee to adjudicate rights concerns and, most importantly, by trained staff and managers. With these supports in place the central stage of the process can be completed, the rights education of people who we hope will become active self-advocates.

OVERVIEW OF THIS BOOK

This book addresses human rights issues reflecting debates that, in some cases, have raged for centuries. Chapter 1 provides a historical overview of the social location of people with intellectual disabilities while Chapter 2 describes the recent development of international legal protections for the rights of people with disabilities. Included is a review of the influential Montreal Declaration on Intellectual Disabilities adopted at the Montreal PAHO/WHO International Conference on Intellectual Disability, October 5–6, 2004. This is a fitting and optimistic start to the review of human rights issues that follows in subsequent chapters.

Chapter 3 provides a review of the complex area of the fundamental right to life and how it has been contested over time. The right to life is a fitting place to start the discussion of specific rights in light of the centuries-old debate over infanticide and eugenics. This debate is raging with renewed fervour in light of recent developments in genetics research, a familiar concern in the history of the field.

The growth of self-determination, referred to briefly above, is described in greater detail in Chapter 4 from a broader, dialogical perspective. This chapter includes an examination of the emerging person-centred planning movement.

The legal system presents some specific challenges for people with disabilities. Justice systems in various jurisdictions around the world are functionally inaccessible for people with disabilities who may wish to be actively engaged in their own defence. The authors of Chapter 5 review these issues and suggest ways in which the legal system may adapt to address the needs of people who have intellectual disabilities.

People who have intellectual disabilities are more likely to interact with the health-care system than are members of the general population as a result of a higher frequency of various health concerns (Jansen *et al.* 2004; Lennox and Kerr 1997; McCarthy and Boyd 2002; US Department of Health and Human Services 2002). However, the extent to which people with intellectual disabilities are afforded the opportunity to exercise their right to active participation in their own health care remains a concern (Sutherland, Couch and Iacono 2002). The authors of Chapter 6 provide an in-depth discussion of these critical issues in the provision of health care.

From the days of Goddard's examination of the Kallikak family and the restrictions inspired by the eugenics movement, restriction of reproduction rights has been central to many policy decisions. Despite advances, there is wide variation in how sexuality rights are viewed internationally. From abuse to contraception, marriage and parenting rights, Chapter 7 addresses the historically controversial issue of sexuality rights.

Chapter 8 examines the rights of people to receive the least, rather than the most, restrictive forms of intervention. The authors of this chapter provide a historical overview of the use of punishment, the growing controversies surrounding the use of aversive interventions and the challenge to balance the right to treatment with freedom from harm.

Chapter 9 returns the reader to the cornerstone of our project, education. The highly contested role of education in promulgating the rights of people with disabilities in meaningful ways is examined. This chapter includes an extensive historical and theoretical review of approaches to inclusive education with a description of international legislative and policy approaches.

The final chapter brings the focus back to the broad systemic context of support provided for people with intellectual disabilities. The emphasis here is on the central importance of organizational support and, especially, the leadership that is necessary to provide a meaningful organizational commitment to the centrality of human rights in all services for people with intellectual disabilities. While rights awareness for individuals who have intellectual disabilities is important, rights are enacted in a social context. Often that context includes support services. The thesis presented by the authors of Chapter 10 is that, to be effective, organizations that wish to build a rights culture must be learning organizations with committed leaders.

A FINAL THOUGHT

Our hope is that the concepts presented in this book will be enlightening, inspirational and, ultimately, transformative in the lives of people who have disabilities, their care providers, families and friends.

October 2008

REFERENCES

Amnesty International (1997) 'First steps: A manual for starting human rights education.' London: Amnesty International. Retrieved from www.hrea.org on June 25, 2007.

Brabeck, M. M. and Rogers, L. (2000) 'Human rights as a moral issues: Lessons for moral educators for human rights work.' *Journal of Moral Education, 29,* 2, 167–182.

Buckingham, J. (1998) *Teaching Human Rights.* Saskatoon: Public Legal Education Association of Saskatoon.

Flowers, N. (1998) *Human Rights Here and Now: Celebrating the Universal Declaration of Human Rights.* Retrieved from www.umn.edu/humanrts/edumat/hreduseries/hereandnow/Part-2/HRE-intro.htm on November 20, 2007.

Freire, P. (1983) *Pedagogy of the Oppressed.* New York: Continuum.

Griffiths, D., Owen, F., Gosse, L., Stoner, K. *et al.* (2003) 'Human rights and persons with intellectual disabilities: An action-research approach for community-based organizational self-evaluation.' *Journal on Developmental Disabilities, 10,* 2, 25–42.

Herbers, S. (1998) 'Remembrance: Adult education at the national civil rights museum.' *Adult Learning, 9,* 4, 8.

Jansen, D. E. M. C., Kroll, B., Groothoff, J. W. and Post, D. (2004) 'People with intellectual disability and their health problems: A review of comparative studies.' *Journal of Intellectual Disability Research, 48,* 93 (10 pages).

Lennox, N. G. and Kerr, M. P. (1997) 'Primary health care and people with intellectual disability: The evidence base.' *Journal of Intellectual Disability Research, 41,* 5, 365–372.

Mazzucchelli, T. G. (2001) 'Feel safe: A pilot study of a protective behaviours programme for people with intellectual disability.' *Journal of Intellectual and Developmental Disability, 26,* 2, 115–126.

McCarthy, J. and Boyd, J. (2002) 'Mental health services and young people with intellectual disability: Is it time to do better?' *Journal of Intellectual Disability Research, 46,* 3, 250–256.

Middlesex Community Living (2000a) *Understanding Your Rights.* Strathroy, ON: Middlesex Community Living.

Middlesex Community Living (2000b) *Supporting People to Understand Their Rights.* Strathroy, ON: Middlesex Community Living.

Middlesex Community Living (2000c) *Forming a Human Rights Committee.* Strathroy, ON: Middlesex Community Living.

Middlesex Community Living (2000d) *Orientation Manual.* Strathroy, ON: Middlesex Community Living.

Owen, F., Griffiths, D., Stoner, K. Gosse, L. *et al.* (2003) 'Multi-level human rights training in an Association for Community Living: First steps toward systemic change.' *Journal on Developmental Disabilities, 10,* 2, 43–64.

Perske, R. (1972) In W. Wolfesnsberger (1972) *The Principle of Normalization in Human Services.* Toronto: National Institute on Mental Retardation (The Roeher Institute) [Reprinted from R. Perske (1972) 'The dignity of risk and the mentally retarded.' *Mental Retardation, 10,* 24–26.]

Pike, G. and Selby, D. (1997) *Human Rights: An Activity File.* Nepean: Bacon and Hughes.

Ramdas, L. (1997) 'Adult education, lifelong learning, global knowledge: The challenge and the potential.' *Convergence, 30,* 4, 34–40.

Sobsey, D. (1994) *Violence and Abuse in the Lives of People with Disabilities: The End of Silent Acceptance?* Baltimore, MD: Paul H. Brookes Publishing.

Sutherland, G., Couch, M. A. and Iacono, T. (2002) 'Health issues for adults with developmental disability.' *Research in Developmental Disabilities, 23,* 6, 422–445.

Tardif-Williams, C.Y., Owen, F., Feldman, M., Griffiths, D. *et al.* (2007) 'Comparison of interactive computer-based and classroom training on human rights awareness in persons with intellectual disabilities.' *Education and Training in Developmental Disabilities, 42,* 1, 48–58.

Tarulli, D., Tardif-Williams, C., Griffiths, D., Owen, F. *et al.* (2004) 'Human rights and persons with intellectual disabilities: Historical, pedagogical, and philosophical considerations.' *Encounters on Education, 5,* 161–181.

US Department of Health and Human Services (2002) *Closing the Gap: A National Blueprint to Improve the Health of Persons with Mental Retardation.* The Report of the Surgeon General's Conference on Health Disparities and Mental Retardation, 5.

1

Historical and Theoretical Foundations of the Rights of Persons with Intellectual Disabilities: Setting the Stage

Frances Owen, Dorothy Griffiths, Donato Tarulli and Jacqueline Murphy

The social location of people who have been variously described as moral imbeciles (cf. Carlson 2001), idiots, morons, feebleminded, defectives (Trent 1994), 'changelings' (Goodey 2001), mentally retarded, learning disabled or as having intellectual disabilities, has been historically and continues to be widely contested, with vast differences in practice being evident around the world. This book examines one particular facet of this contestation: the degree to which people who have been identified as having intellectual disabilities are able to exercise their human rights within the context of their everyday lives as protected in national and international charter. While an exhaustive examination of every aspect of human rights theory and praxis is impossible in a single volume, the overarching theme here is to examine the opportunity for people who have intellectual disabilities to realize their full rights of citizenship, not only in areas that have received extensive public attention, such as the right to life, the right to marry and to have children, and the right to full protection under the law, but also those rights that other citizens may not even consider in these terms: for example, the right to receive treatment using the least restrictive effective interventions and the right to choose with whom you live (Griffiths *et al.* 2003; Owen *et al.* 2003). In the words of Dr. Sev Ozdowski, Australian Human Rights Commissioner and Disability Discrimination Commissioner, in his address to the 13th Congress of Inclusion International:

> Human rights are rights recognised as inherent in each and every one of us by virtue of our common humanity and innate dignity as human beings. They are the rights that must be respected if we are each to fulfil our

potential as human beings. They are not luxuries – they are the basic and minimum necessities for living together in human society. (Ozdowski 2002)

If human rights are, in fact, assumed to be universal simply by virtue of our shared humanity, the need for a book such as this is ironically tragic. Regrettably, despite legislative initiatives at the national and international levels in various parts of the world, rights abuses persist. Even in jurisdictions that have legislative protections, it may well be that many people with disabilities are not aware that these protections exist and do not know how to invoke them with effect (Mazzucchelli 2001). This book was inspired by stories like that of Ed Murphy who, in recounting his experience of life in care services, reported that:

> It really doesn't help a person's character the way the system treats you. One thing that's hard is that once you're in it, you can't convince them how smart you are. And you're so weak you can't convince them how smart you are. And you're so weak you can't really fight back. (Bogdan and Taylor 1982, pp.29–30)

With greater awareness of rights abuses and the ways in which they can be addressed and prevented, Ed Murphy's experience of being voiceless can be avoided for others who have been identified as having an intellectual disability.

To provide a general context for the chapters that follow, this chapter will provide a brief review of some of the historic barriers to full access to human rights that have been experienced by people with intellectual disabilities. The evolution of social attitudes toward disability, including ideologies that have supported rights abuses and dehumanizing institutional practices, will be discussed. The growth of rights movements and self-determination will also be reviewed in relation to social movements and legislative protections that support them.

HUMAN RIGHTS RESTRICTIONS: A BRIEF HISTORY

Histories related to social treatment of people identified as having intellectual disabilities reflect a tension between concern for the protection, development and welfare of those with disabilities and a fear for the public good – a fear that has supported such practices as eugenics (Carlson 2001; Read and Walmsley 2006). In his classic text, *A History of Mental Retardation*, Scheerenberger (1983) describes key historical trends in conceptions of intellectual disability and identifies how persons with intellectual disabilities have been differentially treated in history. As Scheerenberger notes, in prehistoric times, people who were born with disabilities were killed, sometimes with their mothers; and yet there is also archeological evidence of Neanderthal community support for an individual with a physical disability, suggesting that the tribe protected and 'found a protective place' for a person who had a disability (p.5). In Mesopotamia, despite his prescription of dramatically harsh punishments for his subjects, Hammurabi's Code of 282 laws did not identify people with disabilities as negative social targets and suggests a degree of responsiveness to human need. However, in ancient Greece, Aristotle advocated infanticide, and the Spartans insisted on it to protect their vision of perfection in the Spartan population. Centuries after the demise of the Spartan city state, Hitler's advocacy of similar attempts to achieve racial perfection resulted in the death of millions, including people with disabilities.

Through the Middle Ages in Europe, infanticide was frowned upon. The largely agrarian economies of the period demanded a large labour force and high mortality rates made the potential contribution of each person born more valued. While this admittedly utilitarian awareness of the importance of human life was encouraging, as were care facilities such as the Mansur Hospital in Cairo – where two attendants were assigned for each resident, musicians played patients to sleep and actors provided entertainments – more often during this period people with disabilities were warehoused, shackled and enslaved. The 17th and 18th centuries in Europe saw the growth of medical knowledge and philosophy. There was a focus on classification, efforts to understand etiology, and an awareness of the importance of empiricism. Jean Jacques Rousseau's focus on the natural centrality of the senses in human learning, as detailed in his treatise *Emile*, inspired various programs of 'natural education'. However, in everyday life, while some people who had intellectual disabilities might be cared for at home, many were in some kind of residential care or, as was increasingly the case, were simply abandoned. In some places they became objects of perverse entertainment. Institutions such as 'Bedlam' – the Bethlem Hospital given by the sheriff of London to the Bishop and Church of Bethlem in 1247 – 'was [until 1770] one of London's favourite tourist spots. People entered the "penny gates" and were allowed to roam the yards and to be entertained or shocked according to their personal taste and expectations' (Scheerenberger 1983, p.44).

With the rise of industrialization in Europe came a renewed need for labourers, including child workers, many of whom had intellectual disabilities. The 19th century in Europe was a period of massive and rapid change. Industries drew people from the country to the city, scientific knowledge was growing exponentially and there was a focus on the arts. With these changes came an increased understanding of the nature of intellectual disabilities. Progress was achieved in the classification of various medical conditions that laid the foundation for future work. The French psychiatrist and student of Phillipe Pinel, Jean Etienne Dominique Esquirol, made a clear differentiation between intellectual disability and mental illness, and Edouard Séguin, a student of French physician Jean Marc Itard, further differentiated the classification system and was able to demonstrate successful training for people with intellectual disabilities (Scheerenberger 1983).

In the United States of America, in the years immediately following the revolutionary war, people with disabilities were a part of everyday community life. Those who were physically strong worked alongside others. Those who needed more care could find it in the homes of extended family members or in almshouses while those who ran afoul of the law were jailed. People in the new republic who had intellectual disabilities were sometimes looked upon pityingly and tended to be seen as deserving of benevolence. However, as in Europe, the perception of those with disabilities in the new United States was also influenced by social change and economics. With increasing poverty during the economic crisis of the early 19th century the almshouses grew and, over time, differentiated according to the classification of dependent groups (Trent 1994).

By the 1840s, news spread to England and America of the success experienced by Edouard Séguin at the Bicêtre Hospital in the suburbs of Paris. Leaders in the field in America began espousing Séguin's methods. The movement that grew up around the hope for institutional training for people with intellectual disabilities fostered 'the emergence of idiocy as a social and cognitive construct' (Trent 1994, p.16). Séguin himself arrived in America in the 1850s fuelling the emerging focus on training; however, Americans did not accept his conception of idiocy 'as a failure of the will' (Trent 1994, p.16). Instead, they broadened their search to examine the pathology and typology of disability and its degenerative properties. Thus, the earlier focus on education was being replaced by a medicalized conception of intellectual disability.

Early American reformers who developed specialized programs focused their efforts on providing people with disabilities with skills and subsequent community employment; however, by the 1860s, instead of moving out of institutions, many people were remaining as institutional employees. 'Although the original educational function of the institution would remain prominent, once in the institution many feebleminded child-students would become feebleminded adult-workers' (Trent 1994, p.23). Most institutions were growing and even included working farms. The similar growth of institutions in England has been variously attributed to the rise of urban industrialization – although, as Barnes (1991) points out, the movement started before increased urbanization – and to an increased focus of the economy on large factory work and away from agriculture and local industry. However, there was also the 'spirit of Victorian patronage' (Barnes 1991, p.16) that stimulated a differentiated response, one 'which not only separated disabled people from other disadvantaged sections of the community, but also divided them up into specific categories and groups, with differing treatments for each group' (p.16). In the middle of the 19th century the interest in 'mental defectives' grew in France and Switzerland, spreading through Western Europe and to Canada and the United States (The Roeher Institute 1996).

As the old century waned and faded into the new, across America there was a growing focus on the cult of success from Horatio Alger's rags to riches tales to the role of the successful housewife in promoting the well-being of her family. As Trent (1994) explains:

> Being not the rationalistic optimism of a century earlier nor the romantic optimism of the 1840s, faith in progress at the end of the century combined elements of social Darwinism and a better understanding of heredity with a concern for race purification and perfection. (p.135)

These views spawned a growing perception of people with intellectual disabilities as presenting a threat to the moral foundation of America, a threat that could best be managed or controlled through institutional isolation from society in 'feebleminded communities' (p.143). In the early years of the eugenics movement medical scientists believed the route to improving human existence was to eradicate genetic predispositions to disability. New research in genetics and documents, such as Goddard's history of the Kallikak family, fuelled this movement. 'He concluded that because of their lack of control, sexual immorality, fertility and the crime and delinquency they spread, the feeble-minded constituted a menace to society and should be removed, controlled and sterilized' (The Roeher Institute 1996, p.4). In her discussion of what she calls discursive discrimination in 1920s and early 1930s Sweden, Boréus (2006) suggests that this movement was supported by excluding people with disabilities from active discourses relevant to their lives and using the dominant discourse to objectify and marginalize them.

Carlson (2001) has pointed out that prior to the end of the 19th century, when the threat to 'race purification' became a major focus, gender was not a focus of the discourse on intellectual disability. The growing awareness of the impact of genetics and the fears associated with it prompted the focus to shift to the woman with a disability who could bear children and who, in the context of this world view, would perpetuate her disability. The perceived need to regulate procreation for this reason, coupled with the perception that women with disabilities needed protection just as society needed protection from them, resulted in women with disabilities being segregated from men in institutions. Ironically, these same women were often employed to care for children within the institutions, maintaining what Carlson refers to as the institution's 'self-perpetuating mechanism' (p.130):

> There were two competing definitions of her very nature: on the one hand, [the woman with an intellectual disability] was inherently morally defective and the birth of an illegitimate child proved her feeblemindedness; on the other hand, she was seen as able to properly care for children

> – presumably in a morally acceptable fashion – which is why she was em-
> ployed within the institution. (Carlson 2001, p.129)

Institutions thrived well into the 20th century with the predominant view being the necessity for 'social control' of people with mental deficiencies (Dybwad 1996; The Roeher Institute 1996). One of the most devastating and profound manifestations of eugenics informing public policy was in the Holocaust, in which an estimated 90,000 people with disabilities were killed (Brown and Brown 2003; Scheerenberger 1983). Perhaps ironically, on the Allied side of the conflict, when the United States entered the war in 1942 many men who had been identified as being 'mentally retarded' became involved in the war as soldiers or in other war-related occupations (Smith and Lazaroff 2006).

Throughout the 20th and into the 21st centuries, there has been a gradual shift from this focus on social protection to a growth in the self-advocacy movement. This shift has been strengthened by increasing formal commitments by various nation states and national and international organizations to upholding the fundamental human rights of people who have intellectual disabilities. Illustrating this change is the shift in perception represented by Stanley P. Davies' two key texts. In 1930 he published *Social Control of the Mentally Deficient*, a ground-breaking text in the field at the time. However, by 1959 the same author had published *The Mentally Retarded in Society*, a revised version of the former volume. Times were indeed changing (Dybwad 1996).

In the period of the late 1940s and early 1950s the focus on so-called mental age had contributed to people in institutions being dressed and treated as perpetual children. Witness the focus on children in the name of the influential National Association for Retarded Children (now known simply as the Arc of the United States), which was founded in 1953. By the 1960s, this focus on perpetual childhood began to change. Research focused on issues such as self-concept, success in mainstreamed employment, community adjustment, and critiques of prevailing assessment techniques challenged the old notions that supported the need for protection of society and control of people with disabilities (Dybwad 1996).

While the late 19th and early to mid 20th centuries were influenced by the eugenics movement and the commitment to a protectionist stance toward people with disabilities, toward society, and especially protection of the race, the mid to late 20th century saw a strong shift toward deinstitutionalization and the rise of the Community Living movement with people who have disabilities being included in 'normal' life (Radford and Park 1999; Sobsey 1994; Wolfensberger 1972). The formalized notion of normalization emerged first in Denmark. In 1959, that country passed its Mental Retardation Act that focused services on providing life experiences as similar to normal living circumstances as possible. Led by Bank-Mikkelsen in Denmark and Nirje in Sweden, this vision of normalization developed through the 1960s, building on the fundamental concept of

ensuring that the same legal and human rights were afforded to people with intellectual disabilities as to all other citizens (Emerson 1992). Nirje's development of
what became known as the normalization principle evolved from his life with ref-
ugees, with people who had cerebral palsy and from his experiences as an
ombudsman for people with intellectual disabilities. At the celebration of the
25th anniversary of normalization and social role valorization in 1999, Nirje
described how his thinking evolved in response to these experiences and the passage of progressive legislation in Sweden in the 1960s that ensured the right of
people with intellectual disabilities to community and educational services. As
early as 1963 Nirje criticized systems that 'were not "as close to the normal
as possible"' (Nirje 1999, p.24). In 1967 he organized the Stockholm Symposium of the International League on Legislative Aspects of Mental Retardation
that included experts Niels Erik Bank-Mikklsen, Lennart Wessman and Karl
Grunewald. The outcomes of the symposium reflected the growing use of nor-
malization-like language and a clear commitment to rights that was developed
further in the 1968 Jerusalem Declaration of the Rights of the Mentally Handicapped, that later contributed to the 1971 United Nations Declaration on the
Rights of the Mentally Handicapped. Nirje began using the comparison of a
normal day in the life of people with and without disabilities as a way to highlight the need for change. The underlying principles of the normalization
principle arose from the rights movement, international problem solving and,
most importantly 'from the point of view of the people with intellectual disabilities themselves' (Nirje 1999, p.28). Through Nirje's commitment to international
cooperation the word spread and, in 1969, on the advice of Gunnar Dybwad,
Wolf Wolfensberger visited Bengt Nirje and Karl Grunewald to see the Swedish
experience for himself.

In 1972 Wolf Wolfensberger defined the normalization principle as 'Utilization of means which are as culturally normative as possible, in order to establish
and/or maintain personal behaviours and characteristics which are as culturally
normative as possible' (p.28). Wolfensberger reflected on the need for individual
programming and environments to be structured so that people with intellectual
disabilities would learn to display behaviours that were considered normative.
Initially, 'normalization did not develop as an isolated ideal but reflected the
prevalent liberal trends of many Western societies at that time to respond to the
demand for the equal rights of a number of disadvantaged or minority groups'
(Emerson 1992, p.3). Normalization was about rights, quality of life and 'normative lifestyles' (p.3), but not necessarily about integration or inclusion. A similar
conceptual trend was developing in North America but with a somewhat different trajectory. In the 1970s, and with further refinement in the 1980s,
Wolfensberger espoused a shift in how people with disabilities were portrayed by
the public and a shift in the normalization philosophy from a focus on 'culturally
normative practices' to 'socially valued roles' (p.5). The latter led to

Wolfensberger's supplanting of normalization with his conception of 'social role valorization'. Wolfensberger (2000) asserts that social role valorization (SRV), with its grounding in role theory, provides a method for people with intellectual disabilities to improve their quality of life by changing their perceived social roles. From the perspective of SRV, this can be accomplished by emphasizing valued roles held by a person or by helping a person to gain access to valued roles or by enhancing the person's competency. This approach emphasizes issues such as the social stigma associated with labelling, the stereotypes that perpetuate them and the role expectancies associated with them; the importance of raising the consciousness of care providers to insure their awareness of latent social biases; and the 'conservatism corollary' that suggests that 'the more devalued you are, the greater the impact of any further devaluing characteristic' (Emerson 1992, p.7). The service implications of Wolfensberger's approach include a strong emphasis on full integration of devalued people into the valued centre of society. Emerson (1992) contrasts Wolfensberger's scientific social theory of normalization with the earlier Scandinavian emphasis on egalitarianism. He criticizes Wolfensberger for focusing on the need for people with intellectual disabilities to conform to valued social standards rather than emphasizing the centrality of individual choice in the Scandinavian model. In Britain in the 1980s, O'Brien supported a more integrated approach emphasizing quality of life with individual choice (Emerson 1992). Oliver's (1999) criticism of normalization is perhaps even more fundamental. He argues from the perspective of materialist theory that normalization 'offers no satisfactory explanation of why disabled people are oppressed in capitalist societies and no strategy for liberating them from the chains of that oppression' (p.164). Oliver maintains that disability is socially constructed within the capitalist context. He contrasts what he sees as normalization's focus on changing people with the materialist focus on raising the consciousness of people with disabilities and the call to collective political action as evidenced in organizations such as the British Council of Organizations of Disabled People.

Race's (1999) extensive examination of social role valorization and the history of normalization in England chronicles, among other issues, what he sees as the key confusion among English academics of normalization with SRV concepts. For example, he discusses the lingering power of the phrase 'an ordinary life' being associated with SRV although he points out that Wolfensberger did not use this term. However, despite the theoretical controversies that SRV has sparked from groups such as proponents of the Social Model of Disability over many issues including the location and focus of disability in social role devaluation or in broader social and economic factors, Race, Boxall and Carson (2005) argue that the approaches also share some common ground. While proponents of SRV focus on individuals, those oriented to the Social Model emphasize the centrality of action at a societal level; however, in practice, these can converge. For example, Race and his colleagues argue that the English Direct Payments initiative 'as a means of enabling people to have greater control over their own lives' (p.517) is an example of an action based on the application of the Social Model; however, this social program benefits individuals. Race and his colleagues also cite the application of the English *Valuing People* white paper, which they assert is founded to a large extent on SRV principles, as having broad social benefits through the participation of people with disabilities on Planning Boards. This suggests the potential for convergence of benefit across theoretical orientations that can arise from identifying 'where, on the spectrum from *individual* to *social*, an initial focus would be most effective, and therefore what the insights of *both* SRV and the Social Model might be at that level' (p.519).

Conceptual growth moved hand in hand with the development of legislative protections geared with increasing specificity to the needs of people with disabilities. However, even into the 21st century, rights abuses abound, such as the reported legally sanctioned restraints of 'cage beds' in the Czech Republic (Vann and Siska 2006) and reported abuses in the Turkish mental health-care system, including arbitrary detention, use of electroconvulsive therapy (ECT) without anaesthesia, starvation of children in centres and the use of physical restraints (Disability Rights International 2005). In November 2007, Mental Disability Rights International (MDRI) published a report on a four-year (2003–2007) investigation of abuse and rights violations in Serbia, a country that has espoused the belief in segregation of people with intellectual disabilities that has been generally supported in Central and Eastern Europe. During the four years of the MDRI's work, investigators reported that 'Filthy conditions, contagious diseases, lack of medical care and rehabilitation, and a failure to provide oversight renders placement in a Serbian institution life-threatening' (Ahern and Rosenthall 2007, p.iii). The MDRI investigators reported observing infants, children and adults who were housed in cribs in rooms with no stimulation. An investigator who visited the Stamnica Institution reported that:

> There were rows of metal cribs filled with teenagers and young adults. Labelled immobile or bedridden, many of them were kept naked from the waist down on plastic mattresses, covered only with a sheet to facilitate staff clean-up of bladder and bowel incontinence. Staff reported they also eat in the cribs and spend all of their time in the cribs. They never get out. (Ahern and Rosenthall 2007, p.v)

With no regulations restricting physical restraint, MDRI reports some people in Serbia are left in restraints for extended periods of time, even for years. The investigators reported seeing children and adults tied to furniture. They describe the institutions as being understaffed with very limited rehabilitation programs and medical care. Some institutions had limited or no heat, even in winter, and poor sanitary conditions. Serbia has perpetuated its traditional institutional system, replicating old institutions with foreign aid funds and leaving the country with limited if any community services for people with disabilities.

However, there is hope for reform. MDRI's report acknowledges the open approach that Serbia has shown in acknowledging the shortcomings in its care system. In 2005 the Serbian government passed its 'Social Welfare Development Strategy' focused on issues related to poverty and the development of a system to protect human rights, including a focus on the promotion of integration. In 2006 it passed the 'Law on the Prevention of Discrimination Against Persons with Disabilities' designed to eliminate discrimination on the basis of disability and to provide services to protect rights and to promote independent living. The country has worked to develop programs for inclusion, foster care and deinstitutionalization, but it apparently falls short of a total commitment to institutional closure. Ahern and Rosenthall, with their colleagues from MDRI, emphasize that 'Strikingly, the proposed programs fail to address the rights or needs of the people who are most vulnerable to abuse: children and adults with mental disabilities who are now detained in institutions' (2007, p.18). The MDRI report details extensive violations of international rights conventions in Serbia, including Article 19 of the United Nations Convention on the Rights of People with Disabilities that asserts the right of people who have disabilities to live in community settings and to be fully included.

In the long and slow journey toward realization of true rights protections for people with intellectual disabilities, issues reappear in various forms that prompt reexamination of the degree to which true progress has been made. In his examination of 17th century conceptions of intellectual disability from a theological perspective, Goodey (2001) ends with a reference to the 'current eugenicist enthusiasm for human germ-line intervention' (p.25). Referring to Richard Baxter's influence on British thought concerning 'natural disability theory', Goodey reminds us that:

> Baxter was not entirely sure that humans could be perfected, and refrained from making classifications that God alone knew about and determined. Many of today's genetic technicians are more confident about their perfection, and know enough about psychology to determine who will be saved. (p.26)

CODES AND LEGISLATIVE PROTECTIONS

The United Nations Universal Declaration of Human Rights (1948), adopted in the middle of the 20th century following two World Wars and a Great Depression, offered a ray of hope in a world that had been filled with death and darkness. Many rights statements have followed, some of which offer specific protections for people with intellectual disabilities. In 1967, at a meeting of the

International League of Societies for Persons with Mental Handicap (ILSMH, now known as Inclusion International) attended by representatives from the United States and seven European countries, a formal commitment was made to human rights in the symposium's published *Conclusions* (as cited in Dybwad and Bersani 1996):

> The symposium considered that no examination of the legislative aspects of the problem of mental retardation would be complete without general consideration being given to the basic rights of the mentally retarded, not only from the standpoint of their collective rights and those of their families, but also from that of the individual rights of the retarded person as a human being (Dybwad 1996, p.6).

Included in the rights identified in this document were rights associated with living arrangements, recreation, social rights such as the right to marry and to have children, the right to physical safety and the right to a fair trial. With the removal of the reference to the right to marry and have children, proposed by more conservative members, the Declaration of General and Special Rights of the Mentally Retarded was prepared by an ILSMH committee and subsequently submitted to the United Nations through the French Delegation. The document, with the revised title of Declaration on the Rights of Mentally Retarded Persons, was passed by the General Assembly (Dybwad and Bersani 1996). This document built on the 1948 United Nations Declaration of Human Rights and was followed by the 1975 Declaration on the Rights of Disabled Persons.

National declarations, such as the Canadian Human Rights Act (1977), prohibited discrimination on the basis of factors such as physical or mental disability. Subsequently, in 1985, Canada became the first nation to include in its constitution equal legal protections for people with disabilities (Rioux and Frazee 1999). Included in the anti-discrimination protections is a specific prohibition against discrimination on the basis of disability (Neuman 1984). Around the world, the range of legislation protecting human rights varies in specificity and breadth of application, as the following list readily suggests: the Australian Disability Discrimination Act (1992); the Bulgarian Law for Protection, Rehabilitation and Social Integration of Disabled (with 2002 amendments); the Ethiopian The Rights of Disabled Persons to Employment proclamation, no. 101/1994; the Guatemalan Law of Attention to Persons with Disabilities 135–1996; the Hungarian Equalization Opportunity Law (Act no. XXVI of 1998); Indian Persons with Disabilities (Equal Opportunities, Protection of Rights and Full Participation) Act, 1995 (no. 1 of 1996); the Israeli Equal Rights for People with Disabilities Law, 5758–1998; the New Zealand Disabled Persons Employment Promotion (Repeal and Related Matters) Bill (18 May 2004, No. 138–1); the Scottish Disability Rights Commission Act 1999 (c. 17); the Swedish Act Prohibiting Discrimination, SFS 2003: 307; the Thai 1991 Rehabilitation of Disabled

Persons Act to the United Kingdom Disability Rights Act 1999 and The Americans with Disabilities Act of 1990 (ADA). This long list attests to the burgeoning of rights-related legislation in this field in the past 20 years (Disability Rights Education and Defense Fund).

In March 2007, the United Nations Convention on the Rights of Persons with Disabilities was opened for signature. There are eight principles that underlie the new convention:

(a) Respect for the inherent dignity, individual autonomy including the freedom to make one's own choices, and independence of persons.

(b) Nondiscrimination.

(c) Full and effective participation and inclusion in society.

(d) Respect for difference and acceptance of persons with disabilities as part of human diversity and humanity.

(e) Equality of opportunity.

(f) Accessibility.

(g) Equality between men and women.

(h) Respect for the evolving capacities of children with disabilities and respect for the right of children with disabilities to preserve their identities. (United Nations Enable [a])

While this is certainly a major step forward on the international stage, all these manifesto rights, both national and international, have limited impact until structures are established to enact them in a meaningful way. As O'Neill (1996) has suggested:

> Mere insistence that certain ideals or goals are rights cannot make them into rights; but a proleptic rhetoric of rights may be politically useful in working to set up institutions that secure positive rights that constitute (one possible) realization of fundamental imperfect obligations. (p.36)

An example of the disconnect between government policy and implementation is found in Forbat's (2006) analysis of the implementation of the British Department of Health's *Valuing People* strategy. The senior policy and practice personnel she interviewed did not demonstrate consistent use of language associated with the strategy's focus on rights. She found that 'rights are treated as a problematic concept – as what people lack, rather than something that is positively embraced' (p.256). Forbat expressed concern that the policy would not be implemented by front line care providers if their leaders, as in this study, were not embracing it.

For the new UN Convention on Rights of Persons with Disabilities, implementation will be monitored at the level of the member states with UN oversight being handled through the Conference of States Parties, consisting of signatories to the Convention, and the Committee on the Rights of Persons with Disabilities, with its 18 expert members elected from a group nominated by the States Parties. However, implementation is planned to 'be a progressive process that will not happen overnight' (United Nations Enable [b]). Reliance on formal structures alone is not adequate to insure full enactment of human rights. The convergence of formal and informal social forces is necessary for the roots of human rights to grow deep into social structures. The growing trend toward collective self-advocacy and rights education are factors that have the potential to assist in creating the kind of structures that can help to promote meaningful enactment of these manifesto rights.

A CAVEAT: WHO WRITES THE HISTORY, WHO HOLDS THE FUTURE?

Over the course of human history, people identified as having an intellectual disability have experienced discrimination based on 'ableism', a relatively new term with very old roots (Lester 1998). Ableism refers to the view that people with disabilities are inferior and therefore not entitled to the rights assumed to be accessible to others. Fear and threat fed by ignorance, economic need and fluctuating social values have been the building blocks of barriers to human rights faced by people with disabilities. This view has coloured all aspects of social interaction and historical discourse on disabilities. In his 2007 President's Address, Hank Bersani Jr., President of the American Association on Intellectual and Developmental Disabilities (AAIDD), reflected on that organization's name change that saw the shift away from 'mental retardation'. Bersani contrasts the lives of those who devote their professional lives to supporting people labelled as having mental retardation, developmental or intellectual disabilities, and the lives of the people who live with the labels. While care professionals achieve status and success through their work in the field, 'MR [mental retardation] has drawn narrow lives for people defined by it – lives devoid of any of the facets that we find lend our lives dignity, afford us respect, and make our lives comfortable' (Bersani 2007, p.400). Bersani's argument is that the repeated round of name changes that what is now AAIDD has undergone since it was founded in the late 19th century have not changed the lived reality for people who have borne the labels. He emphasizes that changing the label to reduce the stigma associated with it is insufficient; the important change to make is in the lived experience of people identified as having a disability. His argument is that any label will become stigmatized by its association with people whose lives have been marginalized. The key is in addressing the social location of people identified as having an intellectual disability. In this regard, it is worth pointing up the productive possibilities of narrative approaches to both the organization of care and the practice of disability research. Compared to traditional paradigms of care provision or research, in which the voice of the professional or expert is privileged, narrative strategies seek to afford the person with a disability a greater say in the matters that affect their lives. As Atkinson and Walmsley (1999) have noted, people with intellectual disabilities have traditionally been silent (or silenced) about such matters, with the tendency being for others to speak for or represent them. 'Lost voices', quite fittingly, is the expression Atkinson and Walmsley use to describe this history of exclusion. Increasingly, however, and in particular as narrow and constraining assumptions and negative stereotypes about the communicative capacities of persons with intellectual disabilities have been challenged, narrative methods are being proposed as a means by which the perspectives and experiences of persons with intellectual disabilities may be recovered. In rendering audible those otherwise lost voices, narrative approaches clearly carry the potential for empowerment of persons with intellectual disabilities (Walmsley and Johnson 2003). Narratives are in this sense a form of personal liberation. In foregrounding individual experience and subjective meanings, life narratives allow people to emerge and be seen precisely as people, as opposed to 'cases' (Atkinson 2004; Gillman, Swain and Heyman 1997). Atkinson (2005) summarizes the argument in the following terms:

> Life stories, and the opportunity to tell them, are particularly important for people with learning disabilities because often they have been silent, or silenced, while other people – families, practitioners, historians – have spoken on their behalf. Life stories begin to redress that balance as they become a means by which people with learning disabilities have a voice that is theirs. (p.8)

The empowerment afforded by personal narratives stems from a variety of more specific effects. For instance, Ramcharan and Grant (2001) suggest that narrative and life history texts have been particularly effective both in establishing positive principles related to good services, as well as in identifying negative principles associated with people's experiences in service settings. In this connection, they claim that 'certain principles such as "rights, independence, choice and inclusion" appearing centre stage in *Valuing People*…reflect their articulation in life history texts' (p.352). Among the other potential benefits of narrative practices are their promotion of a community identity – their promotion, in other words, of collective empowerment – and hence of the possibility of Freireian conscientization and political affiliation (Ramcharan, Grant and Flynn 2004). Personal narratives can also help to undermine debilitating myths and stereotypes about persons with intellectual disabilities, including, for example, the 'dominant belief…that "these people" form a homogeneous population – "they are all the same"' (Goodley 1996, p.337), or that they suffer from communicative deficiencies that inescapably render them incapable of telling stories (see the work of Booth and Booth 1996 for a critique of this assumption). Finally, life narratives can serve to inscribe unofficial, lost, or hidden histories of intellectual disabilities, and accordingly encourage the individual or collective resistance to the received, conventional, or official histories – histories which, in their privileging of documentary sources, often abstract away the lived, experience-near dimensions of the history of intellectual disabilities (Atkinson 2005).

Since historical records have for the most part been kept by professionals, such as those described by Bersani, and not by people living with a disability, it is difficult to gain anything but a shadowed impression of the true lived experiences of people with disabilities over the centuries. Elizabeth Bredberg's (1999) criticisms of disability history stem from what she sees as an overemphasis on secondary sources. She points out that the majority of histories focusing on disability are written by nonhistorians, usually clinicians or those viewing the field from the perspective of intervention who do not have training in the analysis of primary historical source material. On the other hand, few historians who do have this training have ventured into this subject area. As such, the accounts available generally tend to be rather 'one-sided in their account of the disabled people, presenting them as depersonalised objects of institutional action' (p.191). In their review of special education in London and Bedfordshire, UK between 1890 and 1970, Read and Walmsley (2006) similarly grieve the lack of availability of an 'authentic voice of recipients of early forms of special education' (p.466), forcing reliance on third party, professional accounts.

Similar problems, but resulting from more active resistance than simple lack of availability, are identified by Malacrida (2006) in her effort to gather first-person accounts of people who lived in an institution in Alberta, Canada. In attempting to give voice to those who had resided at an institution for children and adults with developmental disabilities, Malacrida encountered active resistance on the part of those in power. She argues that, while the historical data provided by people who have disabilities has come under scrutiny in light of notions concerning acquiescence and 'false memory', people in positions of social and cultural advantage who are in positions of power in relation to people who have disabilities may not have had their historical recounting subjected to the same degree of scepticism. Nonetheless, she was able to interview 21 people who shared their experiences in the Foucauldian 'gaze' that infused life in the institution where nonconformists were secluded naked and observed through a one-way mirror for days at a time (Malacrida 2005).

Dybwad (1996) also discusses the slow emergence of the first-person voice in his review of the history of the self-advocacy movement. He refers to an early 1962 paper by Sabagh and Edgerton that included direct quotations on the topic of sterilization from people who had been institutionalized, and notes that by 1969, at the National Youth Conference on Mental Retardation, the program included a panel of youth with intellectual disabilities who discussed programs that were available to them. The process of insuring that people with disabilities were being included and heard was starting. Also in 1969, Bengt Nirje described the Swedish Parents' Association's course in parliamentary procedure for young adults with intellectual disabilities and he also described a conference that had been held the previous year at which participants with disabilities discussed a range of issues of importance to them including wage rates at sheltered workshops. At a 1971 conference on volunteerism organized by the ILSMH and the President's Committee on Mental Retardation, participants argued that people with intellectual disabilities should receive leadership training. A 1972 conference held by and for people with disabilities, produced a report entitled *Our Life: A Conference Report*, and the now highly successful People First organization was initiated during conferences in Canada and the United States in 1973 and 1974. Nirje's (1972) description of the 1970 Malmo conference, attended by 50 people with intellectual disabilities from Sweden and Denmark, emphasizes the delegates' opportunity to define their role as people with intellectual disabilities:

> By giving a voice to their common experiences, aspirations, and right to self-determination, they appear to have made the first organized attempts to break through our communication barrier, thus reaching toward a more direct relationship between themselves and the mainstream of society. (p.179)

Nirje identified the focus on self-interest groups at the conference as a normalizing enterprise that could be strengthened by providing participants with group process skill development.

By 1982, the ILSMH began including people with disabilities to speak about their own experiences as part of the conference program and, in 1984, an international self-advocacy conference was held in the United States. Five countries were represented. The formal self-advocacy movement burgeoned through the 1980s and 1990s. Organizations for self-advocates, including People First, Disabled People International and Self-Advocates Becoming Empowered, grew in membership and in influence. By the 1990s, more researchers and practitioners were writing biographical accounts of individuals' experiences and helping people to express their own stories (cf. Edgerton and Gaston 1991; Gillespie 2000; Hingsburger 1992; Smith 1995) as well as engaging in investigation of the experience of people with intellectual disabilities living in relation to the growing systemic focus on community living (Pedlar *et al.* 1999). Gunnar Dybwad offers an optimistic view of this development: 'people with intellectual impairments have – in my lifetime – gone from "feebleminded patients" to empowered agents of social change. They work to make the world better not just for themselves, but for the rest of us as well' (quoted in Dybwad and Bersani 1996, p.16). In addition to the rise of self-advocacy, as discussed in the Introduction to this book, systemically based and systematically delivered rights education may help people who have intellectual disabilities to speak out for themselves and, as Dybwad has suggested, for others as well. Nevertheless, while this progress is encouraging, people with disabilities around the world still struggle to be heard in an authentic way, leaving in question the issue of whose voice will predominate when the histories of the early years of the 21st century are written.

HUMAN RIGHTS IN THE 21ST CENTURY?

Ed Murphy, quoted above, talked about feeling weak and unable to fight back in a system that did not hear him when he was a resident in various services between 1955 and 1972 (Bogdan and Taylor 1982). Bersani's (2007) discussion of the difference between changes in nomenclature and real changes in the lives of people with disabilities, Goodey's (2001) caution of the potential for eugenic resurgence through advances in genetics, and the MDRI report on abuses in Serbia reflect the limited gains that have been made toward meaningful inclusion and true valuing of people who have intellectual disabilities. Yet, the optimism of Gunnar Dybwad (1996) and the recent passage of the United Nations Convention on the Rights of Persons with Disabilities offer hope, as do the developments in human rights research and practice described in the chapters that follow. One wonders whether a person currently involved in care services would have a different experience of personal agency than that described by Ed Murphy.

REFERENCES

Ahern, L. and Rosenthall, E. (2007) *Torment not Treatment: Serbia's Segregation and Abuse of Children and Adults with Disabilities.* Washington, DC: Mental Disability Rights International. Retrieved from www.mdri.org on December 19, 2007.

Atkinson, D. (2004) 'Research and empowerment: Involving people with learning difficulties in oral and life history research.' *Disability and Society, 19,* 7, 691–702.

Atkinson, D. (2005) 'Narratives and people with learning disabilities.' In G. Grant, P. Goward, M. Richardson and P. Ramcharan (eds) *Learning Disability: A Life Cycle Approach to Valuing People.* Maidenhead: Open University Press.

Atkinson, D. and Walmsley, J. (1999) 'Using autobiographical approaches with people with learning difficulties.' *Disability and Society, 14,* 2, 203–216.

Barnes, C. (1991) *Disabled People in Britain and Discrimination: A Case for Anti-Discrimination Legislation.* London: Hurst and Company.

Bersani, H. (2007) 'President's address 2007 – The past is prologue: "MR," go gentle into that good night.' *Intellectual and Developmental Disabilities, 45,* 6, 399–404.

Bogdan, R. and Taylor, S. J. (1982) *Inside Out: Two First-Person Accounts of What It Means to Be Labelled 'Mentally Retarded'.* Toronto: University of Toronto Press.

Booth, T. and Booth, W. (1996) 'Sounds of silence: narrative research with inarticulate subjects.' *Disability and Society, 11,* 1, 55–69.

Boréus, K. (2006) 'Discursive discrimination of the "mentally deficient" in interwar Sweden.' *Disability and Society, 21*, 5, 441–454.

Bredberg, E. (1999) 'Writing disability history: problems, perspectives and sources.' *Disability and Society, 14*, 2, 189–201.

Brown, I. and Brown, R. I. (2003) *Quality of Life and Disability; An Approach for Community Practitioners.* London: Jessica Kingsley Publishers.

Carlson, L. (2001) 'Cognitive ableism and disability studies: feminist reflections on the history of mental retardation.' *Hypatia, 16*, Fall, 124–146.

Davies, S. P. (1930) *Social Control of the Mentally Deficient.* New York: Crowell.

Davies, S. P. (1959) *The Mentally Retarded in Society.* New York: Columbia University Press.

Disability Rights Education and Defense Fund, Country Laws Index. Retrieved from www.dredf.org/international/lawindex.shtml on June 25, 2007.

Disability Rights International (2005) *Behind Closed Doors: Human Rights Abuses in the Psychiatric Facilities, Orphanages and Rehabilitation Centers of Turkey.* Washington, DC: Mental Disability Rights International.

Dybwad, G. (1996) 'Setting the stage historically.' In G. Dybwad and H. Bersani (eds) *New Voices: Self-advocacy by People with Disabilities.* Cambridge, MA: Brookline Books.

Dybwad, G. and Bersani, H. (eds) (1996) *New Voices: Self-advocacy by People with Disabilities.* Cambridge, MA: Brookline Books.

Edgerton, R. B. and Gaston, M. A. (1991) *'I've Seen It All!' Lives of Older Persons with Mental Retardation Living in the Community.* Baltimore, MD: Paul H. Brookes Publishing Co.

Emerson, E. (1992) 'What is normalisation?' In H. Brown and H. Smith (eds) *Normalisation: A Reader for the Nineties.* London: Tavistock/Routledge.

Forbat, L. (2006) 'An analysis of key principles in *Valuing People*: Implications for supporting people with dementia.' *Journal of Intellectual Disabilities, 10*, 3, 249–260.

Gillespie, C. (2000) *Someone Like That: Life Stories.* Edmonton, AB: Rowan Books Inc.

Gillman, M., Swain, J. and Heyman, B. (1997) 'Life history or "case" history: The objectification of people with learning difficulties through the tyranny of professional discourses.' *Disability and Society, 12*, 5, 675–693.

Goodey, C. F. (2001) 'From natural disability to the moral man: Calvinism and the history of psychology.' *History of the Human Sciences, 14*, 3, 1–29.

Goodley, D. (1996) '"Tales of hidden lives." A critical examination of life history research with people who have learning difficulties.' *Disability and Society, 11*, 3, 333–348.

Griffiths, D., Owen, F., Gosse, L., Stoner, K. *et al.* (2003) 'Human rights and persons with intellectual disabilities: An action-research approach for community-based organizational self-evaluation.' *Journal on Developmental Disabilities, 10*, 2, 25–42.

Hingsburger, D. (1992) *I Witness: History and a Person with a Developmental Disability.* Mountville, PA: VIDA Publishing.

Lester, S. (1998) *Claiming Disability.* New York: NYU Press.

Malacrida, C. (2005) 'Discipline and dehumanization in a total institution: institutional survivors' descriptions of Time-Out Rooms.' *Disability and Society, 20*, 5, 523–537.

Malacrida, C. (2006) 'Contested memories: Efforts of the powerful to silence former inmates' histories of life in an institution for "mental defectives".' *Disability and Society, 21*, 5, 397–410.

Mazzucchelli, T. G. (2001) 'Feel safe: A pilot study of a protective behaviours programme for people with intellectual disability.' *Journal of Intellectual and Developmental Disability, 26*, 2, 115–126.

Neuman, E. (1984, February 14) *Human rights and the nursing home resident.* Address to the Institute on Nursing Home Care, Toronto.

Nirje, B. (1972) 'The right to self-determination.' In W. Wolfensberger *Normalization: The Principle of Normalization in Human Services.* Toronto: National Institute on Mental Retardation (The Roeher Institute).

Nirje, B. (1999) 'Formulating the Normalization principle.' In R. J. Flynn and R. A. Lemay (eds) *A Quarter-century of Normalization and Social Role Valorization: Evolution and Impact.* Ottawa: University of Ottawa Press.

Oliver, M. J. (1999) 'Capitalism, disability, and ideology: A materialist critique of the Normalization principle.' In R. J. Flynn and R. A. Lemay (eds) *A Quarter-century of Normalization and Social Role Valorization: Evolution and Impact.* Ottawa: University of Ottawa Press.

O'Neill, O. (1996) 'Children's rights and children's lives.' In R. E. Ladd (ed) *Children's Rights Re-visioned: Philosophical Readings.* Scarborough, ON, Canada: Nelson, Canada.

Owen, F., Griffiths, D., Stoner, K., Gosse, L. *et al.* (2003) 'Multi-level human rights training in an Association for Community Living: First steps toward systemic change.' *Journal on Developmental Disabilities, 10,* 2, 43–64.

Ozdowski, S. (2002) *Human Rights for People with Intellectual Disabilities in Australia: Where to From Here?* Australian Human Rights and Equal Opportunity Commission: Disability Rights. Retrieved from www.hreoc.gov.au/disability_rights/speeches/2002/inclusion.htm on January 7, 2007.

Pedlar, A., Haworth, L., Hutchison, P., Taylor, A. and Dunn, P. (1999) *A Textured Life: Empowerment and Adults with Developmental Disabilities.* Waterloo, ON: Wilfred Laurier University Press.

Race, D. G. (1999) *Social Role Valorization and the English Experience.* London: Whiting & British Ltd.

Race, D., Boxall, K. and Carson, I. (2005) 'Towards a dialogue for practice: Reconciling Social Role Valorization and the Social Model of Disability.' *Disability and Society, 20,* 5, 507–521.

Radford, J. P. and Park, D. C. (1999) 'Historical overview of developmental disabilities in Ontario.' In I. Brown and M. Percy (eds) *Developmental Disabilities in Ontario.* Toronto: Front Porch Publishing.

Ramcharan, P. and Grant, G. (2001) 'Views and experiences of people with intellectual disabilities and their families. (1) The user perspective.' *Journal of Applied Research in Intellectual Disabilities, 14,* 4, 348–363.

Ramcharan, P., Grant, G. and Flynn, M. (2004) 'Emancipatory and participatory research: How far have we come?' In E. Emerson, C. Hatton, T. Thompson and T. R. Parmenter (eds) *The International Handbook of Applied Research in Intellectual Disabilities.* West Sussex: John Wiley and Sons.

Read, J., and Walmsley, J. (2006) 'Historical perspectives on special education, 1890–1970.' *Disability and Society, 21,* 5, 455–469.

Rioux, M. H. and Frazee, C. L. (1999) 'Rights and freedoms.' In I. Brown and M. Percy (eds) *Developmental Disabilities in Ontario.* Toronto: Front Porch Publishing.

Roeher Institute (1996) *Disability, Community and Society: Exploring the Links.* North York, Ontario; The Roeher Institute.

Scheerenberger, R. C. (1983) *A History of Mental Retardation.* Baltimore, MD: Paul H. Brookes Publishing Co.

Smith, J. D. (1995) *Pieces of Purgatory: Mental Retardation In and Out of Institutions.* Pacific Grove, CA: Brooks/Cole Publishing Company.

Smith, J. D. and Lazaroff, K. (2006) '"Uncle Sam needs you" or does he? Intellectual disabilities and lessons from the "Great Wars".' *Mental Retardation, 44,* 6, 433–437.

Sobsey, D. (1994) *Violence and Abuse in the Lives of People with Disabilities: The End of Silent Acceptance?* Baltimore, MD: Paul H. Brookes Publishing Co.

Trent, J. W. (1994) *Inventing the Feeble Mind: A History of Mental Retardation in the United States.* Berkeley, CA: University of California Press.

United Nations Enable (a), Guiding Principles of the Convention. Retrieved from www.un.org/disabilities/default.asp?navid=14&pid=156 on June 25, 2007.

United Nations Enable (b), Relationship between development and Human Rights, Retrieved from www.un.org/esa/socdev/enable/convinfodevhr.htm on June 25, 2007.

Vann, B. H. and Siska, J. (2006) 'From "cage beds" to inclusion: The long road for individuals with intellectual disability in the Czech Republic.' *Disability and Society, 2*, 5, 425–439.

Walmsley, J. and Johnson, K. (2003) *Inclusive Research with People with Learning Difficulties: Past, Present and Futures.* London: Jessica Kingsley Publishers.

Wolfensberger, W. (2000) 'A brief overview of Social Role Valorization.' *Mental Retardation, 38*, 2, 105–123.

Wolfensberger, W. (1972) *The Principle of Normalization in Human Services.* Toronto: National Institute on Mental Retardation (The Roeher Institute).

2

The Emergence of the Human Rights of Persons with Intellectual Disabilities in International Law: The Cases of the Montreal Declaration on Intellectual Disabilities and the United Nations Convention on the Rights of Persons with Disabilities

Jocelin Lecomte and Céline Mercier

INTRODUCTION

It is a sad irony to realize that, historically, persons with intellectual disabilities (ID) have been forgotten by movements working for the recognition of fundamental human rights. This irony is compounded by the fact that there are over 180 disability-related United Nations (UN) human rights documents relevant to persons with ID (Quinn and Degener 2002), as well as the notion that civil rights movements were conceived to alleviate the discrimination that burdened the most vulnerable groups of society.

> The existing human rights system was meant to promote and protect the rights of persons with disabilities, but the existing standards and mechanisms have in fact failed to provide adequate protection to the specific cases of persons with disabilities. It is clearly time for the UN to remedy this shortcoming. (Louise Arbour, United Nations Human Rights Commissioner, 2006)

The problem seems to be aggravated by the reality of persons with ID most often burdened with an invisible disability, unable to speak for themselves and historically relegated to closed institutions. A review of the various international juridical instruments leads one to conclude that the rights of persons with ID, when addressed,[i] have too often been subject to so-called 'progressive' clauses, of the 'when possible' type, or even obscured because amalgamated with persons with disabilities in general (Quinn and Degener 2002).

The last 15 years have witnessed some promising changes regarding the rights of persons with intellectual disabilities. The United Nations, under the guidance of a few special rapporteurs,[ii] have pushed forward a twin strategy of consolidating existing binding treaty-based rights in a disability convention (hard law) while also developing guidelines (soft law) by way of international conferences. The 'hard law' aspect of this approach came to fruition in 2006, with the adoption by the UN General Assembly of the Convention on the Rights of Persons with Disabilities.[iii] This accomplishment was tributary in no small part to the parallel development of guidelines on disability by way of international conferences and declarations. One such declaration, pertaining specifically to intellectual disabilities, is the Montreal Declaration on Intellectual Disabilities[iv] that was adopted in 2004.

These developments are the result of a major paradigm shift in the recognition of the place that the international community now gives to persons with disabilities: these persons have fundamental rights by virtue of being humans, rather than as a result of being disabled. Moving away from a biomedical model, the international community now accepts that individuals with a disability are entitled to rights inherent to their condition as humans, rather than be entitled to rights as a result of them having a disability. This constitutes a change in paradigm, from *objects of rights* to *subjects of rights*, based on the common denominator that all human beings inherently possess fundamental inalienable rights.

In order to examine the emergence of the human rights of persons with ID in international law, two examples will be presented: the Montreal Declaration on Intellectual Disabilities and the UN Convention on the Rights of Persons with Disabilities. Prior to these two examples, a brief review of some basic international and national law concepts and instruments will be presented.

INTERNATIONAL LAW STANDARDS

There are two categories of regulations in international law: binding agreements (hard law) and non-binding agreements (soft law). Binding agreements are of two types: conventions and customary international law. Conventions are state agreements, sometimes called treaties, pacts or covenants, while customary international law is entirely different: it derives from judicial principles or behaviour of States which have long been recognized by the international community. These regulations can also become customary through judicial declarations by bodies such as the International Court of Justice or the Inter-American Commission on Human Rights of the Organization of American States.[v] When an agreement is deemed binding, from this right emanates State obligations to respect, protect and fulfil this treaty and the rights that it contains. *Respect* signifies respecting the right by way of not directly violating it. *Protect* signifies protecting the right by outlawing violations of the right by non-State actors. And *fulfil* means fulfilling the right by making sure that its real exercise is not theoretical.[vi]

The most important difference between hard and soft international law pertains to its sanction. A violation of hard law obligations will result in possible judicial condemnation of the State, whereas non-compliance to soft law documents would not give way to any sanction. Should a soft law instrument become recognized by an international body as customary international law, as is the case with the United Nations Declaration on Human Rights,[vii] then sanctions from a UN body such as the Human Rights Council[viii] could become a real possibility.

Binding international human rights standards or hard law

Binding international laws are numerous but, in the realm of human rights, emanate from three documents referred to as the International Bill of Rights: the Universal Declaration of Human Rights of 1948,[ix] the International Covenant on Civil and Political Rights[x] (ICCPR) and the International Covenant on Economic, Social and Cultural Rights[xi] (ICESCR), both adopted in 1966. The two covenants from 1966 dealt with the fundamental human rights that the Universal Declaration had referred to back in 1948, while expanding on their significance.

The ICCPR protects so-called basic rights or civil liberties such as the right to life, freedom, safety (Article 9), equality, marriage, association, religion, etc., and also prohibits discrimination based on disability (Article 26) and inhuman and degrading treatment (Article 7). The ICESCR protects quality of life rights and exercise of these rights. This covenant covers the right of access to the highest standard of mental and physical health that a society can provide (Article 12), the right to education, quality of life, social protection, cultural and scientific freedom, and the right to enjoy these rights without discrimination (Article 2(2)). States are obliged to make the maximum effort, based on their resources, to progressively achieve full realization of the rights recognized in the ICESCR.

But 1966 was unfortunately during the Cold War and, as such, each opposing bloc championed a covenant for political purposes. Thus, the Western bloc quickly adopted the ICCPR while calling upon the USSR to respect the political and civil rights that it enunciated, while the Cominterm States adopted the ICESCR and confronted the capitalist countries to respect the rights that it contained. Such political play allowed for the severance of the rights of the International Bill of Rights until the end of the Cold War.

It is only with the end of the Cold War that the western international community 'rediscovered' economic, social and cultural rights. The ICESCR is of fundamental importance for persons with an intellectual disability since it is a binding international treaty signed on by the vast majority of the international community.

Recently, Canada was strongly reprimanded by reports by the CESCR on its budgetary social compressions since 1994. The CESCR noted the negative impact of these compressions on services for persons with disabilities:

> 36. The Committee is also concerned about significant cuts in services on which people with disabilities rely, such as cuts in home care, attendant care and special needs transportation systems, and tightened eligibility rules for people with disabilities. Programmes for people who have been discharged from psychiatric institutions appear to be entirely inadequate. Although the Government failed to provide to the Committee any information regarding homelessness among discharged psychiatric patients, the Committee was told that a large number of those patients end up on the street, while others suffer from inadequate housing, with insufficient support services.[xii]

The fact that economic, social and cultural rights are of a 'progressive realization' nature has unfortunately contributed to their somewhat lacklustre enforcement by member States.[xiii] The concept of progressive realization is linked to the available resources by the State, not to its priorities or political imperatives. It should be noted that the absence of economic resources in a State does not constitute justification for a violation of the fundamental rights of persons with an intellectual disability as established by international covenants.[xiv] A State which refuses to use its resources to the maximum to ensure that all citizens enjoy the right to health would be in violation of Article 12 of the ICESCR.[xv]

Although hard international law was somewhat in a bind during almost 45 years, that did not stop the development of hard or soft international law, either instigated by international organizations (the UN has instigated more than 20 multilateral human rights treaties as well as numerous regional treaties[xvi]), or by civil society.

Non-binding international human rights standards or soft law

Soft law emerges from resolutions, declarations, plans of actions, etc. As mentioned, instruments of a soft law nature do not have any binding effects on States, as their aim is to incite them to incorporate if not the text then the intention of the text into their national legislation (Duplessis 2007). Soft law instruments, more often than not, address social, economic and cultural rights. As such, they play on more moral field.

The last decade has witnessed the proliferation of international soft law instruments. While varying tremendously in scope and in nature, and being somewhat oblivious to persons with ID per se, some of these declarations, especially those adopted by the UN General Assembly, have been instrumental in pushing forward the agenda of human rights and disability. The legal effects of resolutions by the United Nations General Assembly are of a 'semi-binding' character: 'thus, a resolution where the General Assembly "recommends", "requests", "urges" or "invites", is obviously not binding, whereas a resolution that "requires", "decides", "affirms", "declares is prescriptive" (David 1985, p.81). Those to whom a resolution is addressed are bound by it if: (i) they accept the resolution; (ii) the resolution is limited to reminding them of a regulation that is already binding; or (iii) the resolution has been respected by all for a certain period of time, thus becoming customary law and, therefore, binding. An example of this last category is the 1948 Universal Declaration of Human Rights.

The UN General Assembly adopted its first such instrument some 30 years ago. The UN Declaration on the Rights of Mentally Retarded Persons (1971)[xvii] played an important role in giving some much needed visibility to persons with ID. Two decades later, the UN General Assembly adopted in 1991 the MI Principles,[xviii] which called for drastic changes in the institutional care of persons with disabilities and, two years later, the United Nations Standard Rules on the Equalization of Opportunities for People with Disabilities,[xix] whose title is very much self-explanatory. The Standard Rules were, until the UN Convention on Persons with Disabilities, by far the most important and comprehensive international instrument guaranteeing the rights of people with disabilities. Moreover, they establish the obligation of States to create conditions enabling persons with disabilities to participate in the legislative process, including persons with an intellectual disability and groups composed of these persons, for any legislation that concerns them:

> National legislation, embodying the rights and obligations of citizens, should include the rights and obligations of persons with disabilities. States are under an obligation to enable persons with disabilities to exercise their rights, including their human, civil and political rights, on an equal basis with other citizens. States must ensure that organizations of persons with disabilities are involved in the development of national legislation concerning the rights of persons with disabilities, as well as the ongoing evaluation of that legislation. (United Nations 1993 Rule 15, 1)

Combined with the MI Principles, they became instrumental in paving the way for a comprehensive treaty on disability rights.

Since the year 2000, the UN treaty-created bodies have also started to formulate observations, formally called General Observations, on matters of concern. As such, the Committee overseeing the Covenant on Economic, Social and

Cultural Rights (CESCR) has produced General Comment 5 that pertains specifically to persons with disabilities.[xx] The content of these General Comments are of a non-binding nature, but are deemed to represent interpretations of the content of the ICESCR. Such interpretations, done by the treaty-created body itself, are highly considered by the international courts when called upon to render judgement on a case that involves ICESC rights. Hence, their influence cannot be overstated (O'Flaherty 2006).

Concurrent to these UN General Assembly declarations and to the UN General Comments, an important number of conferences contributed to the field of human rights and disabilities: Caracas (1990), Vienna (1993), Managua (1993), Yale (1995), Stockholm (2000), Montreal (2004), etc. These conferences were organized either by international organizations, NGOs (non-governmental organizations) or by actors from civil society. The soft law that came out of these conferences, although not binding, is nonetheless important in its contribution to the overall knowledge of specific human rights questions as well as advocacy vehicles to be distributed to these organization's members.

National application of international law

The long-established principle in international law is that treaties only engender rights and obligations for signatory States. This principle does not apply to international instruments related to human rights; these instruments create rights and obligations for signatory States towards their fellow citizens.[xxi]

Several international conventions (or treaties), such as the ICCPR as well as the ICESCR, are by nature binding on States. Application of these conventions is incumbent upon signatory States as a whole, i.e. on all their legislative, political and judicial authorities. Article 27 of the Vienna Convention on the Law of Treaties affirms the principle of the primacy of international law over national law, stating that a party may not invoke the provisions of its internal law as justification for its failure to perform a treaty (Vienna Convention on the Law Treaties 1969, Article 27).

Traditionally, a State introduces a treaty into its internal order, so that it can later apply it. This obligation of introduction constitutes an obligation of result, not of means. The way in which a treaty is introduced may vary greatly from one State to another.

The essential question around the applicability of international human rights instruments is knowing whether their provisions are sufficient. If they are, the instruments are deemed self-executory. If necessary, once the instruments have been ratified, supplementary measures can be taken for their implementation. Thus, a treaty would not be self-executory if it is drawn up in terms which address contracting States as subjects of international law and requires that they take legislative or regulatory measures in order for the treaty to be applied effectively on an internal level.

The introduction of a treaty into the internal order of a State is generally subject to the passing of a special judicial act by the state authority. Execution of a treaty thus requires that certain measures be taken on a national level: vote of special credits, adoption of laws or regulatory acts and modification of existing legislation or regulations. The form and nature of the implementation may vary depending on national systems and this often explains the chronological differences that exist amongst signatory States.

When the application of a treaty is self-executory, that is to say, no particular measures are required prior to its execution, private citizens can claim its application before a national judge without having to wait for the treaty to be incorporated into national legislation. Generally speaking, the overall provisions of international instruments on human rights are drafted with sufficient precision and clarity, following the example of internal legislative or constitutional texts. It is not a matter here of simple principles, but of recognition of an individual's actual rights. Based on this fact, the provisions should have direct application in the internal order.

In Canada, it is the federal government that is the only competent body to sign binding treaties.[xxii] When Canada has ratified an international convention,[xxiii] it is bound by its content[xxiv] throughout the country, regardless of jurisdiction.

> 52. [...] The Committee [CESCR] urges the Federal Government to take concrete steps to ensure that the provinces and territories are made aware of their legal obligations under the Covenant [ICESCR] and that the Covenant rights are enforceable within the provinces and territories through legislation or policy measures and the establishment of independent and appropriate monitoring and adjudication mechanisms.[xxv]

The effective realization of the obligations put forward in treaties falls under the separation of competences between the federal and the provinces, enabled in the Constitutional Act of 1867. Thus, the federal government has to negotiate with the provinces the implementation of treaties that it signs.[xxvi] As this is a somewhat complicated and tiresome process, the provinces are more often than not consulted during the treaty negotiations.

In practice, unfortunately, national judges have been hesitant, and even resistant, in their recognition of the self-executory character of a treaty, even for human rights conventions. Recent decisions by courts throughout Canada seem to have begun reversing this trend. These decisions have established that rules of international law that have not been signed on by Canada can be taken into account by Canadian courts when rendering decisions,[xxvii] as long as these rules of international law do not conflict with internal law and that the aforementioned international law is of a customary nature. In the case of human rights soft law, the courts can take into account the values that have been expressed, especially in the absence of any other relevant international instrument.[xxviii] This should be done on a case per case basis.

THE MONTREAL DECLARATION ON INTELLECTUAL DISABILITIES

Context

The Montreal Declaration on Intellectual Disabilities[xxix] originated as a result of the Montreal Pan-American Health Organization (PAHO) and World Health Organization (WHO) Conference on Intellectual Disability.[xxx] It was adopted and signed on October 6, 2004 by 65 participants and representatives from 17 countries, namely from the Americas but also from major organizations defending the rights of individuals with intellectual disabilities. The Montreal conference brought together experts from the WHO Pan-American region (the Caribbean, Central America, South America and North America), representatives from WHO (Geneva), from PAHO (Washington), from the regional office of WHO-Africa, and from different non-governmental international organizations. These experts (representatives from all levels of governments, leaders of parent associations and associations for individuals with an intellectual disability, experts in international law, human rights, and intellectual disabilities) gathered to discuss the state of the fundamental human rights awarded to persons with ID on a Pan-American level.

The Montreal Declaration on Intellectual Disabilities does not aim to restate all of the basic human rights mentioned in international conventions and declarations that also apply to individuals with intellectual disabilities. Rather it aims to remind the international community that an intellectual disability poses unique problems with respect to the acknowledgement and enforcement of the fundamental human rights of individuals with an intellectual disability. It also hopes to guide civil and public authorities in their attempts to ensure full and complete citizenship to persons with ID (Lecomte and Mercier 2007).

In the three years since its adoption, the Montreal Declaration on Intellectual Disabilities has been quoted in many publications in English, Spanish, French, or Portuguese and has played an important role in the drafting of the UN Convention on the Rights of Persons with Disabilities, especially regarding the legal capacity of persons with ID. It has been cited most favourably by the United Nations Special Rapporteur on the right of everyone to the enjoyment of the highest attainable standard of physical and mental health, Mr. Paul Hunt, in his 2005 report on Mental Health as 'an important first step in redressing the marginalization of persons with intellectual disabilities in relation to the right to health, as well as their other human rights'.[xxxi] The Special Rapporteur lists the Montreal Declaration in the same light as other major human rights documents such as the MI Principles[xxxii] and the Standard Rules.[xxxiii]

The Montreal Declaration on Intellectual Disabilities is currently used in the human rights trainings provided in American countries by the Pan-American Health Organization (PAHO). Among its impacts, mention must given to the fact that it was the object of a memo to the Director General of the United Nations Committee on social development, presented by the Canadian delegation to the United Nations' Ad Hoc Committee on a *Global and Integrated International Convention on the Promotion and Protection of the Rights and Dignity of Handicapped Individuals*, as well as the basis for an executive summary intended for the Canadian delegation to the United Nations' Ad Hoc Committee. It also was pre-eminently mentioned in a response by the The Roeher Institute to the United Nations Educational Scientific and Cultural Organization International Bioethics Committee's *Elaboration of the Declaration on Universal Norms on Bioethics*. The Montreal Declaration was also given full support by the Government of Quebec, in 2004 at the Montreal PAHO/WHO closing ceremony, as well as in 2005 by the Minister of Health and Social Services in a speech in the National Assembly.[xxxiv] This support was linked to available resources.

Content

The Montreal Declaration refers in its Article 2 to the values of dignity, self-determination, equality and social justice (Herr 2003) which, according to a recent study by the United Nations High Commission for Human Rights (Quinn and Degener 2002), constitute fundamental values of the system of international law. These values were influential through the drafting of the Montreal Declaration. Although long recognized by international law, they needed to be put into the perspective of intellectual disabilities.

Through these values, the Montreal Declaration on Intellectual Disabilities can be summarized as emphasizing three fundamental human rights: the right to equality and non-discrimination, the right to health, and the right to make decisions about one's life (self-determination). What follows is an overview of these notions and how they influenced the final content of the Montreal Declaration.

1. The right to equality and non-discrimination for persons with ID
(A) THE RIGHT TO EQUALITY
Omnis definito in jure periculosa est[xxxv]
The concept of right to equality can easily be qualified as one of the founding stones of international law. This concept has been extensively elaborated on,

although not in the context of persons with ID. The right to equality of persons with an intellectual disability is inherent in their humanity, which means that they possess the same rights and obligations[xxxvi] as other citizens. Every human being is a human person (except for embryos) and all human persons inherently possess juridical personality (except for corpses) by virtue of being subjects of law. All human beings are subjects of law, and members of the community in which they are called to participate, based on the opportunities available to them. A subject of law is abstract and has no race, religion, class or disability. His juridical personality, i.e. his capacity for being a subject of law, is inherent in his human condition and is distinct from that of other human persons. This juridical personality is independent by virtue of its nature and its ability to enter into commitments.

Whereas the goal of the law is to regulate relations between citizens, the right to equality is defined as the right to live in society while respecting the value, worth, characteristics and needs of individuals. Respect for the right to equality is therefore a social responsibility (Drapeau 2001). This right applies, therefore, to access to health services[xxxvii] and to the local organization of health services.[xxxviii]

Article 1 of the Montreal Declaration makes reference to the Universal Declaration of Human Rights[xxxix] which accompanies the Charter of the United Nations.[xl] The Universal Declaration of Human Rights is the most famous judicial instrument in the world; its content is now considered to constitute customary international law and is thus binding on all nations. International law is based on this fundamental principle that all persons are equal before the law.

The principle of equality is the cornerstone of international law. This has not always been the case regarding persons with ID, as the UN Declaration on the Rights of Mentally Retarded Persons (1971) can attest when it is stated that: 'All mentally retarded persons have, *to the maximum degree of feasibility*, the same rights as all other human beings'.[xli] With regards to the Universal Declaration of Human Rights, *General Comment 5* is explicit on this point and states: 'All human beings are born free and equal including persons with a disability',[xlii] whereas the Declaration of Vienna[xliii] goes even further by stating that '*or other status*' mentioned in the Universal Declaration of Human Rights[xliv] unequivocally *includes* persons with a physical or *intellectual* disability (Rosenthal 2003).

The exercise of the right to equality must be ensured by the State, in conformity with the obligations that derive from the ICESCR, where protection against discrimination is interpreted as applying to the obligation to promote the integration of persons with an intellectual disability into the community (Rosenthal 2003).

In contrast to most international conventions, conventions on human rights possess a more objective character. This means that these rights are not attributed to individuals by virtue of a particular revocable statute, but are linked in principle to the quality of humanness itself (Sudre 2001). The public character of international instruments on human rights derives from their intrinsic nature. Because they are public in character, national judges must automatically apply their provisions.

With regards to the exercising of these rights, the public character of international instruments on human rights implies a collective and binding control mechanism on all State Parties, so that it is a matter of defending a common patrimony. Each contracting State or each judicially recognized entity of a State Party may invoke this mechanism even though its own nationals are not being adversely affected.[xlv]

The control of the application of the right to equality in international law is usually done by two sets of mechanisms: (i) by periodical reports done by UN treaty created bodies, such as CESCR; (ii) by way of complaints formulated by individuals or organizations.[xlvi]

In this last regard, Article 44 of the American Convention on Human Rights[xlvii] stipulates that: 'Any person or group of persons, or any nongovernmental entity legally recognized in one or more Member States of the Organization, may lodge petitions with the Commission containing denunciations or complaints of violation of this Convention by a State Party.'[xlviii]

(B) EQUALITY OF OPPORTUNITY

Article 5(b) of the Montreal Declaration refers to the paradigm of equality of opportunity.[xlix] Equality of opportunity, along with equality of result and equality of resources, is a variant of the concept of formal equality. Equality of opportunity is a matter of creating conditions where the same opportunities for social participation are available to all, including persons with an intellectual disability.

In spite of the fact that human beings are similar, they are also different as individuals. However, as noted by Marcia Rioux (2003), equality of opportunity is based on a person's individual ability to use, indeed seize, the opportunities presented to him. Thus it can potentially be highly discriminatory for persons with ID if offered in the absence of supports.

What is commonly termed the 'dilemma of equality' lies in the fact that although equality of opportunity means equal chances for all (irregardless of race, sex, disability, etc.), certain legislation is grounded in these very considerations in order to promote measures to combat inequality. Thus, in some cases, equality of opportunity for other citizens would be discriminatory for an intellectually disabled person. Take, for example, the implementation of computerized voting in local elections. Rules stating that everybody must vote alone, by themselves, would constitute indirect discrimination against persons with ID, as they would potentially be in need of some assistance; this besides being a violation of their political rights which are protected by Article 2(1) of the ICCPR.

From the perspective of equality of opportunity, whose specific objective is not simply the general protection of human dignity, but the fight against exclusion, marginalization and social inequity, the right to equality would be ensured by allowing different treatment if, and only if, such measures contributed to combating inequity and reducing exclusion and prejudices related to the causes of discrimination. Different treatment is not, therefore, discriminatory if it is based on egalitarian considerations (Proulx 2001).

What distinguishes the right to equality from other basic rights is its essentially comparative nature. One cannot say if this right has been violated without comparing the treatment received by various persons, in order to determine if some have been treated better or worse than others. Thus, in order to guarantee equality, it is first necessary to demonstrate the existence of a difference in treatment.

Equality of treatment is based on principles of respect for the dignity of the individual, the value of human persons, and the belief that all human beings are of equal value. However, the right to equality cannot be summed up in an affirmation of equality of treatment, enforceable by legislation against discrimination. Derogations from the right to equality are often necessary in the pursuit of equality of opportunity. These objectives require preferential treatment in order to remedy historic injustices, or to allow target groups to benefit from opportunities such as work, independent living or any other form of social participation. This is the foundation for the obligation of accommodation, i.e. taking reasonable measures to respect and protect the right to equality as a way of taking into account the differences amongst individuals, in order to ensure that treatment is truly equitable and there is no form of exclusion.

Equality would then be one of opportunity, but with appropriate accommodations made, so that intellectually disabled individuals are able to make life choices.

2. Discrimination

The Montreal Declaration, in its preamble, refers to the fact that persons with ID experience some of the most difficult living conditions in the world.[1] Although this situation can be attributed in part to issues of poverty, malnutrition and under-development, the main reason for it lays in the systemic discrimination and the absence of judicial protection that persons with an intellectual disability face:

> People with mental disabilities are often deprived of liberty for prolonged periods of time without legal process; subjected to peonage and forced labor in institutions; subjected to neglect in harsh institutional environments and deprived of basic health care; victimized by physical abuse and sexual exploitation; and exposed to cruel, inhuman and degrading treatment. (Rosenthal 2003, p.479)

Under the international human rights framework, discrimination is a breach of a government's human rights obligations. 'In general, groups that are discriminated against tend to be those that do not share the characteristics of the dominant group within a society. Thus discrimination frequently reinforces social inequalities and denies equal opportunities' (Gruskin 2005, p.11). Discrimination stands in opposition to the notion of equality. Equality is a more general concept subdivided into degrees of State obligations,[li] whereas discrimination represents its *a contrario* counterpart and involves prohibitions based on prevailing social values. As such, any form of discrimination against persons with ID is forbidden by a host of international juridical instruments, as the best protection that persons with ID have had, prior to the UN Convention on the Rights of Persons with Disabilities, comes from anti-discrimination treaties.[lii]

Discrimination against persons with an intellectual disability can take various forms. It may be expressed through different and disadvantageous treatment, which constitutes direct discrimination. Direct (*de jure*) discrimination can be recognized immediately because it is based on intellectual disability as the criterion for exclusion. However, discrimination may also take the form of certain seemingly neutral legislative or administrative regulations that are applied in a general way without any distinction being made, but which have a disproportionate or prejudicial impact on persons with an intellectual disability; this constitutes indirect discrimination (*de facto*).

> Both *de jure* and *de facto* discrimination against persons with disabilities have a long history and take various forms. They range from insidious discrimination, such as the denial of educational opportunities, to more 'subtle' forms of discrimination, such as segregation and isolation achieved through the imposition of physical and social barriers. The effects of disability-based discrimination have been particularly severe in the fields of education, employment, housing, transport, cultural life, and access to public places and services.[liii]

Discrimination can result as much from the existence of visible and concrete limitations as from perceptions, myths and stereotypes. Any struggle against discrimination which victimizes persons with an intellectual disability must begin with a social and judicial analysis of the real and perceived response of a civil society towards intellectual disability (Nussbaum 2006).

This concept is recognized in international law by, notably, the Committee on Economic, Social and Cultural Rights in *General Comment 5*.[liv] In Canada, the Supreme Court has recently affirmed that 'reasonable accommodations' should apply in situations of potential direct and indirect discrimination,[lv] in a case per case approach.

Should the notion of reasonable accommodation be applied in an individual fashion? Is the concept of reasonable accommodation the best option to address discrimination and inequalities towards persons with ID?

The concept of reasonable accommodation is based on the work of John Rawls:

> The Rawlsian approach proposes that it is society's responsibility to redress inequalities created between citizens because of natural handicaps or handicaps created by the social milieu of origin or present living conditions. Inequalities of birth are not deserved; a cooperative society will be careful to redress the inequality created by the chance of birth. That is to say that, for Rawls, justice in the form of equity is built on the conjunction of the principles of freedom and equality; each individual has the inalienable right to fundamental liberties which are compatible with the freedom of all. Everyone must have access to equality of opportunity. The second principle is the principle of difference: the existence of social and economic inequities must be accepted to the extent that advantages must be distributed in such a way as to benefit the least favoured, those who are dispossessed. (Massé 2003, p.413)

In our opinion, individual reasonable accommodation is not the best solution to the problem of equality, or discrimination, since it involves making concessions to those who are 'different', rather than discarding the idea of normality and promoting real inclusion.

> If there are no intrinsic boundaries to disability, then deciding whether a person has a disability or not becomes a social, cultural, and political question. If one must draw a line, one should do so with an eye to the broader goals of substantive equality, positive reform, and recognition of universal human variation and difference. Only then may we approach a time when no lines need to be drawn. (Penney 2002, p.215)

Shouldn't we then carefully examine the possibility that reasonable accommodation might create a gulf which divides persons with ID from other citizens, based on disability and reinforcement of stereotypes, while pigeon-holing individuals with rigid and dehumanizing definitions? According to the human rights paradigm, the right to equality for persons with ID must involve the acceptance of their difference, through more global accommodation, rather than as granting of concessions on the basis of their disability. The notion, however, deserves careful consideration, with account taken of the overall situation of persons with ID and emphasis put not on their differences, but on the common interests they share with the rest of society: their fundamental rights.

As stated in Article 5 of the Montreal Declaration, the right to equality for persons with intellectual disabilities should not be only of opportunity, but also may require, when that person wants to, appropriate measures, positive actions, accommodation and supports, on the basis of respect of their differences and of their individual choices.

3. The right to health[lvi]

Historically, the right to health has been one of the last rights to be recognized by the constitutions of States and international documents. The climate of optimism following the Second World War encouraged the rise of a new international judicial and financial order. Concurrently, although an international sanitary law had existed since 1930 for the purpose of preventing the spread of epidemics, the creation of the United Nations allowed for the emergence of a health law which focused on promoting the health of individuals and establishing their rights in the area of international health. The Universal Declaration of Human Rights thus states that 'everyone has the right to a standard of living adequate for the health and well-being of himself'.[lvii] It was to this end that the founding States of the UN agreed to establish the World Health Organization,[lviii] whose constitution affirms that 'the enjoyment of the highest attainable standard of health is one of the fundamental rights of every human being' (Constitution of the World Health Organization 1948). Since its beginnings, the World Health Organization has been given quasi-regulatory authority in the creation of rules of law. These rules of law are by nature binding on Member States of the WHO.[lix]

As a specialized institution within the UN whose objective is 'the attainment by all peoples of the highest possible level of health' (Constitution of the World Health Organization 1948, note 83), the WHO is also concerned with safeguarding health as a human right. The WHO's Alma-Ata Declaration[lx] affirms that the right to health is a fundamental right of persons and that this right, like that of education, constitutes one of the basic responsibilities of the State. Furthermore, the right to health involves the equitable distribution of health services, facilities and materials.[lxi] It should be noted, however, that this right to 'the highest possible level of health' must take into account biological and socio-economic variables as they pertain to individuals; consequently, the right to health '*must be understood as a right to the enjoyment of a variety of facilities, goods, services and conditions necessary for the realization of the highest attainable standard of health*'.[lxii]

The right to health is expressed on an international level by the covenants and acts of international organizations. References to this right are found in the Universal Declaration of Human Rights, but it emanates from Article 12 of ICESCR[lxiii] as well as General Comment 14.[lxiv] As it refers to the highest attainable standard of physical and mental health, it aims at reducing the gap between those who enjoy higher standards of health and quality of services and those who do not, for a variety of civil, political, economical, social or cultural reasons. The right to health encompasses the recognition that health is a human right and that access for all to health-care facilities, services, treatments and goods as well as related readaptation services is part of that right to health. From this right emanates governmental obligations to respect, protect and fulfil this treaty right to health.

> The right to health is closely related to and dependent upon the realization of other human rights, as contained in the International Bill of Rights, including the right to food, housing, work, education, human dignity, life, non-discrimination, equality, the prohibition against torture, privacy, access to information, and the freedoms of association, assembly and movement. These and other rights and freedoms address integral components of the right to health.[lxv]

General Comment 14 also states that human rights and fundamental freedoms are universal, indivisible, inter-dependent, inter-related and applicable to disabled persons.[lxvi] The universality of human rights allowed for the World Conference on Human Rights[lxvii] to state in its *Declaration of Vienna* of 1993 that 'all human rights and fundamental freedoms are universal and thus unreservedly include persons with disabilities'.

The Montreal Declaration goes even further by stating in its Article 4 that 'For persons with intellectual disabilities, as for other persons, the exercise of the right to health requires full social inclusion, an adequate standard of living, access to inclusive education, access to work justly compensated and access to community services'. Thus, the right to health is not only linked to other human rights; they work together, as a whole.[lxviii] Accordingly, you cannot exercise one while having the other negated. The right to education can be impended by the negation of the right to mobility or, reversely, the right to vote for all can be rendered void by the negation of the right to education for women, thus restricting alphabetization to males only.

Human rights abuses can dramatically affect health, while health can be dramatically worsened when human rights are ignored (Gruskin 2005). Another example of this affirmation can be found in the interaction between the ICCPR and the ICESCR regarding the obligation of States to offer persons with intellectual disabilities community-integrated services. In fact, in the absence of such services, the obligation created by the ICESCR could, theoretically, cause institutionalization to be considered arbitrary detention according to the ICCPR.[lxix]

The importance of the right to health for persons with ID cannot be overstated. In many countries of the world, health is often the only point of contact between government services and persons with ID. For international organizations, such as WHO, it is unfortunately sometimes the only available country entry point.

Thus the right to health must be looked upon in a more global way. For persons with ID, this means looking at health services, but also social and readaptation services. A right to health approach is about removing restrictions on delivery of services. It is also about asking if these services are being provided, to whom, in what ways. It is also about asking how persons with ID are able to meaningfully participate in decisions that affect their health.

4. The right to make decisions about one's life

The notion of protection is one which has long been held against persons with ID, as guardianship laws have historically been used to deny persons with ID their right to make decisions and that persons with ID have often been excluded from decisions about their human rights, health and well-being. As such, even though recognized by binding international law instruments,[lxx] the freedoms of persons with ID to make their own choices and take their place in civil life have frequently been unrecognized, ignored, abused or removed. But sometimes, the civil protection of a person with ID per se, or of his/her assets, can be necessary when they are unable to take care of themselves. While the question must be dealt with on a case per case approach, the absence of such legal protection mechanisms can often lead to human right abuses of persons with ID.

Article 6 constitutes the most important and original contribution of the Montreal Declaration: the establishment of common standards on supported decision-making for persons with ID.

6. (a) Persons with intellectual disabilities have the same right as other people to make decisions about their own lives. Even persons who have difficulty making choices, formulating decisions and communicating their preferences can make positive choices and decisions that further their personal development, relationships and participation in their communities. Consistent with the duty to accommodate in paragraph 5(b), persons with intellectual disabilities should be supported to make their choices and decisions, to communicate them and to have them respected. Accordingly, where individuals have difficulty making independent choices and decisions, laws and policies should promote and recognize supported decision-making. States should provide the services and the necessary support to facilitate persons with intellectual disabilities in making meaningful decisions about their own lives;

(b) Under no circumstance should an individual with an intellectual disability be considered completely incompetent to make decisions because of his or her disability. It is only under the most extraordinary of circumstances that the legal right of persons with intellectual disabilities to make their own decisions can be lawfully interrupted. Any such interruption can only be for a limited period of time, subject to periodic review, and pertaining only to those specific decisions for which the individual has been found by an independent and competent authority to lack legal capacity;

(c) That independent and competent authority must find by clear and convincing evidence that, even with adequate and appropriate supports, all less restrictive alternatives to the appointment of a surrogate decision-maker have been exhausted. That authority must be guided by due process, including the individual's right to: notice; be heard; present evidence; identify experts to testify on his or her behalf; be represented by one or more well-informed individuals who he or she trusts and chooses; challenge any evidence at the hearing; and appeal any adverse finding to a higher court. Any surrogate decision-maker must take account of the person's preferences and strive to make the decision that the person with an intellectual disability would make if he or she were able to do so.

This standard was accepted by all Montreal Declaration signatories: self-advocates, leaders of parents' groups, human rights lawyers, governmental representatives, etc. Article 6 is constructed around the principles of self-determination, vulnerability/paternalism and consent.

Self-determination

Self-determination is defined as 'acting as the primary causal agent in one's life and making choices and decisions regarding one's quality of life free from undue external influence or interference' (Wehmeyer 1996, p.24) while acting without any constraint other than that of the good of others (Lachapelle and Wehmeyer 2003; Wehmeyer 1998). The concept of self-determination is somewhat new to the human rights realm. Self-determination is an international law concept born in the 19th century and that became prominent through the decolonization period of the first half of the 20th century. It refers to the right to self-rule. Self-determination for persons with ID is very much linked to the right to agency, which 'means the capacity of individuals to set themselves goals and accomplish them as they see fit' (Ignatieff 2000, p.23).

The concept of self-determination, recognized by the WHO and PAHO, is notably set out in the United Nations MI Principles[lxxi] and Standard Rules,[lxxii] which state that all treatment must be based on preserving and actualizing the person's autonomy. The principle of autonomy requires that any action which has consequences for another person must be subject to the consent of the person involved; without this consent, the action is not legitimate and the use of force in resistance is morally defensible (Hanson as cited by Massé 2003). Ethically speaking, although defining autonomy is highly complex, it appears that all theories on the subject agree on two essential conditions: freedom and agency (Beauchamp and Childress 2001). Both these conditions emphasize freedom of choice, the absence of coercion, and the recognition that individuals are capable of intentional actions (agency).[lxxiii]

Vulnerability and paternalism

According to international soft law, persons with an intellectual disability are vulnerable and, consequently, may be poorly prepared for evaluating the risk factors to which they are exposed:

> 'Vulnerability' refers to a substantial incapacity to protect one's own interests owing to such impediments as lack of capability to give informed consent, lack of alternative means of obtaining medical care or other expensive necessities, or being a junior or subordinate member of a hierarchical group. Accordingly, special provision must be made for the rights and welfare of vulnerable persons.[lxxiv]

What happens, however, when respect for an individual's autonomy is in undeniable opposition to his physical and mental well-being? Does respect for autonomy mean that we are not authorized to imagine a greater good for persons with an intellectual disability than they are able to imagine for themselves? What should we do when protecting the fundamental rights of a person with an intellectual disability is prima facie incompatible with his ability to exercise self-determination and, furthermore, when the best way of protecting the person means denying him any possibility of consent?

Independently of the concept of vulnerability, it remains unassailable that persons with ID are, first and foremost, subjects of rights. The stronger the degree of paternalism, the greater the risk that other principles such as autonomy will be encroached upon. Although paternalism may be acceptable in ensuring the welfare of the person concerned, a form of paternalism which focused on the welfare of a third party such as, for example, a health and social services organization, would not be admissible. The organization, nevertheless, could be paternalistic, which would mean that it would have the moral obligation, to a certain legal degree, to request an intervention if it believed its users to be at risk. The question then is to know whether the vulnerability of persons with an intellectual disability justifies a certain degree of paternalism.

If it is then inevitable, and even desirable, to be paternalistic in order to protect users, it should nonetheless not be forgotten that paternalism implies a priori that certain objective criteria exist for determining what is best for the individual. Furthermore, this way of viewing the relationship between persons and the organization or health professional presupposes that both parties share the same values (Bissonnette and Drouin 1994), or at least are aware of the other's values.

This is where Article 6 of the Montreal Declaration comes into play, in helping to identify these values and also safeguarding the paternalistic interventions.

Consent

Consent is defined as the ability of individuals to choose what they consider best for themselves, insofar as they do not subject others (that is, without their consent) to the consequences of their actions (Cea and Fisher 2003). Acceptance of the individual's autonomy requires that any act of consequence to this individual must be subject to his/her consent. Without this consent, the action is not legitimate (Hanson 2004) and illegal. The difference between obtaining or not consent is important. Without consent, a surgeon is committing an assault with a deadly weapon, a felony. With a proper and valid consent, the same surgeon is proceeding in operating a patient.

The consent of persons with ID must be at the heart of all decisions concerning them and this consent must be both free and informed. Decisions must be free of any constraint and made with knowledge of all necessary information. This principle applies, in theory, to all types of intellectual disabilities where competency is not called into question (Dinerstein, Herr and O'Sullivan 1999). It is important to note before getting to consent, one has to verify if the person with ID can consent. That question of competency to consent is very important, as it has to be based on a case per case approach (Schalock and Luckasson 2005), is not static and can be influenced by stimuli and learning (Khouri and Philips-Nootens 2005).

The principle of autonomy underlines the importance of free and informed consent. In order to obtain consent, all relevant information must be supplied when meeting with the person and simple explanations given, avoiding overly technical terms. Time for reflection must also be given. The person's response should be given verbally or by signing a consent form. But how can one ensure that consent is truly informed? Is this feasible (O'Neill 2003)? And, most importantly, how does one define the term 'informed' in the case of persons with ID?

The Montreal Declaration addressed these questions by stating that under no circumstance should a person with ID be considered completely incompetent to make decisions. Even persons who have difficulty making choices, formulating decisions and communicating their preferences can make decisions.

One of the conditions which would appear essential in obtaining informed consent is that persons with ID understand the issue. The fact that a person may have difficulty in expressing himself verbally does not automatically imply that he is incapable of giving consent. There are various means of communication and consent may be given in a non-verbal way. The MI Principles state, in Principle 11(2), that the right to informed consent includes the right to information about treatment in *a language and manner* (italics ours) understood by the patient. In the same way, General Comment 5 establishes the right to benefit from all the latest scientific advances.[lxxv] These reasons establish that it is the State's duty to ensure that consent is obtained by using all the technical support necessary.

Once it is established by an independent and competent authority that a person with intellectual disability is incompetent to make a specific decision, the Montreal Declaration then establishes guidelines to support the decision-making of the person with ID. After all less restrictive alternatives to the appointment of a surrogate decision-maker have been exhausted, that independent and competent authority must take into account the person with ID's preferences and strive to make the decision he/she would have made if able to do so. This process must notably include the person with ID's right to be heard, be represented by one or more well-informed individuals who he or she trusts and chooses, challenge any evidence at the hearing, and appeal any adverse finding. While these criteria can seem self-evident, they are of crucial importance in numerous countries that do not have any civil protection legislation or that have legislation traditionally used against persons with ID.

Although it is too soon to assess its repercussions, the potential impacts of the Montreal Declaration on Intellectual Disabilities are multiple and transcend political, civil, social, economic and cultural spheres. The Montreal Declaration could serve as a benchmark, or even as a standard, which in time might become a legal source of interpretation for the content of human rights provisions in the context of decision-making for persons with ID. While complementing the UN Convention on the Rights of Persons with Disabilities, the Montreal Declaration could become one of the references in the field of intellectual disability rights and enhance global and national awareness and support for the respect of the fundamental rights of persons with ID.

The UN Convention on the Rights of Persons with Disabilities

While the general protection to which all individuals are entitled is based on the abstract idea of their equality, the special protection recognized by international law as afforded certain groups of persons specifically takes into account the fact that all individuals are not identical and that, in certain matters, their needs and capacities may vary depending on their physical situation, intellectual state, general health, economic situation, etc. The principle of justice, in its most formal acceptation, requires that equals be treated equally and unequals, unequally (Aristotle as cited in Massé 2003). Thus, along with general rights conferred upon the 'abstract' person, specific rights must be recognized to vulnerable populations such as a child and his mother, the elderly person, or persons with disabilities.

Context

On December 19, 2001, the United Nations General Assembly formed an Ad-Hoc committee whose mandate was to draft a *Comprehensive and Integral International Convention to Promote and Protect the Rights and Dignity of Persons with Disabilities.*[lxxvi] One of the first acts of this committee was to give the High Commissioner for Human Rights the mandate to study the potential of existing juridical instruments for protecting the rights of disabled persons. The study[lxxvii] concluded that there was, in fact, no binding international juridical instrument specific to the rights of disabled persons. It naturally followed that this judicial lacuna also applied to persons with an intellectual disability. Indeed, statements on the fundamental rights of persons with an intellectual disability are scattered over 180 treaties, conventions and declarations dealing with subjects as diverse as the right to work, the protection of children, and the prohibition of discrimination against women.[lxxviii] As a result, the Ad-Hoc committee decided to concentrate on gathering and consolidating these rights into a single legally binding treaty.

Six years and eight meetings later, the Convention on the Rights of Persons with Disabilities was adopted by the UN General Assembly. It is the most rapidly negotiated human rights treaty in the history of international law. Following if not the content then the spirit of Article 15 of the UN Standard Rules[lxxix] that says that '[...] States must ensure that organizations of persons with disabilities are involved in the development of national legislation concerning the rights of persons with disabilities, as well as in the ongoing evaluation of that legislation', the Convention is the first treaty that directly, and most successfully, involved NGOs and civil society into the negotiations of its content.

The Convention on the Rights of Persons with Disabilities received its 20th ratification on 3 April 2008, triggering the entry into force of the Convention and its Optional Protocol 30 days later. On May 12, 2008, a commemorative event at the United Nations headquarters in New York celebrated the entry into force. According to United Nations officials, the rapid coming into force of the Convention on the Rights of Persons with Disabilities and its Optional Protocol, which was opened for signature on March 30, 2007, is due to the strong commitment of United Nations Member Countries as well as advocacy by organizations of persons with disabilities, who were instrumental in drafting the Convention. Adopted by the General Assembly in December 2006, the Convention was one of the fastest treaties ever negotiated at the United Nations. The Convention has been ratified by 41 countries at the time of writing (see www.un.org/disabilities for details).

Content and implications for persons with ID

The UN Convention aims at providing an international standard of human rights for persons with disabilities that will be legally binding on any country that commits to it. Disability groups throughout the world have welcomed it as a step forward towards universal recognition of the human rights of disabled people. The most significant impact of the Convention will be a levelling up of provision for persons with disabilities across the world. Inevitably, this means that it will be mostly keenly felt in countries that do not already have legislation protecting the civil and human rights of persons with disabilities. Currently only 45 countries out of 193 UN members have specific legislation that protects persons with disabilities.[lxxx]

The Convention refers to a very broad array of rights, from the specific right to equal recognition of persons with disabilities before the law to more general obligation of States to ensure and promote the full realization of all human rights and fundamental freedoms for all persons with disabilities without discrimination of any kind on the basis of disability. While the Convention does not create new rights, as it aims at consolidating existing ones, its focus is not only on legislation but also attitudes – it places a duty on the Member State to combat negative stereotypes and prejudices against persons with disabilities.

The Convention will apply only to those countries that ratify it. There is no specific compulsion on countries to ratify. The US, for example, has indicated that they will not ratify the Convention because they have disability discrimination laws in place. Once a country has ratified it, they will need to report to the Committee on the Rights of Persons with Disabilities on steps they are taking to promote disability rights, and remove legislation, customs or practices that discriminate against disabled persons. There are no details about what penalties might be in place if a country does not meet this obligation, nor what measures will be used to determine whether a country has made appropriate progress.

Countries that ratify the Convention will begin the process of replacing discriminatory legislation. As the new legislation comes into force, they will have to comply with it. This, however, will be a slow process, and universal minimum standards are unlikely to be a reality for a number of years.

Although composed of 50 articles, participants in the negotiations (States, international organizations and NGOs) were unable to reach a consensus on a definition of disability. They were however able to define in Article 2 the concept of discrimination based on disability:

> 'Discrimination on the basis of disability' means any distinction, exclusion or restriction on the basis of disability which has the purpose or effect of impairing or nullifying the recognition, enjoyment or exercise,

on an equal basis with others, of all human rights and fundamental freedoms in the political, economic, social, cultural, civil or any other field. It
includes all forms of discrimination, including denial of reasonable
accommodation.

Even without encompassing a definition of disability, the Convention still clearly
applies to persons with ID, as it states in its Article 1 that:

The purpose of the present Convention is to promote, protect and ensure
the full and equal enjoyment of all human rights and fundamental freedoms by all persons with disabilities, and to promote respect for their
inherent dignity. Persons with disabilities include those who have
long-term physical, mental, intellectual or sensory impairments which in
interaction with various barriers may hinder their full and effective participation in society on an equal basis with others.

While the impact of the Convention on countries that already have disability legislation in place, such as Canada, seems to be minimal, a closer look at the content
of the Convention seems to indicate that numerous friction points exist with the
actual organization of health and social services to persons with ID and their
families.

A quick examination of Article 19 of the Convention, pertaining to 'Living
independently and being included in the community', raises some questions
when it is stated that States Parties shall ensure that: '[…] persons with disabilities
have the opportunity to choose their place of residence and where and with
whom they live on an equal basis with others and are not obliged to live in a particular living arrangement'. More often than not, the community-based living
arrangements for persons with ID are of a 'when available' nature.

Article 20 of the Convention refers to the obligation of States Parties to take
effective measures to facilitate 'the personal mobility of persons with disabilities
in the manner and at the time of their choice, […]', which again brings up the
question of self-determination of persons with ID in the organization of ID services as well as the capacity of service providers to insure the exercise of these
rights.

These examples, amongst many, show the difficulties that lie ahead in getting
national legislation in step with the UN Convention on the Rights of Persons
with Disabilities. As mentioned, in Canada, it is the federal government that is the
only competent body to sign binding treaties. When it finally ratifies the UN
Convention,[lxxxi] it will be bound by its content, from Newfoundland to Yukon,
regardless of provincial jurisdiction. From the UN Convention will emanate State
obligations to respect, protect and fulfil this Convention and the rights that it
contains.

These examples highlight the importance of drafting legislation, policies and programs that put the support of the choices of persons with ID and their families at the core of their content. Moreover, they also showcase the fact that while the Convention does not create new rights, as it aims at consolidating existing treaty-based ones, it allows for a review of the numerous shortcomings associated with the respect of these existing rights towards persons with ID. One has to wish that the monitoring mechanisms that are part of the Convention will allow Member States to be shamed into action towards addressing historical wrongs pertaining to the real respect and exercise of the human rights of persons with ID.

CONCLUSION – THE ROAD AHEAD

There is no country in the world where major policy and program changes in matters related to the rights of persons with ID are not required.[lxxxii] Furthermore, the existence of laws does not necessarily guarantee that the fundamental rights of persons with ID are protected. In some countries, it is through laws that the fundamental rights of persons with ID are violated.[lxxxiii] The UN Convention on the Rights of Persons with Disabilities seeks to address this situation.

One of the current challenges is to ensure that the recent attention to human rights translates into policies, programs and actions that will effectively impact on the underlying conditions necessary for the respect and enforcement of the human rights of persons with ID. The best way to go forward would be by mainstreaming human rights: assessing the human rights implication of any planned action, including legislation, policies or programs, in all areas and at all levels pertaining to persons with ID. Mainstreaming is thinking about the human rights aspects of every governmental action that affects persons with ID and their families. This holistic approach[lxxxiv] would make human rights an integrated part of the design, implementation, monitoring and evaluation of policies and programs in the political, economical and social spheres. As stated in the Montreal Declaration, States would thus have to guarantee the presence, the availability, the access and the enjoyment of adequate health and social services based on the needs and, in line with Article 25 of the UN Convention on the Rights of Persons with Disabilities, the free and informed consent of persons with ID. Accordingly, persons with ID and their families would always be actively involved in all these processes, whose outcomes should promote the organization of community-based services[lxxxv] that guarantee the enforcement of these rights.

Furthermore, persons with ID and their families must be aware that they share the same rights and freedoms as all other human beings, that they are entitled to due process of law and that ultimately they have the right to a legal recourse or any other effective recourse to a competent court or tribunal for protection against acts that violate their fundamental rights recognized by national and international laws. In the Americas, the national laws of the Member States of the Pan-American Health Organization (PAHO)[lxxxvi] all include anti-discriminatory provisions that may be invoked by persons with an intellectual disability or the groups which represent them.[lxxxvii] Also, several Member States of PAHO have signed the Pan-American Convention on Human Rights,[lxxxviii] as well as the ICCPR and the ICESCR, all of which contain provisions protecting the fundamental rights of persons with an intellectual disability.[lxxxix] Finally, the UN Convention on the Rights of Persons with Disabilities contains such mechanisms, as do most federal and provincial human rights legislation in Canada.

The concept of human rights of persons with ID has been an evolving historical process which, rather than culminating, truly starts with the UN Convention on the Rights of Persons with Disabilities. Intellectual disability is more than ever seen as part of the diversity of the human race. Consequently, questions related to the fundamental rights of persons with an intellectual disability are, in fact, by their universal nature, questions of general interest to all citizens. As such, it is through international law that these fundamental human rights of persons with ID have expanded to encompass a corpus of rights equal to those of all other human beings. The road ahead now leads to States themselves pushing through national recognition of these international law concepts. Only then will persons with ID truly be able to enhance their right to be equal while protecting their right to be different.

REFERENCES

African Charter of Human and Peoples Rights (1982) OAU Doc CAB/LEG/67/3 rev 5, 21 ILM 58.

Alma-Ata Declaration (1978) 'Report of the International Conference on Primary Health Care, Alma-Ata', *WHO: 'Health for all'*, 1, 6–12. WHO: Geneva.

American Convention on Human Rights, O.A.S. Treaty Series No. 36, 1144 U.N.T.S. 123.

Baker c. Canada (Ministère de la Citoyenneté et de l'Immigration) (1999) 2 R.C.S. 817.

Beauchamp, T. L. and Childress, J. F. (2001) *Principles of Biomedical Ethics*, 5th edn. New York: Oxford University Press.

Bissonnette, G. and Drouin, M.-S. (1994) 'Attitudes et rôle du médecin dans une unité de soins palliatifs.' *Le Médecin du Québec*, février, p.56–59.

Bolis, M. (2002) *The Impact of the Caracas Declaration on the Modernization of Mental Health Legislation in Latin America and the English-speaking Caribbean*. PAHO document presented at the *XXVII International Congress on Law and Mental Health*, Amsterdam, The Netherlands, July 9–12.

British Columbia (Superintendent of Motor Vehicles) v. British Columbia (Council of Human Rights) (1999) 3 R.C.S. 868.

Cea, C. D. and Fisher, C. B. (2003) 'Health care decision-making by adults with mental retardation.' *Mental Retardation, 41*, 2, 78–87.

Conclusions and recommendations of the Committee on Economic, Social and Cultural Rights, Canada, U.N. Doc. E/C.12/1/Add.31 (1998).

Constitution of the World Health Organization (1948) 14 R.T.N.U. 204.

David, E. (1985) 'Le droit à la santé comme droit de la personne.' *Revue québécoise de droit international, 81*, 63–116.

Dinerstein, R. D., Herr, S. and O'Sullivan, J. (eds) (1999) *A Guide to Consent.* Washington, DC: AAMR.

Drapeau, M. (2001) 'L'évolution de l'obligation d'accommodement à la lumière de l'arrêt Meiorin'. *Revue du Barreau, 61*, 299–319.

Duplessis, I. (2007) 'La pertinences des instruments internationaux en matière de protection des majeurs', dans *Service de formation permanente du Barreau du Québec, Autonomie et protection, 261*, 1–31, 19.

Form for Presenting Petitions on Human Rights Violations to the Inter-American Commission on Human Rights of the Organization of American States. Retrieved from www.cidh.oas.org/cidh_apps/instructions.asp?gc_language=E on October 28 2008.

General Comment 5 on Persons with disabilities, Report on the Tenth and Eleventh Sessions, U.N. ESCOR 1995, par. 5.

General Comment 14 ICESCR (22nd session, 2000), no. 43.

Gruskin, S. (ed) (2005) *Perspectives on Health and Human Rights.* New York and London: Taylor & Francis Routledge.

Hanson, B. (2001) 'Principe d'autonomie.' In G. Hottois and J.-N. Missa (eds) *Nouvelle Encyclopédie de bioéthique.* Brussels: De Boeck University.

Herr, S. (2003) 'From wrongs to rights: International Human Rights and legal protection' in S. Herr, L. Gostin and H. H. Koh (eds) *The Human Rights of Persons with Intellectual Disabilities.* Oxford: Oxford University Press.

Ignatieff, M. (2000) *The Rights Revolution.* Toronto: House of Anansi Press.

Inclusion International (2006) *World Report on Poverty and Disability: Hear Our Voices: People with an intellectual disability and their families speak out on poverty and exclusion.* London: [www.inclusion-international.org]

International Covenant on Civil and Political Rights, G.A. res. 2200A (XXI), 21 U.N. GAOR Supp. (No. 16) at 52, U.N. Doc. A/6316 (1966), 999 U.N.T.S. 171.

International Covenant on Economic, Social and Cultural Rights, G.A. res. 2200A (XXI), 21 U.N. GAOR Supp. (No. 16) at 49, U.N. Doc. A/6316 (1966), 993 U.N.T.S. 3.

Khouri, R. P. and Philips-Nootens, S. (2005) *L'intégrité de la personne et le consentement aux soins,* 2e édition. Québec: Éditions Yvon Blais.

Lachapelle, Y. and Wehmeyer, M. L. (2003) 'L'autodétermination.' In M. J. Tassé and D. Morin (eds) *La déficience intellectuelle.* Montréal: Éditions Gaëtan Morin.

Lecomte, J. and Mercier, C. (2007) 'The Montreal Declaration on Intellectual Disabilities of 2004: An important first step.' *Journal of Policy and Practice in Intellectual Disabilities, 4*, 1, 66–69.

Manila II (1993, WHO and CIOMS).

Marcil-Lacoste, L. (1994) Les avatars de l'égalité dans la réflexion contemporarire, *Cahiers de Recherche Ethique, 18*, 10. In M. Garon and P. Bosset (2003) *Le droit à l'égalité: des progrès remarquables, des inégalités persistantes.* Commission des droits et libertés de la personne et de la jeunesse, 2003. Retrieved from www.cdpdj.qc.ca/fr/droits-personne/bilan_charte.asp?noeud1=noeude2=16cle=0 on October 28 2008.

Massé, R. (2003) *Éthique et santé publique,* Québec: Les Presses de l'Université Laval.

Nussbaum, M. C. (2006) *Frontiers of Justice.* Cambridge, MA: Harvard University Press.

O.A.S. Treaty Series No. 36, 1144 U.N.T.S. 123, reprinted in Basic Documents Pertaining to Human Rights in the Inter-American System, OEA/Ser.L.V/II.82 doc.6 rev.1 at 25 (1992).

O'Flaherty, M. (2006) 'The concluding observations of UN Human Rights Treaty Bodies.' *Human Rights Law Review 27*, 31.

O'Neill, O. (2003) 'Some limits of informed consent.' *Medical Ethics, 29*, 4–7.

Olmstead v. L.C. ex rel. Zimring 119 S.Ct. 2176 (1999).

Penney, J. (2002) 'A constitution for the disabled or a disabled constitution?' *Journal of Law and Equality, 1*, 1, 84–115.

Principles for the Protection of Persons with Mental Illness and the Improvement of Mental Health Care, adopted in 1991 by the United National General Assembly, G.A. Res. 46/119, 46 U.N. GAOR Supp. (no. 49) Annex at 188–192, U.N. Doc. A/46/49 (1991).

Proulx, D. (2001) 'Les droits à l'égalité revus et corrigés par la Cour Suprême du Canada dans l'arrêt Law: un pas en avant ou un pas en arrière?' *Revue du Barreau, 61*, 185–279.

Quinn, G. and Degener, T. (2002) *Human Rights Are for All: A Study on the Current Use and Future Potential of the United Nations Human Rights Instruments in the Context of Disability.* Geneva: Office of the UN High Commissioner for Human Rights.

Re Legislative jurisdiction of Parliament of Canada to enact Weekly rest in industrial undertakings Act (135, c.14), (1936) R.C.S. 461.

Re Public Service Employee Relations Act (Alb), (1987) 1 R.C.S. 313.

Report of the Special Rapporteur on the right of everyone to the enjoyment of the highest attainable standard of physical and mental health, Paul Hunt, COMMISSION ON HUMAN RIGHTS, E/CN.4/2005/51.

Rioux, M. (2003) 'On second thought: constructing knowledge, law, disability and inequality.' In S. Herr, L. Gostin and H. H. Koh (eds) *The Human Rights of Persons with Intellectual Disabilities.* Oxford University Press.

Rosenthal, E. (2003). 'Recognizing existing rights and crafting new ones: Tools for drafting human rights instruments for people with mental disabilities. In S. Herr, L. Gostin and H. H. Koh (eds) *The Human Rights of Persons with Intellectual Disabilities.* Oxford University Press.

Rosenthal, E. and Sundram, C. J. (2003). *International Human Rights and Mental Health Legislation,* WHO manual, p.19. Oxford: Oxford University Press.

Schalock, R. L. and Luckasson, R. (2005) *Clinical Judgment.* Washington DC: AAMR.

Speech from the delegate Minister to Youth Protection and Readaptation, Mrs. Margaret Delisle, National Quebec Assembly debate, Wednesday, March 16, 2005, Vol. 38, N° 127.

Sudre, F. (2001) 'La Convention Européenne des Droits de l'Homme', in L. Nkopipie Deumeni (ed) Le fonctionnement de la justice pénale et les exigences du droit des droits de l'homme: L'exigence de la célérité, Projet/Justice/PNUD.

The Case of Victor Rosario Congo, Inter-American Commission on Human Rights, Report 29/99, Case 11, 427, Ecuador, Sess. 1424, OEA/Ser/L.V/II.) Doc. 26, March 9, 1997, para. 54.

The Economist, Many rights, some wrongs, March 22 2007 print edition.

The Economist, April 4 2007 print edition.

Universal Declaration of Human Rights, G.A. Res. 217 A (III), G.A. Off. Doc., 3rd session, p.71, U.N. Doc. A/810 (December 10, 1948).

United Nations, *Comprehensive and Integral International Convention to Promote and Protect the Rights and Dignity of Persons with Disabilities,* G.A. Res. 168, U.N. GAOR, 56th Sess, Agenda Item 119(b), U.N. Doc A/RES/56/168 (2001).

United Nations, Standard Rules on the Equalization of Opportunities for Persons with Disabilities, G.A. Res. A/RES/48/96 (December 20th, 1993).

Vienna Convention on the Law of Treaties, 1969, Article 27.

Vienna Declaration and Program for Action, World Conference on Human Rights, Vienna, June 14–25, 1993, U.N. Doc A/CONF.157/23, II (B) (6) (63).

Wehmeyer, M. L. (1996) 'Self-determination as an educational outcome: Why is it important to children, youth and adults with disabilities?' In D. J. Sands and M. L. Wehmeyer (eds) *Self-determination Across the Life Span: Autonomy and Choice for People with Disabilities.* Baltimore, MD: Paul H. Brookes Publishing Co.

Wehmeyer, M. L. (1998) 'Self-determination and individuals with significant disabilities: Examining meaning and misinterpretations.' *Journal of Associations for Persons with Severe Handicaps, 5,* 24.

WHO Mental Health Policy and Service Guidance Package: Mental Health Legislation & Human Rights, 2003.

WHO, *25 Questions and Answers on Health and Human Rights,* Health & Human Rights Publication Series, Issue No. 1, July 2002.

NOTES

i   Very few international documents specifically pertain to intellectual disabilities; the most notable are the UN Declaration on the Rights of Mentally Retarded Persons (1971) and the Montreal Declaration on Intellectual Disabilities (2004).

ii   Most notably MM. Leandro Despouy, Bengt Linqdvist and Paul Hunt.

iii   The text of the Convention can be found at www.un.org/disabilities/ accessed October 28 2008.

iv   The text of the Montreal Declaration can be found at www.montrealdeclaration.com.

v   In this regard, see *The Case of Victor Rosario Congo,* Inter-American Commission on Human Rights, Report 29/99, Case 11, 427, Ecuador, Sess. 1424, OEA/Ser/L.V/II.) Doc. 26, March 9, 1997, para. 54.

vi   Gruskin, S., Harvard Intensive Course on Health and Human Rights, June 2006; notes from the author.

vii   Universal Declaration of Human Rights, G.A. Res. 217 A (III), G.A. Off. Doc., 3rd session, p.71, U.N. Doc. A/810 (December 10, 1948).

viii   The Human Rights Council, based in Geneva, is the UN replacing body of the Commission on Human Rights, as a subsidiary organ of the General Assembly. The Council is responsible for promoting universal respect for the protection of all human rights and fundamental freedoms for all, without distinction of any kind and in a fair and equal manner. The Council can also address situations of violations of human rights, including gross and systematic violations, and make recommendations thereon to the General Assembly. See www.ohchr.org/english/bodies/hrcouncil for more information.

ix   It was a Canadian law professor from McGill University in Montreal, John Humphrey, who was one of the principal architects of the Universal Declaration of Human Rights.

x   G.A. res. 2200A (XXI), 21 U.N. GAOR Supp. (No. 16) at 52, U.N. Doc. A/6316 (1966), 999 U.N.T.S. 171, entered into force March 23, 1976. The ICCPR's supervisory body is the Human Rights Committee.

xi   G.A. res. 2200A (XXI), 21 U.N. GAOR Supp. (No. 16) at 49, U.N. Doc. A/6316 (1966), 993 U.N.T.S. 3, entered into force January 3, 1976. The ICESCR's supervisory body is the Economic, Social and Cultural Rights Committee (CESCR).

xii   Conclusions and recommendations of the Committee on Economic, Social and Cultural Rights, Canada, U.N. Doc. E/C.12/1/Add.31 (1998).

xiii   For more on this debate, see The Economist, *Many rights, some wrongs,* March 22, 2007 print edition, as well as the response by Mrs Louise Arbour, United Nations High Commissioner for Human Rights, in The Economist, April 4, 2007 print edition.

xiv   ICESCR General Comment 14 (22nd session, 2000), no. 30.

xv   Op. cit., note 16.

xvi   See www.ohchr.org/EN/ProfessionalInterest/Pages/InternationalLaw.aspx for complete list.

xvii   Declaration on the Rights of Mentally Retarded Persons, Proclaimed by General Assembly resolution 2856 (XXVI) of December 20, 1971.

xviii   Principles for the Protection of Persons with Mental Illness and the Improvement of Mental Health Care, adopted in 1991 by the United National General Assembly, G.A. Res. 46/119, 46 U.N. GAOR Supp. (no. 49) Annex at 188–192, U.N. Doc. A/46/49 (1991).

xix   United Nations, Standard Rules on the Equalization of Opportunities for Persons with Disabilities, G.A. Res. A/RES/48/96 (December 20, 1993)

xx   General Comment 5 (1994) on Persons with disabilities, Report on the Tenth and Eleventh Sessions, U.N. ESCOR 1995, par. 5.

xxi   Although the concept of erga omnes obligations would seem to be the exception to that rule, as they are obligations owned to the international community as a whole. As such, Member States to human rights treaties could bring forward complaints of violations based on the concept of erga omnes regardless of the nationality of the alleged victim.

xxii   Re: Legislative jurisdiction of Parliament of Canada to enact Weekly rest in industrial undertakings Act (135, c.14), (1936) R.C.S. 461.

xxiii   While the ICCPR and ICESCR were adopted in 1966, Canada ratified them both in 1976.

xxiv   As well as those emanating from UN organizations, such as WHO.

xxv   Op. cit., note 17.

xxvi   One of the most famous examples of this rule was exposed during the 1981 Constitutional Conference. The adoption of the Constitution Act, 1982, marked the repatriation of the Canadian Constitution. Because Canada had a written constitution originally enacted by the Parliament of the United Kingdom in 1867, patriation took place in 1982 by means of the Canada Act, 1982 (UK), Chap. 11; proclaimed in force April 17, 1982 (except s. 23(1)(a) in respect of Quebec). The federal government had convened the Canadian provinces to a constitutional conference in 1981 in order to negotiate the implementation of this Act.

xxvii   Baker c. Canada (Ministère de la Citoyenneté et de l'Immigration), (1999) 2 R.C.S. 817.

xxviii   See the famous opinion on the subject written by Chief Justice Dickson in Re Public Service Employee Relations Act (Alb), (1987) 1 R.C.S. 313.

xxix   Op. cit., note 9.

xxx   This conference was organized by the Montreal PAHO/WHO collaborating centre and its associated partners, the Lisette-Dupras and the West Montreal Readaptation centres for persons with intellectual disability.

xxxi   Report of the Special Rapporteur on the right of everyone to the enjoyment of the highest attainable standard of physical and mental health, Paul Hunt, Commission on Human Rights, E/CN.4/2005/51.

xxxii   MI Principles, op. cit., note 25.

xxxiii   Standard Rules, op. cit., note 26.

xxxiv   Speech from the delegate Minister to Youth Protection and Readaptation, Mrs. Margaret Delisle, National Quebec Assembly debate, Wednesday, March 16, 2005, Vol. 38, N° 127.

xxxv   'Every definition in law is perilous', Javolenus.

xxxvi   Universal Declaration of Human Rights, op. cit., note 12.

xxxvii   ICESCR General Comment 14, op. cit., note 19, no. 19.

xxxviii   Ibid., 'Inappropriate health resource allocation can lead to discrimination that may not be overt. For example, investments should not disproportionately favour expensive curative health services which are often accessible only to a small, privileged fraction of the population, rather than primary and preventive health care benefiting a far larger part of the population.'

xxxix   Universal Declaration of Human Rights, op. cit. note 12.

xl   Charter of the United Nations, June 26, 1945, 59 Stat. 1031, T.S. 993, 3 Bevans 1153, entered into force October 24, 1945.

xli   This clause is today very much incompatible with international treaties as well as national charters and laws.

xlii   General Comment 5, op. cit., note 28.

xliii   Vienna Declaration and Program for Action, World Conference on Human Rights, Vienna, June 14–25, 1993, UN Doc A/CONF.157/23, II (B) (6) (63).

xliv   Universal Declaration of Human Rights, op. cit., note 12. Article 2: Everyone is entitled to all the rights and freedoms set forth in this Declaration, without distinction of any kind, such as race, colour, sex, language, religion, political or other opinion, national or social origin, property, birth or other status.

xlv   See examples of this in Article 24 of the European Convention on Human Rights, as well as Article 49 of the African Charter of Human and Peoples Rights, OAU Doc CAB/LEG/67/3 rev 5, 21 ILM 58 (1982).

xlvi   The ICESCR does not yet receive individual complaints, although a UN committee is considering such a mechanism.

xlvii   American Convention on Human Rights, O.A.S. Treaty Series No. 36, 1144 U.N.T.S. 123 Entered into force 18 July 1978.

xlviii   www.cidh.oas.org/Basicos/English/Basic3.American%20Convention.htm

xlix   Equality of opportunity is also found in General Comment 14, where it is related to the *highest attainable level of health*. See ICESCR General Comment 14, op. cit. note 19.

l   See the report by United Nations Special Rapporteur on Disability, Bengt Lindqvist, at: www.un.org/esa/socdev/enable/dismsre1.htm. See also Leandro Despouy, Special Rapporteur, *Final Report*, 3, U.N. Doc. E/C4/Sub2/1991/31 (12 July 1991); Inclusion International (2006). World Report on Poverty and Disability: 'Hear Our Voices: People with an Intellectual disability and their families speak out on Poverty and Exclusion', London: [www.inclusion-international.org]; E. Rosenthal and C. Sundstram in *The Human Rights of Persons with Intellectual Disabilities*, in S. Herr, L. Gostin and H. H. Koh (eds) Oxford University Press, 2003, 551pp. For a more detailed description of human rights abuses against persons with ID, see Mental Disability Rights International Reports available at www.MDRI.org as well as the International Disability Rights Monitor (IDRM) project at www.ideanet.org.

li   Marcil-Lacoste has inventoried, in 20th-century writings, no fewer than 140 ways of defining equality. Marcil-Lacoste (1994) in M. Garon and P. Bosset (2003) *Le droit à l'égalité: des progrès remarquables, des inégalités persistantes*. www.cdpdj.qc.ca/fr/publications/docs/bilan_charte_etude_2.pdf.

lii   International Covenant on Economic, Social and Cultural Rights (ICESCR); International Covenant on Civil and Political Rights (ICCPR); Convention against Torture and Other Cruel, Inhuman or Degrading Treatment or Punishment (CAT); International Convention on the Elimination of All Forms of Racial Discrimination (CERD); Convention on the Elimination of All Forms of Discrimination against Women (CEDAW); Convention on the Rights of the Child (CRC), The International Convention on the Protection of the Rights of All Migrant Workers and Members of Their Families (Migrant Convention).

liii   General Comment 5, op. cit., note 28.

liv   General Comment 5, op. cit., note 28.

lv   British Columbia (Superintendent of Motor Vehicles) v. British Columbia (Council of Human Rights) (1999) 3 R.C.S. 868.

lvi   This section is based on a presentation done by the author (Lecomte) at the XIV Congreso Mundial de Inclusión Internacional, in Acapulco, México on November 7, 2006, under the heading: In theory and in practice: The need to link health to human rights regarding the situation of persons with an intellectual disability.

lvii   Universal Declaration of Human Rights, op. cit. note 12. art. 25.

lviii   The World Health Organization was founded in 1948, at which time its Constitution was ratified by 26 states.

lix   It is interesting to note that, in spite of the existence of the WHO, all the organizations in the UN system intervene directly and indirectly in the area of health. For example, the policies/directives/interventions of the Food and Agricultural Organization (FAO), the World Bank, the International Labour Organization (ILO), the United Nations Organization for Industrial Development (UNIDO), the OECD, UNESCO, etc.

lx   Alma-Ata Declaration, Report of the International Conference on Primary Health Care, Alma-Ata, September 6–12, 1978, in WHO: 'Health for all', No. 1, WHO, Geneva, 1978.

lxi   ICESCR General Comment 14, op. cit., note 43

lxii   Ibid.

lxiii   Op. cit., note 16.

lxiv   ICESCR General Comment 14, op. cit., note 19.

lxv   Ibid.

lxvi   Ibid.

lxvii   Vienna Declaration, op. cit., note 57.

lxviii   See World Health Organization, 25 WHO Questions and Answers on Health and Human Rights, Health & Human Rights Publication Series, Issue No. 1, July 2002.

lxix   This example is taken from Eric Rosenthal and Clarence J. Sundram, International Human Rights and Mental Health Legislation, WHO manual, p.19.

lxx   Most notably the International Bill of Rights that encompasses the Universal Declaration of Human Rights, the ICCPR and the ICESCR.

lxxi   MI Principles, op. cit., note 25.

lxxii   Standard Rules, op. cit., note 26.

lxxiii   Massé, op. cit., note 78, p. 148.

lxxiv   Definition of vulnerability according to the Declaration of Manila (1993) made jointly by the World Health Organization (WHO) and the Council for International Organizations of Medical Sciences (1993, WHO and CIOMS).

lxxv   General Comment 5, op. cit., note 28.

lxxvi   United Nations, Comprehensive and integral international convention to promote and protect the rights and dignity of persons with disabilities, G.A. Res. 168, U.N. GAOR, 56th Sess, Agenda Item 119(b), U.N. Doc A/RES/56/168 (2001).

lxxvii   Quinn, G., op. cit., note 4.

lxxviii   For more details, see www.umn.edu/humanrts/instree/ainstls1.htm.

lxxix   Standard Rules, op. cit., note 26.

lxxx   http://news.bbc.co.uk/1/hi/world/5274354.stm.

lxxxi   Canada officially announced on March 31, 2007 that it will ratify the UN Convention on the Rights of Persons with Disabilities. Unfortunately, Canada has a long history of signing treaties but not implementing them through legislation. See interview with Mr. Peter Leuprecht, director of the Institut d'études internationales de Montréal in Journal du Barreau, June 2007.

lxxxii   General Comment 5, op. cit., note 28.

lxxxiii   See the WHO Mental Health Policy and Service Guidance Package: Mental Health Legislation & Human Rights, 2003.

lxxxiv   A holistic approach to health was initially developed by WHO in its 1978 report entitled 'Primary Health Care Involving a Paradigm Shift'. The concept was developed in relation to the community health approach and involved the participation of the community in the broad sense of organization of health services. Its objective was to promote concerted action amongst various social systems such as health, social services, justice and education. Intersectorality fosters interaction amongst individuals from various milieus and integrated interventions for society as a whole, rather than for individuals or target groups. In this approach, emphasis is placed on factors, which determine health. New public health (WHO 1989).

lxxxv   Since the Declaration of Caracas in 1990, community integration of institutionalized individuals has been established as a sine qua non of their welfare and, more specifically, as a fundamental right. This right to community integration was recognized as a basic right in General Comment 5 and, most notably, in the United States Supreme Court ruling in Olmstead v. L.C. ex rel. Zimring (Olmstead v. L.C. ex rel. Zimring 119 S.Ct. 2176 (1999)). Recently, international experts studying the question have concluded that mental health services offered exclusively in an institutional and segregated fashion border on discrimination, according to international law. The same would seem to hold true for institutional ID services. See Mónica Bolis, *The Impact of the Caracas Declaration on the Modernization of Mental Health Legislation in Latin America and the English-speaking Caribbean*, PAHO Document presented at the *XXVII International Congress on Law and Mental Health*, Amsterdam, The Netherlands, July 9–12, 2002.

lxxxvi   World Health Organization's Regional Office for the Americas. PAHO also works very closely with the Organization of American States.

lxxxvii   See the Form for Presenting Petitions on Human Rights Violations to the Inter-American Commission on Human Rights of the Organization of American States at www.cidh.org.

lxxxviii   O.A.S. Treaty Series No. 36, 1144 U.N.T.S. 123. Entered into force July 18, 1978, reprinted in Basic Documents Pertaining to Human Rights in the Inter-American System, OEA/Ser.L.V/II.82 doc.6 rev.1 at 25 (1992). The list is available at www.cidh.org/Basicos/English/Basic4.Amer.Conv.Rabbif.htm

3

Right to Life

Shelley L. Watson and Dorothy Griffiths

INTRODUCTION

> There are historical and contemporary reasons to believe that the life of a
> person with mental retardation has not had, and still does not have the
> same value for everyone everywhere. Even in an affluent society, moral
> perspectives and self-interest often decide who lives and who dies; who
> receives available resources and who is left without – who, in effect, is al-
> lowed to join the moral community of humanity in which equality of
> opportunities is held forth as the normative ideal (Noble 2003, p.389)

'In a perfect world, one would need to go no further than the elegant phrases contained in the Universal Declaration of Human Rights' (Herr 2003, p.19). The
Universal Declaration of Human Rights (United Nations 1948) rose in the after-
math of World War II to articulate 'the equal and inalienable rights of all members
of the human family' (p.2). Within this document, the rights of persons with disabilities to an adequate standard of life were ensured.

The Universal Declaration of Human Rights was a landmark document that
punctuated the future from a time during World War II where humanity had witnessed unprecedented evidence of abuse of freedom, dignity, and security. One of
the populations, that represents a seemingly unknown group of victims of these
atrocities, was individuals with intellectual disabilities. Hitler called people with
disabilities 'useless eaters' because they consumed the resources of the nation and
gave, in his mind, nothing back (Scheerenberger 1983). As a product of his
regime and the propaganda that followed, persons with intellectual disabilities
were identified, institutionalized, denied medical treatment and basic nutrients
and exposed to the gas chambers. His euthanasia program was so effective that
physicians and families became convinced that disabled children were better
dead than to live a life with a disability (Scheerenberger 1983). This event,
however shocking, was not an isolated incident.

At the beginning of the last century, persons with intellectual disabilities
throughout various parts of the world were the targets of the eugenics social

movement. The eugenics movement was conceived by Goddard (1920). The term 'eugenics' is derived from the Greek word for 'well born', a phrase coined in 1883 by Francis Galton, cousin of Charles Darwin. It refers to:

> the science of improving the stock, which is by no means confined to questions of judicious mating, but which, especially in the case of man, takes cognizance of all the influences that tend in however remote a degree to give the more suitable races or strains of blood a better chance of prevailing speedily over the less suitable than they otherwise would have had. (Galton 1907, p.17)

Eugenics brings together the study of heredity with some particular doctrines about the value of human lives (Russell 2001). The eugenics advocates sought to purify the human race from elements that reduced the intellectual and social welfare capacity of society. This movement had far-reaching implications to the procreation rights of individuals considered not 'well born' and to the more startling implications related to their right to life itself.

As a result of this movement, widespread sterilization laws were passed that allowed governments to legally and permanently ensure that thousands of young people with intellectual disabilities would not procreate. The movement was based on the belief that persons with intellectual disabilities would give birth to children who were disabled, and since disability, mental health risks, and criminality were all considered inter-related, the social fabric of society would be protected through sterilization laws. Although the theory had many scientific flaws, the practice of eugenics continued throughout much of North America until the 1970s.

The American Breeders' Association (cited in Scheerenberger 1983) summarized the views of the eugenics movement in its 1913 statement:

> The following classes must be generally considered as socially unfit and their supply should be if possible eliminated from the human stock if we would maintain or raise the level of quality essential to the progress of the nation and our race: (1) the feebleminded, (2) paupers, (3) criminaloids, (4) epileptics, (5) the insane, (6) the constitutionally weak, (7) those predisposed to specific diseases, (8) the congenitally deformed, and (9) those having defective sense organs. (p.154)

This Association explored various means to improve the race, including segregation and institutionalization, sterilization, restrictive marriage laws and customs, and euthanasia.

Since this time there has been the United Nations Declaration on the Rights of Mentally Retarded Persons (1971) and the Declaration on the Rights of Disabled Persons (1975). As a result, persons with intellectual disabilities have experienced more than a quarter century of equal rights and freedoms that has produced significant positive changes in the lives of persons with intellectual disabilities. Flynn and Lemay (1999), in reviewing the changes in social policy regarding persons with intellectual disabilities for the previous quarter century, note that there has been enormous improvement in the field since the formulation and adoption of the principles of normalization. Normalization requires that services make provisions that afford individuals with disabilities the same opportunities in life as nondisabled persons.

Although most Western countries support in principle the belief that any citizen has a right not to be deprived of life, liberty, or security except in accordance with the principles of fundamental justice, people with intellectual disabilities have endured and continue to endure gross violations of this right in the form of euthanasia and murder. Hollander (1989) cautioned that there is a current wave of:

> large-scale death making of afflicted people...which includes abortion of potentially handicapped fetuses, the withholding of basic (and potentially life-saving) medical procedures, and massive overdoses of psychoactive drugs. These place ever-increasing numbers of people with mental handicaps at risk for euthanasia. (pp.53–54)

Within the field, institutionally grounded practices such as sterilization, abortion, denial of life-saving medical treatment, and genetic engineering have come under attack for the real and potential threats they pose to this fundamental set of rights (e.g. Hollander 1989; Rioux 1996; Sobsey, Donnellan and Wolbring 1994; Ticoll 1996).

In this chapter the authors will explore the dimensions of the right to life debate as it relates to both historical and contemporary society.

SEMANTICS AND THE RIGHT TO LIFE

Ethicist Jan Narveson (1995) suggests that many of the issues around life and death are clouded in semantic distinctions that require clarification. She notes that, at the very least, there is a distinction between biological life and experiential or conscious life. The latter requires awareness, thought, feeling, sensation and emotion. However, 'the sort of life that most people have in mind as being valuable is life in our second sense' (Narveson 1995, p.61).

Narveson (1995) posits:

> spending thousands of dollars to keep a body functioning when no mind is attached to it would be regarded by most as pointless. But spending thousands to enable us to continue to have experience is something we do all the time, and that makes perfectly good sense to us. (p.61)

The challenge however to this distinction is that others are making determination for persons with intellectual disabilities as to whether their life experience is of value. It is the debate over the quality of life of persons with intellectual disabilities that has historically led to the death of persons with intellectual disabilities, often in the name of euthanasia.

Euthanasia is often called second-party assisted suicide. Euthanasia can be active or passive; the distinction is actively killing someone or passively letting the person die. It is typically thought of as 'easing the death', assuming first that there is suffering and second that the individual would wish to end life. However, others refer to euthanasia as 'the intentional putting to death of a person with an incurable or painful disease' (Stedman 1990, p.544). Sobsey (1994) suggests these definitional distinctions are critical. Using the former definition, starving a newborn with a disability or murdering a child with severe disabilities could not be determined as euthanasia but as murder because there would be no evidence of consent. The latter definition provides no distinction between euthanasia, eugenics and outright murder.

Narveson (1995) proposes that no one else can determine for another whether their life is worth living and to second-guess whether another is suffering sufficiently to want to end their life. In the example of Nazi Germany, the motivation for killing appeared to be contrary to the definition of euthanasia. Hitler spoke of creating a superior race and advocated the practice of selective breeding to eliminate the weak, ill and disabled from society; the disabled carried no value in Hitlarian society, except to drain on the resources of the state. In this case, the motivation appeared to be based in economics and the eugenic belief. If the motivation for the killing was for gain (i.e. financial), then the act was murder; if the motivation was based upon the eugenic propaganda of protecting the genetic pool in society, then the killings were genocide. Genocide is the systematic elimination of a specific group of individuals. This latter distinction appears more closely to describe the Nazi policy where persons with intellectual disabilities were allowed to die or murdered because of their disability.

The right to life for persons with disabilities continues to be debated in our contemporary society. Some of the issues that still emerge involve the question of who determines whether someone's life is worth living and whether we, as a society, have a right to make that determination for others. If there is a right to life, is it absolute? If we have a positive right to life, then society has a responsibility to keep people alive if it is possible. If we believe that there is a negative right to life, then it only forbids us from killing people, but permits withholding of life-saving intervention thereby depriving them of life (Narveson 1995). Such is the distinction that pervades many of the dimensions of the right to life debates that occur in contemporary society. In this chapter the authors will explore seven dimensions to the right to life.

RIGHT TO LIFE

The right to life can be looked at in many ways.

The right:

- to be conceived

- to be born

- to not have one's life terminated at birth because of social devaluation

- to receive the nurturance and provision of elements of life to sustain life to its fullest

- to safety and security of one's life

- to continue life through appropriate medical treatment and support

- to choose life.

Although the dimensions are somewhat indistinct, each dimension has some unique aspects worthy of exploration.

Right to be conceived

Today advocates caution that there is a new eugenics movement. Like the Victorian era eugenic movement, this one too is grounded in science. The current movement arises out of the discoveries of the Human Genome project, which has allowed scientists to identify the genetic codes for various forms of genetic-based diseases and disabilities. The Human Genome Initiative promises great potential for understanding the nature of diverse disabling conditions and enhancing the potential for improved quality of life for many persons with disabilities (Griffiths and Watson 2004). However, critics of the project have argued that this potential scientific benefit to persons with disabilities does not come without a counterbalancing risk to the same population. More specifically, concerned advocates have countered that as the knowledge of the genetic location of various disabling conditions becomes known, this information may be applied to either enhance the quality of life of persons with disabilities or to introduce a New Eugenics movement to eliminate individual persons with disability or to eliminate disability from society altogether. Advocates fear that once the genetic etiology of a specific disability can be identified through genetic counselling or in utero, families could be pressured to choose to avoid pregnancy or to abort a fetus with a disability, or to alter the genes of the fetus to eliminate the disability. The pressure for this may come from many sources: personal, economic, professional, societal, and even governmental (Asch, Gostin and Johnson 2003). Its critics argue that the science of the Human Genome project could therefore conceivably be used to eliminate the life of children with disabilities, thus serving as a new form of eugenics.

The birth of a child with a disability is often seen as nothing other than a tragedy for the family and for the child (Fletcher 2001). There are numerous articles written about 'agonizing choices' made by parents. The decision to terminate a life is usually presented as in the best interests of the child; the life of a person with a genetic condition is one of such suffering that it is better not to be born. Therefore, while bringing a child with a disability into the world remains a choice, it becomes a selfish action causing suffering (Fletcher 2001).

This belief has led some individuals to file so-called 'wrongful life' or 'wrongful birth' lawsuits. To clarify these terms, 'wrongful life' means the child sues the mother or medical practitioners for being born. In a 'wrongful birth' lawsuit, the mother sues a medical practitioner or institution for allowing the child with a disability to be born. Such suits are typically genetic or prenatal malpractice suits. Many of these lawsuits have been successful and many American judges have talked about the right of a child to be born as a whole functional human being (Liu 1987). In France, a court of appeals let children born with disabilities sue doctors for not having detected their disabilities while in the womb (Reynolds 2000). There has been one successful lawsuit in Canada where a physician was ordered to pay a divorced couple $325,000 for the 'distress and expense' of giving birth to a child with Down syndrome. The doctor was found negligent when he did not order an amniocentesis; the parents indicated that had they known their child was going to be born with Down syndrome, they would have aborted the child. Cases like these are awarded worldwide, being highly publicized in the United States, France, Korea, and the Netherlands (Pritchard 2005).

Arguments for termination of fetuses with disabilities have also been posed from the perspective of benefit to the fetus (Sheldon and Wilkinson 2001). The Fetal Interests Argument claims that termination benefits the fetus by saving it from a life that would involve intolerable suffering (Pritchard 2005). As stated by Harris (2000), 'deliberately to make a reproductive choice knowing that the resulting child will be significantly disabled is morally problematic, and often morally wrong…it is wrong to bring avoidable suffering into the world' (p.96). This is further endorsed by Purdy (1996) who states, 'it is morally wrong to reproduce when we know there is a high risk of transmitting a serious disease or defect' (p.124) and individuals at risk for the disease have a 'moral duty to try not to bring affected babies into the world' (p.128). Some researchers feel that there are now enough reproductive options available so that this duty need not impede a family's reasonable desires (Purdy 1996). This thus brings us to the issue of pregnancy termination if there is a genetic diagnosis.

Right to be born

Similar to the right to be conceived, advocates for the rights of persons with intellectual disabilities have also criticized certain contemporary medical practices for the rights violations they perpetuate. For example, amniocentesis – a routine medical procedure, particularly for women who are older – is used to determine if the fetus might develop Down syndrome. In some circumstances, the practice may be used to prepare a parent to be informed about how best to care for and understand the needs of their newborn child with Down syndrome, while in others the parents, so advised, may choose abortion.

Genetic counselling and prenatal diagnosis have become common occurrences when a couple or woman decides to have a baby. Breakthroughs in the Human Genome project have allowed for diagnosis of multiple disorders before a child is even born. The prenatal diagnostic process seeks to facilitate informed and autonomous decision-making, appreciation of the inheritance of a genetic condition, integration of genetic information into a useful framework, and improvement in the emotional well-being of those affected or their family members (Bernhardt 1997; Clarke 1991). However, prenatal screening practices are presented as a necessary intervention in the case of fetal abnormality (The Roeher Institute 2002) and several provinces in Canada have instituted province-wide programs aimed at reducing the number of babies born with disorders associated with intellectual disability.

Ethicists, human rights organizations, and genetic counsellors alike have their opinions regarding this controversial issue and consensus does not exist regarding which genetic applications are 'good' and which are 'bad' (The Roeher Institute in Cooperation with Inclusion International 1999). Disability rights activists note that as we move toward the quest for the perfect child, stigmatization against individuals with disabilities is evident (Shakespeare 1999; Turnbull 2000). Alternative views suggest that selective termination does not discriminate against people with disabilities because fetuses and individuals with disabilities are morally different entities (Gillam 1999). Finally, many researchers assert that genetic testing is simply eugenics in disguise (e.g. Black 2003; Turnbull 2000). As Hubbard (1997) so poignantly states, 'at base are similar principles of selection and eradication of life' (p.196).

Prenatal genetic testing cannot be discussed without addressing the issue of termination of pregnancy and the topic of this chapter, the right to life. Many feel that when testing reveals a disability, the only course of action is termination (Harris 2000). However, as discussed by Chen and Schiffman (2000), there is great debate as to what level of disability, if any, justifies pregnancy termination. Further, this points to the issue of quality of life and what constitutes a 'life worth living'.

Prenatal testing is carried out so routinely that we rarely question its existence. However, many writers have questioned why we engage in it (Kaplan 1993; Shakespeare 1998; Turnbull 2000). The most frequently given reason is that we are trying to *prevent* or ameliorate medical or disabling conditions that are genetically based. Once a genetic syndrome or condition is diagnosed in a fetus, there are three types of prevention that can be taken: (i) prevention of the birth through abortion; (ii) prevention or amelioration of the disability through methods such as treatment through dietary changes or supplements for the mother (e.g. (PKU)); and (iii) prevention of family disruption through prenatal preparation by family members. At first glance, these appear to be worthy and common sense intentions, but in fact the issue is not that simple.

The fundamental question remains 'Why do we want to prevent the birth of fetuses with disabilities?' (Kaplan 1993, p.607). Many reasons have been provided for the prevention of the birth of a child with a genetic disability, but the five most prevalent are: (i) the economic impact on families; (ii) the economic impact on society; (iii) potential disruption to families; (iv) the quality of life of a child or person with a disability; and (v) not being a 'perfect child' (Kaplan 1993). The economic impact on families and the disruption to families appear to be worthy or harmless reasons because they will allow the family to become prepared for the birth of their child. Advance knowledge also allows the family to make a decision that having a child with a disability is perhaps not an experience they are financially or emotionally prepared for. These goals of prenatal genetic testing will not be discussed further, but for further reading on this topic, please see Griffiths and Watson (2004). The quality of life of a person with a disability, which is not as clear cut, will be addressed later in the chapter. However, the economic impact on society and the issue of the perfect child point to eugenic principles, which are at the heart of the debate regarding prenatal genetic testing. This thus brings us to a discussion of eugenics and the relationship between prenatal genetic testing and historical eugenics.

Many argue that eugenics is an issue of the past and no longer a concern in society. On the other hand, there are differing opinions regarding the place of eugenics and whether or not current genetic testing perpetuates eugenic ideologies. According to the Genetic Interest Group (GIG 1999), the new genetics is concerned more with identifiable medical diseases than with personality traits and behaviours, therefore it is not eugenic. According to this group of researchers, the new genetics represents a biological approach to biological problems, not a reductionist approach to the whole human being. They further assert that leading researchers in the field understand the limited contribution of many different genes and their study is primarily individual variation, not purported race or social group differences. Moreover, they contend that very few researchers working in the field link genetics to ideas of racial or national success and failure. The GIG (1999) does acknowledge, however, that:

some people do interpret some areas of genetics in ways akin to historical eugenics – although cultural theories of group difference and degeneration are more popular today than genetic ones – but that is purely an interpretation of the science and not the science itself. To conflate the science with historical eugenics does a disservice both to modern genetics and to history. (p.8)

In GIG's (1999) view, both the philosophy and the science of medical genetics are different from historical eugenics. According to this group, medical genetics is neither 'reductionist' nor morally discriminatory. Rather, the underlying ethos of the field is to consider people equal as human beings, while recognizing that some have or are at risk of producing children with a medical condition. The general feeling of the new genetics is to alleviate disease and suffering, which often takes the form of section termination because cures are not available.

Disability rights activists, on the other hand, argue that prenatal genetic testing is simply eugenics. According to Lippman (1991), 'whatever else, prenatal diagnosis *is* a means of separating fetuses we want to develop from those we wish to discontinue. Prenatal diagnosis does approach children as consumer objects subject to quality control' (p.23). Moreover, 'all of these practices have the effect of reducing genetic disease or improving the health of newborn babies, but will they lead us down the slippery slope to the eugenic ideals experienced earlier in the twentieth century?' (Iredale 2000, p.211). As stated by Elizabeth (cited in Chapman 2002), a woman with a genetic disability, 'I mean it is really the last acceptable form of eugenics, isn't it?' (p.202).

As Russell (2001) comments, once we have stripped away the technical issues, we are faced with a very basic debate about whether we believe some unborn infants have more value than others. Further, the debate is essentially about predicting the future. However, no one can foretell the medical advances that will be achieved in the upcoming years, nor can one predict the quality of life for another individual (Yagel and Anteby 1998).

As mentioned above, the economic impact has been used as a reason for preventing children from being born with disabilities. Addressing testing for fragile X syndrome, the second leading genetic cause of intellectual impairment, White (1997) reports an estimated cost of over £90,000 for each case detected. In the United Kingdom, routine antenatal screening for fragile X syndrome is three times as expensive as that for Down syndrome. However, White (1997) endorses routine testing in order to prevent fragile X syndrome because this sum must be offset against the costs of lifetime care for a child with fragile X syndrome, which exceeds £700,000 (White 1997).

The cost of having a child with Down syndrome has also been addressed in recent literature; due to technological advances there is an increased life expectancy of individuals with this syndrome and a subsequent cost to care. Glasson *et al.* (2002) found that the life expectancy of individuals with Down syndrome is approaching that of the general population, but accompanied by a range of significant midlife health problems. They conclude that these findings are of relevance to all developed countries and have considerable implications in terms of the counselling information provided to families at risk of having a child with Down syndrome. Glasson *et al.* (2002) highlight the earlier age at which individuals with Down syndrome experience the onset of chronic disorders and the fact that a large majority of individuals with Down syndrome remain at home with their families, who care for them. They discuss the fact that care providers may 'be themselves age incapacitated and eventually unable to cope with the burden of an increasingly dependent relative' (p.392).

Glasson *et al.* (2002) further declare, 'despite the ready availability of prenatal diagnosis in most Western countries, the prevalence of Down Syndrome amongst live births appears to have stabilized' (p.393). Such a view is also evident in Olsen *et al.* (2002) who state that 'prenatal diagnosis has prevented an increase in Down Syndrome live birth prevalence but has not been sufficient to reduce live birth prevalence significantly' (p.991). Both of these groups of authors therefore see a primary goal of genetic counselling as reducing the number of individuals born with genetic disorders.

Kitcher (1997) believes that Western democracies practise 'laissez-faire eugenics'. Each parent or couple is free to make their own decisions. She cautions there is danger in retaining the most disturbing aspect of past eugenics – the tendency to try to transform the population in a particular direction to reflect a set of social values. Parental choice is often used as an argument that prenatal genetic screening is not eugenics; it is the parents' choice to terminate the pregnancy and parental choice is not mandated by government legislation (GIG 1999), therefore the spirit that drives parental choices has nothing in common with that which drove the old eugenics. Hampton (2005) therefore calls this 'family eugenics'. She chooses this term because ethical decisions made by the medical profession and state pass the final decision onto prospective parents and their families.

'Governments provide genetic services with expectation of health gain from the avoidance of disability. There is nothing wrong with this, so long as, unlike under the eugenics of old, parents remain free to make their own choices' (GIG 1999, p.8). However, disability advocates state that scientists and physicians are once more engaged in developing the means to decide what lives are worth living and who should and should not inhabit the world. The difference now is that they provide only the tools; pregnant women have the responsibility to make the final decisions, 'euphemistically' called choices (Hubbard 1997, pp.195–196).

This therefore brings us to the question, is it really a choice if there are societal pressures to have prenatal testing and, if the tests reveal a genetic condition, parents experience pressures to terminate the pregnancy?

When undergoing prenatal genetic diagnosis, parents are not always given real choices with full information about the technologies and treatments available (The Roeher Institute in Cooperation with Inclusion International 1999). Two ways have been cited in which women's autonomy in decision-making is compromised; the increased routinization of prenatal screening programs and the information they are presented with regarding disabilities (Kerr and Shakespeare 2003). In a study by the Canadian Royal Commission on new reproductive technologies, one in four women felt pressure from hospital staff to undergo amniocentesis (Glover and Glover 1996). Consequently, they are not always in a position to make free and informed decisions. As some geneticists and counsellors themselves have recognized, the consumer-oriented model in prenatal genetic counselling, whereby couples are left to make their own decisions, often conflicts with broader policy goals that focus on measures of efficiency and define 'successful' prevention in terms of termination of the pregnancy. Second, as discussed by Chadwick (2001), the amount of genetic information forthcoming, which is often poorly understood, may turn out to be a burden to parents rather than of assistance. Turnbull (2000) states that genetic counselling is a profession deeply committed to the furtherance of genetic medicine. Given such a commitment and imbued with medical authority, genetic counselling does not merely describe genetic reality to clients, it dictates genetic reality for them and in so doing radically alters their conceptions of the future. This genetic reality, however, presents a very biased picture of the genetic condition. Negative stereotypes and lack of recognition or awareness of the richness of the lives people with disabilities may enjoy when they are well supported also portray a bleak depiction of disability (The Roeher Institute 2002).

Medical professionals and genetic counsellors may themselves perpetuate these perceptions because of their own biases, because they are not well enough informed to challenge them, or because, out of concern for 'autonomous' decision-making, they attempt to be nondirective in their approach, leaving women in a moral and ethical vacuum (The Roeher Institute 2002). This is not always the case. Many trained genetic counsellors and informed physicians who have had positive experiences with disability make efforts to share these with the couples they counsel. However, trained counsellors do not provide most genetic counselling (The Roeher Institute 2002). Family doctors, obstetricians, and medical geneticists provide much of the initial counselling, and the counselling ability of these various professionals has been found lacking by several studies (see Marteau and Dormandy 2001). It has also been suggested that termination of life may be up to 50 per cent higher when counselling is done by a medical professional rather than by a trained genetic counsellor (Marteau, Drake and Bobrow 1994; The Roeher Institute 2002; Shakespeare 1998).

Parents must also face eugenic pressures from society and from individuals around them. A social environment hostile or indifferent to certain forms of disability does not facilitate genuine choice. Genetic diagnosis may also lead to blaming parents. As we begin to shift toward a search for a genetic cause of disability, this results in the blaming of parents who have 'caused' the disability. It is felt that parents are to blame by either not being screened for genetic conditions or by choosing to carry a pregnancy to term after screening reveals the existence of a targeted genetic trait (Kaplan 1993). Likewise, social pressure may lead to families being blamed for making 'wrong' decisions (Russell 2001). These pressures contribute to family difficulties or disruptions and social ostracism (Kaplan 1993). This is due in part to the belief that the life of a person with a genetic condition is one of such suffering and that it is better that they are not born. As Harris (1995) argues:

> not only is it not wrong, but indeed it is right to prefer to produce a non-disabled individual rather than a disabled one where there is a genuine choice...attempts to eradicate disability are not the same as attempts to eradicate the disabled, even where these attempts constitute preferring not to create individuals with disability. (p.233)

From a disability advocacy perspective, the reality of genetic advances is that a climate of medically endorsed intolerance against individuals with disabilities is being cultivated (Turnbull 2000). Intrinsic to this is eugenic pressure, which is inherently discriminative, violating international and national human rights legislation. However, eugenic pressure primarily focuses on fetal life, which is not covered by human rights legislation (Turnbull 2000). Until birth, the fetus is not considered an autonomous person and therefore cannot benefit from human rights (Flegel 1998). Since genetic science has not discovered any significant remedies for the 'genetic needs' of fetuses, termination is typically the obvious route. Yet clearly this only masks the problem and does not deal with it. Terminating a fetus with a genetic condition insults individuals with the same genetic condition. By locating the *problem* in the fetal and the female body, the social dimension of eugenics is masked by science (Turnbull 2000).

Right to not have one's life terminated at birth because of social devaluation

Scheerenberger (1983) describes historical evidence that the Greek philosophers Plato and Aristotle both advocated that children with disabilities should be put to death. In Sparta, infanticide was regulated by the state; newborns were examined by a state counsel and a child who was deemed defective was thrown from a cliff. Infanticide has been widely and routinely practised until recently on every continent and every civilization throughout history (Williamson 1978). In the book *Born to Die*, Shelp (1986) suggests there are three reasons why infanticide has been carried out: (i) to maintain a balance between economic resources and population, (ii) to eliminate children with disabilities, (iii) sociocultural reasons such as maintaining genetic purity, or religious reasons. For example, Martin Luther had suggested that children with disabilities were devils and should be drowned (Sobsey 1999a). Early in the 20th century there was a call to end lives 'not worth living' (Binding and Hoche 1920), changing the focus of the killing to one of quality of life, to prevent suffering and allow choice. However, Daly and Wilson (1988) suggest that disability is the most commonly accepted reason for infanticide in many societies.

In the late 19th to early 20th century, the decision to terminate a live birth had a more singular focus, eugenics. To increase the breeding stock of the nation and to eliminate forces that would deter from controlled breeding, the science of breeding became the new rationale for the elimination of persons with disabilities (Sobsey et al. 1994). One of the most noted violations of this right to life was witnessed in the Nazi regime that adopted a state policy in 1939 to systematically grant death of mercy to anyone whose condition, according to human judgement, was incurable. Physicians were permitted to kill patients with specific diagnoses that were incurable or if they had been institutionalized for more than five years (Sobsey et al. 1994). It should be noted however that at the Nuremberg Trial, where this and other practices were rendered crimes against humanity, Karl Brant, the head of the program, professed that his actions were to ease their suffering and indicated he acted out of beneficence. Under the application of this policy, 100,000 persons who were deemed mentally handicapped were put to death, such that in the 1960s in post-war Germany there were relatively few mature adults with mental retardation (Hollander 1989). Some of the individuals died of lethal injections; many simply had food and medical care withheld. Later there were gas chambers developed by the T4 program staff to look like showers so that the persons with disabilities would easily cooperate in their own death march.

The systematic murder of persons with intellectual disabilities was, however, not limited to what Hollander (1989) called the 'warped thinking of Nazi zealots' (p.53). Pernick (1996), the author of *Black Stork: Eugenics and the Death of Defective Babies in American Medicine and Motion Pictures since 1915*, details the eugenics movement. He described numerous instances where physicians refused to treat and thereby facilitated the death of newborns with disabilities and birth defects. Newspaper accounts publicized the withholding of life-saving treatment of babies with disabilities during the decade after 1925, and movies propagating the eugenic agenda became quite common. Hollander (1989), too, cites examples early in the last century where physicians would openly suggest that death would be preferable for persons with disabilities. Physicians proposed death by morphine, chloroform or carbonic acid gas as means to provide the painless extinction of persons with intellectual disabilities in the US. In 1941, a program was proposed to the American Psychiatric Society to sanction mercy killing for those who were considered hopelessly unfit; the program was, however, never officially adopted although seriously considered (Hollander 1989). This dialogue occurred just months before the United States was drawn in to World War II.

Even in recent years, euthanasia thinking and practice has continued. Van der Wal *et al.* (1982) reported that in the Netherlands, 26 per cent of the physicians surveyed indicated that they falsified the cause of death to indicate natural causes rather than euthanasia. Fletcher (2001) argued that some persons with disabilities lack the essentials of personhood and thus have no rights to life. He felt an IQ of 40 was questionable, below 20 was definitive of a lack of personhood. In the Yale-New Haven Hospital, Duff and Campbell (1973) reported that 14 per cent of the babies who died did so because of discontinued treatment. They noted 'decisions that are made not to treat severely-defective infants' are familiar in special care facilities (p.892).

Today, with the advent of neonatal intensive care units, children whose lives might have naturally terminated because of medical complications may now have potential for survival because of science. The new technology leads to discussion about when to provide treatment or select no treatment for newborns with disabilities. Judgement regarding corrective surgery involves decisions about the future prospect of quality of life of the newborn as well as the quality of life of the family. The topic has resulted in a wealth of literature on the topic and considerable debate among bioethicists.

Some bioethicists believe that there is no moral basis for not choosing to treat a child with a disability, citing discrimination, and noting that the right to life should take precedence over typical mitigating factors such as future potential, family impact or economic reasons (Ramsey 1978). However, more extreme ethicists suggest if there is no potential for cognitive life then killing newborns with disabilities is in most cases desirable and morally permissible (Tooley 1984). Singer (1979), an Australian bioethicist, suggests that 'killing a defective infant is not morally equivalent to killing a person' (p.13).

In some countries, due to 'a mixture of traditional practices, beliefs and superstitions...infanticide is still practiced in cases of serious birth disabilities' (Noble 2003, p.391). However, Noble continues that the 'practice of infanticide through selective non-treatment is probably very widespread throughout the world'. While the UN Declaration on the Rights of Mentally Retarded Persons suggests that persons with disabilities are deserving of full participation in the society to whatever degree is feasible, Noble cautions that the issue of feasibility allows for the discretionary judgement of whether this is feasible for a nation or for a family. Moreover, he suggests that, internationally, the Western standards of human rights are not shared.

Discussions in the United Nations have shown that internationally this is not merely a practice in history. 'During the last quarter century, the UN has taken an increasingly proactive role in working for global recognition of the human rights of people with intellectual disabilities' (Mittler 2003, p.37). In 1997, W. Eigner, President of Inclusion International to the UN High Commission on Human Rights, presented evidence where the lives of the newly born with severe impairments were being legally terminated.

Wolfensberger (1989) has suggested that massive death-making of persons with intellectual disabilities was still occurring in the United States in the late 20th century, estimating 200,000 to 400,000 lives were being terminated each year. He further suggests that withholding medical treatment from severely impaired newborns is addressed in isolation, as if there were no connections between this and the death resulting from other means such as withholding of sustenance or abortion.

Right to receive the nurturance and provision of elements of life to sustain life to its fullest

The denial of nurturance and the supports to sustain life occurs in two similar but slightly different versions: passive or cold euthanasia and neglect. Wolfensberger (1989) has termed these death-making.

Passive or cold euthanasia, as it is often termed, occurs when individuals are killed not by the action of another, but because of a lack of action. Passive euthanasia involves failure to provide the necessities to sustain human life (Sobsey 1994). Most of these forms of death-making are subtle and indirect (Wolfensberger 1989). In the Yale-New Haven hospital, it was discovered that of 299 newborns who died, 86 per cent had died despite medical efforts and 14 per cent died because of withheld or discontinued treatment. The 14 per cent who were denied supports to sustain life had disabilities (Duff and Campbell 1973). The stated motivation and outcome for passive euthanasia is the same as for active euthanasia; death is rendered because it is felt that the person should be provided an easy death. Often the justification given is that the person was 'better off dead'. This sentiment can be seen in the statement by Wimarth (cited in Hollander 1989), the superintendent of the Wisconsin Home for the Feeble-Minded, who described 'it is not uncommon for a person of a kindly and sympathetic nature, as he passes through an institution for the care of the mentally defective, to say that it would be a kindness to them if they were deprived of life' (p.57).

The second type of death-making is the withdrawal of care through negligence. Negligence is a form of abuse that occurs when the individual is denied the supports and care to sustain life. The motive for negligent abuse can be emotional, personal or sometimes financial. The following case illustrates this form of death-making.

Kay Lynn Kuffer, a 15-year-old with cerebral palsy, died weighing 15 pounds 1 ounce. She died from malnutrition and dehydration. She had not seen a doctor in 5 years. The mother reportedly responded to the child's death saying 'everybody has to go sometime.' She asked detectives to keep her name out of the paper because she did not want people to know she had a child. The child had not been out of the house in six years. The mother was charged with neglect leading to death of the child but was released on her own recognizance and a bond of only $10,000. (Sobsey 1999a)

Persons with intellectual disabilities are at higher risk for all forms of abuse, including negligence (Sobsey 1994; Wilson and Brewer 1992). 'Neglect is perhaps the most insidious form of abuse; in extreme form it may be one of the most damaging' (Sobsey 1994, p.34). Neglect can be physical (nutritional and physical needs are not met), emotional (deprivation of basic human interactions), medical (denial of appropriate medical treatment), or educational (failure to provide educational opportunities appropriate for growth).

For individuals with disabilities, neglect or abuse by omission is the most frequent form of abuse. Moreover, the more significant the disability, the more likely the abuse will remain unreported (Wilson and Brewer 1992). The victimization of persons with intellectual disabilities is often perpetrated within the very system in which they are supported and by the individuals who are empowered to support them (Luckassson 1992; Sobsey and Varnhagen 1988).

In the Kay Kuffer death, her lawyer noted that he had received dozens of calls of support for the mother. The minister who presided over Kay's funeral supported the mother by asking the media to stop demonizing her. However, as one noted authority on abuse wrote:

Kay Kuffer needed help as she slowly starved to death over the last six years. If her mother could not help her; maybe human services or child welfare should have. Maybe the health care system should have done something. Maybe the schools should have. I have no doubt that the health, education and social service systems share some of the blame with the mother. That does not make it okay. (Sobsey 1999a)

Right to safety and security of one's life

There is no more glaring example of the disregard for the life of a person with disability than the story of Amar Ahmed Mohammed, a 19-year-old with Down syndrome, who was befriended by a group of men. After gaining his trust they strapped him with explosives and sent him into a voting station in Iraq where he was detonated (Reynolds 2005).

This type of situation typically generates outrage from most individuals, regardless of one's political interests; however, most of the murders for apparent personal benefit are not so harshly judged by the public. In fact many of the murders of children with disabilities are often justified by the murderer and the public as understandable or justifiable. Let's explore some of the recent cases of children who have been murdered by their parents.

> Lisa Thompson attempted to murder her daughter Brandy Leigh, age 6, with a massive drug overdose in her daughter's feeding tube; she received a conditional sentence. (Sobsey 1999b)

> Rachel Craig murdered her daughter Chelsea; Chelsea had Rett's syndrome. (Reynolds 2001)

> Tracy Latimer was placed in her father's truck as he piped carbon monoxide poisoning into the cabin while the rest of the family went to church. He then placed her back in her bed and awaited the return of his family. Tracy was 12 years old and had cerebral palsy. (Eckstein 1996)

> Ryan Wilkinson, 16, was killed by carbon monoxide poisoning by his mother Cathy, who also killed herself; Ryan had cerebral palsy and was deaf and blind. (Skoutajan 1995)

> Oto Orlik stabbed and killed his daughter Lenka, 14; Lenka had multiple disabilities. (Sobsey 1998)

> Daniela Dawes was released on a five year bond, similar to probation, for murdering her 10-year-old son Jason, who had autism. Dawes pinched his nose and mouth closed until he suffocated to death. The judge who commuted her sentence from murder to manslaughter explained that she had 'suffered enough' and that there was no sentence he could give that would compare to the punishment she had inflicted on herself. (Reynolds 2004)

Rights advocates point to the unsettling number of incidents where parents have been accused of the murder or attempted murder of their children with intellectual disabilities, in some cases claiming they are performing euthanasia. The University of Alberta, in collaboration with Temple University, has uncovered 1000 cases throughout the world of homicide committed against people with disabilities (Sobsey 1999b). Sobsey (1999b) notes that the homicides show a pattern of leniency on the part of the courts, suggesting that the murder of children with disabilities is understandable. Moreover, the public has often responded with compassion to the parents who have committed these murders. In fact, there are several websites in support of Robert Latimer, regarding the 'unfair sentence he received for an act committed out of love by euthanizing his severely disabled daughter' (RobertLatimer.net, n.d.). Sobsey (cited in Reynolds 2002) reports that between 1990 and 1994, the average number of Canadian murder cases in which parents killed their children was 34 each year. Between 1994 and 1998, the average rate of such deaths was 49, with 62 cases in 1997 alone. Sobsey attributes this increase in deaths to the case of Robert Latimer and the support he has received publicly.

The grandfather of Brandy Leigh Thompson perhaps best exemplifies the sentiment often heard, 'I can understand how it happened. I think you know what I mean...I would have done it six years ago' (Canadian Press, November 10, 1998). Similarly, friends and supporters of Cathy Wilkinson commented that they were not surprised by the murder; the stress of raising a deaf and blind child at home drove someone to such drastic action.

Advocates clearly and vehemently oppose these practices, and warn that the message they convey to society recalls the underlying message of the eugenics movement – that the individual with a disability, the family of that person, and society would prefer that this person was not born and that disability did not exist in our society.

Right to continue life through appropriate medical treatment and support

A major concern regarding the right to life is denial of appropriate medical treatment and support. 'There is a tremendous amount of work to be done in order that children with disabilities in Canada receive medical treatment as would any other child' (Blanchet 1995, p.71). Clinicians have long-since noted that persons with intellectual disabilities often have medical challenges, which have been neglected or undiagnosed (Ryan 2001). Wolfensberger (1980) notes that:

> In hospitals (even those run by religious bodies), mentally retarded people, people with other handicaps, and elderly people are commonly denied relatively elementary life supports such as antibiotics, basic resuscitation. Or even the simplest medical procedures. In fact the likelihood is relatively high that persons afflicted with multiple devalued conditions will not leave a hospital alive – even if their affliction and/or illness is relatively moderate. (p.171)

Medical neglect is often the result of communication challenges with the persons who have disabilities, or 'diagnostic overshadowing'. Diagnostic overshadowing occurs when the disability foreshadows further exploration of medical issued (Reiss, Levitan and Szyszko 1982). In some cases, negligence is intentional. In 1983 Stephen Dawson, aged six years, was being denied medical treatment to repair a blocked shunt because the presiding physician convinced the family that his quality of life was insufficient to warrant the procedure. Local advocates were able to convince the courts to override the family and medical decision, and were successful in gaining the required medical treatment for Stephen (S.D. 1983).

Blanchet (1995) suggested that intentional medical neglect is the result of 'conscious or unconscious value judgments made by professionals about the quality of life of people with a disability, particularly those with severe disabilities' (p.75). Even the overarching medical organizations often resist restrictions on 'privatized death-making of impaired newborns' (Wolfensberger 1989, p.63). Life of the person with a disability is a value that is calculated against the economic factors of costly medical treatment and the societal estimation of who is most deserving of scarce resources. The latter situation is illustrated in a Canadian example. A young man with Down syndrome, Terry Urquhart, was initially refused a heart transplant, not because of medical reasons such as compatibility or viability, but deservedness. The medical decision was later overturned when the family challenged the decisions in the courts (Canadian Council of Canadians with Disabilities n.d.).

Persons with intellectual disabilities present with a greater probability of associated health issues than the population in general. Yet internationally, there have been reports about the challenges associated with access to health prevention and intervention resources for people with intellectual disabilities (Lennox and Kerr 1997). People who have intellectual disabilities, by virtue of their disabling conditions, often have increased likelihood of requiring medical care as well as increased likelihood of having their medical conditions misunderstood or ignored. Consequently researchers and advocates such as Feldman *et al.* (2005) argue there is an increased need to emphasize educational programs to teach medical self-advocacy to people with intellectual disabilities.

The above issue is illustrated in a study by Garth and Aroni (2003). They interviewed mothers of children with cerebral palsy about their experiences with medical professionals. The mothers suggested that a key factor in accessing medical care was continuity, whereby the physician can become aware of the person as a whole, not just their disability. They suggested that continuity was critical in realizing improved communication. As one mother noted, 'Even though…he [the child] mightn't understand it all but she [the general practitioner] still makes an effort by not talking baby talk but by talking to him at the level she thinks he will understand' (p.572).

Right to choose life

The link in the chain of life events is the right to choose life over death. Does a person with a disability have a right to choose whether to live or not? We all have the option of choosing when to refuse emergency medical care through a designated living will. For the purpose of this chapter we are not referring to situations where someone is requesting assistance to commit suicide. Assisted suicide, the choice to actively terminate one's life when there is imminent long-term illness or pain, goes well beyond the scope of this chapter. The aspect that we will however address is discussion of who chooses when someone would wish to have medical procedures that would allow an individual to sustain life.

> John was a man who had a great quality of life in his group home. He was beginning to develop some medical problems and was approached by his family to sign a 'living will'. The will stated that the staff should not call for medical care if he should have a heart attack. The family informed the agency that John had signed the will. The agency were uncomfortable with the role the family had asked them to play and felt that failure to call medical help would be negligent on their part. The staff further noted that John was becoming increasingly despondent and they wondered if he had been coerced into signing or signed out of deference to his family. The latter was the case and the will was revoked.

For whatever reason, John's family felt that his life was not worth saving if medical challenges arose. Their reasons may have been to ease his pain and suffering and long-term palliative care.

However, should it have been their decision to make? Many individuals today choose to produce a living will to ease the pressures and decisions upon those that are left behind and to make sure our personal wishes are respected. However, John was not asked but told what his right to life should be. The decision to continue life under these circumstances was not his but that of his family. In this case, John was capable of making this determination, but what about situations where the individual is not competent to make such a decision?

Kuhse and Singer (1985) suggest that if the person cannot make a determination if their life is worth living, then others more competent should make that decision for them. Other party decisions however bring question as to in whose best interest is the decision being made.

Blanchet (1995) notes that:

> In examining the issues affecting the rights of children with disabilities to medical treatment, one serious problem is the 'No Code' practice. In this practice, it is decided, often before a child requires life-saving or any other medical intervention, that the child will not receive any treatment except comfort measures or that no resuscitation will take place in the event of cardiac arrest. Children (with disabilities) are subject to this practice in ambulance services, in hospital emergency wards and in intensive care units. (p.74)

The following serves as a common example:

> Louis was automatically deemed by medical judgment as a DNR, do not resuscitate him when he fell into a coma in the hospital. The medical staff on duty assumed that there should be a DNR because he was a person with an intellectual disability. Only because of the questioning of one of the staff was this judgement challenged and medical attention was received. Louis lives a full and happy life now nearly ten years after this incident.

A second example perhaps serves as a conclusion for this chapter. Much of the discussion regarding right to life has been based on a decision about quality of life and whose life is worth living.

> Reg went to the hospital with stomach pains and was dismissed with medication to ease constipation. After several more trips, he was diagnosed with cancer. He quickly deteriorated and the question was posed by the medical staff, 'What is his life like?' The question had obvious meaning to his care workers. They knew that the doctor was asking, 'Is his life worth saving?' The staff very quickly described a vital man, important and involved in his community. They described a man who loved life and those around him, and who was deeply cared for by all. The Do Not Resuscitate Order (DNR) was not instilled. However, despite the vigilant care of his personal staff, who never left his side, and attentive medical attention, Reg passed away

> Reg was a man who loved people and he loved to go to church to listen to the music. His funeral took place in his local church that held about 400 persons. His minister had organized the music that Reg liked most and he provided a wonderful eulogy along with some staff and friends. It was one of the nicest funerals one of these authors has been to. In the eulogy the minister spoke of Reg and the impact that he had on the lives of so many. He had no family, yet the church was filled with people whom he had touched in a very meaningful way. His life had quality and his life had meaning to everyone in that room. Although he was unable to recover from the cancer, it was critical that to the very moment of his death his right to have that wonderful life was upheld.

CONCLUSION

From the time of Plato to the Holocaust, to current and emerging practice in the scientific community, the controversy of right to life of individuals with intellectual disabilities has been and continues to be a matter of debate and practice in our society. The right to life of persons with disabilities, although sanctioned by law, is not actualized in practice. Wolfensberger (1989) believes that there is need to act at many levels to end the death-making of persons with disabilities. He suggests the public must be more aware of the facts, educated about the realities, confronted about prejudice and practice, made accountable in the courts, and that there needs to be a commitment to challenge the laws and practices that have and continue to jeopardize the right to life of persons with disabilities.

Disability presents an enormous dilemma for the individual and the community. For, as Stiker (1997) suggests, disability introduces doubt into the social world of the individual and the community. Individuals, families, and communities are unprepared to recognize and seldom ready to accept disability. 'Disability is far from merely being a medical problem that can be "cured". On the contrary, it is mainly a cultural and sociopolitical problem' (Reindal 2000, p.92). Disability shatters preconceived expectations and norms and calls accepted values and notions of well-being into question (Albrecht and Devlieger 1999).

Reducing suffering and preventing impairment are goals that most people would support. Nevertheless in our focus on disability, we should not ignore people and relationships. Disability is a fact of life (Shakespeare 2001). As Suzuki (1999) asserts, it is the diversity of the human genome that gives us the resilience and ability to stave off extinction. Diverse genetic characteristics allow a species to adapt to new and unpredictable conditions. Suzuki (1999) questions what might be the ramifications of eliminating one of these genes from the human genome? Further, as poignantly stated by Gill (1992), if we eliminate individuals with disabilities, 'what group would be the next to be judged too imperfect' (p.42)?

REFERENCES

Albrecht, G. L. and Devlieger, P. J. (1999) 'The disability paradox: High quality of life against all odds.' *Social Science and Medicine, 48,* 8, 977–988.

Asch, A., Gostin, L. O. and Johnson, D. M. (2003) 'Respecting persons with disabilities and preventing disability: Is there a conflict?' In S. S. Herr, L. O. Gostin and H. Hongju Koh (eds) *The Human Rights of Persons with Intellectual Disabilities: Different but Equal.* New York: Oxford University Press.

Bernhardt, B. B. (1997) 'Empirical evidence that genetic counselling is directive: Where do we go from here?' *American Journal of Human Genetics, 60,* 1, 17–20.

Binding, K. and Hoche, A. (1920) *Die Freigabe der Vernichtung lebensunwerten Lebens.* Leipzig: Felix Meiner.

Black, E. (2003) *War Against the Weak: Eugenics and America's Campaign to Create a Master Race.* New York: Four Walls Eight Windows.

Blanchet, A. (1995) 'The rights of children with disabilities to medical treatment: The Canadian Scene.' In G. Allan Roeher Institute (eds) *As If Children Matter: Perspectives on Children, Rights and Disability.* Toronto: The Roeher Institute.

Canadian Council of Canadians with Disabilities. (n.d.) 'Consumers with disabilities speak out on health issues.' Retrieved from www.ccdonline.ca/publications on November 27, 2007.

Canadian Press (November 10, 1998) 'Mom gets bail in girl drugging case.' *The Tribune.* Welland, Ontario.

Chadwick, R. (2001) 'Whose choice? Whose responsibility? Ethical issues in prenatal diagnosis and learning disability.' In L. Ward (ed) *Considered Choices: New Genetics, Old Prejudices?* London: British Institute of Learning Disabilities.

Chapman, E. (2002) 'The social and ethical implications of changing medical technologies: The views of people living with genetic conditions.' *Journal of Health Psychology, 7,* 2, 195–206.

Chen, E. A. and Schiffman, J. F. (2000) 'Attitudes toward genetic counseling and prenatal diagnosis among a group of individuals with physical disabilities.' *Journal of Genetic Counseling, 9,* 2, 137–152.

Clarke, A. (1991) 'Is non-directive counselling possible?' *Lancet, 338,* 998–1001.

Daly, M. and Wilson, M. (1988) *Homicide.* New York: Aldine de Gruyter.

Duff, R. and Campbell, A. G. M. (1973) 'Moral and ethical dilemmas in the special-care nursery.' *The New England Journal of Medicine, 289,* 890–894.

Eckstein, C. M. (1996) 'One of our children is dead.' Retrieved from www.chninternational.com/one_of_our_children_is_dead.html on November 27, 2007

Feldman, M., Owen, F., Griffiths, D., Tarulli, D. *et al.* (2005) 'Facilitating health care and mental health care access of persons with intellectual disabilities: One element of systemic change.' *The NADD Bulletin, 8,* 4: 71–76.

Flegel, K. M. (1998) 'Society's interest in protection for the fetus.' *Canadian Medical Association Journal, 158,* 7, 895–896.

Fletcher, A. (2001) '"Three generations of imbeciles are enough": Eugenics, the new genetics, and people with learning difficulties.' In L. Ward (ed) *Considered Choices: New Genetics, Old Prejudices?* London: British Institute of Learning Disabilities.

Flynn, R. J. and Lemay, R. A. (eds) (1999) *A Quarter-Century of Normalization and Social Role Valorization: Evolution and Impact.* Ottawa: University of Ottawa Press.

Galton, F. (1907) *Inquiries into Human Faculty.* London, UK: J. M. Dent and Sons.

Garth, B. and Aroni, R. (2003) 'I value what you have to say: Seeking the perspective of children with a disability, not just their parents.' *Disability and Society, 18,* 5, 561–576.

Genetic Interest Group (GIG) (1999) Genetic Testing, Screening and 'Eugenics' [online]. Retrieved from www.gig.org.uk/docs/gig_eugenics.pdf on November 13, 2003.

Gill, C. (1992) 'Life, death, and disability: How eugenics and abortion puts activists in a quandary.' *Mainstream, 16,* 3, 38–42.

Gillam, L. (1999) 'Prenatal diagnosis and discrimination against the disabled.' *Journal of Medical Ethics, 25,* 163.

Glasson, E. J., Sullivan, S. G., Hussain, R., Petterson, B. A., Mongomery, P. D. and Bittles, A. H. (2002) 'The changing survival profile of people with Down's syndrome: Implications for genetic counselling.' *Clinical Genetics, 62,* 5, 390–393.

Glover, N. M. and Glover, S. J. (1996) 'Ethical and legal issues regarding elective abortion of fetuses with Down Syndrome.' *Mental Retardation, 34,* 4, 207–214.

Goddard, H. H. (1920) *Human Efficiency and Levels of Intelligence.* Princeton, NJ: Princeton University Press.

Griffiths, D. M. and Watson, S. L. (2004) 'Demystifying syndromes associated with developmental disabilities.' In D. Griffiths and R. King (eds) *Demystifying Syndromes: Clinical and Educational Implications of Common Syndromes Associated with Persons with Intellectual Disabilities.* Kingston: NADD Press.

Hampton, S. J. (2005). 'Family eugenics.' *Disability and Society, 20,* 5, 553–561.

Harris, J. (1995) 'Should we attempt to eradicate disability?' *Public Understanding of Science, 4,* 233–242.

Harris, J. (2000) 'Is there a coherent social conception of disability?' *Journal of Medical Ethics, 26,* 2, 95–100.

Herr, S. S. (2003) 'From wrongs to rights: international human rights and legal protection.' In S. S. Herr, L. O. Gostin and H. Hongju Koh (eds) *The Human Rights of Persons with Intellectual Disabilities: Different but Equal.* New York: Oxford University Press.

Hollander, R. (1989) 'Euthanasia and mental retardation. Suggesting the unthinkable.' *Mental Retardation, 27,* 2, 53–61.

Hubbard, R. (1997) 'Abortion and disability: Who should and who should not inhabit the world?' In L. J. Davis (ed) *The Disability Studies Reader.* New York: Routledge.

Iredale, R. (2000) 'Eugenics and its relevance to contemporary health care.' *Nursing Ethics, 7,* 3, 205–214.

Kaplan, D. (1993) 'Prenatal screening and its impact on persons with disabilities.' *Clinical Obstetrics and Gynecology, 36,* 3, 605–612.

Kerr, A. and Shakespeare, T. (2003) *Genetic Politics: From Eugenics to Genome.* Cheltenham, New Clarion.

Kitcher, P. (1997) *The Lives to Come: The Genetic Revolution and Human Possibilities.* Harmondsworth: Penguin Books.

Kuhse, H. and Singer, P. (1985) 'What's wrong with the sanctity of life doctrine?' In *Should the Baby Live: The Problem of Handicapped Infants.* Oxford: Oxford University Press.

Lennox, N. G. and Kerr, M. P. (1997) 'Primary health care and intellectual disability: A review.' *Primary Care Special Edition of the Journal of Intellectual Disability Research. Special Issue IASSID Congress, 4,* 5, 365–372.

Lippman, A. (1991) 'Prenatal genetic testing and screening: Constructing needs and reinforcing inequities.' *American Journal of Law and Medicine, 17,* 1–2, 15–50.

Liu, A. N. C. (1987) 'Editorial.' *Journal of Medical Ethics, 13,* 69–73.

Luckasson, R. (1992) 'People with mental retardation as victims of crime.' In R.W. Conley, R. Luckasson and G. N. Bouthilet (eds) *The Criminal Justice System and Mental Retardation.* Baltimore, MD: Paul H. Brookes Publishing Co.

Marteau, T. M. and Dormandy, E. (2001) 'Facilitating informed choice in prenatal testing: How well are we doing?' *American Journal of Medical Genetics, 106,* 185–190.

Marteau, T., Drake, H. and Bobrow, M. (1994) 'Counselling following diagnosis of a fetal abnormality: The differing approaches of obstetricians, clinical geneticists, and genetic nurses.' *Journal of Medical Genetics, 31,* 11, 864–867.

Mittler, P. (2003) *Working Towards Inclusive Education: Social Contexts.* London: David Fulton Publishers.

Narveson, J. (1995) *Moral Matters.* Peterborough, Canada: Broadview Press.

Noble, J. H. (2003) 'The economics of equality: an exploration of country differences.' In S. S. Herr, L. O. Gostin and H. Hongju Koh (eds) *The Human Rights of Persons with Intellectual Disabilities: Different but Equal.* New York: Oxford University Press.

Olsen, C. L., Cross, P. K., Gensburg, L. J. and Hughes, J. P. (2002) 'The effects of prenatal diagnosis on population and changing fertility rates on the low birth prevalence of Down syndrome in New York State, 1983–1992.' *Prenatal Diagnosis, 16,* 11, 991–1002.

Pernick, M. S. (1996) *Black Stork: Eugenics and the Death of Defective Babies in American Medicine and Motion Pictures since 1915.* New York: Oxford Univeristy Press.

Pritchard, M. (2005) 'Can there be such a thing as a "wrongful birth"?' *Disability and Society, 20,* 1, 81–93.

Purdy, L. M. (1996) 'Genetics and reproductive risk: Can having children be immoral?' In M. Purdy (ed) *Reproducing Persons: Issues in Feminist Bioethics*. Ithaca, NY: Cornell University Press.

Ramsey, P. (1978) *Ethics at the Edges of Life: Medical and Legal Intersections*. New Haven, CT: Yale University Press.

Reindal, S. M. (2000) 'Disability, gene therapy and eugenics – a challenge to John Harris.' *Journal of Medical Ethics, 26*, 89–94.

Reiss, S., Levitan, G. W. and Szyszko, J. (1982) 'Emotional disturbance in mental retardation: Diagnostic overshadowing.' *American Journal of Mental Deficiency, 86*, 567–571.

Reynolds, D. (2000) Family wins "wrongful birth" decision. Retrieved from www.inclusiondaily.com/news/advocacy/wrongfulbirths.htm on October 20, 2008.

Reynolds, D. (2001) *Mother Charged with Poisoning Teenage Daughter*. Retrieved on November 27, 2007 from www.inclusiondaily.com/news/crime/capracraig.htm.

Reynolds, D. (2002) *Sympathy for Robert Latimer Linked to Increase in Child Murders*. Retrieved from www.inclusiondaily.com/news/crime/latimer.htm on November 27, 2007.

Reynolds, D. (2004) *Prosecutors call Daniela Dawes Sentence 'Manifestly Inadequate'*. Retrieved on November 27, 2007 from www.inclusiondaily.com/archives/04/07/01.htm#dawes

Reynolds, D. (2005) *Insurgents Used Teen with Down Syndrome as Human Bomb on Election Day*. Retrieved from www.inclusiondaily.com/archives on November 27, 2007.

Rioux, M. (1996) 'Reproductive technology: A rights issue.' *Entourage*, 5–7.

RobertLatimer.net (n.d.) Retrieved from www.robertlatimer.net/court_transcripts/judge_nobles_ruling.htm on November 27, 2007.

Roeher Institute in Cooperation with Inclusion International (1999) *Genomes and Justice: Reflection on a Holistic Approach to Genetic Research, Technology and Disability*. Toronto: The Roeher Institute.

Roeher Institute (2002) *The Construction of Disability and Risk in Genetic Counselling Discourse*. Toronto: The Roeher Institute.

Russell, O. (2001) 'Supporting families to make informed decisions: How can we safeguard genetic diversity while respecting parents' "right to choose"?' In L. Ward (ed) *Considered Choices: New Genetics, Old Prejudices?* London: British Institute of Learning Disabilities.

Ryan, R. (2001) *Handbook of Mental Health Care for Persons with Developmental Disabilities*. Quebec: Diverse City Press.

Scheerenberger, R. C. (1983) *A History of Mental Retardation*. Baltimore, MD: Brookes.

S.D., (1983) 3 W. W. R. 597 (Provincial Court) and 618 (Supreme Court of B.C.)

Shakespeare, T. (1998) 'Choices and rights: Eugenics, genetics, and disability equality.' *Disability and Society, 13*, 5, 665–681.

Shakespeare, T. (1999) '"Losing the plot"? Medical and activist discourses of contemporary genetics and disability.' *Sociology of Health and Illness, 21*, 5, 669–688.

Shakespeare, T. (2001) 'Foreword.' In L. Ward (ed) *Considered Choices: New Genetics, Old Prejudices?* London: British Institute of Learning Disabilities.

Sheldon, S. and Wilkinson, S. (2001) 'Termination of pregnancy for reason of fetal disability: Are there grounds for special exceptions?' *Medical Law Review, 9*, 2, 85–109.

Shelp, E. E. (1986) *Born to Die? Deciding the Fate of Critically Ill Newborns*. New York: The Free Press.

Singer, P. (1979) *Practical Ethics*. Cambridge: Cambridge University Press.

Skoutajan, H. F. (1995) *Christian Century, 112*, 20, 948–950. Retrieved from http://findarticles.com/p/articles on November 27, 2007.

Sobsey, D. (1994) *Violence and Abuse in the Lives of People with Disabilities: The End of Silent Acceptance?* Baltimore, MD: Paul H. Brookes Publishing Co.

Sobsey, D. (1998) *Displacement and Homicide*. Retrieved from www.ualberta.ca/~jpdasddc/abuse/ICAD/digests/vol1no32.html on November 27, 2007.

Sobsey, D. (1999a) *The Kay Kuffer Starvation*. Retrieved from www.freedaemonhosting.com/ftp/afs/ualberta.ca/dept/jpdas/ICAD/ICAD.1999–02 on November 27, 2007.

Sobsey, D. (1999b) *Attempted Murder Sentence in Ontario*. Retrieved from www.freedaemonhosting.com/ftp/afs/ualberta.ca/dept/jpdas/ICAD/ICAD.1999–12 on November 27, 2007.

Sobsey, D., Donnellan, A. and Wolbring, G. (1994) 'Reflections on the holocaust: Where did it begin and has it really ended?' *Developmental Disabilities Bulletin, 22,* 2, 120–135.

Sobsey, D. and Varnhagen, C. (1988) *Sexual Abuse and Exploitation of People with Disabilities*. Ottawa: Health and Welfare Canada.

Stedman, R. L. (1990) *Stedman's Medical Dictionary* (25th edn.). Baltimore, MD: Williams and Wilkins.

Stiker, H. J. (1997) *A History of Disability*. Michigan: The University of Michigan Press.

Suzuki, D. (1999) 'The importance of human diversity.' In The Roeher Institute in Cooperation with Inclusion International (eds) *Genome(s) and Justice: Reflections on a Holistic Approach to Genetic Research, Technology and Disability*. Toronto: The Roeher Institute.

Ticoll, M. (1996) 'The human genome project: A challenge for the new millennium.' *Entourage,* 10–12.

Tooley, M. (1984) *Abortion and Infanticide*. Oxford: Oxford University Press.

Turnbull, D. (2000) 'Genetic counselling: Ethical mediation of eugenic futures?' *Futures, 32,* 9–10, 853–865.

United Nations (1948) *Universal Declaration of Human Rights*. Retrieved from www.un.org/Overview/rights.html on December 4, 2007.

Van der Wal, G., van Eijk, J. Thm., Leenen, H. J. J. and Spreewenberg, L. (1982) 'Euthanasia and assisted suicide. I. How often is it practiced by family doctors in the Netherlands?' *Family Practice, 9,* 2, 130–134.

White, M. R. (1997) 'Respect for autonomy in genetic counselling: Analysis and proposal.' *Journal of Genetic Counseling, 6,* 3, 297–313.

Williamson, L. (1978) 'Infanticide: An anthropological analysis.' In M. Kohl (ed.) *Infanticide and the Value of Life,* pp.61–75. Buffalo, NY: Prometheus.

Wilson, C. and Brewer, N. (1992) 'The incidence of criminal victimization of individuals with an intellectual disability.' *Australian Psychologist, 27,* 2, 114–117.

Wolfensberger, W. (1980) 'A call to wake up to the beginning of a new wave of "euthanasia" of severely impaired people (Editorial).' *Education and Training of the Mentally Retarded, 15,* 2, 171–173.

Wolfensberger, W. (1989) 'The killing thought in the eugenic era and today: A commentary on Hollander's essay.' *Mental Retardation, 27,* 2, 63–74.

Yagel, S. and Anteby, E. (1998) 'A rational approach to prenatal screening and intervention.' *Human Reproduction, 13,* 5, 1126–1128.

4

Self-Determination and the Emerging Role of Person-Centred Planning: A Dialogical Framework

Donato Tarulli and Carol Sales

INTRODUCTION AND OVERVIEW

This chapter proposes a conceptualization of self-determination as a situated event or accomplishment enabled by or constituted in a particular form of dialogue between self and other. To pursue this dialogical approach to self-determination is, by implication, to eschew individualistic ontological frameworks that antagonistically position the agency or autonomy of the self against the constraining influence or authority of the other. Rather, we acknowledge that autonomy, agency, and control – hallmarks of self-determination – necessarily emerge in relational, dialogical contexts. We readily acknowledge, however, that dialogue is not a monolithic, unambiguously benevolent category, and accordingly see the need to distinguish the dialogue of autonomy and self-determination from modes of dialogue that have traditionally silenced or denied the voices of persons with intellectual disabilities.

Toward this end, in the first part of the chapter, we draw a parallel between three waves of the disability movement, as identified in Bersani's (1996) historical account of leadership in developmental disabilities, and three corresponding forms of the I–Thou/self–other relation, as described in Gadamer's (1989) philosophical hermeneutics. As we elaborate below, corresponding to the 'professionalism' of the First Wave is a mode of dialogue that silences and disempowers the other through a process of objectification: in effect, the person with an intellectual disability becomes the mute, passive object of the professional gaze. In terms of the communicative relation between professional and 'patient', we might say that the professional in this instance speaks not so much *for* or *with* the individual in his or her charge, but rather *about* him or her, from a distanciated, objective position. Corresponding to the Second Wave or the 'parent movement' is a form of dialogue that retains the power imbalance of the first, but which replaces its cold professionalism with a stance of care and protection (societal, familial, or otherwise) and a paternalistic logic of 'acting in the best interests'; this attitude and logic give rise to a form of dialogue in which the other speaks on behalf of or *for* the other. The Third Wave, corresponding to the 'self-advocacy movement', suggests – indeed, necessitates – a mode of dialogue that we take to be fundamental to the constitution of autonomy and self-determination. It is a dialogue that involves speaking *with* the other, a dialogue characterized more specifically by openness, risk, and mutual trust.

In the second part of the chapter we examine the extent to which the dialogical qualities of this third mode of the self–other relation are embodied in the contemporary practice of person-centred planning. In exploring the constitutive link between the person-centred approach to the organization of care and the self–other dialogue, we also have occasion to reflect on the assumptions inherent in two competing notions of autonomy: the first of these envisions autonomy as emancipation, as a matter of the self's disengagement from the other; the second, which presupposes an understanding of the self or *autos* as a dialogically constituted story or narrative, sees autonomy as a relational accomplishment. We conclude with a consideration of the implications of this latter dialogical formulation for the person-centred planning process.

WAVES OF THE DISABILITY MOVEMENT

In an influential paper, Bersani (1996) identifies three phases in the history of the disability movement. Bersani refers to these phases more specifically as waves, a rather effective metaphor for suggesting the fuzzy boundaries and overlap that invariably exist between stages in the historical development of any phenomenon. With this brief caveat in place, we draw on and elaborate Bersani's reading of the three waves of the disability movement with a view to establishing, in a subsequent section, the conceptual link between each wave and a particular mode of dialogue or, equally, a particular mode of experiencing the other in the I–Thou relation.

First Wave: professionalism

The First Wave, extending from the mid-19th to mid-20th century, is that of *professionalism*. According to Bersani (1996), the label aims to capture the emphasis placed during this period on the expertise of professionals in fields of medicine, psychology, education, special education and social work and the role of such expertise in determining appropriate courses of action in matters pertaining to persons with intellectual disabilities. People with intellectual disabilities had few if any rights and, accordingly, little opportunity to exercise control over their own lives. The power to determine the fate of individual 'patients' fell largely in the hands of medical practitioners and other professionals. As Bersani (1996) observes, professionals:

> decided on who got therapy, what therapy they got, and when such therapy was pointless. They determined who went to school and who could not benefit from school. They said who could learn to work and who was 'non-feasible' for rehabilitation. They set the criteria to evaluate who was ready for the community and who would never be ready to live in the community. (pp.259–260)

On the disciplinary front, too, professionals established the academic agenda of the day: they determined what issues were worth pursuing and defined the field of 'mental retardation' in their own terms (Bersani 1996; Wehmeyer, Bersani and Gagne 2000). The growing role of science in the lives of people in this case meant applying 'science to better understand the causes and possible cures of the "deficiency"' (Bersani 1996, p.260). By definition, persons with intellectual disabilities – the 'mentally defective' – were disempowered, with nothing to contribute either to their own treatment or to the emergent field of mental retardation. 'To most professionals,' writes Bersani (1996), 'they were "subjects" in experiments, and the objects of studies' (p.260).

Through the work of Edouard Séguin in the mid-19th century, people with intellectual disabilities – 'idiots' as they were often labelled – were positioned predominantly as objects of educational intervention, as cases to be cured. Séguin's program of 'physiological education', over which the educator was to have total control, was designed to remediate the failure of the will, a failure which was believed to be at the root of 'idiocy'. Séguin depicted his typical charge as 'one who knows nothing, thinks nothing, wills nothing, and can do nothing, and [claimed that] every idiot approached more or less this *summum* of incapacity' (Séguin 1846, as cited in Trent 1994, pp.45–46). The educator's task, accordingly, was to awaken the will through exercise and moral training, the latter defined more specifically as 'the systematic action of a will upon another, in view of its improvement; in view for an idiot, of his socialization' (Séguin 1866, cited in Trent 1994, p.51). Here, the emphasis is clearly on the teacher's authority over the student; indeed, the heteronomy inherent in this relation of constraint is proffered as the very mechanism required to activate the will and excite a natural but otherwise dormant 'natural curiosity', and thereby to promote a level of social functioning and independence that would make reintegration into society possible.

As the medical model of late 1850s gradually began to replace the educational model of 1840s and early 1850s, persons with intellectual disabilities came increasingly to be regarded as objects of clinical diagnosis. Where Séguin stressed the educational, rehabilitative intervention required to facilitate social integration, those in American medical circles stressed the pathological basis of idiocy – 'degenerative and polymorphous heredity' (Trent 1994, p.18) – and the formalism of emerging classification schemes and medical typologies. Within this climate, 'idiocy became types of idiocies' (Trent 1994, p.17), a multiple category which, in Hervey Wilbur's (1852, cited in Trent 1994) formulation, for example, encompassed labels such as simulative idiocy, higher-grade, lower-grade, and incurables.

Second Wave: the parent movement

The Second Wave, the origin of which Bersani (1996) locates at the midpoint of the 20th century, was marked by the increasing investment of parents in the lives of children with intellectual disabilities, and for that reason the wave is aptly referred to by Bersani as the *parent movement*. In the post-World War II period in the US, many were beginning to enjoy greater prosperity and, consequently, also the luxury to focus on more than just economic survival. The beginnings of the baby boom, in addition to scientific and medical advances, meant that there were more children with intellectual disabilities being born and surviving past childhood. As the numbers of children went up, families began to form their own groups, first locally and eventually at the state and national levels. While they emerged initially as a means of providing mutual support, they later became tools of advocacy by parents for children and themselves (Bersani 1996).

In 1950, a voice for parents and relatives emerged in the form of the NARC (National Association for Retarded Children) (later renamed, without acronym, The Arc). While oppressive stereotypes continued to exist, more humane views also came to the fore, largely through the activism and writings of parents (Trent 1994; Wehmeyer *et al.* 2000). The NARC's message was that people should not fear or be ashamed of children with intellectual disabilities, for with the proper environmental and educational supports many of these children could realize their potential (Trent 1994).

Where in the First Wave, authority remained unambiguously in the hands of professionals, during the parent movement the balance of power began to shift to parents. Trent (1994) summarizes the early years of this parent movement in the following terms:

> NARC parents in their first decade shaped the agenda of retardation around themselves and their children as victims. But as 'angry lobbyists,' they also became a powerful source of change, causing concern among professionals who had so long dominated the field of mental deficiency. (p.241)

Indeed, in its reaction against the experience of stigma, the NARC was character-ized by its 'determination to maintain parent dominance at all levels, its strong resistance to professionalization of the group's leadership, and its mistrust of both the medical profession and the more established social welfare agencies' (Castles 2004, p.354).

As parents began to position themselves as leaders, and as their organizations proliferated and their writings became more widely disseminated in the lay and professional communities, their impact on the field of mental retardation became more pronounced. As Bersani (1996) observes, the formative influence of both parent groups and professionals sympathetic to the cause was felt in changes to the discourse of the field, in the themes addressed at academic conferences, and in the subjects treated in professional journals. Equally important was the impact of the parent movement on the proliferation and availability of services and legisla-tive protections for children. During the 1950s and into the 1970s, models of service provision were based increasingly on the needs, wishes, and experiences of families, and not on the research of medical professionals and academics. Brockley (2004) similarly argues that during the period from 1940 to 1965 in America, activist parents played a pivotal role in the reform and expansion of ser-vices for people with intellectual disabilities. The focus of these efforts was often on finding ways to make their children's existence count, making them useful, and acknowledging their possible contributions to society, such as their serving as an impetus for novel advances in medicine, prevention, and social services.

Parents made a most dramatic difference in how mental retardation was por-trayed in the media and other public outlets. After World War II parent groups in the US contributed to and changed the cultural discourse on the meaning of mental retardation by pointing up its social foundations. As Castles (2004) writes:

> NARC activists sought to deflect blame from the children themselves to the larger society, arguing that better public understanding of mental re-tardation and greater community acceptance of their children were key factors in preventing the problems associated with mental retardation. They located the problem not in the presence of the retarded child but in the community's failure to accept and accommodate that presence. In fighting the stigmatization of mental retardation, parent activists found themselves challenging not only the old eugenic understanding of men-tal retardation as lower-class social deviance but also the more basic assumptions that underlay the medical model of disability. They called into question the idea that both problems and solutions could be found in the disabled individual alone. (p.364)

Interestingly, this externalization of disability foreshadows features of what is now known as the social model of disability. The model locates disability not in individual pathology, but rather in the social and physical barriers 'out there', in the objective, material structures that reflect a community's inability to accept and engage difference.

Wehmeyer *et al.* (2000) note that the parent movement was also of historical importance in the emergence of self-advocacy, with many parents reminding professionals that as care providers and consumers of services they spoke for their sons and daughters and represented their best interests. To be sure, professional expertise remained important, but it was no substitute for parents' more immediate, day to day knowledge of their children. Accordingly, parents demanded a voice in matters pertaining to the organization of care for their children – seeking, for example, to be included in meetings of professionals aimed at determining the needs of children with intellectual disabilities (Bersani 1996).

While parents' groups did much to establish mental retardation as a social problem worthy of interest and sympathy, 'the new rhetoric of the retarded child could be deployed in different ways, not all of them particularly progressive or beneficial to individuals with mental retardation' (Castles 2004, p.353). In particular, the emergent discourse often drew on past images which likened individuals with intellectual disabilities to eternal children, whose enduring innocence and lasting dependence effectively placed them beyond the pale of development. 'This model of mental retardation,' adds Castles (2004):

> not only fit perfectly with the prevailing poster-child style of disability advocacy but also strengthened parents' own positions as spokespersons for their children. As long as individuals with mental retardation could still be viewed as helpless children, parents' roles in representing their children's interests and speaking for their children remained intact. (p.360)

Alongside the discourse of the eternal child was a rhetoric that continued to position the child as a problem that threatened the entire family. In some regards, then, and despite the predominance of the language of benevolent care, the emergent NARC discourse also 'echoed and reinforced the fear that these children were dangerous, not by virtue of poor genetics or antisocial behaviour but simply as disruptive presences in otherwise stable families' (Castles 2004, p.363), a view which 'could easily shade into a conviction that the family needed to be rescued from the child's presence. It was only a short step from imagining the family's imminent disintegration to demonizing the young child as an unacceptable threat to his brothers, sisters, and parents' (Castles 2004, p.360). Medical professionals accordingly advocated institutionalizing children at an early age to protect parents and nondisabled siblings. While later activists would certainly challenge this paternalistic equation of adults with intellectual disabilities and children, and resist medical professionals' overemphasis on institutionalization, it is not surprising to conclude that 'in many ways, the new model of mental retardation reflected the interests of middle-class parents far better than the interests of individuals with mental retardation' (Castles 2004, p.360).

Third Wave: self-advocacy

Bersani (1996) identifies the *self-advocacy movement* of the 1970s and 1980s as the Third Wave of the disability movement. Marked by the realization among family members and professionals alike that persons with intellectual disabilities could speak for themselves, this period is associated with increased opportunities for self-determination (Wehmeyer *et al.* 2000). The new emphasis on making choices, self-assertion, self-knowledge, self-efficacy, self-regulation, autonomy and independence – which Wehmeyer *et al.* (2000) attribute to the emergence of the independent living movement and the popularization of the normalization principle – went far to undermine the lingering stereotypes of persons with intellectual disabilities as eternal children or holy innocents (Wehmeyer and Berkobien 1996).

By the early 1970s, people with intellectual disabilities, often with the help of family members and other community allies, began to organize themselves (Bersani 1996). In a manner parallel to the development of parent groups earlier in the century, local, state, and national associations of persons with intellectual disabilities 'formed partly in reaction to the attitudes promoted by parent and professional associations, but also in an effort to emulate the effective advocacy approaches of these groups' (Bersani 1996, p.262). As stated in the introductory chapter, this increasing trend toward self-representation and self-advocacy culminated in the creation of People First in Canada and the United States in 1973 and 1974.

Bersani (1996) concludes his analysis with a sobering reminder that the fruits of the Third Wave were earned despite the difficulties self-advocates encountered along the way – difficulties which included reluctance among professionals to concede power to parents, and in turn reluctance among parents and parent groups to share their power with the persons for whom they were speaking. In this latter regard, Bersani points to the continued existence of parent groups like The Voice of the Retarded, which according to its website 'advocates that the final determination of what is appropriate depends on the unique abilities and needs of the individual and desires of the family and guardians' (www.vor.net/about_us.htm). Here again, under the guise of paternalistic benevolence, people with intellectual disabilities risk being denied a real voice and the opportunity to speak on their own behalf. Ultimately, groups like this 'oppose self-determination…fight progress…deny the obvious. They are stuck in the Second Wave' (Bersani 1996, p.264).

MODES OF EXPERIENCING THE OTHER

What do these waves suggest about the nature of the relation between professionals or parents and persons with intellectual disabilities? As we argue more fully below, each of the waves identified by Bersani (1996) articulates and supports a particular form of dialogue. To explore this connection, we draw on Gadamer's (1989) description of three modes of the self–other or I–Thou relation. Presented as part of his exposition of the hermeneutic experience of understanding, each of these modes describes a particular way of experiencing the other or Thou.

The other as object

Gadamer's (1989) first mode stresses themes that are readily identifiable in the wave of professionalism as it has been described above. Prominent among these is the authoritative expertise and control of professionals. On the traditional model of the patient–professional relation, the dominant stance toward the patient/other is one of paternalism, the patient's care falling completely in the expert and benevolent hands of professionals (Arnason 2000). Implicit in this characterization is the assumption that the self can know the other objectively and with the assurances of scientific predictability. As Gadamer (1989) writes, 'we understand the other person in the same way that we understand any other typical event in our experiential field – i.e., he is predictable. His behavior is as much a means to our end as any other means' (p.358). There is no effort here to appreciate the world from the other's vantage point or experiential horizon. Accordingly, this mode of the self–other relation may be more aptly described as a monologue than a dialogue, a mode of *observation* rather than of interaction and *communication* (Arnason 2000, p.18). It is, to use an alternate idiom, a one-sided relation in which 'the intellect contemplates a thing and expounds on it. There is only one subject here – cognizing (contemplating) and speaking (expounding). In opposition to the subject there is only a *voiceless thing*' (Bakhtin 1986, p.161) – to wit, an object.

This process of objectification is associated with the tendency to depict persons with intellectual disabilities in a way that finalizes them, that is, in a way that sees them merely as embodiments of a perspective that is typical to a person or social group of this or that sort. As particular instantiations of typical perspectives or medical categories, persons with intellectual disabilities become predictable, the meaning of their activities ultimately predetermined by an overarching professional meaning. Here, a person's autonomy, creativity, and freedom is essentially closed off by the monologic voice of the professional. There is certainly no sense that the professional is engaging persons in a reciprocal fashion, that one is allowing them to speak in a way that might even challenge one's (i.e. the professional's) assumptions and expectations. Ultimately, the contemplating, categorizing intellect of the professional 'denies the existence outside itself of another consciousness with equal rights and equal responsibilities, another *I* with equal rights' (Bakhtin 1984, p.292). Within this framework:

> *another person* remains wholly and merely an *object* of consciousness, and not another consciousness. No response is expected from it that could change everything in the world of my consciousness. Monologue is finalized and deaf to the other's response, does not expect it and does not acknowledge in it any *decisive* force. (Bakhtin 1984, p.293)

The other, in short, is not construed as an independent voice whose difference from the self might constitute the enabling ground of a dialogically emergent meaning. The focus on the other's typicality and predictability essentially divests the other of her otherness and hence of any power actively to contribute to these possibilities to mean. For Gadamer (1989), the self who approaches the other in this way ultimately fails to understand, for understanding proceeds not from free and uninvolved contemplation, but rather relationally, with and through the specific bond one forms with the other.

The other as a form of self-relatedness

In the second mode of dialogue described by Gadamer, the other is construed as other, but that otherness is understood as analogous to one's own experience. The assumption is that I and Thou are speaking from the same horizon, namely the horizon of the I. Hence the experience and understanding of the other amounts to a 'form of self-relatedness' (Gadamer 1989, p.359). Such an understanding is embodied in the notion that one can faithfully know and express the other's claim – indeed even understand the other better than the other understands him- or herself.

Within this mode of experiencing the Thou, it is assumed that differences between self and other constitute potential barriers to understanding and that it is only through a sympathetic mode of listening and apprehension – in which one seeks to inhabit the other's point of view – that one can overcome such differences. This further assumes, somewhat problematically for Gadamer, that we can disentangle ourselves from our own interpretive horizons, from the particularity and uniqueness of our own position in the world. To the extent that this sort of self-forgetfulness is impossible, however, we risk interpreting the other in our own terms. In effect, in pretending to know the other in the other's own terms, we risk reducing the other to a mirror reflection of ourselves. We fuse or merge with the other and consequently the 'Thou loses the immediacy with which it makes its claim. It is understood, but this means it is co-opted and preempted reflectively from the standpoint of the other person' (Gadamer 1989, p.359). So while the other is acknowledged as an other, which is to say as a subject in his or her own right, with his or her own needs and preferences, this subject is not afforded the power to mean autonomously, to mean differently. The putative understanding that occurs here amounts to a form of control whereby one robs the other of a voice and a justification of his or her own claims.

Within this mode of the I–Thou relation, finally, the appeal is not, as it is in the first mode, to objectivity – which in any event makes no pretence to recognizing the otherness or subjectivity of the other – but rather to the possibility of knowing the other precisely as other, as a person, and to acting in a way that is for and in the best interests of that person. In this 'best interests' ethos, reminiscent of the discourse of many parent groups, the person's voice is simply not sufficiently valued or privileged. While it is true that the parent movement paved the way for the later emphasis on self-advocacy for persons with intellectual disabilities, in their insistence on speaking for the child or adult with intellectual disabilities, and in their assumption that they know all they need to know about the other, parent groups risk overlooking the claims of those for whom they advocate, or at least risk interpreting those claims in self-focused ways.

The other as other

We noted above that neither of the preceding modes of experiencing the other constitutes a dialogue as such. Both forms privilege a single voice or horizon: that of distanced and dispassionate objectivity in the first case, and that of benevolent paternalism in the second. What we wish to propose here – albeit tentatively and with reservations to come – is that the third mode of dialogue discussed by Gadamer (1989) is most apposite to the themes of self-determination associated with the Third Wave of the disability movement. In this third mode of dialogue, which Gadamer sees as synonymous with the form and content of authentic understanding, the emphasis is on shared deliberation and joint decision-making in a relationship of mutual trust and respect (Arnason 2000).

The third mode of experience, the Thou, is preeminently an ethic and ethos of democratic listening:

> In human relations the important thing is…to experience the Thou truly as a Thou – i.e., not to overlook his claim but to let him really say something to us. Here is where openness belongs… Without such openness to one another there is no genuine human bond. Belonging together always also means being able to listen to one another. (Gadamer 1989, p.361)

In Gadamer's hermeneutical framework, openness to experience and to learning from what is other requires a willingness to concede that one does not know, a willingness to recognize the inescapably limited, partial, and incomplete knowledge afforded by one's own horizon of expectations. In short, for Gadamer authentic listening, and hence authentic dialogue, requires that we risk our preconceptions and the cozy familiarity and security they otherwise afford. Indeed, to understand, or, equally, to be open to new experience, is to inhabit a place of perpetual risk where 'I myself must accept some things that are against me, even though no one else forces me to do so' (Gadamer 1989, p.361). Only by engaging our horizon of intelligibility with the other's claims do we become aware of the limitations of our knowledge and beliefs – if only ever partially, as understanding is never final or complete.

Gadamer's (1989) third mode of dialogue suggests that experiencing another person as a Thou requires recognizing the singularity and uniqueness of the other's subject position – of the other's story, so to speak. This understanding might usefully be elaborated by foregrounding what Bersani (1996) argues are the central messages of people in the Third Wave: namely, that self-advocates have different values and concerns than professionals or even parents; that they value choice, independence and risk; and that they have dreams for their futures, dreams which lend direction to their lives. As we argue more fully below, these messages resonate clearly with the principles of person-centred planning.

PERSON-CENTRED PLANNING

Person-centred planning (hereafter PCP) is an approach to organizing assistance for people with intellectual disabilities which encompasses a variety of specific forms, each bearing a particular family resemblance, each premised on a set of common assumptions regarding the provision of individualized assistance. In keeping with the message of self-advocates stated above, PCP is a process which takes into account the unique circumstances of the individual in both the determination and implementation of a service plan. In contrast to traditional approaches, which often privilege the voices of clinical experts and in which the person's input is often tokenistic and subjugated to the professional perspective (O'Brien, O'Brien and Mount 1997), PCP privileges the voice of the person or service user. It establishes a communicative context that, in principle at least, allows for the expression and understanding of what is important to a person – his or her goals, aspirations, dreams. In short, it is a means of providing assistance that understands itself, appropriately enough, as being centred on the person.

Below we briefly outline some of the other defining features and assumptions of approaches that fall under the rubric of PCP:

1. The expression of goals and plans is a collective accomplishment, one that requires the mobilization of the person's social and community network. Family members, friends, and others in the person's social network are included in the determination of goals. This tack is premised on the assumption that family and friends may know the person best – compared to, say, agency staff – and be most strongly committed to the

person (Mansell and Beadle-Brown 2004). In dialogue with the person with intellectual disabilities, this team identifies areas for change and development. This process is understood as entailing some form of intersubjective agreement. As O'Brien (2002) puts it, the person and his or her allies strive 'to align around a common understanding of what is desirable for the person now and in the future' (p.402). It is assumed, moreover, that this network of individuals close to the person can bring in resources and the continuity of relationships that formal service systems often cannot.

2. PCP stresses the provision of support to achieve goals expressed by the person in dialogue with his or her allies; it is not limited to goals that can be accommodated by pre-established residential, educational, employment settings and existing service schedules. 'Instead of fitting the person into existing service options, a group of people focus on an individual and her hopes and dreams… It requires listening and learning, focusing on what is important to someone now, and what she will want and need in the future' (Mercer 2003, pp.3–4). In other words, PCP understands itself as a creative process: rather than accept the status quo as far as existing services are concerned, it endeavours to match the uniqueness of a person's goals and aspirations with an equally unique set of supports. Just like individual dreams and aspirations, support plans are unique to person rather than common across people.

3. PCP reflects several inter-related values. As articulated by O'Brien and Lyle (1987), these include the following: (i) community presence: participating in community life to the extent of a person's choosing; (ii) choice, control, and decision-making: being free to make decisions pertaining to both big and small aspects of daily life, to express lifestyle preferences, and to choose preferred modes of support; (iii) competence: establishing opportunities to engage in meaningful activities with whatever level of assistance is required and identifying areas for growth and development; (iv) reputation/respect: fulfilling respected roles and living with dignity, focusing on positive dreams, plans, strengths, and capacities as opposed to deficits and problems; and (v) relationships (social, romantic, and otherwise): giving and receiving love and affection and feeling needed, all of which establish an enabling context for participation in self-chosen activities.

PCP and self-determination

This overview of the elements and assumptions of PCP is enough to suggest the link between it and self-determination. Self-determination, which 'is about control over one's life and one's destiny' (Wehmeyer *et al.* 2000, p.114), is both a value and outcome of PCP. Wehmeyer (2002) explains this confluence of aims by observing that both flow out of the self-advocacy movement and its emphasis on empowering people with intellectual disabilities to achieve control over decision-making and the choices that affect their quality of life. 'These principles – the value for personal control, the emphasis on improving quality of life, and the emphasis on empowerment – underlie efforts to promote self-determination' (Wehmeyer 2002, p.54).

While self-determination and PCP are certainly closely related, they are not in Wehmeyer's (2002) formulation synonymous terms. He argues that, in the first instance, self-determination is not enabled solely by increased opportunities, as often assumed by PCP practices, but rather requires the capacity to make complex decisions and to harness the knowledge needed to take control. According to Wehmeyer, PCP does not put enough stress on teaching skills or capacities related to self-reliance and self-sufficiency. His own stance on self-determination is that it is most likely to be manifested when three conditions are in place: achieving self-determination requires capacity, opportunities to exercise choice and control, and environmental supports (Wehmeyer *et al.* 2000).

For neither Wehmeyer nor proponents of PCP is self-determination about doing it alone. Exerting control is not necessarily nor primarily about independent performance. What is most critical, rather, is 'being the causal agent in one's life and making things happen in accordance with one's preferences, wants, needs, and interests' (Wehmeyer 2002, p.59). To be sure, intellectual impairments may limit the skills a person can perform, but the person can still be the centre of the decision-making process – that is, decisions can still be made on the basis of the person's preferences and interests, and this is so even if the person does not independently make the decisions. In this regard, Wehmeyer readily acknowledges that decision-making is in many instances a group process, an interdependent accomplishment – a fact that is also congenial to the principles and practices of PCP. However, Wehmeyer (2002) goes on to add that 'this does not mitigate the need to do everything possible to ensure that it is the person, to the greatest extent feasible, who is the plan maker' (p.59). He cautions, in fact, that in some instances this fundamental principle may be compromised. For example, he notes that particularly when a person's cognitive limitations effectively prevent that person from adequately communicating his or her dream and vision to others or from fully comprehending the range and nature of the options available, it very often becomes the task of the members of the PCP team to assist in the construction of that dream and vision. This necessary reliance on others' descriptions and insights may be problematic, however, because it:

> introduces the possibility that the dream or vision represents the other
> person's dreams more than those of the person for whom planning is

occurring. A similar concern exists in determining the preferences of people with significant cognitive disabilities. Interviewing significant others about their perceptions of the person's preferences is an important component in supporting choice making, but there is a need to go beyond that step by implementing additional ways to more objectively evaluate preferences through direct observations or systemic evaluations of preferences… The point is not that parents, family members, or friends purposely subjugate the individual's dreams with their own but that it can be very difficult to make an external determination of a person's dreams, however well one knows that person. (Wehmeyer 2002, p.60)

To further support his concerns about the possibility of others supplanting the person's dreams with their own, Wehmeyer (2002) presents arguments about the need to cultivate both opportunity and ability in the promotion of self-determination. On the issue of an individual's abilities and communicative capacities, he writes:

A means is put into place to check the legitimacy of the visioning process by ensuring that part of the action plan emerging from person-centered planning is to promote skills and knowledge related to areas such as problem solving, decision making, goal setting, self-advocacy, self-regulation, self-management, and self-knowledge. More accurately, perhaps, a mechanism is put into place to better enable people, through successful experiences, to refine and individualize those visions and dreams and to make them known to others. (p.62)

While we feel that Wehmeyer's concerns serve as a very important check on PCP practices that might unwittingly engender a dialogue of domination – a dialogue in which a person with intellectual disabilities risks being subjected to the monological representations of others – our interest here is in showing how these concerns, however reasonable and well-intentioned, betray an allegiance to a particular understanding of self-determination, one which rests more specifically on a conception of autonomy as emancipation or disengagement from others. This understanding of autonomy might usefully be distinguished from that which we see as implicit in received descriptions of PCP: a conception of autonomy as a relational, dialogical accomplishment. Before exploring the constitutive link between PCP and this latter view, let us examine the two conceptions of autonomy and their related assumptions about the self in more detail.

TWO CONCEPTIONS OF AUTONOMY

In his reflections on the nature of autonomy, Meininger (2001) distinguishes among three conceptions of the *autos* (self) implicit in notions of autonomy.

These are captured metaphorically in Meininger's account as the *garden*, the *way*, and the *story*, the latter two of which are especially pertinent to the distinction, intimated above, between autonomy as emancipation and autonomy as relationship.

The *autos* as way

Conceptions of the self as 'the way' assume that the self, or human nature more generally, is 'a continuing process to ever more self-determination' (Meininger 2001, p.243), a constant developmental journey from dependence to independence. Implicit in this conception is the assumption that the other is always primarily a source of potential subjugation, an opponent, a source of constraint. Meininger (2001) adds:

> From the perspective of this conception of the self autonomy is primarily conceived as freedom: the freedom to determine one's own life. Heteronomy, the tutelage of others, is here considered to be the basic form of violence in human relations… The emancipatory character of this conception is a clear expression of the necessity of a right to autonomy in order to protect the weak from the unbridled and authoritarian self-realization of the strong. As in professional care relations the caregiver *per definitionem* is the stronger party, the right to autonomy and the respecting of that right must promote the view that this relation is guided by the priorities of the care-receiver rather than by those of the caregiver. (p.244)

Attendant on this conception is an adherence to abstract and general principles of equality and justice and to a discourse of individual rights. These are predominantly rights that protect one from the unwelcome interference of others. This is a juridical, contractual formulation of the self–other relation that infuses it with an oppositional, litigant tone (Meininger 2001).

From an ontological perspective, this emphasis on emancipation and autonomy-as-freedom-(from) suggests that the self is, at root, capable of existing without the other. Indeed, the moral imperative underlying this ontological claim requires that if I am to live authentically and in accordance with my original way of being in the world, I must embrace 'that unique form of being human that I have come to recognize as mine' (Meininger 2001, p.244). In this formulation, self-determination presents the positive possibility of accessing this moral ideal of authenticity. Such access is possible because we are primordially self-sufficient, not just occasionally so. Self-relatedness defines the most fundamental quality of the self, relations with others being relegated to a secondary status, playing no ineradicably formative or constitutive role in the life of the *autos*. Indeed, as intimated above, relations with others are seen in terms of their potential to interfere with this originary self-sufficiency. In this regard, we are reminded of Wehmeyer's (2002) understanding of the role of the other in self-determination. For Wehmeyer, that role is not essential. The other's participation in the exercise of self-determination is not an ontological necessity, but rather a matter of choice, desire, and circumstance, forever carrying the potential to manifest itself as benevolent paternalism or, at worst, malevolent constraint or subjugation. Hence the need for those individual rights and legal protections that would safeguard the self against the other's interference (Meininger 2001), or hence the need, in Wehmeyer's specific formulation, for the cultivation of those individual skills and capacities for self-determination that may protect the person against externally imposed descriptions.

The *autos* as story

The self or *autos* may also be described using the metaphor of the story. As Meininger (2001) elaborates:

> From the perspective of this conception the *autos* manifests itself in a history, an intrigue, a plot. In a story the principal character is involved with others in finding the 'good life with and for others.' This implies that the other is also involved in the movement towards self-esteem which characterizes human existence. My movement towards self-esteem may be understood as a story about what I experience in others and about the full range of signification and meaning these encounters may have for me…
> A story is the reconstruction of a movement towards self-esteem which goes by way of the other and his or her own movement towards self-esteem. This movement transcends categories like self interest, mutual interest or contract. It is about my involvement with others and about their involvement with me. It is about the 'sense' and the 'meaning' which may be derived from this involvement. (p.245)

The emphasis here is clearly on the situated, relational nature of autonomy. One's autonomy manifests itself not despite the other but precisely in virtue of the other. Accordingly, the monological conception of the self suggested by the notion of autonomy as emancipation gives way in this case to the sense of a dialogically constituted self, a self that emerges most fully through its encounters with others. The path to the self – to self-esteem, to use Meininger's idiom – passes necessarily through the other. Autonomy and identity go hand in hand: I am autonomous in the measure to which I act in conformity with my dialogically constituted identity and feel at home in the things I do (Meininger 2001).

A person's achievement of autonomy requires that we listen to the person's story, that we understand the person's aspirations, values, and dreams – in short, the person's identity or sense of self. That story, moreover, implicates others: 'As soon as I meet the other I am included in his or her story, as conversely the other is included in my story. Then, I am unable to be excluded from the adventures, the intricacies, the plot in the story of the other' (Meininger 2001, p.247). In this regard, the metaphor of the self as story foregrounds the mutually constitutive nature of the self–other relation. 'The other is neither an opponent nor an instrument, but the other is the one to whom I owe my existence and who is a constitutive moment in that unique story which is mine' (Meininger 2001, p.247). That story requires the other's recognition and appropriation, the other's participation and engagement. In this aspect, we can say that understanding – be it of the world or of ourselves – unfolds in our openness to the other, through a relationship best described in terms of Gadamer's (1989) third mode of experiencing the Thou. In telling one's story, one invariably implicates oneself in a series of social identities that reflect membership in various spheres of life: family, friends, community, and so on. The stories we tell take shape, evolve, and are transformed in our encounters with the stories of others. In short, stories connect us to the social world (Gillman, Swain and Heyman 1997).

PERSON-CENTRED PLANNING, NARRATIVE, AND THE PROMISE OF DIALOGUE

Narratives and life histories are being increasingly used as a resource in care and support settings to facilitate the process of self-expression in persons with intellectual disabilities (e.g. Hewitt 2000). Meininger (2006) suggests that the use of life stories in this regard is a reaction against traditional practices of care which have privileged purely functional and instrumental approaches to problems. Narratives and life histories disclose the uniqueness and concrete particularity of a person's identity and foreground the meaning of experiences – this in contrast to standard practices of care which, in the quest to secure an evidence base for service planning, often emphasize depersonalized and generalized accounts of objectifiable deficits (Meininger 2006). While revealing the typical, formalizable dimensions of human functioning, the professional discourses of diagnosis and treatment may conceal what is unique about a client's identity. Through experience-near stories, in contrast, one gets to know a person in his or her singularity, as a person situated in a concrete temporal flow that includes past experiences, current circumstances, and aspirations for the future – all of which are appreciated in the context of the person's day-to-day social relationships.

In an analysis that emphasizes issues of power and hegemony in the practice of care, Gillman et al. (1997) argue that, unlike experientially empty 'case histories', the life stories we tell ourselves and others help us to resist colonization at the hands of professional discourses. When experientially rich and unique narratives are subordinated to more formal case histories, one risks imposing a generalized identity on people with intellectual disabilities and thereby contributing to their ongoing marginalization, stigmatization, and homogenization (Gillman *et al.* 1997).

This brief description of the possible functions of narrative practice in service settings is enough to bring to mind the nature and aims of PCP as they were described earlier. For instance, the temporal sensibility we see in narrative practices is quite clearly reflected in claims that the task of members of the PCP team is:

> to understand the life that the person has experienced to this point, to understand more clearly the life that he or she is experiencing now, and to envision the kind of life that he or she wants to pursue and experience in the future. (Kincaid and Fox 2002, p.30)

As a means of affording voice to personal goals and dreams, or, equally, as a means of constituting and communicating who one is and what it means for one to lead a meaningful life, PCP also resonates with narrative and life-history approaches to service provision.

Within the PCP literature, O'Brien (2002) has recently made the connection quite explicit in his claim that PCP is an "expression of the narrative mode... It is about composing and enacting good stories" (p.408). Elaborating on this link to narrative practices, he adds:

> Story is a foundation for phronesis, the practical wisdom necessary to make decisions that apply generally understood values in particular circumstances and draw a sensible balance among competing goods (e.g. freedom and safety). Story provides a channel for imagination to discover and broadcast the hopeful possibility that alternative realities are possible... People with developmental disabilities come alive when attention is given to their stories. Person-centered planning can provide a social space for appreciating a person's story in a way that leads to meaningful new chapters. A decent community life begins with hearing and changing the stories of people who have been mindlessly excluded and controlled because of disability. Person-centered planning can provide a social space for shaping and learning from positive stories of community life for people with disabilities. (pp.412–413)

In these remarks, we see an incipient narrative framework for thinking about the unique potentials of PCP. Quite clear in O'Brien's account is the sense that stories – and not generic care plans, statistics, manualized procedures, or objective, evidence-based outcomes – should form the foundation of practical decisions regarding the planning and provision of assistance. Only through an appreciation of the details about a human life that a story provides are we able to apprehend, if only provisionally, the context – social, emotional, physical, or otherwise – that establishes the meaning of people's hopes and dreams. In other words, stories offer us a sense of "'the human being behind the disability'", "the essence of a person", "the unique individuality", "the meaning of feelings and life events'" (Meininger 2005, p.108). Such a stance recalls the importance in the practice of care of what Aristotle called phronesis or practical judgement, an orientation to decision-making and action that calls for one's attentiveness to the concrete particularities of specific situations (cf. Polkinghorne 2004).

What of the dialogical dimensions of PCP? If PCP can be seen as a process that involves constructing and acting on narratives, can that process be reasonably defined as a dialogical one? The collaborative, multivoiced processes that are, in principle, central to PCP practice certainly suggest the sort of openness and attentiveness to the other's claims that defines Gadamer's (1989) third mode of experiencing the Thou. The narratives disclosed in PCP contexts are clearly understood as joint, dialogical constructions: the stories one tells take shape, evolve, and are transformed in one's encounters with the stories of others. As utterances, stories are directed toward the other's responsive understanding, and indeed this anticipated response enters the utterance from within, having a material effect on the form, content, and tone of that utterance (Bakhtin 1986; Volosinov 1986).

But to what extent are such dialogues reciprocally transformative? Perhaps the most critically defining feature of the third mode of dialogue is its insistence on the self's own potentials for transformation in the encounter with the other. Meininger (2006) comments on the possibility of such transformation as a result of life story work:

> By assisting their son, daughter, brother or sister to tell their own life story or to compose a life story book, their consciousness may be raised about their own relationship to their family member with learning disabilities. Often they feel inspired to tell more about their own life story which is always interwoven with the life story of the family member who has learning disabilities. (p.187)

The key in this is to follow the hermeneutic injunction to listen, and this means to engage the other's claims with a stance of humility and openness, that is, with the sober recognition that one does not already and self-assuredly know the other outside of that moment of engagement. In narrative terms, 'you have to meet the challenge to retell your own life story in the light of the life story of the person you encounter' (Meininger 2006, p.187). This entails not simply the acknowledgement of the other's otherness – a *tolerance* for otherness, if you will – but a willingness actively to engage the other's horizon with one's own so that a new, different understanding will emerge. The point of such dialogue is not self-verification or self-confirmation, but to listen and be transformed in one's self-understanding by an openness to what is other.

In principle, PCP would certainly require this attentiveness to the other. Indeed, 'listen and learn' seems to be the rallying cry for many proponents of the practice. This call must not, however, be interpreted methodologically, that is, simply as an injunction to hone one's technical or clinical skills so that one is better able to document the person's needs, wishes, and wants, but rather must be seen as a call for the risk-laden, unpredictable, non-methodical movement of dialogue and open, authentic engagement. As O'Brien (2002) puts it, PCP carries with it an ethical injunction to create 'a context for the kind of listening that invites engagement in another person's life' (p.400). Of course, stories themselves carry this demand to be heard, and as such may mitigate against the possibility of distancing oneself from the other. This listening and learning, moreover, need not be limited simply to what one comes to know and understand about the other, but can be understood more reflexively as an invitation to self-knowledge and self-transformation – say, to an elucidation of one's own otherwise unacknowledged assumptions and biases, such as those that underlie the expectations one holds for the other or which inform one's beliefs regarding what is possible in the world of service provision. This self-reflexivity and self-questioning – motivated by our encounter and engagement with the other – will, in turn, establish a more open and hospitable communicative context for the other's expression of his or her strengths and capacities.

We do not mean to idealize or romanticize the communicative processes in PCP. We seek only to point up its potentials for cultivating authentic dialogue. That principle and practice often pass each other by must certainly be kept in mind. As Mansell and Beadle-Brown (2004) recently argue in their analysis of the 'implementation gap' in PCP, the discourse of 'reciprocity, mutual interdependence, and community' (p.3) that characterizes the practice may point to an unattainable ideal. In a related vein, there is also the real danger that even the most benevolent, well-intentioned, respectful invitations to dialogue carry the potential for domination. For the time being, and notwithstanding these very important concerns, we wish to point not to what presently is but to what might reasonably be. Toward that possible end, we encourage proponents of PCP to begin to reflect more critically and self-consciously on the dialogical potentials of their work.

REFERENCES

Arnason, V. (2000) 'Gadamerian dialogue in the patient-professional interaction.' *Medicine, Health Care and Philosophy, 3,* 1, 17–23.

Bakhtin, M. (1984) *Problems of Dostoevsky's Poetics* (C. Emerson, ed. and trans.). Minneapolis, MN: University of Minnesota Press.

Bakhtin, M. M. (1986) *Speech Genres and Other Late Essays* (C. Emerson and M. Holquist eds, V. W. McGee trans.). Austin, TX: University of Texas Press.

Bersani, H., Jr. (1996) 'Leadership in developmental disabilities: Where we've been, where we are, and where we're going.' In G. Dybwad and H. Bersani Jr. (eds) *New Voices: Self-advocacy by People with Disabilities*. Brookline, MA: Brookline Books.

Brockley, J. (2004) 'Rearing the child who never grew: Ideologies of parenting and intellectual disability in American history.' In S. Noll and J. W. Trent Jr. (eds) *Mental Retardation in America: A Historical Reader*. New York: New York University Press.

Castles, K. (2004) '"Nice, average, Americans": Postwar parents' groups and the defense of the normal family.' In S. Noll and J. W. Trent (eds) *Mental Retardation in America: A Historical Reader*. New York: New York University Press.

Gadamer, H. G. (1989) *Truth and Method* (2nd rev. edn) (J. Weinsheimer and G. Marshall trans.). New York: Continuum Press.

Gillman, M., Swain, J. and Heyman, B. (1997) 'Life history or "case" history: The objectification of people with learning difficulties through the tyranny of professional discourses.' *Disability & Society, 12,* 5, 675–693.

Hewitt, H. L. (2000) 'A life story approach for people with profound learning disabilities.' *British Journal of Nursing, 9,* 1, 90–95.

Kincaid, D. and Fox, L. (2002). 'Person-centered planning and positive behaviour support.' In S. Holburn and P. M. Vietze (eds) *Person-centered Planning: Research, Practice, and Future Directions.* Baltimore, MD: Paul H. Brookes Publishing Co.

Mansell, J. and Beadle-Brown, J. (2004) 'Person-centred planning or person-centred action? Policy and practice in intellectual disability services.' *Journal of Applied Research in Intellectual Disabilities, 17,* 1, 1–9.

Mercer, M. (2003) *Person-centered Planning: Helping People with Disabilities Achieve Personal Outcomes.* Homewood, IL: High Tide Press.

Meininger, H. P. (2001) 'Autonomy and professional responsibility in care for persons with intellectual disabilities.' *Nursing Philosophy, 2,* 3, 240–250.

Meininger, H. P. (2005) 'Narrative ethics in nursing for persons with intellectual disabilities.' *Nursing Philosophy, 6,* 2, 106–118.

Meininger, H. P. (2006) 'Narrating, writing, reading: Life story work as an aid to (self) advocacy.' *British Journal of Learning Disabilities, 34,* 3, 181–188.

O'Brien, J. (2002) 'Numbers and faces: The ethics of person-centered planning.' In S. Holburn and P. M. Vietze (eds) *Person-centered Planning: Research, Practice, and Future Directions.* Baltimore, MD: Paul H. Brookes Publishing Co.

O'Brien, J. and Lyle, C. (1987) *Framework for Accomplishment.* Decatur, GA: Responsive System Associates.

O'Brien, C. L., O'Brien, J. and Mount, B. (1997) 'Person-centered planning has arrived...or has it?' *Mental Retardation, 35,* 6, 480–484.

Polkinghorne, D. (2004) *Practice and the Human Sciences: The Case for a Judgment-based Practice of Care.* Albany, NY: SUNY Press.

Trent, J. W., Jr. (1994) *Inventing the Feeble Mind: A History of Mental Retardation in the United States.* Berkeley, CA: University of California Press.

Volosinov, V. N. (1986) *Marxism and the Philosophy of Language* (L. Matejka and I. R. Titiunik trans.). Cambridge, MA: Harvard University Press.

Wehmeyer, M. L. (2002) 'The confluence of person-centered planning and self-determination.' In S. Holburn and P. M. Vietze (eds) *Person-centered Planning: Research, Practice, and Future Directions.* Baltimore, MD: Paul H. Brookes Publishing Co.

Wehmeyer, M. and Berkobien, R. (1996) 'The legacy of self-advocacy: People with cognitive disabilities as leaders in their community.' In G. Dybwad and H. Bersani Jr. (eds) *New Voices: Self-advocacy by People with Disabilities.* Brookline, MA: Brookline Books.

Wehmeyer, M., Bersani, H., Jr. and Gagne, R. (2000) 'Riding the third wave: Self-determination and self-advocacy in the 21st century.' *Focus on Autism and Other Developmental Disabilities, 15,* 2, 106–115.

5

Legal Rights and Persons with Intellectual Disabilities

Voula Marinos, Dorothy Griffiths, Leanne Gosse,
Jennifer Robinson, J. Gregory Olley
and William Lindsay[i]

INTRODUCTION

Article 6 of the United Nations Declaration of Human Rights states that 'everyone has the right to recognition everywhere as a person before the law'. Moreover, Article 7 of the same declaration states that 'all are equal before the law and are entitled without any discrimination to equal protection under the law'. Clearly it is critical that any justice system is predicated on the basis of equality regardless of gender, race, class or dis/ability. As Sobsey notes, 'access to the justice system is one of the most fundamental rights of all citizens, because, without this access, individuals cannot legally defend any of their rights and are forced to become dependent on others to advocate on their behalf' (Sobsey 1994, p.284).

While these are fundamental human rights, the praxis of such rights are, at times, dubious. Reiman (1998) contends that the criminal justice system is one of fairness and equality wherein it ensures the protection of the rights of all and proportionately punishes those who violate such rights and interests. However, the justice system, on occasion, deviates from such goals, jeopardizing the legal rights of individuals in contact with the system and further perpetuating social inequalities.

It is generally accepted that persons with intellectual disabilities represent 2–3 per cent of the population throughout North America (Petersilia 2000). They are generally law-abiding citizens of society; however, due to a complex number of factors they are often over-represented in the legal system, both as victims and defendants (Conley, Luckasson and Bouthilet 1992; Griffiths and Marini 2000). However, our literature search has revealed no data on the prevalence of persons with disabilities as participants in the judicial process in either civil or criminal cases.

Individuals with intellectual disabilities become entangled in the legal process for the same range of complex cognitive, social, emotional and economic reasons as nondisabled persons. Additionally, there are specific risk factors that appear to relate strongly to the life experiences of persons with intellectual disabilities that increase their vulnerability to be both perpetrators and victims of certain crimes (Conley *et al.* 1992; Griffiths and Marini 2000). For example, they may have poor cognitive judgement, and increased risk of psychiatric disorder or challenges (Prem-Stein and Gambioli 2003). However, there are also throughout Canada, the United States, and the United Kingdom disability-specific civil cases that reflect action to protect the rights of the person with disability or to gain compensation for previous rights infringements.

The focus of this analysis is on the rights of persons with intellectual disabilities as they interact with the court process in Canada, the US and UK. Although all individuals regardless of class, gender, race or disability are guaranteed rights in law, persons with intellectual disabilities are more likely than others to experience vulnerability in interacting with persons in authority, to confess, be found incompetent to testify or stand trial, be led by the interviewer, be denied bail, and be sentenced to incarceration. In this chapter the authors provide an analysis of some of the psychological and social factors known about persons with intellectual disabilities, as they may relate to the courtroom experience. The chapter also includes a section on ways in which persons with intellectual disabilities can be supported as they interact with the court system. The culmination of these supports can increase the knowledge of criminal justice professionals to recognize and effectively provide persons with intellectual disabilities their inherent rights in the court process.

SOURCE OF RIGHTS

Persons with intellectual disabilities may interact with the judicial system in one of three ways: as litigants, victims, or accused. We discuss the concept of rights and accommodations to persons with intellectual disabilities in the context of the court process in general – criminal or civil – and from an international perspective. In this section, we provide examples of sources of legal rights within Canada, the US, and the UK to emphasize the point that respecting human rights of persons with disabilities in any court process is similar across jurisdictions to a large extent, and therefore the accommodations that we suggest are likely applicable in multiple contexts.

In the Canadian criminal process, for example, there are a couple of major legal contexts to consider when examining the experiences of individuals as accused or complainants/victims in the criminal justice process. The Canadian Charter of Rights and Freedoms guarantees all Canadians in contact with the justice system fair and equitable treatment, and outlines the state's powers relating to rights of the accused; individuals are guaranteed legal rights such as life, liberty and security of the person (section 7), the right to be secure against unreasonable search and seizure (section 8), the right against arbitrary detention (section 9), the right to instruct counsel on arrest or detention (section 10b), the right to be informed of being charged with an offence without unreasonable delay (section 11a) and others. When an individual believes that a Charter right has been violated, the court can be asked for a remedy under section 24. The Human Rights Code of Ontario guarantees protection of all vulnerable individuals' rights. It is public policy to recognize the dignity and worth of each person and to provide for equal rights and opportunities without discrimination. Further, section 17 (1) explains that a 'right of a person under this Act is not infringed for the reason only that the person is incapable of performing or fulfilling the essential duties or requirements attending the exercise of the right because of disability'.

In the criminal justice system in the United States, much like Canada, there are a few central frameworks to consider in examining the rights and liberties of the accused in the criminal justice process. The Constitution of the United States of America secures for all US citizens fair treatment within the justice system and delineates the responsibilities of the state and rights of the citizens. Within the US Constitution, the Bill of Rights guarantees individuals legal rights, such as freedom of speech and religion, the right to be free from cruel and unusual punishment, and the right to protection from unreasonable search and seizure. The Fifth and Sixth Amendments are central to the criminal justice process. They guarantee due process and the right to a speedy public trial with an impartial jury and assistance of counsel.

The Americans with Disabilities Act of 1990 (42 U.S.C. § 12101 et seq.) is a wide-ranging civil rights law that aims to prohibit discrimination based on disability. The Act is divided into five sections: Employment, Public Services, Public Accommodations, Telecommunications, and Miscellaneous Provisions. It affords similar protections against discrimination to the Civil Rights Act of 1964, which made discrimination based on race, religion, sex, national origin, and other characteristics illegal. Disability is defined as 'a physical or mental impairment that substantially limits a major life activity'. The determination of whether any particular condition is considered a disability is made on a case by case basis.

In the UK persons with intellectual disabilities are protected under a number of sources, primarily under the Human Rights Act (1998) respecting the European Convention on Human Rights (ECHR) (1950). Additionally the Disability Discrimination Act (c.50) (DDA) (1995) and (2005) provides disabled persons with rights within education, employment, buying or renting land or property, access to everyday goods and services, and motoring and transport. 'Disability' and 'disabled person' under the DDA includes any person who has 'a physical or mental impairment which has a substantial and long-term adverse effect on his ability to carry out day-to-day activities' (Part 1, section 1). Articles 5, 6 and 7 of the European Convention on Human Rights are directly related to traditional rights of due process such as the right to liberty and security of the person, unlawful detention, to be informed of reasons for arrest and charge against him in a language he understands, habeas corpus, speedy trial, right to counsel and defence, including legal aid and an interpreter if required.

More recently, the United Nations Convention on the Rights of Persons with Disabilities was passed in March 2007. 'Discrimination on the basis of disability' means any distinction, exclusion or restriction on the basis of disability which has the purpose or effect of impairing or nullifying the recognition, enjoyment or exercise, on an equal basis with others, of all human rights and fundamental freedoms in the political, economic, social, cultural, civil or any other field. It includes all forms of discrimination, including denial of reasonable accommodation. Article 5, in particular, relates to equality before the law and the prohibition of discrimination based upon disability. Article 13 guarantees access to justice:[ii]

1. States Parties shall ensure effective access to justice for persons with disabilities on an equal basis with others, including through the provision of procedural and age appropriate accommodations, in order to facilitate their effective role as direct and indirect participants, including as witnesses, in all legal proceedings, including at investigative and other preliminary stages.

2. In order to help ensure effective access to justice for persons with disabilities, States Parties shall promote appropriate training for those working in the field of administration of justice, including police and prison staff.

Therefore concerns about the welfare and discrimination of persons with disabilities has reached world-wide attention in the 21st century and appropriate supports and accommodations are meant to be developed to assist in their treatment and participation within the judicial process.

Persons with intellectual disabilities as litigants: the example of forced sterilization

The reproductive rights of persons with intellectual disabilities have historical civil law significance. In the previous century, the reproductive control of persons with intellectual disabilities resulted in institutionalization, mass sterilization, intrusive reproductive research involving castration, and even mass murder (Scheerenberger 1983). In Canada, until the 1970s, persons with intellectual disabilities were victims of legalized mass sterilization; within that mandate atrocities occurred where persons with Down syndrome, who are typically sterile, were the targets of intrusive research related to reproduction. Moreover, as late as 1976, in the US, 26 states still permitted involuntary sterilization of the mentally ill, 24 permitted sterilization of persons with intellectual disabilities and 14 permitted such actions for those with epilepsy (Pfohl 1994).

In light of the above, it is no wonder that in the past few decades, there have been two landmark civil cases in Canada regarding persons labeled as intellectu- ally disabled with regards to issues of reproduction and sterilization. The case of Eve v. Mrs. Eve (1986), heard by the Supreme Court of Canada, protected Eve's rights not to be subjected to non-therapeutic sterilization for the purpose of con- traception. Eve's mother requested the sterilization procedure. The court decided that although a third party (parens patriae) may be appropriate for some consent procedures, such an irreversible and intrusive procedure that affected bodily integrity could not be provided under this principle.

In a more recent case of Muir v. Alberta (1996), Muir brought legal action against the Province of Alberta for forced sterilization while she resided at the Michener Center in Red Deer Alberta. The suit was won on the grounds that the decision to sterilize was not justified according to the statute (Alberta Steriliza- tion Act) and that a proper process was not followed. Other suits followed.

In the United States, the foundation/legal framework relating to persons with disabilities as litigants is illustrated by the history of eugenic sterilization. Buck v. Bell, 274 U.S. 200 (1927), was the US Supreme Court ruling that upheld a statute instituting compulsory sterilization of the mentally retarded 'for the pro- tection and health of the state'. It was predominantly seen as an endorsement of eugenics – the attempt to improve the human race by eliminating 'defectives' from the gene pool. The effect of Buck v. Bell was to legitimize eugenic steriliza- tion laws in the US as a whole. While many states already had sterilization laws, their use was erratic and effects practically non-existent in every state except Cali- fornia. After Buck v. Bell, dozens of states added new sterilization statutes or updated their constitutionally non-functional ones with statutes that more closely mirrored the Virginia statute upheld by the Court.

Sterilization rates under eugenics laws in the US climbed from 1927 until Skinner v. Oklahoma, 316 U.S. 535 (1942). While Skinner v. Oklahoma did not specifically overturn Buck v. Bell, it created enough of a legal quandary to dis- courage many sterilizations. By 1963, sterilization laws were almost wholly out of use, though some remained on the books for many years.

Across the US more than 65,000 people were documented to have been ster- ilized under eugenics laws, based on the idea that society would be improved if people with mental retardation, mental illness, or 'undesirables' were not allowed to spread their 'problems' on to their children. During the 1960s, most of those sterilized in North Carolina were young black women. Over the last 15 years of its operation, 99 per cent of the 'victims' were women; more than 60 per cent were black. In April 2003, Governor Easley signed a law that officially put an end to forced sterilization in North Carolina.

Persons with intellectual disabilities as complainants/victims of crimes

Although persons with disabilities are more likely to be the victims of crime rather than perpetrators, crimes against persons with disabilities typically go unreported (Sobsey 1994; Wilson and Brewer 1992). The rate of violence and abuse endured by people with a disability is significantly higher than that of people without such disabilities; a common finding in Canada, the US and Australia (Petersilia 2000; Wilson and Brewer 1992).

In Canada it was reported that the rate of violent crimes against persons with intellectual disabilities is 4–10 times higher than rates against the general population (Sobsey, Lucardie and Mansell 1995). The more severe the disability, the more likely the crime is to be unreported. Wilson and Brewer (1992) reported that in Australia, 71 per cent of crimes against persons with more severe disabilities went unreported, compared to 40 per cent in the group with moderate levels of disability. If reported, crimes against persons with intellectual disabilities are less likely to result in charges or convictions (Prem-Stein and Gambioli 2003). For example, in Alberta, Canada, 39 per cent of the sexual assaults against persons with intellectual disabilities were reported but of those reported only 8 per cent led to prosecution. Persons with severe or multiple disabilities, who represent the most vulnerable population (Wilson and Brewer 1992), are the least likely to have access to the justice system when they are victims of crime (Doe 1995).

Persons with intellectual disabilities are vulnerable to the full range of crimes that affect nondisabled persons but they also bear increased vulnerability as victims of crimes perpetrated because of their disability (Luckasson 1992). Persons with disabilities often require increased institutional support, and their systems of support can at times increase their vulnerability. In the US, it was reported that persons with intellectual disabilities are 2.9 times more likely to be assaulted, 10.7 times more likely to experience sexual assault, and 12.7 times more likely to be robbed (Prem-Stein and Gambioli 2003). Persons with intellectual disabilities may experience more victim-risk factors than nondisabled persons because of their disabling condition (i.e. impaired judgement, lack of adaptive behaviour, or physical disability) and/or because of the nature of their environments, care provision, or lack of education. Researchers found that most crimes against persons with disabilities occur in Canada within the specialized environments in which they are supported and are perpetrated by known persons, often care-providers (Sobsey and Varnhagen 1988). For example, although 56.9 per cent of sexual abuse of persons with intellectual disabilities occurs in relationships similar to those common to nondisabled victims (family members, acquaintances, paid generic service providers, strangers, or dates), 43.7 per cent of the offences against disabled persons involve relationships prompted by the victim's disability (i.e. caregiver, support or professional staff, and other persons with disabilities) (Sobsey and Varnhagen 1988). Persons with intellectual disabilities who live in institutions, group homes, or who were living alone, experienced the highest rates of victimization (Wilson and Brewer 1992).

Accused persons with intellectual disabilities

Persons with intellectual disabilities are greatly over-represented in the criminal justice system on the whole, although their involvement at different stages is not consistent. In Canada, for example, statistics reveal that the percentage of mentally disordered accused entering the criminal justice system has been escalating at a minimum of 10 per cent annually over the last decade or more. (Schneider 1999). This is likely a result of mental health diversion programs.

The picture of over-representation is similar in the correctional system. Studies in the US, for example, have demonstrated that approximately 10 per cent of adults in prison have an intellectual disability (Petersilia 2000). In the UK, McBrien, Hodgetts and Gregory (2003) contend that persons with an intellectual disability are not over-represented in the prison population; however, they are over-represented at most other stages of the criminal justice system. Data were not available from any site searched regarding the number of persons with intellectual disabilities who enter the civil law process. It may be that individuals with intellectual disabilities are often diverted from many civil suits because the agencies that support them will intervene to resolve conflicts prior to court.

Although the criminal offences committed by persons with intellectual disabilities are generally less severe than that of nondisabled persons (Day 1997), they have an exaggerated presence in the justice system because they are more likely to be apprehended, confess to the crime, incriminate themselves, be led by the interviewer, plead guilty, waive their rights without full comprehension of the process, and less likely to plea bargain or appeal judgement, understand the implications of their statements or be able to afford appropriate defence counsel (Abel and Rouleau 1990; Brown and Courtless 1971; Hayes 1994; McGee and Menolascino 1992; Moschella 1982; Murphy, Coleman and Haynes 1983; Santamour and West 1977).

Some researchers argue that these statistics are falsely low, asserting that the numbers do not take into consideration cases where the intellectual disability is not detected and where the individual interacts with agencies other than the justice system (Day 1994). Other researchers (Denkowski and Denkowski 1985) estimate that in their US national sample the prevalence of intellectual disability within the prison system, assessed by intelligence testing alone, was only 2 per cent. They claimed the reduced rate was due to enhanced court diversion programs, whereby the individuals would be diverted to other systems or options. For example, research has shown that many persons with intellectual disabilities who commit a crime are diverted from the correctional facility to restrictive residential care facilities for persons with an intellectual disability or mental illness, or within supervised community residential settings (Day 1994; Lakin *et al.* 1982, as cited in Noble and Conley 1992). Additionally, the data do not account for many cases where a person with intellectual disabilities is accused of committing a crime but not brought to court because the person is found incompetent to testify or unfit to stand trial. This subgroup of individuals with intellectual disabilities may be required to reside in a residential institution, presumably for rehabilitation or habilitation, sometimes indefinitely without a process of redress (Fedoroff *et al.* 2000).

The above statistics are also confounded by the method of evaluation of cognitive functioning. For example, Hayes and McIlwain (1988) found, using a definition of intellectual ability that included social and adaptive skills as well as intelligence levels, that the rate of incarcerated persons with intellectual disabilities was as high as 13 per cent. They further found that many of these individuals, particularly the women, were dually diagnosed with mental illness and intellectual disability. Although individuals with intellectual disabilities commit the same range of offences as nondisabled persons, their offences are typically less severe. The majority of the offences are property related, public nuisance, or less serious violent crimes (Day 2000).

Persons with intellectual disabilities and the courtroom: challenges and accommodations

Given the roles and complex interactions that persons with intellectual disabilities face when involved in the court process, there has been increasing interest in assisting them. However, there is little empirical research on this subject (Griffiths and Marini 2000), and the literature that is available has not decisively identified a path to ensure an easier interaction with the legal system for people with intellectual disabilities. In the section that follows, the authors provide some of the psychological factors known about persons with intellectual disabilities as they relate to the courtroom experience. Evidence pertaining to persons with intellectual disabilities as it may relate to the courtroom are discussed in the following order: (i) identifying persons with intellectual disabilities in the courtroom, (ii) identifying when there may be a need for assessment for a intellectual disability, (iii) skills needed to engage in court proceedings, (iv) the implications of a low IQ or mental age, (v) the relationship between intellectual disability and the person's ability to be witness in court, (vi) providing testimony, (vii) the relationship between intellectual ability and memory, (viii) implications for the interaction of the person with intellectual disabilities in court, and (ix) strategies to enhance the retrieval process for persons with intellectual disability.

1. Identifying persons with intellectual disabilities in the courtroom

Individuals with intellectual disabilities often enter the judicial system without evaluation or consideration as to how the nature of their disabling condition may have affected commission of the crime, understanding of rights, pre-trial testimony, understanding of possible outcomes, or their ability to provide consistent and accurate testimony (Griffiths and Marini 2000). One study found that most individuals with intellectual disabilities are not labelled by the court prior to arraignment (52.4%), trial (9.1%) or imprisonment (9.1%) and only 27.3 per cent are identified at the time of arrest (McAffe and Gural 1988). Indeed, many individuals go undetected. When an intellectual disability is recognized by the court, the severity of delay is often more extreme and the accused is frequently hospitalized rather than sent to prison.

It is not always apparent that a person in the court has an intellectual challenge. Society is familiar with obvious disabilities such as Down syndrome, the most common chromosomal abnormality that produces intellectual disability; however, even some persons with Down syndrome may present with a mosaic effect that lacks many of the characteristic features. Other genetic or chromosomal abnormalities present with visual differences but the general population cannot identify these. Still, many individuals with intellectual disabilities have no or minimal outward physical features that might alert the court to an intellectual challenge. They may show, however, some subtle signs in their manner of dressing, physical coordination, communication, or social or emotional behaviours.

2. Identifying when there may be a need for assessment of intellectual disability

If the above circumstances cause suspicion, the court might explore some basic features of the individual's background that tend to be associated with persons having impaired intellectual functioning:

- Did the person attend school, and to what age? If the person quit early or went through the public system to the age of 21 these could indicate a special education system.

- Did the person grow up in the natural family? In the past persons with intellectual disabilities were more likely to be removed from their families and placed in congregate living situations; this is happening less in recent decades.

- Did the person attend school in the same neighbourhood as siblings? Inclusion in the neighbourhood school is considered best practice but is still not in place in all communities.

- Does the person have a history of involvement in the social service network or receiving government disability benefits?

These events are inconclusive in isolation but may provide additional support for observed inconsistencies in court appearance.

Some countries have adopted a screening tool for use in the courts. For example, Australia and the UK apply the Hayes Ability Screening Index (Hayes 2000) as a quick reference tool. The Hayes Ability Screening Index (Hayes 2000) was designed for use in the justice system to identify persons early and possibly requiring additional assessment. It involves gathering some background information and conducting observations of behaviour. It can be administered quickly and consists of self-report questions, a spelling subset, a 'join the dots' puzzle, and a clock drawing subset. It can be adjusted to be jurisdiction-specific.

3. Skills needed to engage in court proceedings

If the accused is a person with an intellectual disability, then the consideration of fitness to stand trial may be raised. In Canada, section 2 of the *Criminal Code* defines 'unfit to stand trial' as unable 'on account of mental disorder' to conduct a defence because of an inability 'to understand the nature or object of the proceedings, understand the possible consequences of the proceedings, or communicate with counsel'. Mental disorder has been defined by the Supreme Court of Canada in R. v. Oommen (1994), establishing that '[t]he accused must possess the intellectual ability to know right from wrong in an abstract sense. But he or she must also possess the ability to apply that knowledge in a rational way to the alleged criminal act' (p.516).

Accused persons with intellectual disabilities may be deemed unfit to stand trial for three reasons. First, accused persons with intellectual disabilities may be unfit because of a mental disorder, but the condition is sensitive to rehabilitation, such as depression. Second, unfitness might be a permanent state that is the result of cognitive impairment that would not be sensitive to rehabilitation or education. Third, they may be unfit due to ignorance of the court proceedings, expectations and roles. In this case the accused may become fit if it can be demonstrated that they have acquired knowledge of the nature and object of the court proceedings, the consequences of the proceedings, and can communicate with counsel. Areas that may be covered in fitness restoration training are the differences between available pleas, the nature or purpose of the proceedings, and the roles of the judge, jury and counsel.

In the US, the equivalent concept to 'unfitness' or 'fitness' is 'competence'. The concept of competence in the US can apply to any aspect of participation in court proceedings (e.g. competence to testify, competence to be sentenced). The specific case of competence to stand trial is governed by the 'Dusky standard' (Dusky v. US362 U.S. 402 80 S.Ct. 788 1960). In this case, the US Supreme Court ruled that a defendant must have adequate ability to consult lucidly with his or her attorney and to have rational and factual comprehension of the charges against him or her in order to be found competent to stand trial.

In the UK, 'fitness to plead' is the relative equivalent to the American concept of competency to stand trial, relating specifically to the capacity to understand the proceedings. A person may have an intellectual disability that caused the person to be 'unfit' at the time of the alleged offence, but being fit to plead relates only to mental state at the time of trial. As Exworthy (2006) points out, the test of fit to plead is 'explicitly an intellectual one and the criteria assess the defendant's level of comprehension and communication' about the charge and its consequences, the trial process, and the potential to participate and work with his/her lawyer. Fitness to plead is related to Article 6 of the European Convention on Human Rights and the right to a fair trial.

The authors were not able to find formal, validated procedures to evaluate 'fitness to stand trial' for persons with intellectual disabilities for use in the Canadian court system. In the US and the UK, the Competence Assessment for Standing Trial for Defendants with Mental Retardation (CAST-MR) is a measure, validated by Everington and Luckasson (1992) and again by Everington and Dunn (1995) for use with this population. These tools however are sensitive to jurisdictional differences and as such must be developed locally. The CAST-MR was used by 45 per cent of psychologists surveyed about practices used when evaluating juvenile competence to stand trial (Ryba, Cooper and Zapf 2003). In the UK the next most frequently used assessment instrument is the MacArthur Competency Assessment Tool – Criminal Adjudication and the Competency Screening Test. The research evidence validating competence assessment is sparse and is even sparser in the area of defendants with intellectual disability, compared with juveniles or with accused persons with mental illness. Some of the limitations of competency assessment instruments are summarized by Otto et al. (1998), and include the lack of underlying conceptual structure, lack of standardized administration, lack of criterion-based scoring, lack of quantitative indices of discrete competence related abilities, and limited norms.

In Canada, 'unfit' in the mental health field is assumed to be potentially alterable with rehabilitative treatment (i.e. psychoactive medication or therapy); however, 'unfit' for persons with intellectual disabilities may be a permanent state, unresponsive to rehabilitation in the same way. That being said, the evaluation of fitness may be altered if appropriate environmental factors are changed and supports provided (Ericson, Perlman and Issacs 1994) or if fitness restoration training is provided.

One of the great challenges to the legal system is that persons with intellectual disabilities are being assessed for fitness or competence and trained to achieve fitness or competence by individuals from the mental health field. Mental health professionals may or may not be educated in working with persons with intellectual disabilities; this is a subspecialty known as 'dual diagnosis'. The general mental health professional may have limited knowledge of persons with intellectual disabilities and little if any real experience in interviewing, questioning, or evaluating the real abilities of someone so labelled. Thus a major obstacle to court-appointed experts is ensuring both sides are equally neutral or as knowledgeable about persons with intellectual disabilities.

Court preparation for a witness, complainant, or accused with an intellectual disability is important. It relates to both competence to witness and fitness to stand trial, although each require some overlapping and some different skill sets as a burden of proof. Witnesses, complainants and accused with intellectual disabilities need familiarity with the expectations of them upon entering the courtroom, including an understanding of the role of the judge, counsel, jury (if applicable) and courtroom decorum.

Although in Canada it is no longer necessary for witnesses or complainants to swear an oath, but rather to promise to tell the truth, people who are unable to communicate that they understand a promise may be denied the opportunity to give testimony even if they can communicate what happened to them and they can show that they have not fabricated a story (Richler 1995). Witnesses and complainants need to demonstrate understanding of either 'what is an oath?' or 'what is a promise?', and commit to tell the truth. As such they must clearly understand truth from lie and why it is important to tell the truth.

In the US, the Federal Rules of Evidence as they pertain to competency of witnesses disqualifies a witness if he or she 'is (i) incapable of expressing himself concerning the matter as to be understood, either directly or through interpretation by one who can understand him, or (ii) incapable of understanding the duty of a witness to tell the truth' (Rule 601).

The Dusky standards are the basis for the previously mentioned Competence Assessment for Standing Trial for Defendants with Mental Retardation (CAST-MR) (Everington and Luckasson 1992), an instrument designed to assess competence to stand trial for people with mental retardation (intellectual disability). In practice, the courts generally limit both the number and kind of competencies that are considered. This is because the Dusky case makes up so much binding precedent in the case law of competency.

State laws specify the next steps if a defendant lacks capacity to proceed. As in Canada, defendants who are found not competent to stand trial can be required to participate in educational activities that may result in competency. In general, the court may dismiss the charges when it appears that the defendant will not gain capacity to proceed or when the defendant has been substantially deprived of his or her liberties for a time equal to the maximum time that he or she would have been confined if found guilty of the crime.

In the US, if an accused is deemed incompetent to stand trial then s/he may be hospitalized for lengthy periods of time, violating his/her constitutional right to due process. To counter such concerns, an option may be training for competency within the legal system. For example, in California, an accused deemed incompetent to stand trial may be required to partake in a court competency training program, which is designed to improve competency to stand trial through educational training in class activities, video presentations, and weekly assignments. Through a quasi-experimental program evaluation of this particular resource, Bertsch, Younglove and Kerr (2002) found, using the Competency Assessment Instrument (CAI), that previously incompetent accused were found competent to stand trial after six months of training.

Further, in a similar American treatment/training program designed for competency, Siegel and Elwork (1990) found that with training/treatment, accused with intellectual disabilities could be rendered competent to stand trial. The treatment under question in this study entailed cognitive problem solving, focusing on communication skills, increasing knowledge of the court process and a psycho-educational intervention utilizing video, court models and discussion groups. Results of this study demonstrate the effectiveness of such training programs, which may uphold defendants' rights to due process and promote a more reasonable and proficient justice system (Siegel and Elwork 1990).

Unfitness to plead in the UK can be distinguished between lower courts and 'Crown courts', where more serious offences are heard. In lower courts, Exworthy (2006) outlines that in a situation in which an accused's fitness outweighs the 'interests of justice', the individual can be hospitalized under the Mental Health Act. If the individual cannot be treated to be fit, then the court can order hospitalization for a period of time without imposing a conviction. Concern has been raised, however, since there is no requirement to test the strength of the evidence; an individual may be found not guilty had s/he proceeded to trial and is hospitalized nonetheless.

4. The implications of a low IQ or mental age

Young children are usually considered prima facie incapable of committing a crime. This argument, although appealing to apply to persons with intellectual disabilities with a similar mental age, assumes that all individuals with intellectual disabilities would not appreciate the significance of their behaviour, in the manner assumed for children (Fitch 1995). However, Fitch suggested that place-ment of persons with intellectual disabilities within the same category as children would not allow appropriate consequences for individuals, particularly those with mild and moderate intellectual disabilities, to assume responsibility and to learn from the consequences of their behaviour. Moreover, the accused's intellec-tual disability may have served as a mitigating circumstance regarding commission of a crime, competency to witness, fitness/competency to stand trial, and sentencing considerations, and as such is an important consideration.

The results from a standardized and individually administered intelligence test are often used to determine the general level of intellectual functioning of the individual. Such a test is generally described as an IQ (intelligence quotient), as a label (borderline, moderate, severe, profound) and a mental age (e.g. MA of seven years, two months). It is vital that the mental health professional, who provides the psychometric evaluation of the cognitive functioning of the person with an intellectual disability, understands that an evaluation of a cognitive ability is more than just an IQ score. The court might exercise caution in the evidence of 'experts' who base their assessments on the IQ alone. An IQ score and the associated mental age are indicative of the person's performance at that point in time on a test of intelligence. However, the IQ is not just a number but a continuum of skills that represent quantitative and qualitative differences in abilities, which results in a different developmental pattern, in both timing and degree (McGee and Menolascino 1992). An individual with an intellectual disability may be able to function fairly independently in society and may appear socially competent.

Mental age refers to the average chronological age, from a large sample of individuals who answered the same number of questions on the test of intelli-gence as the individual being tested. Because the cognitive constraints *appear* similar to those of children, mental age is frequently used to describe the behav-iour and global functioning of adults with intellectual disabilities. It is however difficult to rule out other factors, related to such things as maturation and life experience, that could be important in circumstances of a crime or that may either hinder or enhance functioning in a court of law (Valenti-Hein and Schwartz 1993). For example, a 42-year-old man may have an IQ that acquires him a label of intellectual disability and a mental age equivalent to that of a child, but this should not be interpreted to mean that this man has the thoughts, experiences, or general knowledge of a child. This man has lived 42 years on earth and has those experiences and level of maturation. Intelligence tests predict academic achieve-ment but 'claims concerning the ability of psychological tests to predict behavior must be made cautiously' (Aiken 1994, p.97).

For now, we can only extrapolate from a database that indirectly addresses the needs of people with intellectual disabilities and make educated guesses that could help them interact with the legal system (Valenti-Hein and Schwartz 1993).

5. The relationship between intellectual disability and the person's ability to be a witness in court

Historically, persons with intellectual disabilities have been considered aberrant witnesses due to the perceived limitations of cognitive functioning (Perlman *et al.* 1994). For example, the Canada Evidence Act, section16.(1) provides that with a witness whose mental capacity is in question, the court must inquire into whether the person understands the nature of an oath or solemn affirmation, and is able to communicate the evidence. However, many individuals with intellectual disabilities may well be able to communicate the evidence without understanding the concept of oath or solemn affirmation. Section 16.(3) accommodates individuals who can communicate evidence but lack the understanding of oath by allowing them to give unsworn testimony on the condition that they promise to tell the truth. R. v. Leonard (1990), a case involving a child witness, stands for the proposition that the witness must be able to differentiate truth from fabrication and understand that it is important to tell the truth. The individual must understand the responsibility to give evidence as part of normal social conduct and within the court, and appreciate what happens in a court, practically and morally, as a result of a lie. The Canadian Criminal Code (2005) suggests these criteria would be difficult to establish without a sworn oath. However, R. v. Farley (1995), a case involving an adult witness with a severe intellectual disability, confirms that the ability to witness is contingent only upon a meaningful promise to tell the truth. In that case, the witness's ability to testify was based on demonstration of a duty to tell the truth in everyday social conduct. This understanding may be at a basic level of moral development, such as: if you tell a lie you might get punished or telling a lie would be wrong because it is a court or because it would hurt someone (the accused). Additionally, the witness must demonstrate understanding of the nature of a promise and commitment to tell the truth (R. v. Ferguson (1996); R. v. McGovern (1993); R. v. B. (R.J.) (2000) respectively).

In 1960 in the United States, the US Supreme Court ruled in Dusky v. US that a defendant must have adequate ability to consult lucidly with his attorney and to have rational and factual comprehension of the charges against him in order to be found CST (competent to stand trial) (see Table 5.1).

The particular issue of providing evidence in court has been recognized in England and Wales with proposed provisions in trials that include persons with intellectual disabilities (Kebbell and Davies 2003; O'Kelly *et al.* 2003). Most recently the Youth Justice and Criminal Evidence Act 1999 outlines the provision of special measures to witnesses who require assistance because of age or incapacity in order to improve the quality of evidence provided to the court. Outside of this legislation, some have argued that the UK lacks specific guidelines to assist witnesses (Jones 2005).

Table 5.1 Abilities related to the notion of competency

To understand the current legal situation	To comprehend instructions and advice
To understand the charges	To maintain a collaborative relationship with counsel and help plan legal strategy
To understand relevant facts	
To understand the legal issues and procedures	To follow testimony for contradictions or errors
To understand potential legal defences	To testify relevantly and be cross-examined if necessary
To understand possible dispositions, pleas, and penalties	To tolerate stress at the trial and while awaiting trial
To appraise the likely outcome	
To appraise the roles of the defence counsel, prosecutor, judge, jury, witnesses and defendant	To refrain from irrational and unmanageable behaviour during trial
	To disclose pertinent facts surrounding the alleged offence
To identify witnesses	
To relate to counsel in a trusting and communicative fashion	To protect oneself and utilize legal safeguards available

6. Providing testimony

There are several factors in relation to the testimony of persons with intellectual disabilities that may present reasons for caution: learned compliance/deference to authority, projection of false feelings, projection of competence when it does not exist, stress and surrender of defences.

Learned compliance/deference to authority figures: Persons with intellectual disability who are being interviewed may be more prone to tell the interviewer what the interviewer wants, or what is perceived to be what is wanted in order to be compliant or avoid perceived criticism. Consequently, such individuals may be more likely to confess, incriminate themselves, plead guilty, or waive rights without full comprehension of the process (Brown and Courtless 1971; Moschella 1982).

Persons with intellectual disabilities have learned to be over-compliant to authority figures; as such they engage in outward-directed behaviour, by which they look for clues for the desired answer or respond in the affirmative to questions seeking 'yes' responses. Part of this phenomenon is the presentation of an overly pleasant façade, the avoidance of anger in threatening situations, and the active engagement in tasks to gain social interaction from authority figures. Persons with intellectual disabilities want to be liked, especially by persons who are nondisabled; the social interaction may take precedence over the information that is being transferred.

The amount of power the interviewer exercises in questioning is called 'valence' (Garbarino and Stott 1992). If the interviewer exercises too much control, the individual may refuse to respond or respond in one-word sentences. Alternatively, the intellectually disabled person may simply be developmentally unable to do what the interviewer is requesting and, therefore, may give a response in order to comply, even though s/he does not have the answer. Persons with intellectual disabilities are particularly vulnerable to threats and coercion, as well as friendliness (Bazelteton *et al.* 1963, as cited in McGee and Menolascino 1992). Research has shown that in interviewing it is best to maintain a balance so that the individual can say what they want to say about the topic and then respond to more narrow and directed probes (Garbarino and Stott 1992). However, this is not the nature of the legal context. The courtroom can often be very adversarial as counsel explore the reliability of the evidence and seek to discredit opposing witnesses. The use of misleading or intent-laden questioning is common in the court proceeding; this confrontational and adversarial environment makes it very difficult for most individuals with intellectual disabilities to maintain cognitive consistency.

Projection of false feelings: Research has shown that persons with intellectual disabilities will often tolerate unacceptable rules, restrictions and limitations, long past the point that nondisabled persons would allow (Flynn *et al.* 1985). Learned tolerance of intolerable situations is often manifested by blind obedience to authority figures. This can present itself in the courtroom as being nice to the very person who is being accused of abusing them or smiling when telling of a story of horror. The court could be misled to believe that the abuse did not occur because the person did not demonstrate the expected emotion to a given situation.

Projection of competence where it does not exist: While most people from time to time feign competence, Edgerton (1967) noted that persons with intellectual disabilities were especially skilled at projecting competence where it does not exist. The concept of denial or projecting a lack of disability is referred to as wearing a 'cloak of competence' (Edgerton 1967). If asked 'Are you intellectually disabled (or mentally retarded)?', many individuals would fail to disclose or even deny it for fear that an affirmative answer would have negative repercussions (Lustig 1995, as cited in Prem-Stein and Gambioli 2003). If asked 'Do you understand what I have just said?', the answer would generally be 'yes'; the person would deny a lack of understanding. Ericson *et al.* (1994) noted that if the person with disabilities does not know what is expected s/he will often construct an answer based on their own meaning or interpretation. Others may engage in more cavalier behaviour towards questioning that may register outwardly as disrespect for the court.

An individual's ability to provide information will depend on the strength of the interviewee's need to be competent and to please the interviewer, compared to the often competing need to defend oneself against potential negative consequences or feelings (Garbarino and Stott 1992). Garbarino and Stott reported that when children are repeatedly interviewed about an event, they may begin to alter their evidence if they interpret the repetition as an indication that they gave the wrong answer. Chong *et al.* (2000) found a similar pattern in persons with intellectual disabilities, who when repeatedly questioned on an event were likely to change their answers 62 per cent of the time. The shift in testimony is assumed to be an attempt to comply with the perceived wishes of the interviewer. Research has shown that individuals with disabilities are also highly motivated for social reasons, and as such may act to gain approval or to avoid the negative judgement of others.

Moral development level: Based on Kohlberg's (1969) moral development scale, it appears that individuals with intellectual disabilities may present at the lower moral development levels (those based on the principles of morality and based on reinforcement and punishment). This does not mitigate the truthfulness of their statements, but only the motivation base for their moral judgements. For example, persons with disabilities may be more likely to accept blame for an event even if the event was accidental. In this case they would ascribe guilt based on the outcome ('bad things happened and I was responsible'), compared to the potential argument for exemption from guilt when the event is accidental or unintentional. Additionally the individual may seek to avoid punishment by denial of certain facts.

Stress and the surrender of defences: Under stress, individuals with intellectual disabilities may demonstrate 'cognitive disintegration', a term used to refer to stress-induced deterioration in information processing which might result in a bizarre and even psychotic-like behavioural presentation (Sovner and Hurley 1986). They suggest that stress may 'overload their cognitive functioning, and produce breakdowns in reality testing' that results in stress-induced intellectual and emotional decompensation (p.46).

Cognitive disintegration can influence the perception of the person's competency in two ways. First, it can directly influence the cognitive ability of the person to testify. Second, it can also change the person's psychosocial presentation. An interviewer's perception of the person being interviewed can be influenced by a display of unusual behaviour, rambling, inconsistent or contradictory details, speed of speech. If the accused has a disability, these behaviours may affect the perception that the accused is innocent and could not have committed a crime (The Roeher Institute 1995).

The interview with a police officer or a lawyer is decidedly stressful from two perspectives. First, there is stress regarding the interview itself because persons with disabilities are rarely interviewed for their opinions. Usually, questions put to them are rhetorical, posed by authority figures seeking compliance, or as a method of demonstrating the individual has learned a verbally correct response. Second, not only the nature of the interview but the content of this interview will elicit stress. The person being interviewed may be a potential defendant in a crime. Highly anxious persons are less accurate and express less confidence in their ability to recall a task compared to participants with low anxiety.

Preparation for the court process and accommodations within the court process regarding rules of evidence may further reduce the stress associated with questioning. Preparation prior to court can assist the individual to understand court proceedings (i.e. exposure to materials that will acquaint the individual with the procedures of the courtroom and the expectations). An example is a booklet with pictures and Bliss symbols called *After You Tell* by Ludwig (1995). Additionally, the individual may benefit from physical exposure to the courtroom and role-playing regarding the anticipated event. Caution needs to be taken in all of the above situations to ensure that the individual is being trained about the court process rather than the content of the specific evidence that will be presented at court.

7. The relationship between intellectual ability and memory

Cognitive abilities can affect how information is encoded (Sperber and McCauley 1984) and retained or lost (Ellis and Meador 1985). In Canadian courts, for example, a witness must be able to communicate at the trial and demonstrate:

1. that at the time of the event the person had the capacity to witness, understand, recall, and also communicate the events (R. v. Marquard (1993) and

2. appreciation for the need to answer all questions in accordance with his/her recollection of what occurred (R. v. Farley 1995).

For the most part, the major cognitive factors that affect the interaction between persons with intellectual disabilities and the legal system can be narrowed down to three factors: (1) the development of memory, (2) linguistic abilities, and (3) knowledge base (Griffiths and Marini 2000). Of these, Griffiths and Marini suggest memory is by far the most critical factor.

Memory is vital to the provision of evidence before the court (Griffiths and Marini 2000). If the person cannot recall the events in a convincing manner, then their testimony adds little to the proceedings (Sobsey 1994) and may indeed detract from the natural outcome. Memory, however, is fragile and susceptible to suggestion, distortions and even failure (Loftus 1991).

Recent research demonstrates that the act of remembering is a dynamic process, in which the strength and organization of the stored memory can change over time in response to intervening experiences and events, both real and otherwise (see Bruck and Ceci 1999; Ceci and Bruck 1993; Principe *et al.* 2000).

Memories may be much more malleable than previously thought. Because memory is not a static, but dynamic factor, recall depends on the strength of stored memory and how it is organized. It depends on factors antecedent to the event such as prior knowledge, the relevance or value of the event, and how the person understands or absorbs the event because of stress or dissonance. Experiences following the incident such as natural loss due to memory disintegration or events that may have distorted or interfered with recollection also play a role.

Remembering involves two basic processes – storage of information and retrieval:

Storage of information: There are many factors that can affect information storage. The more central issue for many persons with disabilities may be how the event was originally encoded (the knowledge, meaning, and interest with which the person stored the information) and the relationship of the event to incongruous or dissonant events. Information is stored into long-term memory when the event is salient and within the person's understanding. The more elaborate the level of understanding of a type of event, the more likely it is that information is understood, properly stored and accurately retrieved (Griffiths and Marini 2000). This is quite relevant to cases involving sexual offences where persons with intellectual disabilities are victims or the accused. The person's sexual knowledge and understanding can play a significant role in how they perceive and remember the offence and how they communicate their evidence. However, memory can be altered by duration or repetitiveness of the event and the individual's age or role as witness or victim (Whitcomb 1992). The circumstances of the event could tamper how information is stored. If the event is cognitively dissonant to the person's understanding then the individual will have difficulty storing the dissonant concepts – 'My staff member is there to help me/my staff member hurt me.'

Retrieval: While the conditions under which information is stored may not be within the control of the participants or the people trying to help them, the retrieval process is (Griffiths and Marini 2000). The manner in which individuals are questioned about their stored memory can affect how it moves from storage to retrieval (see Loftus 1991). Persons with intellectual disabilities:

> present with reduced vocabulary and understanding of abstract words and ideas, and in general demonstrate challenges with attention span, short-term memory and abstraction. Thinking tends to be concrete or literal in the understanding of situations and questions. There is greater difficulty deriving inference and understanding concepts or situations that require the ability to process and integrate complex information. (Ericson *et al.* 1994, p.104)

Thus, an important factor for the court is whether the interviewing conditions and nature of questioning under which recollection was obtained was leading, misleading, or created undue stress that could affect memory of the person with a disability. Additionally, intervening experiences or changing knowledge that could affect the recollection, reconstruction or reproduction of the events can affect the validity of the memory retrieved (see Table 5.2).

8. Implications for the interaction of the person with intellectual disabilities in court

There is an inherent challenge when people with intellectual disabilities interact with the law. The challenge is to maximize the cognitive and social factors that may help the participants interact with the courts and at the same time satisfy the requirements of the legal system (Perlman *et al.* 1994). Court adaptations for persons with intellectual disabilities are vital if they are to add substantively to the fact- or truth-finding mission of the trial. The court, however, is challenged by the need to ensure that the prejudicial effect of these accommodations does not outweigh the probative value of their evidence.

Several provisions within the Canadian Criminal Code, for example, provide guidance in this pursuit.[iii] A judge or justice, on application of the prosecutor or a witness with an intellectual disability, can order a support person of the witness's choosing to be permitted to be present and close to the person while testifying (Section 486 (1.2)). However, section 486 (1.4) allows the court to sanction this communication. The presence of a support person may be vital to the witness's ability to present their evidence in a forum that may be extremely intimidating to the person with a disability.

The Canada Evidence Act creates provision for witnesses who have difficulty due to physical or mental disability to permit a witness to give evidence by any means that enables the evidence to be intelligible (sections 486(1) and 486(2)). Persons with intellectual disabilities often experience significant delays in their acquisition of verbal language and may have communication marked by echolalia (repeating), reversal of pronouns, idiosyncratic phrases or words, and challenges in typical conversation (APA 2000). Individuals with intellectual disabilities may employ assistive devices to aid their communication, such as manual sign language, picture boards, voice output computers, gesture, and Bliss symbols. The reliance on these devices with this population may be a function of their cognitive disability or to an associated impairment in hearing, sight, or mobility (Ericson *et al.* 1994). Persons with intellectual disabilities have been taught to independently and spontaneously use these systems to request interaction, a change in environment, or to communicate desires and wishes (Bomba *et al.* 1996).

Prior knowledge about the individual's abilities and language needs will help the court to prepare more effectively for the interview. It is important to use whatever form of communication is familiar to the individual and be constantly alert

Table 5.2 Strengths and challenges when questioning persons with intellectual disabilities

Strengths	Challenges
Are often able to understand the discussion in a legal interview	May need time and support to provide adequate answers; may appear unresponsive to questioning, when they actually just need more time to respond. In some cases responses may come some time later in the conversation.
Can provide recalled information if hinged in a contextual framework	May have difficulty recalling temporal order or duration when remembering events because of their cognitive challenges relative to time and date, without context being provided.
Are able to recall long-term events and forget at about the same rate as nondisabled persons	Recall less using unstructured recall-type tasks, likely to fabricate more on misleading short-answer questions and more prone to errors on false leading specific and statement questions due to the demands of the situation and the desire to conform to the authority figure. If given a list of options the person is likely to choose the last one provided.
Provide accurate and salient information regarding the key elements	Provide less salient information and fewer details.
Are able to recall similar to persons without disabilities when structured interview formats were used	Give less complete responses when asked to freely recall or to recall using generalized or short-answer questions.
Able to correct information when presented with leading, specific, and statement questions	Are less able to correct information if given misleading recall questions or false leading specific and statement questions. May be less accurate and less confident in recall if highly anxious; stress can create disassociation and suggestibility, especially when questions are posed to try to trip the person up.

(Adapted from Ericson, Isaacs and Perlman 1999; Perlman *et al.* 1994; Perlman and Ericson 1992; The Roeher Institute 1995.)

to misunderstandings (Garbarino and Stott 1992). In some circumstances, where the person with a disability utilizes an alternative communication strategy, the interviewer may need to have access to someone who can assist them in interpreting during the interview process (i.e. someone who can understand sign or gestures or picture boards). It is helpful if the interpreter is familiar with the individual, as long as the individual could not be accused of bias in their interpretation and as such should be at arm's length from the event under investigation.

In the UK, the Police and Criminal Evidence Act (1984) (PACE) authorizes that an 'appropriate adult' be included in police questioning of a youth or 'mentally vulnerable' suspect detained in police custody to ensure that s/he understands what is occurring, the reasons why, and that any questions asked of the individual are fair, clear, comprehensible and not confusing. The appropriate adult is authorized to be present at all stages of the police proceedings, including the interview, search of his/her person, fingerprinting and other related procedures. A solicitor can be called if the individual wishes; however, unlike the lawyer–client privileged relationship, conversations with the detained individual are not protected by legal privilege (Home Office 1984).

A challenge for the court comes in determining that the mediated communication represents the views of the witness and not that of the interpreter or assistant. In most cases the interpreter is reflecting the individual's communication by way of a standardized language pattern (i.e. manual sign language, Bliss symbols, picture boards). In other cases, the interpreter or assistant will be present to clarify for the court some aspects of the communication that would otherwise be unintelligible or confusing. However, in some cases the individual may have a communication method that is unique to themselves (personally developed gestures) and only understood by those who know the person well. This latter case requires greater caution in the interpretation of section 6.1.

In the 1990s, a unique debate emerged in the courts regarding the validity of 'facilitated communication' (FC) as an accepted means of conveying the evidence of individuals with intellectual disabilities and those with autism spectrum disorder. FC occurs with a 'facilitator' supporting the hand or arm of the individual while the person types a message on a keyboard or uses a picture system to communicate (Crossley 1992). The supporters of this method suggested that the physical support enabled individuals, especially those with autism, to overcome neuromotor difficulty to allow them then to express previously inaccessible thoughts. The challenge to this system was that the empirical research failed to find evidence to support that FC added additional communication beyond that demonstrated through other methods and that the facilitator was not influencing the outcomes (Mostert 2001). As a result, this method of communication has been discredited as a tool for use in courts in the US and Canada because independence from the facilitator cannot be established.

In Canada, a complainant or witness who has difficulty communicating evidence due to mental disability can be ordered by the judge to testify outside the courtroom or behind a screen or other device that would allow the complainant or witness not to see the accused (Part XV of the Canadian Criminal Code (Special Procedure and Powers), section 486 (2.1)).[iv] In such cases the accused, judge or justice and the jury observe the testimony by means of closed circuit television or otherwise, and the accused must be able to communicate to counsel while watching the testimony (section 486 (2.2)). In contrast, testifying behind a screen in the US has been found to violate the sixth Amendment right to a public trial.[v]

For sexual offences, in Canada the law further allows a witness or complainant with a mental disability who has difficulty communicating to enter into evidence a videotape describing the 'acts complained of' (section 715.2). The videotape must have been made within a reasonable time after the alleged offence and the individual must then, while testifying, adopt the content of the statement. Adoption means that the witness recalls giving the statement and that they were attempting to be truthful and honest when giving the statement. The witness or complainant's testimony therefore can be provided in an environment that is conducive to gaining the most accurate account.

In England and Wales, the Youth Justice and Criminal Evidence Act includes provisions for persons with intellectual disabilities in the court system. Such provisions include pretrial preparation, friend-in-court schemes, pretrial hearings, breaks, clearing of the public gallery and videotaped interview evidence (Kebbell and Davies 2003).

It is important to make one note of caution here. When persons with intellectual disabilities are brought into the criminal justice system as victims of sexual assault, the court may be faced with interview tapes where the person has described their story of the event. Sometimes 'props', such as anatomically correct dolls, are used to assist the individual to expand the information given. However, these materials should never be used as the first course of inquiry regarding an event, but rather as a method to assist the person to expand on an already disclosed incident. Additionally, only individuals trained in the use and interpretation of these materials should use this approach. Materials such as anatomically correct dolls have been the subject of contradictory research regarding their suggestibility to children (see Boat and Everson 1988) and persons with intellectual disabilities.

Regardless of the accommodations made to allow persons with disabilities to provide evidence, the witness or complainant will still be subject to cross-examination and the stressors attached to that experience. It is at this stage that persons with intellectual disabilities often lose credibility in the court. We suggest that criminal justice professionals 'at the gate' of the system – specifically police and (Crown) prosecutors – be trained to detect, if possible, when a person may have an intellectual disability that makes comprehension of the process difficult. Police and (Crown) prosecutors ought to alert relevant assistance if an individual is accused, detained, or a witness or victim requires assistance to understand the processes, reasons and implications for particular procedures that are undertaken.

9. Strategies to enhance the retrieval process for persons with intellectual disability

The testimony of persons with intellectual disabilities may lack the depth and breadth that might be present in nondisabled persons. Nonetheless their communication is often far more forthcoming than that of nondisabled persons (McGee and Menolascino 1992). The method of communication, however, may require some adaptation.

A person's understanding of the language used by the court system to investigate the retrieval of information may affect the accuracy of the reported events. Interviewers should be aware that persons with intellectual disabilities may misunderstand or reverse such terms as 'guilty' and 'not guilty' (Smith 1993). Furthermore, limited language production may result in a misunderstanding or misinterpretation of the verbal report by the interviewer. Ericson *et al.* (1994) noted that persons with intellectual disabilities: (i) rarely say that they do not understand the meaning of a word or question unless they are asked, (ii) have difficulty following run-on sentences or multiple questions, and (iii) may not use pronouns either correctly or in a way that gives the listener a proper context.

People with disabilities are rarely interviewed in social contexts of their choosing, and questions are usually rhetorical. If questions are given by authority figures, persons with intellectual disabilities have learned that the authority figure is generally seeking verbal acknowledgement of learning or compliance. Thus the individual with an intellectual disability may require an adapted questioning environment in which the story that they know can be told without prejudice.

The validity of the interview depends on the following. In order to ensure that the legal rights of a person with an intellectual disability are protected, interviewers should:

1. Ensure communication adaptations have been made appropriate to the individual.

2. Create as stress-free an interaction as possible.

3. Give the person permission to say 'I don't know'. Individuals with disabilities will try to comply to the question even if that means attempting to create meaning where there is none.

4. When asking questions provide a context in which the person can place the event.

5. When shifting topics identify that the area of inquiry is now changing to reduce apparent perseverance.

6. Ask questions in as direct a manner as possible and speak directly and clearly to the person.

7. Persons with cognitive challenges may have difficulty with:

   ○ abstract words or terms

   ○ leading questions

   ○ the use of pronouns (use names or titles in questions)

   ○ long, run-on sentences or multiple questions (persons with intellectual disabilities may have shorter attention span and so it is important to keep testimony to the critical issues)

   ○ questioning that requires recall of temporal order or duration (individuals with intellectual disabilities may have cognitive challenges relative to time and date, fail to understand that two events can share the same duration, or that events which may appear incongruous could happen – i.e. my care provider abused me but my care provider is there to care for me)

   ○ lists from which the person must select (often, intellectually disabled persons will simply choose the last item).

8. Check for understanding by requesting the information in a different way rather than asking if the person understood or repeating the same question. If the person is asked the same question a second time there is a tendency to assume the first answer may have been incorrect and so the person may try to alter the question to meet what they think the interviewer wants.

In summary, questioning techniques such as free recall combined with specific questions is the most beneficial. In contrast, short-answer questions, especially misleading ones, and leading statement questions should be avoided. Ceci, Bruck and Rosenthal (1995, p.494) contend that 'weakly suggestive interview techniques do not pose serious hazards' to the accuracy of testimony; rather 'repeated suggestions coupled with stereotyped inductions, atmospheres of accusations, and confirmatory biases' do pose such a threat.

CONCLUSIONS

Persons with intellectual disabilities are over-represented in the legal system as accused, witnesses or litigants. Their ability to engage effectively in the judicial process is often dependent upon support from the court to identify, accommodate and understand their disability as it relates to their performance in the court and as it relates to the event that brought them into court. Without due diligence to these issues the legal rights of persons with intellectual disabilities are routinely jeopardized. Much can be done to be sensitive to, support, and accommodate persons with intellectual disabilities as they participate in the court process.

NOTES

[i]   The authors gratefully acknowledge feedback from Justice Richard Schneider, Ontario Court of Justice, and Ted Kelly, Legal Counsel, Toronto, Ontario. Additionally J. Gregory Olley would like to thank Andrew Lincoln for his valuable assistance in the preparation of the chapter.

[ii]   www.un.org/esa/socdev/enable/rights/ahc8adart.htm#art13.

[iii]   See sections 486 (1.2) and 486 (2.1); section 715.2; and sections 6(1) and 6(2) of the *Canada Evidence Act.*

[iv]   These provisions apply to cases where the accused is charged with an offence under sections 151, 152, 153, 151, 1, 155 or 159, subsection 160(2 or 3) or section 163.1, 170, 171, 172, 173, 210, 211, 212, 213, 266, 267, 268, 271, 272 or 273).

[v]   See U.S. v. Anita Yates, Anton f. Pusztai, US Court of Appeals Eleventh Circuit, November 24, 2004, see www.ca11.uscourts.gov/opinions/ops/200213654.pdf.

REFERENCES

Abel, G. G. and Rouleau, J. (1990) 'The nature and extent of sexual assault.' In W. Marshall, D. R. Laws and H. E. Barbaree (eds) *Handbook of Sexual Assault.* New York: Plenum Press.

Aiken, L. R. (1994) *Psychological Testing and Assessments,* 8th edn. Toronto: Allyn and Bacon.

American Psychiatric Association (APA) (2000) *Diagnostic and Statistical Manual of Mental Disorders,* 4th ed. – TR. Washington, DC: American Psychological Association.

Bertsch, J. M., Younglove, J. A. and Kerr, M. G. (2002) 'A pilot study of the Porterville Developmental Center's Court Competency training program.' *Criminal Justice Policy Review, 13,* 3, 65–77.

Boat, B. W. and Everson, M. D. (1988) 'The use of anatomical dolls among professionals in sexual abuse evaluations.' *Child Abuse and Neglect, 12,* 2, 171–179.

Bomba, C., O'Donnell, L., Markowitz, C. and Holmes, D. L. (1996) 'Evaluating the impact of facilitated communication on the communitive competence of fourteen students with autism.' *Journal of Autism and Developmental Disorders, 26,* 1, 45–58.

Brown, B. S. and Courtless, R. F. (1971) *Mentally Retarded Offender.* Washington, DC: National Institute of Mental Health.

Bruck, M. and Ceci, S. J. (1999) 'The suggestibility of children's memory.' *Annual Reviews of Psychology, 50,* 419–439.

Ceci, S. J. and Bruck, M. (1993) 'The suggestibility of the child witness: An historical review and synthesis.' *Psychological Bulletin, 113*, 3, 403–439.

Ceci, S. J., Bruck, M. and Rosenthal, R. (1995) 'Children's allegations of sexual abuse: Forensic and scientific issues: A reply to commentators.' *Psychology, Public Policy, and Law, 1*, 2, 494–520.

Chong, I., Yu, D. C. T., Martin, G. L., Harapiak, S. and Garinger, J. (2000) 'Response switching to repeated questions by individuals with developmental disabilities during interviews.' *Developmental Disabilities Bulletin, 28*, 1, 56–66.

Conley, R. W., Luckasson, R. and Bouthilet, G. N. (1992) *The Criminal Justice System and a Developmental Disability: Defendants and Victims.* Baltimore, MD: Paul H. Brookes Publishing Co.

Crossley, R. (1992) 'Lending a hand: A personal account of the development of facilitated communication training.' *American Journal of Speech-Language Pathology, 1*, 3, 15–17.

Day, K. (1994) 'Male mentally handicapped sex offenders.' *British Journal of Psychiatry, 165*, 5, 630–639.

Day, K. (1997) 'Clinical features and offence behavior of mentally retarded sex offenders: A review of research.' In R. J. Fletcher and D. Griffiths (eds) *Congress Proceedings – International Congress II on the Dually Diagnosed.* New York: NADD.

Day, K. (2000) 'Treatment and care of mentally regarded offenders.' In A. Dosen and K. Day (eds) *Treating Mental Illness and Behaviour Disorders in Children and Adults with Mental Retardation.* Washington, DC: American Psychiatric Press.

Denkowski, G. C. and Denkowski, K. M. (1985) 'The mentally retarded offender in the state prison system: Identification, prevalence, adjustment and rehabilitation.' *Criminal Justice and Behavior, 12*, 1, 55–70.

Doe, T. (1995) 'Access to justice and children with disabilities.' In The Roeher Institute (ed) *As If Children Matter: Perspectives and Children, Rights and Disability.* Toronto: The Roeher Institute.

Dusky v. US 362 U.S. 402, 80 S.Ct. 788 (1960)

Edgerton, R. (1967) *The Cloak of Competence.* Berkeley, CA: University of California Press.

Ellis, N. R. and Meador, I. M. (1985) 'Forgetting in retarded and nonretarded persons under conditions of minimal strategy use.' *Intelligence, 9*, 1, 87–96.

Ericson, K., Isaacs, B. and Perlman, N. (1999) 'Enhancing communication: The special case of interviewing victim-witnesses of sexual abuse.' In I. Brown and M. Percy (eds) *Developmental Disabilities in Ontario.* Toronto: Front Porch Publishing.

Ericson, K., Perlman, N. and Isaacs, B. (1994) 'Witness competency, communication issues and people with developmental disabilities.' *Developmental Disabilities Bulletin, 22*, 2, 101–109.

Everington, C. T. and Dunn, C. (1995) 'A second validation study of the Competence Assessment for Standing Trial of Defendants with Mental Retardation (CAST-MR).' *Criminal Justice and Behavior, 22*, 1, 44–60.

Everington, C. T. and Luckasson, R. (1992) *Competence Assessment for Standing Trial for Defendants with Mental Retardation: CAST-MR.* Worthington, OH: International Diagnostic Services.

Exworthy, T. (2006) 'Commentary: UK perspective on competency to stand trial.' *The Journal of the American Academy of Psychiatry and the Law, 34*, 4, 466–471.

Fedoroff, J. P., Griffiths, D., Marini, Z. and Richards, D. (2000) 'One of our clients has been arrested for sexual assault: Now what? – The interplay between developmental and legal delay.' In A. Poindexter (ed.) *Bridging the Gap Proceedings 17th Annual NADD Conference.* Kingston, NY: NADD.

Fitch, W. L. (1995) 'A developmental disability and criminal responsibility.' In W. W. Conley, R. Luckasson and G. N. Bouthilet (eds) *The Criminal Justice System and Mental Retardation: Defendants and Victims.* Baltimore, MD: Paul H. Brookes Publishing Co.

Flynn, M. C., Reeves, D., Whelan, E. and Speake, B. (1985) 'The development of a measure for determining the mentally handicapped adult's tolerance of rules and recognition of rights.' *Journal of Practical Approaches to Developmental Handicap, 9*, 2, 18–24.

Garbarino, J. and Stott, F. M., Faculty of the Erikson Institute (1992) *What Children Can Tell Us – Eliciting, Interpreting and Evaluating Critical Information From Children.* San Francisco, CA: Jossey-Bass.

Government of Canada (1985) Canada Evidence Act, R.S.C c.C.5 am. R.S. 1985. C. 19 (3d Supp.), ss. 17,18; 1992. C1.S. 142.

Government of Canada (1985) Criminal Code of Canada, R.S.C. c. C-46. Ottawa, CA: Federal Government of Canada.

Griffiths, D. and Marini, Z. (2000) 'Interacting with the legal system regarding a sexual offence: Social and cognitive considerations for persons with developmental disabilities.' *Journal of Developmental Disabilities, 7*, 1, 77–121.

Hayes, S. (1994) 'The criminal law and the person with intellectual disability.' *Australia and New Zealand Journal of Developmental Disabilities, 19*, 4, 287–292.

Hayes, S. (2000) *Hayes Ability Screening Index.* Sydney: Faculty of Medicine, University of Sydney.

Hayes, S. and McIlwain, D. (1988) *The Prevalence of Intellectual Deficit Among the New South Wales Prison Population: An Empirical Study.* Canberra: Criminology Research Council.

Home Office, United Kingdom (1984) Guidance for 'appropriate adults' under The Police and Criminal Evidence Act (1984) (PACE). Retrieved from http://police.homeoffice.gov.uk/operationalpolicing/powers-pace-codes/custody.html/ on October 28 2008.

Jones, R. (2005) 'Capacity to give evidence in court: Issues that may arise when a client with dementia is a victim of crime.' *Psychiatric Bulletin, 29*, 9, 324–326.

Kebbell, M. and Davies, G. (2003) 'People with intellectual disabilities in the investigation and prosecution of crime.' *Legal and Criminological Psychology, 8*, 2, 219–222.

Kohlberg, L. (1969) 'Stage and sequence: The cognitive developmental approach.' In D. Goslin (ed.) *Handbook of Socialization Theory and Research.* Chicago, IL: Rand McNally.

Loftus, E. F. (1991) 'Commentary: When words speak louder than actions.' In J. Doris (ed.) *The Suggestibility of Children's Recollections.* Washington, DC: American Psychological Association.

Luckasson, R. (1992) 'People with a developmental disability as victims of crime.' In R. W. Conley, R. Luckasson and G. N. Bouthilet (eds) *The Criminal Justice System and Mental Retardation: Defendants and Victims.* Baltimore, MD: Paul H. Brookes Publishing Co.

Ludwig, S. (1995) *After You Tell.* Toronto: Sexual Information and Education Council of Canada.

McAffe, J. and Gural, M. (1988) 'Individuals with mental retardation and the criminal justice system: The view for the State Attorneys-General.' *Mental Retardation, 6*, 5–12.

McBrien, J., Hodgetts, A. and Gregory, J. (2003) 'Offending and risky behaviour in community services for people with intellectual disabilities in one local authority.' *The Journal of Forensic Psychiatry and Psychology, 14*, 2, 280–297.

McGee, J. and Menolascino, F. J. (1992) 'The evaluation of defendants with a developmental disability in the criminal justice system.' In R. W. Conley, R. Luckasson and G. N. Bouthilet (eds) *The Criminal Justice System and Mental Retardation: Defendants and Victims.* Baltimore, MD: Paul. H. Brookes Publishing Co.

Moschella, S. (1982) 'The mentally retarded offender: Law enforcement and court proceedings.' In M. B. Santamour and P. S. Watson (eds) *The Retarded Offender.* New York: Praeger.

Mostert, M. P. (2001) 'Facilitated communciation since 1995: A review of puiblished studies.' *Journal of Autism and Developmental Disorders, 31*, 287–313.

Muir v. Alberta (1996). (Muir vs. the Queen in right of Alberta), 132 D.L.R.(4th) 695, Court of Queen's Bench.

Murphy, W. D., Coleman, E. M. and Haynes, M. (1983) 'Treatment and evaluation issues with the mentally retarded sex offender.' In J. Greer and I. Stuart (eds) *The Sexual Aggressor: Current Perspectives on Treatment.* New York: Van Nostrand Reinhold.

Noble, J. H. and Conley, R. W. (1992) 'Toward an epidemiology of relevant attributes.' In R. W. Conley, R. Luckasson and G. N. Bouthilet (eds) *The Criminal Justice System and Mental Retardation: Defendants and Victims.* Baltimore, MD: Paul H. Brookes Publishing Co.

O'Kelly, C. M. E., Kebbell, M., Hatton, C. and Johnson, S. D. (2003) 'Judicial intervention in court cases involving witnesses with and without learning disabilities.' *Legal and Criminological Psychology, 8,* 2, 229–240.

Otto, R. K., Poythress, N. G., Nicholson, R. A., Edens, J. F. *et al.* (1998) 'Psychometric properties of the MacArthur Competence Assessment Tool – Criminal Adjudication.' *Psychological Assessment, 10,* 4, 435–443.

Perlman, N. B., Ericson, K. I., Esses, V. M. and Isaacs, B. J. (1994) 'The developmentally handicapped witness: Competency as a function of question format.' *Law and Human Behavior, 18,* 2, 171–188.

Perlman, N. and Ericson, K. (1992) 'Interviewing developmentally handicapped persons: The ability of developmentally handicapped individuals to accurately report on witnessed events.' In J. Casselman (ed.) *Law and Mental Health.* Brussels: Leuven.

Pfohl, S. (1994) *Images of Deviance and Social Control: A Sociological History.* Toronto: McGraw-Hill Inc.

Petersilia, J. (2000) *Doing Justice? Criminal Offenders with Developmental Disabilities.* Berkeley, CA: California Policy Research Center, University of California.

Prem-Stein, J. and Gambioli, N. (2003) *Developmental Disabilities and the Justice System. A Training Package.* Vancouver: The Law Courts Education Sourcing of BC and the Kindale Developmental Association.

Principe, G. F., Ornstein, P. A., Baker-Ward, L. and Gordon, B. N. (2000) 'The effects of intervening experiences on children's memory for a physical examination.' *Applied Cognitive Psychology, 14,* 1, 59–80.

R. v. B. (R. J.) (2000), 77 Alta. L.R. (3d) 1, 33 C.R. (5th) 166 (Alta. C.A.).

R. v. Farley (1995), 99 C.C.C. (3d) 76, 40 C.R. (4th) 190, 23 O.R. (3d) 445 (C.A.).

R. v. Ferguson (1996), 112 C.C.C. (3d) 342.

R. v. Leonard (1990), 54 C.C.C. (3d) 225, 37 OAC 269 (C.A.).

R. v. Marquard (1993), 25 C.R. (4th) 1, 85 C.C.C. (3d) 193 (S.C.C.).

R. v. McGovern (1993), 88Man R. (2d) 18 at 21 (Man. C.A.).

R. v. Oommen (1994) 2 S.C.R. 507.

Reiman, J. (1998) *The Rich Get Richer and the Poor Get Prison.* Toronto: Allyn and Bacon.

Richler, D. (1995) 'The United Nations Convention on the Rights of the Child: A tool for advocacy.' In The Roeher Institute (ed.) *As If Children Matter: Perspectives on Children, Rights and Disability.* Toronto: The Roeher Institute.

Roeher Institute (1995) *Harm's Way: The Many Faces of Violence and Abuse Against Persons With Disabilities.* Toronto: The Roeher Institute.

Ryba, N. L., Cooper, V. G. and Zapf, P. A. (2003) 'Juvenile competence to stand trial evaluations: A survey of current practices and test usage among psychologists.' *Professional Psychology: Research and Practice, 34,* 499–507.

Santamour, W. and West, B. (1977) *The Mentally Retarded Offender and Corrections.* Washington, DC: US Department of Justice.

Schneider, R. D. (1999) 'Sentencing mentally ill offenders.' In J. V. Roberts and D. P. Cole (eds) *Making Sense of Sentencing.* Toronto: University of Toronto Press.

Scheerenberger, R. C. (1983) *A History of Mental Retardation.* Baltimore, MD: Paul. H. Brookes Publishing Co.

Siegel, A. M. and Elwork, A. (1990) 'Treating incompetence to stand trial.' *Law and Human Behavior, 14,* 1, 57–65.

Smith, S. A. (1993) 'Confusing the terms "guilty" and "not guilty": Implications for alleged offenders with mental retardation.' *Psychological Reports, 73,* 2, 675–678.

Sobsey, D. (1994) *Violence and Abuse in the Lives of People with Disabilities: The End of Silence Acceptance?* Baltimore, MD: Paul H. Brookes Publishing Co.

Sobsey, D., Lucardie, R. and Mansell, S. (1995) *Violence and Disability: An Annotated Bibliography.* Baltimore, MD: Paul H. Brookes Publishing Co.

Sobsey, D. and Varnhagen, C. (1988) *Sexual Abuse, Assault, and Exploitation of People with Disabilities.* Ottawa: Health and Welfare Canada.

Sovner, R. and Hurley, A. D. (1986) 'Four factors affecting the diagnosis of psychiatric disorders in mentally retarded persons.' *Psychiatric Aspects of Developmental Disability Reviews, 5,* 9, 45–49.

Sperber, R. and McCauley, C. (1984) 'Sematic processing efficiency in mentally retarded.' In P. N. Brooks, R. Sperber and C. McCauley (eds) *Learning and Cognition in the Mentally Retarded.* Hillsdale, NJ: Lawrence Erlbaum Associates.

Valenti-Hein, D. C. and Schwartz, L. D. (1993) 'Witness competency in people with mental retardation: Implications for prosecution of sexual abuse.' *Sexuality and Disability, 11,* 4, 287–294.

Whitcomb, D. (1992) *When the Victim is a Child* (2nd edn). US Department of Justice: Office of Justice Programs.

Wilson, C. and Brewer, N. (1992) 'The incidence of criminal victimization of individuals with an intellectual disability.' *Australian Psychologist, 27,* 2, 1114–1117.

6

Medical Rights for People with Intellectual Disabilities

Yona Lunsky, Paul Fedoroff, Kajsa Klassen,
Carolyn Gracey, Susan Havercamp,
Beverly Fedoroff and Nicholas Lennox

Medical rights are a fundamental aspect of human rights of people with intellectual disabilities. The right to health is described in the UN Constitution and international human rights treaties as 'the right to the highest attainable standard of health' (U.N. ESCOR 2000, General Comment Number 14). The aim of most health-care systems is to support that right by providing health promotion and illness prevention as well as diagnosis, treatment, rehabilitation and palliative care. Medical ethics are essential in making sure the medical rights are protected in individuals with intellectual disabilities. One factor that is critical to this discussion is the involvement of caregivers in addition to the health-care provider and the patient, when the patient has an intellectual disability. This forms a *communication triad* (i.e. patient with disability, health-care provider, caregiver) where each component of the triad has a critical role in ensuring the medical rights are met with the outcome of good health.

In discussing the issues particular to the rights of people with intellectual disabilities, this chapter will review the basic principles of medical ethics (beneficence, non-maleficence, autonomy and justice) and the implications of these principles for individuals with intellectual disabilities. If indeed these basic principles were applied to these individuals consistently, there would likely be no medical rights violations.

MEDICAL RIGHTS

Ethical principles

Beauchamp and Childress (2001) describe the four fundamental principles of biomedical ethics: *Beneficence* (*salus aegroti suprema lex*): health-care professionals must always act in the best interest of the patient to provide the best possible care. *Non-maleficence* (*primum non nocere*): health-care professionals must 'first do no harm'. *Autonomy* (*voluntas aegroti suprema lex*): the patient's rights come first and the health-care professional supports their ability to make decisions autonomously. The patient has the right to consent to treatment as well as the equal right to refuse treatment. *Justice* (*justitia*): synonymous with 'fairness', this principle is most often invoked in discussions of the fair and equitable distribution of resources. Meeting the medical rights of people with intellectual disabilities means ensuring they receive the best possible care, that care providers do no harm, that the patient has an autonomous voice when it comes to decision-making and that distribution of medical services is done fairly and equitably.

There are many situations where the four principles are at odds with one another and the relative merits of each principle must be carefully weighed based on the particular situation. The following vignette is based on the formative experience early in the career of one of the chapter authors (PF). It demonstrates how easy it can be to violate these principles and illustrates the relative roles of the triad (i.e. the individual with intellectual disabilities, the caregiver, and the health-care provider).

Clinical vignette

A family doctor received a page from the clinical manager of a residential facility for individuals with intellectual disabilities one evening because a resident was having a 'very bad day'. She had refused her supper and had become increasingly irritable. Some furniture had been broken and she had been restrained in her bed as a result. The staff asked if it would be possible to get an order for something to settle the patient down.

When the doctor suggested that the woman be seen in hospital, the astonished staff thanked him, but said that really wasn't necessary as it might make the resident's 'attention seeking' worse. The doctor asked if the residential nurse had taken the woman's vital signs and was told that she was too uncooperative to do so. 'All the more reason that she be taken to hospital then', the doctor said. She was brought into emergency by ambulance, in restraints with one knee drawn up and her forehead was warm to touch. Although it appeared as though there was something the patient desperately wanted to say, her level of intellectual disability was sufficiently severe that she was unable to speak more than one or two words. The emergency physician asked for help to examine the patient's abdomen and with some assistance was able to expose her belly. The patient glared as the doctor told her he was going to touch her stomach. He very gently pressed down on the right side of the patient's abdomen in a place known as McBurney's point and withdrew his hand suddenly. The patient let out a scream. 'What was that?' asked the staff member. ' *That* was Blumberg's sign, and *this* is acute appendicitis', the doctor answered. She was operated on immediately and made a full recovery.

Application of four principles to this case

The beneficence principle applies to this case because it was the doctor's responsibility to help the patient by discovering the cause of the symptoms, rather than assuming they were strictly 'attention-seeking behaviours' or just a common demonstration of what might be seen in someone with an intellectual disability ('diagnostic overshadowing'; Reiss and Szyszko 1983). This included seeing the patient, collecting observations from staff, and making a differential diagnosis, taking all the information at hand into account. This was to be done in a sensitive and gentle manner but as efficiently as possible in case it was an emergency, as it turned out to be.

The do no harm principle is relevant to the vignette as well. The patient required assessment and treatment in a way that kept him and others safe but this was to be done without unnecessary invasive procedures. It is possible that a different approach, applying the do no harm principle, may not have required restraints to the degree that they were used. Even if restraints were required for safety reasons, do no harm would mean that staff would comfort and support the restrained client in emotional distress as much as possible (i.e. role of the caregiver). Although the institution staff may have thought 'chemical restraint' (sedation) was in the best interest of the patient and others around her (conflict of beneficence and do no harm), standard medical practice is to avoid any interventions that might mask symptoms leading to the correct diagnosis. The rationale is that it is better to obtain an accurate diagnosis that may be life saving than to provide temporary relief of symptoms that may lead to a life-threatening misdiagnosis.

In terms of autonomy, the staff and doctor needed to think about how they could best include the patient in the process of the medical decisions that took place. The first inclination of staff was to request prescription of a particular treatment from the doctor that the staff could then administer, without giving voice to what the patient may have wanted. Due to her limited language capability and her level of distress, it was challenging to understand the patient's needs and wishes and allow her to exert her autonomy. As a first step, the doctor examined the patient. Finally, in terms of the justice principle, this patient was entitled to fair treatment, which included a right to be examined, visited by a physician, and an opportunity to receive the same diagnostic tests and treatments available to individuals without intellectual disabilities. There is a fine balance between the needs and views of the caregiver, health-care provider, and the patient. Without attention to beneficence, adherence to the apparent rights of autonomy may have meant no exam and no treatment, resulting in a possibly fatal outcome (i.e. undiagnosed ruptured appendix).

With regard to autonomy, it is often the case that individuals with intellectual disabilities require the support and guidance of others in order to make decisions regarding their own health care (Sullivan and Heng 2005). Nonetheless, it is important that they are given the opportunity to actually participate to the extent of their ability in their health care.

HEALTH, AGENCY AND SELF-DETERMINATION

The following section briefly reviews the current status of efforts to promote autonomy in people with intellectual disabilities as it relates to health. These ideas will be revisited in the conclusion of the chapter in the discussion on health rights and examples of interventions.

In a discussion paper for the WHO Commission on the Social Determinants of Health, Solar and Irwin (2005) point to the bi-directional relationships of agency and health suggested by Marmot (2001), and reiterate that 'health enables agency, but greater agency and freedom also yield better health' (p.7). Agency or enacted self-determination, in turn, refers to people having the skills, opportunities and supports to act as causal agents in their lives (Shogren *et al.* 2006).

Efforts to promote self-determination have the potential to affect health both directly and indirectly (Shogren *et al.* 2006). On a physiological level, having greater autonomy and control is associated with immunologic and endocrine response to disease (Shogren *et al.* 2006). On a psychosocial level, self-determination has the potential to enable people with disabilities to manage their own health and health care, and consequently achieve better health outcomes (Shogren *et al.* 2006).

International policy recognizes the importance of self-determination as it relates to people with intellectual disabilities (Beange, Lennox and Parmenter 1999; Department of Health 2001c; Sullivan *et al.* 2006; US Department of Health and Human Services (USDHHS) 2002). Self-determination is essential to giving people with intellectual disabilities greater control and choice in their own health care (Shogren *et al.* 2006). There is a need to find ways to encourage and support people with intellectual disabilities to play an increasingly active role in their health and health care, rather than assume the passive patient role they have historically adopted (Lennox, Beange and Edwards 2000; Lennox and Edwards 2001; Shogren *et al.* 2006).

Health disparities

Measurable differences or variations in health between populations are referred to as 'health disparities' or 'health inequalities' (Dahlgren and Whitehead 1991). In the widely cited paper *The Concepts and Principles of Equity and Health*, Whitehead (1992) further describes health *inequity* as follows: 'The term inequity has a moral and ethical dimension. It refers to differences which are unnecessary and avoidable, but in addition are also considered unfair and unjust' (Whitehead 1992, p.430). We will examine whether the health differences noted in current research between people with intellectual disabilities and the general population qualify as unfair or unjust (Ouellette-Kuntz 2005).

The growing body of international literature on the health of people with intellectual disabilities points to a larger number of health needs as compared to the general population. Far too often, these health needs are described as potentially correctable but unrecognized and therefore unmet (Beange *et al.* 1999). A brief summary of what we know about unmet health needs of individuals with intellectual disabilities is provided here under two headings: *Mortality* and *Morbidity and common health problems*. This research helps us understand the unique health needs of persons with intellectual disabilities. Once these needs are identified we can explore how to reduce health disparities with knowledge of where to focus efforts.

Mortality

Life expectancy of people with intellectual disabilities has increased parallel to that of the general population over the last three decades (Barr *et al.* 1999; Patja *et al.* 2000). Despite this positive trend, people with intellectual disabilities tend to have shorter life expectancies in comparison to the general population.

The most common causes of death for people with intellectual disabilities differ from those of the general population. Within the general population, the leading cause of death is cancer, followed by ischemic heart disease, cerebrovascular disease and stroke. For people with intellectual disabilities, respiratory disease followed by cardiovascular disease (related to congenital heart disease) are the leading causes of death (National Health Service 2004). Patterns of cancers are also different with lower rates of lung, prostate and urinary tract cancers and higher rates of esophageal, stomach, gallbladder cancer and leukemia (National Health Service 2004). Predictors of premature death in people with intellectual disabilities include: severity of intellectual disability, reduced mobility, feeding difficulties, Down syndrome, epilepsy (Eyman *et al.* 1990; Forsgren *et al.* 1996; Yang, Rasmussen and Friedman 2002).

Morbidity and common health problems

Morbidity studies highlight specific health needs of people with intellectual disabilities. Compared to the general population, there is a higher prevalence rate of both mental and physical disorders. The most common health needs encountered by people with intellectual disabilities are briefly reviewed below. The list is based on current literature and reflects the common physical health problems discussed in depth at the Toronto Colloquium on the Primary Care of Adults with Disabilities (Cameron 2005).

OBESITY

The prevalence of obesity is high among persons with intellectual disabilities (Beange, McElduff and Baker 1995; Van Schrojenstein Lantman-de Valk *et al.* 1997) and estimates range from 33 to 57 per cent (Lewis *et al.* 2002; Rubin *et al.* 1998), twice as high as the general population. Obesity can lead to a greater risk for other medical problems such as diabetes and hypertension. Some researchers argue that increasing levels of moderate to vigorous physical activity among people with intellectual disabilities would be the single most effective intervention to improve the overall health of members of this population (Robertson *et al.* 2000a), but fitness programs are not always available to persons with disabilities.

SENSORY IMPAIRMENTS

Adults with intellectual disabilities have a high prevalence of *visual impairment* (Cassidy, Martin and Martin 2002; Janicki *et al.* 2002). McCulloch *et al.* (1996) found that 12 per cent of mildly disabled people, more than 40 per cent of severely disabled and 100 per cent of profoundly disabled people had poor visual acuity. In a recent study, The Special Olympics program screened large numbers of athletes with intellectual disabilities for vision problems and found 40 per cent to have ocular abnormalities, with almost 20 per cent reporting never having had an eye examination (Woodhouse, Adler and Duignan 2004).

Likewise, *hearing impairment* is very common among people with intellectual disabilities and can be a major contributor to communication difficulties. For example, Evenhuis *et al.* (2001) identified hearing loss in 21 per cent of a residential sample of 672 people with intellectual disabilities and Lowe and Temple (2002) reported a rate of 66 per cent in a community sample of individuals with developmental disabilities. Researchers point out that sensory impairments often go undetected by support staff. For example, Kerr *et al.* (2003) in a study in the UK found that caregivers assessed vision as 'perfectly normal' for 49 per cent of their clients, although less than 1 per cent were found to have normal vision on a physical exam. Similarly, staff reported 74 per cent to have normal hearing, while formal assessment indicated only 11 per cent to have normal hearing, with 61 per cent having mild hearing loss, 15 per cent having moderate to severe hearing loss and 13 per cent having profound or severe loss. Prevention, identification, and correction of hearing and vision impairments requires screening by competent staff and may involve straightforward interventions like removing impacted earwax (Kerr *et al.* 2003; Sullivan *et al.* 2006).

DENTAL HEALTH

Several studies have found dental disease to be far more prevalent among people with intellectual disabilities compared to the general population (Balogh, Hunter and Ouellette-Kuntz 2004; Beange *et al.* 1995; Cummella *et al.* 2000; Scott, Marsh and Stotes 1998). For example, Scott *et al.* (1998) noted that various types of dental disease were up to seven times more frequent. Poor oral hygiene and lack of preventative care are implicated as the primary causes of dental disease (Cummella *et al.* 2000; Lewis *et al.* 2002). Furthermore, it is important to recognize the impact of the side effects (e.g. reduced salivation) of psychotropic medications (especially anticholinergic medication) on dental health.

GASTROINTESTINAL DISEASE

Gastro-esophageal reflux disease (GERD) and dysphasia have been identified as a major cause of suffering and morbidity among people with intellectual disability (Beange *et al.* 1995; Bohmer *et al.* 1997). The overall prevalence of reflux esophagitis in people with intellectual disabilities has been estimated at 10–15 per cent compared to 2 per cent in the general population. However, GERD symptoms are often overlooked and underestimated (Bohmer *et al.* 1997).

Heliobacter pylori infections (HPI) are increased in children and adults with intellectual disabilities. This infection can cause diseases such as peptic ulcer, gastric carcinoma, and may be associated with gastritis and esophagitis (Ouellette-Kuntz 2005). Chronic constipation is also very common among people with intellectual disabilities and can be the cause of many physical and behavioural difficulties (Bohmer *et al.* 2001; Lennox and Edwards 2001). Bohmer *et al.* (2001) found that constipation was demonstrated in almost 70 per cent of people with intellectual disabilities. As in the general population, both physical inactivity and medications including anticonvulsants, neuroleptics, anticholinergics, and antidepressants may cause constipation. As with GERD, symptoms are not always recognized and, if left untreated, can lead to serious complications (Bohmer *et al.* 2001; Jancar and Speller 1994) and even death (Heng and Sullivan 2003).

OSTEOPOROSIS

Osteoporosis has been shown to occur with high prevalence among people with intellectual disabilities (Centre, Beange and McElduff 1998). Risk of fractures in this population is particularly high, possibly as a result of an increased risk of falling. In addition, long-term use of anticonvulsants to treat epilepsy may lead to osteoporosis and therefore raise the risk of fractures (Tohill 1997; Wagemans *et al.* 1998). Van Schrojenstein Lantman-de Valk *et al.* (2000) found that fractures were three times more frequent in people with intellectual disabilities than those without intellectual disabilities.

EPILEPSY

Epilepsy occurs 15–30 times more frequently in people with intellectual disabilities compared with the general population (Van Schrojenstein Lantman-de Valk *et al.* 1997) and it is often inadequately monitored and reviewed (Beange *et al.* 1995). Epilepsy can affect both morbidity and mortality. Physical sequelae from seizures, possible fractures and soft tissue injury may lead to the need for hospitalization. Research has identified epilepsy as a possibly avoidable cause of sudden death in people with intellectual disabilities (Forsgren *et al.* 1996). Inappropriate treatment may also result in worsening of behaviour or impaired cognitive function (Forsgren *et al.* 1996).

THYROID DISEASE

Thyroid disease is both a cause and a complication of intellectual disability but it is generally quite easy to treat (Beange *et al.* 1999). There are higher rates for certain groups (e.g. Down syndrome) and its presentation may be very hard to recognize (Wilson and Haire 1992). Often the only symptom is reported by a support person who observes that the person's behaviour has changed in some non-specific way (Wilson and Haire 1992). Diagnosis, therefore, can be easily missed, causing significant deterioration in health, behaviour and functional ability (Beange *et al.* 1999).

MENTAL HEALTH PROBLEMS AND POLYPHARMACY

Compared to the general population, individuals with intellectual disabilities have higher rates of mental health problems, that are often undiagnosed (e.g. USDHHS 2002). Sometimes, their mental health difficulties are misattributed to their disability ('diagnostic overshadowing', Reiss and Szyszko 1983). Although rates of mental health problems tend to vary from study to study, certain disorders are consistently less common (e.g. addictions) and other disorders are more prevalent (e.g. behaviour disorders, autism, psychotic disorders) (Borthwick-Duffy and Eyman 1990; Cooper 1997; Cooper *et al.* 2007; Deb, Thomas and Bright 2001; Tonge and Einfeld 2000). Biological, psychological and social risk factors have been identified as accounting for the increased risk of mental health issues in this population (Deb, Thomas and Bright 2001).

Sometimes, individuals with intellectual disabilities attempt to communicate either emotional distress related to a life event or pain related to a medical issue through their behaviour (see case report above). This behaviour is then misdiagnosed as 'psychiatric' and the person is prescribed psychotropic medication (Bradley and Hollins 2006). Other times, the psychiatric diagnosis is appropriate but the medication follow-up does not occur as it should. Polypharmacy (the use of multiple and excessive amounts of medications) and inadequate medication review are acknowledged problems in persons with intellectual disabilities (Beange *et al.* 1995; Reiss and Aman 1997). Polypharmacy increases the risk for drug interactions and may lead to sedation, increased confusion, constipation, postural instability, falls, incontinence, weight gain, sex steroid deregulation, endocrine or metabolic effects, impairment of epilepsy management and movement disorders (Sommi *et al.* 1998).

A number of studies have reported on polypharmacy and intellectual disability (e.g. Beange *et al.* 1995; Burd *et al.* 1997; Kerr *et al.* 2003; Lewis *et al.* 2002; Lunsky, Emery and Benson 2002; Molyneux, Emerson and Caine 1999; Radouco-Thomas *et al.* 2004; Robertson *et al.* 2000b). In one study (Kerr *et al.* 2003), 22 per cent of individuals discharged from an institution in the UK were prescribed seven or more medications. In a US study (Lewis *et al.* 2002), of those receiving psychotropic medications, only 24 per cent had received a psychiatric consultation and 36 per cent were receiving medication without an accompanying psychiatric diagnosis. Simultaneous receipt of two or more antipsychotics was not uncommon. In Lunsky *et al.*'s (2002) study of community-residing adults with intellectual disabilities, 22 per cent of adults taking psychotropic medications had no idea why they were taking those medications; others offered only vague explanations such as 'to keep me calm' or 'to control my behaviour'.

SEXUAL HEALTH

Women with intellectual disabilities are less likely than other women to receive appropriate breast screening (Havercamp, Scandlin and Roth 2004; Lewis *et al.* 2002). In addition, women with intellectual disabilities are less likely to have a cervical (pap) test presumably due to the assumption that they are not sexually active (McCarthy 1999). Kerr, Richards and Glover's (1996) audit of medical records found that less than one in four women with intellectual disabilities had undergone a pap test compared to four out of five women in the general population. Perhaps as a result of these factors, cancer and other diseases tend to be diagnosed in later, less treatable stages in the population with intellectual disabilities (Cooke 1997).

In identifying women's health as a priority, the Centers for Disease Control and Prevention motivated and funded much of the existing research on women with disabilities. No such champion has emerged for men's health. Hence, the health status of men with intellectual disabilities has received virtually no research attention and is relatively unknown.

EQUITY IN HEALTH-CARE ACCESS AND UTILIZATION

In theory, people with intellectual disabilities who live in industrialized nations have equal access to essential health services (Evenhuis *et al.* 2001). In practice, evidence shows that this is frequently not the case. Barriers to health-care access exist on many levels and are multi-dimensional and complex (Lennox, Diggens and Ugoni 1997; Ziviani *et al.* 2004). Research has identified several barriers to access and utilization in health care specific to individuals with intellectual disabilities. For every major barrier to health care, we propose applicable medical health rights (in bold) and outline steps toward overcoming the barrier.

Systemic barriers

Access to health promotion
Effective health promotion strategies can go a long way towards decreasing health inequities among people with intellectual disabilities if they are offered in a way that is accessible, relevant and appropriate for this population. Jobling (2001) contended that people with intellectual disabilities are ill-prepared for the responsibilities that are involved with understanding the health issues and the choices that need to be made in order to maintain their own health. Tones (1991) breaks health promotion down into three broad areas: health education, disease prevention and health surveillance. Unfortunately, in each of these areas, individuals with intellectual disabilities are on the poor end of a health promotion disparity. For example, programs and public service messages developed to reduce obesity and smoking and to encourage healthy nutrition and exercise are rarely accessible to persons with intellectual disabilities (Webb and Rogers 1999). Furthermore, people with intellectual disabilities are less likely to access routine immunizations and blood pressure checks (Beange and Durvasula 2001). In each of the morbidities reviewed earlier, there are strategic roles for the individual, caregiver, and health-care professional that can aid in the reduction of health disparities and reinforce the process of health promotion amongst individuals with intellectual disabilities (see Table 6.1).

Table 6.1 The role of the triad in the process of health promotion

Triad	Common health problems			Role
	Dental care	Obesity	Polypharmacy	
Client	• improve knowledge and skills in hygiene • practise hygiene skills as part of appointments with guidance/feedback	• increase participation in recreational activities • be knowledgeable about decision-making and lifestyle choices	• be knowledgeable about medication use and side effects • monitor side effects and report to caregiver	• be knowledgeable about importance of maintaining good health practices • play an active role in decision-making
Caregiver	• assist in hygiene • advocate for more cleanings • provide support and comfort during examinations	• be knowledgeable about weight control and access to recreational activities • promote maintenance of nutrition and exercise	• promote compliance with treatment plan • be knowledgeable about medication use and side effects	• provide support and assistance during activities and examinations • encourage communication both with the health-care provider and between the client and the health-care provider • promote maintenance of good health practices
Health-care provider	• regular check-ups • screen for those at high risk	• monitor body weight • provide information about benefits of eating well and exercise	• monitor by means of regular medication reviews	• adopt appropriate techniques for working with this population • empower the client and use caregiver appropriately

The adoption of a healthy lifestyle requires specific skills and health knowledge and, more importantly, attitudes and values that foster taking responsibility to regulate one's own health behaviour.

> Equity, when applied to people with intellectual disability, would lead us to provide them with more resources to maintain and promote their health, because of their greater needs, than we would provide to the general population. We would spend more-than-average time explaining to them the value of not smoking, of eating well and of having their blood pressure checked. More than that, we would work affirmatively to promote their health goals. (Leeder and Dominello 2005, p.98)

Not only do individuals with intellectual disabilities have the right to equitable access to health care, they are entitled to equitable access to health promotion as well.

Finding innovative ways to encourage this kind of understanding should be a primary goal in effective health promotion for this population.

Reactive health-care system

The reactive health-care system relies largely on the ability of individuals to identify and report a problem or illness and then seek out consultation (Lennox *et al.* 1997, 2000). Health-care systems are typically geared to patients who are able to 'complain' and to tell their health-care providers what is wrong and what they think they require. This can be problematic for people with intellectual disabilities who may have difficulty first of all recognizing and naming the problem and, second, knowing exactly how to go about accessing care (Alborz *et al.* 2003).

To deal with this problem we need a more proactive system of screening for health problems and teaching both patients and caregivers to be involved in screening processes (Lennox *et al.* 2007). Strategies such as health education for people with intellectual disabilities and their caregivers may positively influence decision-making about access. Difficulties identifying and communicating health needs on the part of people with intellectual disabilities may be overcome by providing proactive strategies to identify need (Alborz *et al.* 2003). *Ultimately, individuals with intellectual disabilities have the right to a proactive system beyond standard health promotion activities, where everyone plays a role in screening.* However, this will likely require compromise of the ethical principle of autonomy. As will be discussed in the next section, a truly proactive system has a role for the individual, the caregiver, and the health-care provider.

Time constraints

Another barrier to effective health care involves the limitations of short consultation times on history taking and diagnosis (Beange 1996; Lennox *et al.* 1997). For individuals with intellectual disabilities, extra time is often needed for examinations, tests, procedures and health teaching. If health-care providers are not adequately reimbursed for the extra time needed, a disincentive is created that can result in a reluctance to treat people with intellectual disabilities (Beange 1996; Lennox and Kerr 1997). A fee-for-service model may not make allowances for the extra time needed to ensure comprehensive care for people with intellectual disabilities (Ouellette-Kuntz 2005; Solar and Irwin 2005). *Individuals with intellectual disabilities have the right to appropriate time for appointments.* While booking double-length appointments has been suggested as a possible way of tackling the barriers imposed by time constraints, the feasibility of doing so has not yet been investigated or researched (Alborz *et al.* 2003; Lennox *et al.* 1997). However, this modification has been recently implemented in Australia where health-care practitioners are provided with a structured clinical framework that allows for extra time to ensure that the overall health of an individual with an intellectual disability is fully assessed (Department of Health and Ageing 2007).

Lack of coordination and collaboration between health-care services

It is common for people with intellectual disabilities to receive health services from multiple clinicians. At times, however, health-care professionals may work in parallel with each other but be unaware of each other's involvement (Lennox and Edwards 2001). At other times, if a person is treated by more than one health-care professional, for example a GP and a specialist, both may view the other as taking responsibility for the management of care (Horwitz *et al.* 2001) described by Fletcher, Beasley and Jacobson (1999) as a *diffusion of responsibility.* In both cases, the lack of collaboration and coordination of care can have serious negative health implications for the person with an intellectual disability. *Individuals with intellectual disabilities have the right to coordinated health care.* Physicians and caregivers need guidance on how to make this happen and on how to keep the individual at the centre of their own care.

Environmental barriers

Physical constraints

People with mobility and sensory problems face physical barriers to accessing buildings and treatment rooms. More specifically, people with intellectual disabilities may be unable to participate in physical examination and diagnostic interventions because of their individual physical conditions and abilities. Even simple screening procedures such as weight measurement, blood tests, visual exams, and auditory examinations may be inaccessible to persons with disabilities (Barr *et al.* 1999). Written signs and instructions are inaccessible to many individuals with intellectual disabilities and low literacy skills. *Individuals with intellectual disabilities have the right to access facilities and information on how to prepare and participate for medical procedures.* In order to help overcome physical barriers, accommodations can be made such as offering blood work at home or booking exams at a more suitable time of the day.

Role barriers

The triad of the person with an intellectual disability, the support person and the health-care provider creates unique challenges for effective communication and health-care access and utilization.

Individual

As outlined earlier, people with intellectual disabilities face unique health challenges that often go unnoticed and therefore untreated. In recognizing rights, it is important to identify not just external barriers, but also personal barriers (i.e. limitations due to the disability) that impact access and uptake of services. These factors require support and accommodations.

Perception of pain, discomfort or change: having an intellectual disability can hinder the ability to recognize and interpret signals from the body and this can create the very first barrier in accessing health care (Alborz *et al.* 2003).

Communication impairments: communication difficulties may include problems with *expression* – intelligibility, fluency and rate of speech and the ability to use language to clarify, negotiate, and express needs, choices and decisions; as well as *reception* – hearing, recalling and comprehending spoken and/or written language (Byng *et al.* 2003; Van der Gaag 1998). These difficulties can occur to varying degrees depending upon the type and extent of intellectual disability and depending upon the presence of any associated physical disabilities such as cleft palate, cerebral palsy or hearing impairment (Van der Gaag 1998).

Memory: Jansen *et al.* (2004) describe *inadequate anamnesis,* or the poor recollection of one's health or medical history, as an additional factor contributing to insufficient health-care communication for people with intellectual disabilities. This is particularly problematic when a complete record of the medical history does not exist.

Fear: people with intellectual disabilities sometimes do not bring health problems to the attention of health professionals because they may be frightened of the consequences. Whether it be the result of previous unpleasant experiences or due to unfamiliarity with physical examination and screening procedures, confusion, fear and anxiety can be tremendously inhibiting (Law *et al.* 2005). These feelings can further manifest themselves into difficulty in cooperating with examinations and procedures (Evenhuis *et al.* 2001). *Due to their disability and their circumstances, people with intellectual disabilities have a right to the skills and supports necessary to communicate their health needs and wishes.* Although communication difficulties remain an issue for this population, steps have been taken in recent years to educate and ultimately improve communication between the triad within the health-care setting (e.g. ASK diary; Lennox *et al.* 2004).

Caregiver/ support person

It would be a mistake to promote the ethical value of autonomy without recognizing that persons with intellectual disabilities need supports to function as autonomously as possible. Because these individuals experience an increased risk of medical problems but greater difficulty in communicating their needs, it is often the support person (i.e. paid caregiver, family member) who takes on the essential role of ensuring that the health status of a person with an intellectual disability is the best it can be. However, this 'only works successfully if their agent is trained and empathetic and does not underestimate their complaints' (Beange 1996, p.159).

Initially, a support person has to suspect or agree that there is a need to seek out care (Alborz *et al.* 2003). The support person's knowledge, both of the general condition and of the usual health and behaviour of the individual, is critical. Individual perceptions of the support person directly affect both the recognition of the need to access health care and the decision to act on that need. As Alborz *et al.* (2003) point out, when and if health care is accessed may be dependent on the point at which the support person 'considers that a sign or symptom is of significance and needs monitoring, requires action to alleviate distress, or requires health advice from a professional' (p.121).

Clearly, the decisions of support persons are crucial in seeking timely and appropriate health services for people with intellectual disabilities. It is critical that the support person knows the person well. Furthermore, caregivers are often needed to schedule an appointment, ensure transportation is available, and then often be present to act as a mediator between the person with an intellectual disability and the health-care provider.

Within a health-care consultation, the support person needs to balance the responsibility of supporting and encouraging the direct communication between the health-care provider and the individual and ensuring that the information needed to make the necessary diagnosis is made clear. Support persons can play an instrumental role in ensuring that the health-care provider focuses on the individual rather than on them and in such instances can assist the health-care provider by advising effective ways of asking and explaining. As Edwards *et al.* (2005) assert:

> The involvement of a significant other in the clinical encounter can improve health outcomes for people with developmental disability. Third parties who act as advocates for patients with developmental disability can be paid or unpaid, and often involve support persons who are family members or friends. The roles and responsibilities of health advocates for people with intellectual disabilities are clearly associated with the promotion of patient rights and the safeguarding of autonomous decision making. Advocates should aim to make patients' needs and views better heard and respected in the clinical encounter. Advocates should also aim to redress the power imbalance in doctor–patient interactions by encouraging persons with intellectual disabilities to participate actively in their healthcare. (p.211)

Thus, the caregiver plays a role in accessing health care and health promotion activities, by minimizing the barriers experienced by the person with an intellectual disability.

The caregiver must have the information and the skills to promote autonomy. They can be a teacher as they model and educate the clinician and person with the intellectual disability and they can act as an advocate by compensating for communication difficulties, memory impairments, perception problems, and anxiety/fear. Depending on the situation, the role of the caregiver can shift between promoting autonomy and practising beneficence; playing a supportive spectator or participant in a dialogue between two parties or a mediator between all three. The support person is a critical health promotion agent, promoting such activities as teeth cleaning, diet, hygiene, exercise and routine health screening. Ultimately, the caregiver helps to balance the roles of autonomy/choice and beneficence. *Individuals with intellectual disabilities have the right to supportive caregivers who strike the balance between the four ethical principles.* Caregivers need the knowledge, skills and comfort level to play this role.

Health-care provider

Entrenched stereotypical beliefs and negative attitudes toward people with intellectual disabilities by health-care providers still exist and as Lennox and Edwards (2001) astutely point out 'barriers that exist in people's minds are notoriously difficult to remove' (p.35). Such negative attitudes can often result in a 'hands off approach' to patients with intellectual disability (Davis *et al.* 2002) and a greater reluctance to provide care and treatment because they are perceived to be 'more difficult to manage' (Gill, Stenfert-Kroese and Rose 2002, p.1446). Furthermore, inaccurate assumptions may be made about health-related behaviours that can lead to under-recognition of health problems. For example, health-care providers may believe that people with intellectual disabilities do not smoke, drink, experience stress or have sexual relationships (Bond *et al.* 1997).

> Attitudes or beliefs may influence treatment choices, the effort or associated energy that empowers or drives a health intervention, and finally how much confidence that the health care provider displays or draws upon in their particular course of action or inaction. (Lennox and Edwards 2001, p.36)

Negative attitudes and beliefs can lower expectations of people with intellectual disabilities and their support person on the type of treatment, care, support and service they can expect (Law *et al.* 2005). As Marks and Heller (2003) point out, 'changing the attitudes of health care providers is paramount in ensuring that their services enable and empower individuals to have control over their health' (p.210).

A lack of knowledge and training for health-care providers creates huge obstacles to health care for this population. This lack of training has been identified by physicians (e.g. Lennox *et al.* 1997; Millar, Chorlton and Lennox 2004), nurses (e.g. Melville *et al.* 2005), service providers and family members (e.g. Reichard and Rutherford-Turnbull 2004) as a significant barrier to providing good care.

> People with developmental disabilities complain about doctors who: shout, talk to them as if they are not here, do not explain what is happening, treat them as if they are stupid, do not listen to what they are trying to say, pretend to understand when they obviously do not, do not give enough time to the consultation. (Burbridge 1999, p.3)

Lack of training can lead to 'diagnostic overshadowing', attributing abnormalities to one diagnosis, the person's intellectual disability (Gill *et al.* 2002; Reiss and Szyszko 1983). Holland (2000) described it as 'dismissing changes in behaviour, personality or ability that would be taken very seriously in a person without a learning disability' (p.28). Diagnostic overshadowing cannot only lead to problems in diagnosis, but also to problems in treatment delivery.

Hand (1999) states:

> Listening to people with intellectual disabilities describe their everyday joys and challenges and what they see as affecting their health and well-being, will help health care providers better able to 'be in tune' to

the individual's needs, become more observant and more likely to achieve an accurate diagnosis when problems do arise. (p.71)

Health-care providers need to 'expand their repertoire of communication and observational skills' (Hand 1999, p.74) and take time to fully understand the individual person. Health-care providers need the time to do this work and with appropriate reimbursement, the education on how to meet the needs of people with intellectual disabilities, and the skills to work as part of a healthy triad in order to support the person with an intellectual disability, to meet his or her medical needs and to be comfortable with the medical process. *Individuals with intellectual disabilities have the right to receive treatment from professionals who are trained to work with them with appropriate knowledge, skills and comfort level.*

In summary, certain health conditions, including preventable health conditions, are more common amongst individuals with intellectual disabilities than in the general population. Ultimately, individuals with intellectual disabilities have the right to treatment access, good care, and autonomy.

Informed consent

Consent and choice in medical treatment
Informed consent and intellectual disability refers to a shared decision-making process between the patient and health-care provider. The provider must establish that the patient (i) understands the proposed treatments, risks, benefits, side effects, and reasonable alternatives, (ii) is competent to give consent and (iii) freely and voluntarily does so. Capacity to give informed consent varies with each individual and potential procedure. This means that an individual may be able to provide informed consent for one procedure but not another (see Hurley and O'Sullivan 1999). Consent to treatment in intellectual disability is a complicated issue and clinicians do not always seek consent when performing tests or treatment, but rather base their decisions on assumptions (see Keywood *et al.* 1999 in Carlson *et al.* 2004). Sometimes caregivers give proxy consent even when they are not legally able to do so and sometimes treatments are denied because of consent complexities (see Curran and Hollins 1994). One element of capacity to consent is health literacy, the degree to which individuals have the capacity to obtain, process, and understand basic health information and services needed to make health decisions (Baur 2007).

Individuals have a right to *informed* voluntary consent. This means that when they make a decision to participate in a particular treatment option, they have been informed about what the procedure is, the benefits of doing so and the potential risks both of accepting and refusing treatment. It also means that the person can independently choose to accept treatment or not. The ethical values of autonomy and justice can conflict with beneficence here. The person may be informed and may opt out of a treatment. In our efforts to protect individuals with intellectual disabilities, we may take a paternalistic approach and prevent them from making decisions that are not in their best medical interest. The 'dignity of risk' construct is relevant here (Perske 1972), whereby we allow individuals with intellectual disabilities to voluntarily make a health-care decision if they have the capacity to do so, even if we do not agree with that decision (see also Morris, Neiderbuhl and Mahr 1993 and Bannerman *et al.* 1990 on balance of protection from harm and self-determination).

A special issue of informed consent concerns medications that tend to be overprescribed for individuals with intellectual disabilities and even used as chemical restraint. Unfortunately, individuals with an intellectual disability and their substitute decision-makers are not always fully informed about the risks/benefits of their medications and are not always followed properly to monitor such risks (see Aman *et al.* 2007). Individuals with intellectual disabilities and their substitute decision-makers have a right to know what medications are suggested and their potential side effects. In addition, medications should be monitored and quickly withdrawn if the side effects are significant or the benefits are not evident.

Access to participation in medical research

One commonly cited example of a medical rights violation is the Willowbrook study where children with intellectual disabilities were infected with viral hepatitis without their knowledge so that researchers could observe the natural history of the disease. In this historic and notorious study, the nature of the informed consent obtained from their parents was unethical (Beecher 1966). Individuals at risk for exploitation through medical research need protection in light of past atrocities. Medical research committees take extra efforts currently to protect vulnerable populations, such as those with intellectual disabilities, from potential harm. Obviously, individuals have a right to such protections.

However, this need to protect must be balanced with the need to include individuals with intellectual disabilities in research that may be of benefit to this population. This can be done ethically by seeking substitute decision-making under ethically approved guidelines when individuals cannot provide consent themselves. The danger of excluding certain people from research because of their presumed lack of decisional capacity is that research findings will not generalize to them (see Iacono 2006).

The same principles for informed consent to treatment apply to informed consent to medical research. Accurate and balanced information on the research must be conveyed in a way that is understood by the person with an intellectual disability, the person making the decision must be capable of informed choice, and their decision must be made autonomously and voluntarily. As was discussed in the section above on treatment capacity, researchers are obligated to perform an assessment of capacity to consent to research on a project-specific basis.

Many researchers have questioned whether people with intellectual disabilities can make decisions voluntarily when they have so few opportunities to do so and hence lack the skills (see Morris et al. 1993). In addition, researchers have highlighted the concern that these individuals are vulnerable to acquiescing or agreeing to participate in research because it would please their caregiver, doctor, or the researcher. One strategy that has been proposed to combat acquiescence is to ask the person why they agree to participate (for those that can articulate this; Dresser 1996). Other strategies include involving a caregiver as well as friends or advocates in the process (i.e. supported decision-making; Bach and Rock 1996) and explaining projects in a more comprehensible and accessible manner (e.g. using video; see Arscott, Dagnan and Stenfert-Kroese 1998; Dye, Hare and Hendy 2007; Morris et al. 1993). Current approved guidelines require that consent to participate in research protocols be obtained by someone other than the treating physician. Internationally endorsed guidelines for research in intellectual disability were recently developed by the International Association for the Scientific Study of Intellectual Disability (Dalton and McVilly 2004), which emphasize issues regarding consent.

Right to life-saving medical interventions

Not only should individuals with intellectual disabilities have equity of access to standard medical care, but also the right to access life-saving procedures, such as organ transplants (see also Chapter 3 in this volume). Prior to the 1990s, having an intellectual disability was considered a contraindication for solid organ transplant operations because of the assumption that people with intellectual disabilities had a poor quality of life and that they would lack the skills to comply with post-transplant regimens (Martens, Jones and Reiss 2006). This way of thinking is changing due to a number of high profile cases (e.g. Sandra Jensen) and strong advocacy (e.g. National Work Group on Disability and Transplantation in the US). In thinking about the role of patient, health-care provider and caregiver in this situation, patients have a right to be candidates and thus need support from the health-care provider as well as the caregiver to ensure that the organ transplant is successful. Caregivers are fundamental in assisting with compliance with post-transplant treatment. More work is needed to educate patients along with their caregivers on how to access transplants and how to cope with the stress of having had a transplant. No research has been done to date on the role of caregiver in this regard (Martens et al. 2006). Lives Worth Saving in the US is an example of a national program providing outreach, technical assistance, and research toward reaching the national goal of equal access.

Health interventions to meet medical rights

Efforts at promoting the health rights of people with intellectual disabilities have significantly increased in recent years. The remainder of the chapter will provide some examples of health interventions aimed at ensuring that rights of individuals with intellectual disabilities are recognized.

Health-care guidelines are an excellent example of how unique needs of people with intellectual disabilities can be recognized. Etiological specific guidelines exist, such as Down syndrome health-care guidelines (Cohen 1999) as well as broader guidelines such as the Australian Management Guidelines (Lennox and Diggens 1999) or the Canadian Primary Care Guidelines (Sullivan *et al.* 2006). Content-specific guidelines also exist such as the psychopharmacology guidelines (Deb, Clarke and Unwin 2006), mental health assessment guidelines (Deb *et al.* 2001) or the emergency room guidelines (Bradley *et al.* 2002). Such guidelines serve to educate and inform health-care providers on intellectual disability specific issues including medical rights.

Resources are available to help assess and improve health literacy. The national public health plan in the US developed a specific action plan to promote health literacy (Healthy People 2010 Health Literacy Action Plan – *Communicating Health: Priorities and Strategies for Progress*; USDHHS 2003) and the US Department of Health and Human Services National Library of Medicine developed a health literacy bibliography (*Understanding Health Literacy and Its Barriers*; USDHHS 2004).

Similar guidelines and tools are needed for caregivers and for people with intellectual disabilities. Examples might include the ASK (Lennox *et al.* 2004), the women's health-care curriculum (Lunsky, Straiko and Armstrong 2002), medication education booklets (Project MED; see Aman *et al.* 2007) or guidelines on consent developed in the UK and Australia for clients and caregivers (Department of Health 2001a, b; Lennox *et al.* 2004).

A number of studies support the use of primary care based health assessments in adults with intellectual disabilities (Aronow and Hahn 2005; Cooper *et al.* 2006; Hahn and Aronow 2005; Lennox *et al.* 2007). Most recently, a randomized controlled trial of such health-care assessments found significant increases in health screening and health maintenance activities, and a trend towards greater identification of unrecognized disease in the individuals that received these assessments (Lennox *et al.* 2007). The intervention used was called the Comprehensive Health Assessment Program (CHAP) and improved health care by addressing some of the barriers described above, such problems with access, communication and education of health-care providers (Lennox *et al.* 2007). The

CHAP seeks to empower the members of the triad of health care including the person with an intellectual disability.

Furthermore, mental health guidelines (Gratsa *et al.* 2007) have been developed that not only provide a valuable resource, but also highlight important rights that are of specific concern to both families and caregivers involved in the general health care of individuals with intellectual disabilities. Most recently, faculty at Brock University have developed a curriculum that helps people with intellectual disabilities and their caregivers advocate for their medical rights (3Rs: Rights, Respect and Responsibility project mentioned in the Introduction of this book).

CONCLUSION

This chapter reviewed four basic ethical principles in medicine and considered their application in promoting the medical rights of people with intellectual disabilities. Common health problems, barriers to health-care access and utilization were reviewed, taking into consideration the triad of the person with an intellectual disability, the caregiver, and the health-care provider. The chapter concluded with some directions for future work in this area and examples of promising medical rights interventions.

It is clear that we cannot have equity, promote good treatment, and prevent harm if it is not done through the lens of autonomy. As Shogren *et al.* (2006) state:

> encouraging self-determination in health care may well be a key strategy for reducing health disparities experienced by people with intellectual disabilities. Self-determination has the potential to significantly alter many of the issues that are most commonly identified as the sources of health disparities, including health system factors (how health care is financed and structured, and how health promotion programs are designed and delivered), patient level factors (how well patients understand and follow through on health promotion activities and medical advice) and patient/provider communication issues (how effectively patients can communicate their health needs and develop a trusting relationship with their physician). (p.109)

REFERENCES

Alborz, A., McNally, R., Swallow, A. and Glendinning, C. (2003) *From the Cradle to the Grave: A Literature Review of Access to Health Care for People with Learning Disabilities Across the Lifespan.* Report for the National Co-ordinating Centre for NHS Service Delivery and Organization R and D (NCCSDO). London: NCCSDO.

Aman, M. G., Benson, B. A., Farmer, C., Hall, K. and Malone, K. (2007) 'Project MED: Effects of a Medication EDucation booklet series for individuals with intellectual disabilities.' *Intellectual and Developmental Disabilities, 45*, 1, 33–45.

Aronow, H. U. and Hahn, J. E. (2005) 'Stay well and healthy! Pilot study findings from an in home preventive healthcare programme for persons ageing with intellectual and/or developmental disabilities.' *Journal of Applied Research in Intellectual Disabilities, 18*, 2, 163–173.

Arscott, K., Dagnan, D. and Stenfert-Kroese, B. (1998) 'Consent to psychological research by people with an intellectual disability.' *Journal of Applied Research in Intellectual Disabilities, 11*, 1, 77–83.

Bach, M. and Rock, M. (1996) *Seeking Consent to Participate in Research from People Whose Ability to Make an Informed Decision Could Be Questioned: The Supported Decision-making Model.* An Occasional Paper from The Roeher Institute, York University. Ontario: The Roeher Institute.

Balogh, R., Hunter, D. and Ouellette-Kuntz, H. (2004) 'Regional variation in dental procedures among people with an intellectual disability, Ontario, 1995–2001.' *Journal of Canadian Dental Association, 70*, 10, 681.

Bannerman, D. J., Sheldon, J. B., Sherman, J. A. and Harchik, A. E. (1990) 'Balancing the right to habilitation with the right to personal liberty: The rights of people with developmental disabilities to eat too many doughnuts and take a nap.' *Journal of Applied Behavior Analysis, 23*, 1, 79–89.

Barr, O., Gilgunn, J., Kane, T. and Moore, G. (1999) 'Health screening for people with learning disabilities by a community learning disability nursing service in Northern Ireland.' *Journal of Advanced Nursing, 29*, 6, 1482–1491.

Baur, C. (2007) 'Health literacy and adults with I/DD: Achieving accessible health information and services.' *State of the Science in Aging with Developmental Disabilities: Charting Lifespan Trajectories and Supportive Environments for Healthy Community Living.* Atlanta, GA.

Beange, H. (1996) 'Caring for a vulnerable population.' *Medical Journal of Australia, 164*, 159–160.

Beange, H. and Durvasula, S. (2001) 'Health inequalities in people with intellectual disability: strategies for improvement.' *Health Promotion Journal of Australia, 11*, 1, 27–31.

Beange, H., Lennox, N. and Parmenter, T. R. (1999) 'Health targets for people with intellectual disability.' *Journal of Intellectual and Developmental Disability, 24*, 4, 283–297.

Beange, H., McElduff, A. and Baker, W. (1995) 'Medical disorders of adults with mental retardation: A population study.' *American Association of Mental Retardation, 99*, 6, 595–604.

Beauchamp, T. and Childress, J. (2001) *Principles of Biomedical Ethics* (5th edn). Oxford, New York: Oxford University Press.

Beecher, H. (1966) 'Ethics and clinical research.' *New England Journal of Medicine, 274*, 24, 1354–1360.

Bohmer, C. J. M., Klinkenberg-Knol, E. C., Niezen-de Boer, M. C. and Meuwissen, S. G. (1997) 'The prevalence of gastro-oesophageal reflux disease based on non-specific symptoms in institutionalized, intellectually disabled individuals.' *European Journal of Gastroenterology and Hepatology, 9*, 2, 187–190.

Bohmer, C. J. M., Taminiau, J. A., Klinkenberg-Knol, E. C. and Meuwissen, S. G. (2001) 'The prevalence of constipation in institutionalized people with intellectual disability.' *Journal of Intellectual Disability Research, 45*, 212–218.

Bond, L., Kerr, M., Dunstan, F. and Thapar, A. (1997) 'Attitudes of general practitioners toward health care for people with intellectual disability and the factors underlying these attitudes.' *Journal of Intellectual Disability Research, 41*, 5, 391–400.

Borthwick-Duffy, S. and Eyman, R. (1990) 'Who are the dually diagnosed?' *American Journal on Mental Retardation, 94*, 6, 586–595.

Bradley, E., Burke, L., Drummond, C., Korossy, M., Lunsky, Y. and Morris, S. (2002) *Guidelines for Managing the Client with Intellectual Disability in the Emergency Room.* Toronto, ON: Centre for Addiction and Mental Health. Retrieved from www.camh.net/Publications/CAMH_Publications/guide_manageclient_inteldisorder.html on September 28, 2008.

Bradley, E. and Hollins, S. (2006) 'Assessment of patients with intellectual disabilities.' In D. S. Goldbloom (ed) *Psychiatric Clinical Skills.* Philadelphia, PA: Mosby Elsevier.

Burbridge, M. (1999) 'How to communicate with your patient.' In N. Lennox and J. Diggins (eds) *Management Guidelines: People with Developmental and Intellectual Disabilities,* 1st edn. Melbourne: Therapeutic Guidelines Limited.

Burd, L., Williams, M., Klug, M. G., Fjelstad, K., Schimke, A. and Kerbeshian, J. (1997) 'Prevalence of psychotropic and anticonvulsant drug use among North Dakota group home residents.' *Journal of Intellectual Disability Research, 41,* 6, 488–494.

Byng, S., Farrelly, S., Fitzgerald, L., Parr, S. and Ross, S. (2003) 'Having a say: Promoting the participation of people who have communication impairments in health care decision-making.' Final Report to the NHS Health in Partnership Research Programme. Department of Health.

Cameron, D. (2005, November) *Common Physical Problems, Atypical Presentations, and Management Strategies.* Paper presented at the 2005 Colloquium in Primary Care for Adults with Intellectual Disabilities.

Carlson, T., Hames, A., English, S. and Wills, C. (2004) 'Referrals to a learning disability service and consent to treatment.' *Learning Disability Review, 9,* 11–17.

Cassidy, G., Martin, D. and Martin, G. (2002) 'Health checks for people with learning disabilities: community learning disability teams working with general practitioners and primary health care teams.' *Journal of Learning Disability, 6,* 2, 123–136.

Centre, J., Beange, H. and McElduff, A. (1998) 'People with developmental disability have an increased prevalence of osteoporosis: A population study.' *American Journal on Mental Retardation, 103,* 19–28.

Cohen, W. (1999) 'Health care guidelines for individuals with Down syndrome: 1999 revision.' *Down Syndrome Quarterly, 4,* 1, 1–15. Retrieved from www.downsyn.com/guidelines/healthcare.html.

Cooke, L. B. (1997) 'Cancer and learning disability,' *Journal of Intellectual Disability Research, 41,* 312–316.

Cooper, S.-A. (1997) 'Epidemiology of psychiatric disorders in elderly compared with younger adults with learning disabilities.' *British Journal of Psychiatry, 170,* 4, 375–380.

Cooper, S.-A., Morrison, J., Melville, C., Finlayson, J. *et al.* (2006) 'Improving the health of people with intellectual disabilities: Outcomes of a health screening programme after 1 year.' *Journal of Intellectual Disability Research, 50,* 9, 667–677.

Cooper, S.-A., Smiley, E., Morrison, J., Williamson, A. and Allan, L. (2007) 'Mental ill-health in adults with intellectual disabilities: Prevalence and associated factors.' *British Journal of Psychiatry, 190,* 1, 27–35.

Cummella, S., Ransford, N., Lyons, J. and Burnham, H. (2000) 'Needs for oral care among people with intellectual disability not in contact with community dental services.' *Journal of Intellectual Disability Research, 44,* 1, 45–52.

Curran, J. and Hollins, S. (1994) 'Consent to treatment and people with learning disability.' *Psychiatric Bulletin, 18,* 691–693.

Dahlgren, G. and Whitehead, M. (1991) *Policies and Strategies to Promote Social Equality in Health.* Stockholm: Institute for Future Studies.

Dalton, A. and McVilly, K. (2004) 'Ethics guidelines for international, multicenter research involving people with intellectual disabilities.' *Journal of Policy and Practice in Intellectual Disabilities, 1,* 1, 57–70.

Davis, R., Iacono, T., Humphreys, J. and Chandler, N. (2002) *Targeted Health Initiatives for Country People with Developmental Disability*. Final report on Rural Health, Support, Education and Training Grant to the Department of Health and Aged Care. Melbourne: Monash University.

Deb, S., Clarke, D. and Unwin, G. (2006) *Using Medication to Manage Behaviour Problems Among Adults with a Learning Disability: Quick Reference Guide (QRG)*. University of Birmingham, Mencap, London. Retrieved from www.id-medication.bham.ac.uk/qrg.pdf_ on October 31, 2008.

Deb, S., Matthews, T., Holt, G. and Bouras, N. (2001) *Practice Guidelines for the Assessment and Diagnosis of Mental Health Problems in Adults with Intellectual Disability*. Brighton: Pavilion.

Deb, S., Thomas, M. and Bright, C. (2001) 'Mental disorder in adults with intellectual disability. 1: Prevalence of functional psychiatric illness among a community-based population aged between 16 and 64 years.' *Journal of Intellectual Disability Research, 45*, 6, 495–505.

Department of Health (2001a) *Consent – A Guide for People with Learning Disabilities*. London: Department of Health Publications. Retrieved from www.dh.gov.uk/en/Publicationsandstatistics/Publications/ PublicationsPolicyAndguidance/DH_4006066 on September 28, 2008.

Department of Health (2001b) *Consent – What You Have a Right to Expect. A Guide for Relatives and Carers*. London: Department of Health Publications. Retrieved from www.dh.gov.uk/en/Publicationsandstatistics/Publications/PublicationsPolicyAndGuidance/DH_4005443 on September 28, 2008.

Department of Health (2001c) *Valuing People: A New Strategy for Learning Disability for the 21st Century. A White Paper*. Her Majesty's Stationery Office, London, UK. Retrieved from www.archive.officialdocuments.co.uk/document/cm50/5086/5086.htm on September 28, 2008.

Department of Health and Ageing (2007) *Medicare Benefits Schedule July 2007 Supplement: Annual Health Assessment for People with an Intellectual Disability (Items 718 and 719)*. Australia: Australian Government. Retrieved from www.scdgp.org.au/content/Document/July%202007.pdf on September 28, 2008.

Dresser, R. (1996) 'Mentally disabled research subjects: The enduring policy issues.' *Journal of the American Medical Association, 276*, 1, 67–72.

Dye, L., Hare, D. and Hendy, S. (2007) 'Capacity of people with intellectual disabilities to consent to take part in a research study.' *Journal of Applied Research in Intellectual Disabilities, 20*, 2, 168–174.

Edwards, N., Lennox, N., Taylor, M., Nugent, M., Maxwell, J. and Cooling, N. (2005) 'Advocacy.' In N. G. Lennox and J. McDowell (eds) *Management Guidelines: Developmental Disability*. Melbourne: Therapeutic Guidelines.

Evenhuis, H. M., Theunissen, I., Denkers, H., Vershuure, H. and Kemme, H. (2001) 'Prevalence of visual and hearing impairments in a Dutch institutionalized population with intellectual disability.' *Journal of Intellectual Disability Research 45*, 5, 457–464.

Eyman, R. K., Grossman, H. J., Chaney, R. H. and Call, T. L. (1990) 'The life expectancy of profoundly handicapped people with mental retardation.' *New England Journal of Medicine, 323*, 9, 584–589.

Fletcher, R. J., Beasley, J. and Jacobson, J. W. (1999) 'Support service systems for people with dual diagnosis in the USA.' In N. Bouras (ed.) *Psychiatric and Behavioural Disorders in Developmental Disabilities and Mental Retardation*. Cambridge: Cambridge University Press.

Forsgren, L., Edvinsson, S. O., Nystrom, A. L. and Blomquist, H. K. (1996) 'Influence of epilepsy on mental retardation: An epidemiologic study.' *Epilepsia, 37*, 10, 956–963.

Gill, F., Stenfert-Kroese, B. and Rose, J. (2002) 'General practitioners' attitudes to patients who have learning disabilities.' *Psychological Medicine, 32*, 8, 1445–1455.

Gratsa, A., Spiller, M., Holt, G., Joyce, T., Hardy, S. and Bouras, N. (2007) 'Developing a mental health guide for families and carers of people with intellectual disabilities.' *Journal of Applied Research in Intellectual Disabilities, 20*, 2, 77–86.

Hahn, J. E. and Aronow, H. U. (2005) 'A pilot of a gerontological advanced practice nurse preventive intervention.' *Journal of Applied Research in Intellectual Disabilities, 18,* 2, 131–142.

Hand, J. (1999) 'The care of individuals with mental retardation: Lessons from the New Zealand experience.' *International Review of Psychiatry, 11,* 1, 68–75.

Havercamp, S. M., Scandlin, D. and Roth, M. (2004) 'Health disparities among people with developmental disabilities, adults with other disabilities, and adults not reporting disability in North Carolina.' *Public Health Reports, 119,* 4, 418–426.

Heng, J. and Sullivan, W. (2003) 'Ethical issues relating to consent in providing treatment and care.' In I. Brown and M. Percy (eds) *Developmental Disabilities in Ontario* (2nd edn). Toronto: Ontario Association on Developmental Disabilities.

Holland, A. J. (2000) 'Ageing and learning disability.' *The British Journal of Psychiatry, 176,* 1, 26–31.

Horwitz, S. M., Kerker, B. D., Owens, P. L. and Zigler, E. (2001) 'The health status and needs of individuals with mental retardation.' Washington DC: Special Olympics, Inc.

Hurley, A. and O'Sullivan, J. (1999) 'Informed consent for health care.' In R. Dinerstein, S. Herr and J. O'Sullivan (eds) *A Guide to Consent.* Washington, DC: American Association on Mental Retardation.

Iacono, T. (2006) 'Ethical challenges and complexities of including people with intellectual disability as participants in research.' *Journal of Intellectual and Developmental Disability, 31,* 3, 173–179.

Jancar, J. and Speller, C. J. (1994) 'Fatal intestinal obstruction in the mentally handicapped.' *Journal of Intellectual Disability Research, 42,* 429–433.

Janicki, M. P., Davidson, P. W., Henderson, C. M., McCallion, P. *et al.* (2002) 'Health characteristics and health service utilization in older adults with intellectual disability living in community residences.' *Journal of Intellectual Disability Research, 46,* 5, 409–415.

Jansen, D., Krol, B., Grothoff, J. W. and Post, D. (2004) 'People with intellectual disability and their health problems: A review of comparative studies.' *Journal of Intellectual Disability Research, 48,* 2, 93–102.

Jobling, A. (2001) 'Beyond sex and cooking: Health education for individuals with intellectual disability.' *Mental Retardation, 39,* 4, 310–321.

Kerr, A. M., McCulloch, D., Oliver, K., McLean, B. *et al.* (2003) 'Medical needs of people with intellectual disability require regular reassessment, and the provision of client- and carer-held reports.' *Journal of Intellectual Disability Research, 47,* 2, 134–145.

Kerr, M. P., Richards, D. and Glover, G. (1996) 'Primary care for people with an intellectual disability. A group proactive survey.' *Journal of Applied Research in Intellectual Disability, 9,* 4, 347–352.

Law, J., Bunning, K., Byng, S., Farrelly, S. and Heyman, B. (2005) 'Making sense in primary care: Levelling the playing field for people with communication difficulties.' *Disability and Society, 20,* 2, 169–164.

Leeder, S. R. and Dominello, A. (2005) 'Health, equity and intellectual disability.' *Journal of Applied Research in Intellectual Disabilities, 18,* 1, 97–100.

Lennox, N., Bain, C., Rey-Conde, T., Purdie, D., Bush, R. and Pandeya, N. (2007) 'Effects of a comprehensive health assessment programme for Australian adults with intellectual disability: A cluster randomized trial.' *International Journal of Epidemiology, 36,* 1, 139–146.

Lennox, N. G., Beange, H. and Edwards, N. S. (2000) 'The health needs of people with intellectual disability.' *Medical Journal of Australia, 173,* 6, 328–330.

Lennox, N. and Diggens, J. (eds) (1999) *Management Guidelines: People with Developmental and Intellectual Disabilities.* Melbourne: Therapeutic Guidelines Limited.

Lennox, N. G., Diggens, J. and Ugoni, A. M. (1997) 'The general practice care of people with an intellectual disability: Barriers and solutions.' *Journal of Intellectual Disability Research, 4,* 5, 380–390.

Lennox, N. and Edwards, N. (2001) *Lessons from the Labyrinth: Views of Residential Care Officers on Barriers to Comprehensive Health Care for Adults with an Intellectual Disability.* Queensland: University of Queensland, Developmental Disability Unit, School of Population Health.

Lennox, N. G. and Kerr, M. P. (1997) 'Primary health care and people with an intellectual disability.' *Journal of Intellectual Disability Research, 41,* 5, 365–372.

Lennox, N., Taylor, M., Rey-Conde, T., Bain, C., Boyle, F. and Purdie, D. (2004) *'Ask for it:* Development of a health advocacy intervention for adults with intellectual disability and their general practitioners.' *Health Promotion International, 19,* 2, 167–175.

Lewis, M. A., Lewis, C. E., Leake, B., King, B. H. and Lindemann, R. (2002) 'The quality of health care for adults with developmental disabilities.' *Public Health Reports, 117,* 2, 174–184.

Lowe, C. and Temple, V. (2002) 'Identifying hearing loss in adults with developmental disabilities.' *Journal of Speech-Language Pathology and Audiology, 26,* 1, 20–26.

Lunsky, Y., Emery, C. and Benson, B. (2002) 'Staff and self-reports of health behaviours, somatic complaints, and medications among adults with mild intellectual disability.' *Journal of Intellectual and Developmental Disability, 27,* 2, 125–135.

Lunsky, Y., Straiko, A. and Armstrong, S. (2002) *Women Be Healthy: A Curriculum for Women with Mental Retardation and Other Developmental Disabilities.* (Revised by S. M. Havercamp, C. Kluttz-Hile and P. Dickens.) Chapel Hill, NC: North Carolina Office on Disability and Health. Retrieved from www.fpg.unc.edu/~ncodh/WomensHealth/Womenshealthpub.cfm. on September 28, 2008.

Marks, B. A. and Heller, T. (2003) 'Bridging the equity gap: Health promotion for adults with intellectual and developmental disabilities.' *The Nursing Clinics of North America, 38,* 2, 205–228.

Marmot, M. (2001) 'Economic and social determinants of disease.' *Bulletin of the World Health Organization, 79,* 10, 988–989.

Martens, M., Jones, L. and Reiss, S. (2006) 'Organ transplantation, organ donation and mental retardation.' *Pediatric Transplantation, 10,* 6, 658–664.

McCarthy, M. (1999) *Sexuality and Women with Learning Disabilities.* London: Jessica Kingsley Publishers.

McCulloch, D. L., Sludden, P. A., McKeon, K. and Kerr, A. (1996) 'Vision care requirements among intellectually disabled adults: A residence based pilot study.' *Journal of Intellectual Disability Research, 40,* 3, 140–150.

Melville, C., Finlayson, J., Cooper, S., Allan, L. *et al.* (2005) 'Enhancing primary health care services for adults with intellectual disabilities.' *Journal of Intellectual Disability Research, 49,* 3, 190–198.

Millar, L., Chorlton, M. C. and Lennox, N. (2004) 'People with intellectual disability: Barriers to the provision of good primary care.' *Australian Family Physician, 33,* 8, 657–658.

Molyneux. P., Emerson, E. and Caine, A. (1999) 'Prescription of psychotropic medication to people with intellectual disabilities in primary health-care settings.' *Journal of Applied Research in Intellectual Disabilities, 12,* 1, 46–57.

Morris, C., Neiderbuhl, J. and Mahr, J. (1993) 'Determining the capability of individuals with mental retardation to give informed consent.' *American Journal on Mental Retardation, 98,* 22, 263–272.

National Health Service – Scotland (2004) *Health Needs Assessment Report: People with Learning Disabilities in Scotland.* Glasgow: NHS Health Scotland.

Ouellette-Kuntz, H. (2005) 'Understanding health disparities and inequities faced by individuals with intellectual disabilities.' *Journal of Applied Research in Intellectual Disabilities, 18,* 2, 113–121.

Patja, K., Iivanainen, M., Vesala, H., Oksanen, H. and Ruoppila, I. (2000) 'Life expectancy of people with intellectual disability: A 35-year follow-up study.' *Journal of Intellectual Disability Research, 44,* 5, 591–599.

Perske, R. (1972) 'The dignity of risk.' In W. Wolfensberger (ed.) *Normalization: The Principle of Normalization in Human Services.* Toronto: National Institute on Mental Retardation.

Radouco-Thomas, M., Brisson, A., Brassard, P., Fortier, L. and Thivierge, J. (2004) 'Pilot study on the use of psychotropic medication in persons with mental retardation.' *Progress in Neuro-Psychopharmacology and Biological Psychiatry, 28,* 5, 879–883.

Reichard, A. and Rutherford-Turnbull, H. (2004) 'Perspectives of physicians, families and case managers concerning access to health care by individuals with developmental disabilities.' *Mental Retardation, 42,* 30, 181–194.

Reiss, S. and Aman, M. G. (1997) 'The international consensus process on psychopharmacology and intellectual disability.' *Journal of Intellectual Disability, 41,* 6, 445–448.

Reiss, S. and Szyszko, J. (1983) 'Diagnostic overshadowing and professional experience with mentally retarded persons.' *American Journal of Mental Deficiency, 87,* 396–402.

Robertson, J., Emerson, E., Gregory, N., Hatton, C. *et al.* (2000a) 'Lifestyle-related risk factors for poor health in residential settings for people with intellectual disabilities.' *Research in Developmental Disabilities, 21,* 6, 469–489.

Robertson, J., Emerson, E., Gregory, N., Hatton, C. *et al.* (2000b) 'Receipt of psychotropic medication by people with intellectual disability in residential settings.' *Journal of Intellectual Disability Research, 44,* 6, 666–676.

Roosendaal, J. (ed.) (1992) *Mental Retardation and Medical Care.* Zeist: Uitgeverij Kerckebosch.

Rubin, S. S., Rimmer, J. H., Chicoine, B., Braddock, D. and McGuire, D. E. (1998) 'Overweight prevalence in persons with Down syndrome.' *Mental Retardation, 36,* 3, 175–181.

Scott, A., Marsh, L. and Stotes, M. (1998) 'A survey of oral health in a population of adults with developmental disability: Comparison with a national health survey of the general population.' *Australian Dental Journal, 43,* 4, 257–261.

Shogren, K. A., Wehmeyer, M. L., Reese, R. M. and O'Hara, D. (2006) 'Promoting self-determination in health and medical care: A critical component of addressing health disparities in people with intellectual disabilities.' *Journal of Policy and Practice in Intellectual Disabilities, 3,* 2, 105–113.

Solar, O. and Irwin, A. (2005) *Towards a Conceptual Framework for Analysis and Action on the Social Determinants of Health.* Discussion paper for the Commission on the Social Determinants of Health.

Sommi, R., Benefield, W., Curtis, J., Lott, R., Saklad, J. and Wilson, J. (1998) 'Drug interactions with psychotropic medications.' In S. Reiss and M. Aman (eds) *Psychotropic Medications and Developmental Disabilities: The International Consensus Handbook.* Columbus, OH: The Nisonger Center UAP.

Sullivan, W. and Heng, J. (2005, November) 'Patient-centered primary care on a friendship model: Values and methods for selecting practice guidelines in developmental disabilities.' In W. Sullivan (Chair) *Colloquium on the Primary Care for Adults with Developmental Disabilities.* Toronto, Ontario.

Sullivan, W., Heng, J., Cameron, D., Lunsky, Y. *et al.* (2006) 'Consensus guidelines for primary health care of adults with developmental disabilities.' *Canadian Family Physician, 52,* 1410–1418. Retrieved from www.cfpc.ca/cfp/2006/Nov/vol52-nov-cme-sullivan.asp on September 28, 2008.

Tohill, C. (1997) 'A study into the possible link between anti-epileptic drugs and the risk of fractures in Muckamore Abbey Hospital.' *Journal of Intellectual and Developmental Disability, 22*, 4, 281–292.

Tones, K. (1991) 'Health promotion, empowerment and the psychology of control.' *Journal of the Institute of Health Education, 29*, 19, 17–25.

Tonge, B. and Einfeld, S. (2000) 'The trajectory of psychiatric disorders in young people with intellectual disabilities.' *Australian and New Zealand Journal of Psychiatry, 34*, 80–84.

U.N. ESCOR (2000) *The Right to the Highest Attainable Standard of Health*, General Comment No. 14, U.N. ESCOR, Comm. On Econ., Soc. and Cult. Rts., 22nd Sess.

US Department of Health and Human Services (2002) *Closing the Gap: A National Blueprint to Improve the Health of Persons with Mental Retardation: Report of the Surgeon General's Conference on Health Disparities and Mental Retardation.* Rockville, MD: Department of Health and Human Services, Public Health Service, Office of the Surgeon General.

US Department of Health and Human Services (USDHHS) (2003) *Communicating Health: Priorities and Strategies for Progress.* Action Plans to Achieve the Health Communication Objectives in Healthy People 2010. Washington, DC: Retrieved from http://odphp.osophs.dhhs.gov/projects/healthcomm/objective2.htm on September 28, 2008.

US Department of Health and Human Services (USDHHS) (2004) *Understanding Health Literacy and its Barriers.* Washington, DC: USDHHS. Retrieved from www.nlm.nih.gov/pubs/cbm/healthliteracybarriers.html on September 28, 2008.

Van der Gaag, A. (1998) 'Communication skills and adults with learning disabilities: Eliminating Professional Myopia.' *British Journal of Learning Disabilities, 26*, 1, 1–11.

Van Schrojenstein Lantman-de Valk, H. M. J., Metsemakers, J., Haveman, M. J. and Crebolder, H. (2000) 'Health problems in people with intellectual disability in general practice: A comparative study.' *Family Practice, 17*, 6, 405–407.

Van Schrojenstein Lantman-de Valk, H. M. J., van den Akker, M., Maaskant, M. A., Haveman, M. J. *et al.* (1997) 'Prevalence and incidence of health problems in people with intellectual disability.' *Journal of Intellectual Disability Research, 41*, 1, 42–51.

Wagemans, A., Fiolet, J., van der Liden, E. and Menheere, P. (1998) 'Osteoporosis and intellectual disability: Is there any relation?' *Journal of Intellectual Disability Research, 42*, 5, 370–374.

Webb, O. J. and Rogers, L. (1999) 'Health screening for people with intellectual disability: The New Zealand experience.' *Journal of Intellectual Disability Research, 43*, 6, 267–503.

Whitehead, M. (1992) *The Concepts and Principles of Equity and Health.* Geneva: World Health Organization.

Wilson, D. N. and Haire, A. (1992) 'Health care screening for people with mental handicap in the United Kingdom.' In J. Roosendaal (ed.) *Mental Retardation and Medical Care.* Zeist: Uitgeverij Kerckebosch.

Woodhouse, J. M., Adler, P. and Duignan, A. (2004) 'Vision in athletes with intellectual disabilities: The need for improved eyecare.' *Journal of Intellectual Disability Research, 48*, 8, 736–745.

Yang, Q., Rasmussen, S. A. and Friedman, J. M. (2002) 'Mortality associated with Down's syndrome in the USA from 1983 to 1997: A population-based study.' *Lancet, 359*, 9311, 1019–1025.

Ziviani, J., Lennox, N., Allison, H., Lyons, M. and Del Mar, C. (2004) 'Meeting in the middle: Improving communication in primary health care consultations with people with an intellectual disability.' *Journal of Intellectual and Developmental Disabilities, 29*, 3, 211–225.

7

Sexuality and Human Rights of Persons with Intellectual Disabilities

Deborah Richards, Nancy Miodrag, Shelley L. Watson,
Maurice Feldman, Marjorie Aunos, Diane
Cox-Lindenbaum and Dorothy Griffiths

INTRODUCTION

The history of people with intellectual disabilities and their sexual rights can be described as a combination of neglect, prejudice, disapproval, and misunderstanding. Overall, societal value and opinion has assumed that individuals with intellectual disabilities are incapable of expressing their sexuality. These constant obstacles and struggles make assurance of the sexual rights of people who have an intellectual disability especially challenging. In theory and under the rule of law, it is presumed that sexual rights are guaranteed regardless of disability. However, the violation of human rights is nowhere more evident for individuals who have intellectual disabilities than in the area of sexuality (Watson *et al.* 2002). This violation can be attributed largely to Quinn and Degener's (2002) identification of the phenomenon of the 'invisibility' of people with disabilities, which suggests that they are viewed as objects rather than as subjects.

People with intellectual disabilities have been alarmingly marginalized, discriminated against, and underserved in relation to their right to sexual intimacy, sex education, procreation, parenting, marriage, and even loving another person of their choice, if it at all resembles a sexual relationship. Is this denial of sexual rights a social barrier, a systemic problem, and/or a historical perception of false belief that has disallowed people with intellectual disabilities the entitlements others have taken for granted?

The authors of this chapter will present the issues, both past and present, relating to sexual rights violations by challenging the traditional beliefs. First, the history of how people with intellectual disabilities have been denied their sexuality and the result of that denial will be critiqued. Second, an examination of various topics concerning sexual rights and how they have influenced the lives of people with intellectual disabilities will be addressed. This will be followed by a discussion about societal attitudes evidenced in systems, professionals, caregivers, and the carry-over effects that these attitudes have had that ultimately affect quality of life for individuals with intellectual disabilities. In the final section, the authors set out to build a 'framework for change' that aims to promote sexual equality regardless of disability.

HISTORICAL PERSPECTIVE

Historically, individuals with intellectual disabilities were prevented from carrying out sexually productive and full lives. This was a result of false beliefs held by negative societal assumptions and attitudes regarding their potential criminality, promiscuous behaviour, and sexual perversion and deviance (Di Giulio 2003; Lumley and Scotti 2001). The consequence of such prejudice and sexual stigmatization was known as the practice of selective breeding or eugenics, spurred by the Eugenics Movement from 1880 to 1940 (Griffiths and Lunsky 2000; Karellou 2003; King and Richards 2002; Lumley and Scotti 2001). During that same period in history, in the case of Buck v. Bell, 274 U.S. 200 (1927), the United States Supreme Court upheld the constitutionality of involuntary sterilization of individuals with mental retardation. Oliver Wendel Holmes affirmed that 'three generations of imbeciles are enough' (p.207). This belief continues to be held by many people today, and directly impacts their perception of the sexuality and sexual rights of individuals with disabilities.

It was not until the 1970s, sparked by Wolfensberger's normalization movement, that groups began to advocate for individual choices and desires for people who had intellectual disabilities. This movement supported the right of people with intellectual disabilities to live with, work with, and love people of both sexes. The normalization movement created an atmosphere for providers to examine and reflect on their personal and professional attitudes (Wolfensberger 1983). Karellou (2003) emphasizes that, historically, people with intellectual disabilities have been cast into roles that limited and distorted their sexual lives and feelings. Moreover, society did not acknowledge their sexuality and perceived them to be eternal children, incapable of having sexual feelings (Horgos 1998).

For many years, it was believed that individuals with intellectual disabilities were incapable of falling in and out of love, did not seek emotional satisfaction, and were not interested in marriage or having children. Today, in spite of the normalization and deinstitutionalization movements in Western culture that helped to change these ignorant and fearful attitudes, persons with intellectual disabilities are still denied complete sexual rights and emancipation because of the persistence of such disapproving attitudes (Stinson, Christian and Dotson 2002).

Real and assumed rights

In North America, people with intellectual disabilities are guaranteed or implied equality with all other citizens with regard to their rights to sexual self-expression. In Canada, the right to be free from discrimination based on disability is guaranteed in the Canadian Charter of Rights and Freedoms (Department of Justice Canada 1982) under section 15 (1 and 2). Canada was the first country in the world to include equality rights for persons with disabilities in a fundamental constitutional document (Rioux and Prince 2002). The Charter provides a framework for the fundamental treatment of *all* Canadians while ensuring equality and full citizenship for individuals with disabilities. In the United States, President John F. Kennedy declared, in 1963, that persons with disabilities should be granted the same rights as persons without disabilities under the American Bill of Rights, and, by 1973, this was reiterated in the Rehabilitation Act. These implied rights include treatment and education, privacy, choice of marital status, and freedom to procreate and raise a family.

Other documents, such as the Valencia Declaration of Sexual Rights (Instituto de Sexologia Y Psicoterapia Espill 1997), include the right to sexual equity, and refer to the freedom from all forms of discrimination, paying due respect to the protection of sexual diversity for all, regardless of sex, gender, age, race, social class, religion, and sexual orientation. All persons are sexual and are endowed with dignity and self-worth, regardless of race, sex, disability, sexual orientation, or medical condition (SIECUS, cited in Medlar 1998). Globally, the United Nations Declaration of Rights for Retarded Persons (1971) declared that people with intellectual disabilities had the right to cohabitate and to marry. Although these sexually related rights are legally assumed, they have been routinely denied to people with intellectual disabilities.

In the United States, the concept of consent to sexual expression for persons with disabilities is guided by Constitutional law, civil law, and criminal law. These laws are often conflicting, with governmental obligations to recognize certain rights to sexuality and at the same time, to protect from harm, persons with mental disability. It is, therefore, difficult to strike a balance between individual rights and the duty of social institutions to protect people with disabilities. Since the President's Commission for the Study of Ethical Problems in Medicine and Bio Medical and Behavioral Research, it is becoming more commonplace in the treatment of mental disabilities to utilize treatment teams or committees in ethics in order to address this fundamental conflict (Stavis 1991).

Outcomes of denying one's sexual rights

Healthy sexuality is a criterion for mental wellness (The World Health Organization; WHO 1975) and includes two components. The first is the capacity to enjoy and control sexual and reproductive behaviour within the parameters of social and personal ethics. The second is freedom from fear, shame, or other psychological factors that may inhibit sexual expression.

The opportunity for healthy sexuality is typically abused for persons with intellectual disabilities (Griffiths *et al.* 2002). Persons with intellectual disabilities are rarely provided with choice regarding their sexuality or reproduction. They are routinely restricted, and receive punishment and/or recrimination for sexual expression. They are often denied privacy, opportunity, knowledge, and choice about their sexual expression. Rowe and Savage (1987) suggest that it is common for persons with disabilities to be treated as sexually incompetent. Service providers 'discourage relationships between clients in both overt and subtle ways' (p.138), which includes insisting on parental consent for education, having sex-segregated settings, and taking punitive measures for sexual activity, all of which are infringements on the universal rights of people with intellectual disabilities. McConkey and Ryan (2001) conducted a study in Ireland and identified that only one in five staff members surveyed had received any training in sexuality. Moreover, if they were trained, the concentration was on policy training concerning vulnerable adults and the protection from abuse, which, in turn, discouraged any form of sexual expression for fear of the potential for any sexually abusive situations.

Not only is the right to develop a healthy sexuality typically neglected, but researchers suggest that people with intellectual disabilities are also more likely to be victims of sexual abuse (The Roeher Institute 1994). Sexual abuse is defined as unwanted or forced sexual contact, unwanted touching or displays of sexual parts, threats of harm or coercion in connection with sexual activity; it also includes denial of sexuality, denial of sexual education and information, and forced abortion or sterilization (The Roeher Institute 1994). Researchers show the following about the victims of sexual abuse:

- The US Department of Justice reports that 68 per cent to 83 per cent of women with developmental disabilities will be sexually assaulted in their lifetime and less than half of them will seek assistance from legal or treatment services (Guidry Tyiska 2001).

- Females with intellectual disabilities are 1.5 times more likely than persons without disabilities to experience unwanted sexual advances in their lives; men are more likely to experience assault (Doucette 1986; Jacobson 1989; Kohan, Pothier and Norbeck 1987; Ridington

1989; Sobsey *et al.* 1991; Stimpson and Best 1991; The Roeher Institute 1988; Ticoll and Panitch 1993).

- Women experience higher rates of abuse than men (62%: 38%), although males with disabilities experience higher rates of abuse than males without (Sobsey 1994).

- Sexual abuse is four times more common in institutional settings (Blatt and Brown 1986).

- Abuse of persons with disabilities typically occurs more than once in their lives (53.8%) and is repeated by the same offender (10.3%) (Mansell, Sobsey and Calder 1992). Only 19 per cent of victims report single abuse events or events that have occurred two to ten times.

- Children with disabilities are sexually abused at a rate 2.2 times higher than children without disabilities (Cross, Kaye and Ratnofsky, cited in Murphy and Elias 2006).

- 39–68 per cent of girls and 16–30 per cent of boys had been subjected to sexual abuse before the age of 18. American estimates show that one in three children and one in four adolescents with learning disabilities have been sexually abused (Ticoll 1994).

Researchers show the following about the offenders:

- Typically, they are male and known to the victim (e.g. family member, neighbour, care provider, babysitter) (Mansell *et al.* 1992; Sobsey 1994).

- Offenders in the role of care providers gain access to their victims through the disability services; this represents the greatest percentage of offenders (26.3%).

- Other offender groups include natural, foster, and step-family (23%), neighbours or acquaintances (13.5%), other service providers not related to disability services (10.5%), strangers (9%), other persons with disabilities (8.3%), transportation providers (6%), and dates (3%) (Mansell *et al.* 1992).

- Persons with disabilities may also be at increased risk of abuse at the hands of other persons with disabilities who offend because vulnerable individuals are often clustered with potential victimizers in residential programs (Gust *et al.* 2002).

- Offences typically occur in environments where care is provided, such as private homes (57.3%), group homes (8.5%), institutions (7.7%), hospitals (1.7%), and rehabilitation services (4.3%) (Mansell *et al.* 1992).

In the past few decades, researchers have shown that persons with intellectual disabilities are being severely and chronically sexually abused and exploited (Sobsey 1994). Given the prevalence of this risk, strategies need to be put into place to provide accurate and up-to-date information about sexuality, and what to do if abuse occurs. Without such information, individuals remain vulnerable to victimization.

SPECIFIC RIGHTS INFRINGEMENTS

Sex education and training

Despite improvements in society's attitude toward the sexuality of individuals with intellectual disabilities, information is often not provided and there are limitations on what is actually discussed (McCabe 1999). Negative feelings in relation to sexuality often develop (McCabe 1999), resulting in low levels of sexual expression. Although society's attitudes are more positive today than in the past, McCabe (1999) and Szollos and McCabe (1995) contend that information on actual sexual expression and attitudes toward sexuality is largely unavailable.

The Valencia Declaration of Sexual Rights (Instituto de Sexologia Y Psicoterapia Espill 1997) includes the right to sexual health, the right to wide, objective, and factual information on human sexuality, and the right to comprehensive sexuality education. Not providing sex education to individuals with disabilities is a direct violation of this declaration of human rights. As with individuals without disabilities, individuals who have disabilities have the same rights to information, services, and to a health service provider who has adequate knowledge, sensitivity, and experience in sexual development. Self-empowerment, life skills, parenting, and medical concerns are common to all, but these issues may require special attention for individuals with disabilities (Cole and Cole 1993). Individuals with intellectual disabilities require sexuality education because of the movement toward deinstitutionalization and community living, the increased incidence of sexual abuse, and the advent of Human Immunodeficiency Virus (HIV) and Acquired Immune Deficiency Syndrome (AIDS). People with intellectual disabilities have also expressed an interest in learning more about their sexuality (Whitehouse and McCabe 1997). Equally important, they have major gaps in their sexual knowledge, showing it to be partial, inaccurate, inconsistent, and even improbable (Gillies and McEwen 1981; McCabe 1999;

McCabe and Cummins 1996; McCabe and Schreck 1992; Szollos and McCabe 1995). Although there is limited research on the sexual attitudes of people with intellectual disabilities, researchers have found them to be poorly informed and hold largely negative attitudes toward the expression of their sexuality (Heshusius 1982; McCabe 1993, 1999; McCabe and Cummins 1996; McCabe and Schreck 1992; McCarthy 1996; Szollos and McCabe 1995). Sexual education is also pivotal to the development of positive self-image, interpersonal skills, and feelings of social competence in the area of sexuality (Rowe and Savage 1987). It is thus imperative that the sexuality of individuals who have intellectual disabilities no longer be denied or ignored and that programs be designed specifically to enhance their quality of life and to fulfil their basic human rights.

Contraception/birth control options

The 1986 case of 'Eve' was a monumental point in history for people with intellectual disabilities. Justice LaForest of the Supreme Court of Canada passed down a decision that denied third party authorization of nontherapeutic sterilization of individuals with intellectual disabilities (King and Richards 2002; Rioux 1996). This was the first time in Canadian history that the natural rights of all women, with and without disabilities, took precedence over society's right to perform sterilization procedures without the consent of the woman involved. As of 1986, people with intellectual disabilities had the right to control their own body (King and Richards 2002; Price 1990; Rioux and Yarmol 1987). Recently, the principle of self-determination, that is, having the skills, knowledge and beliefs that allow people to set goals for themselves, and to take the initiative to reach these goals (Field *et al.* 1998), became paramount in the lives of people with disabilities, who have markedly embraced the ideas of self-direction and consumer control (Ward and Meyer 1999).

Today, the Canadian Supreme Court ruling protects people with intellectual disabilities from forced sterilization. However, other countries differ significantly in their medical attitudes and approaches toward sterilization laws, ranging from advocating for sterilization to absolute rejection (Servais *et al.* 2002). Roets, Adams and Van Hove (2006) recently published the story of Marie, a Belgian woman with disabilities who was informed by medical professionals that sterilization was essential because such a procedure would prevent her from having bladder difficulties, would reduce her cholesterol level, and would cease her menstruation. However, medical professionals did not explain the procedure, nor would they discuss the issue of sterilization with the woman. Servais *et al.* (2002) concluded in their study that the final choice of contraception is dictated by neither medical nor rational factors, but is ultimately an institutional factor. In other words, people with intellectual disabilities are not provided with the opportunity to make contraceptive decisions, because the facility's particular contraceptive method of choice tends to override individual rights.

Historically, in the United States, women with disabilities have been forced into sterilization regardless of their own desires or ability to care for children. A premise for increased sterilization was that men and women who were sterilized could eliminate future generations of people with disabilities. This premise also assumed that sterilization would eliminate sexual activity (Irvine 1988).

In 1969, a Texas court refused to order the sterilization of a woman with disabilities and the test of that appeal was challenged (Frazier v. Levi 440 SW 2nd 293, Texas Civil Appeals, Houston 1969). In 1996, the American Congress amended the law to include forced sterilization as grounds for refugee status (United Nations Enable 2002a). When US courts have authorized sterilization, they have done so for three reasons:

- if it is the only effective means of preventing pregnancy

- on the grounds that 'incapacitated' women have a right not to bear children and

- if the court does not exercise its authority to order sterilization, the right would be denied to the woman whether it is in her best interest, and whether she would choose sterilization if she were competent.

Most American courts require the following procedures to be followed to justify an order for forced sterilization. Courts usually require proof of *some* or *all* of the following elements:

- that the woman would consent if she were able to

- that she will not develop sufficiently in the foreseeable future to make an informed decision about sterilization; sterilizations of young women are often denied on this basis, particularly if they have not received adequate training to assist them in making such a decision

- that she is physically capable of procreation and is engaging in sexual activities that are likely to result in pregnancy; many persons with disabilities are not sexually active or are sterile. These women should not be subjected to sterilization

- that, because of her disability, she is permanently incapable of caring for a child, even with reasonable assistance

- that she will not suffer psychological or psychiatric harm if she is sterilized

- that the guardians (if any) consent to the sterilization

- that the operative and long-term medical risks of the proposed method of sterilization are minimal and medically acceptable

- that the proposed method of sterilization is the least invasive of the person's body; for example, tubal ligation is preferred over hysterectomy because it is less invasive

- that the current state of medical knowledge suggests that no reversible sterilization or other workable, less drastic contraceptive method will shortly be available.

Many persons have full guardians when, in fact, they are capable of understanding and handling some aspects of their daily life, including making the decision about sterilization. These persons may not need guardianship, or may only need a limited guardianship. A full guardianship may be terminated by court order, and a limited guardianship substituted if necessary (Advocacy, Inc. 2000). Only by terminating her full guardianship can a woman, who has previously been found to be incapacitated, consent to sterilization. Clinical experience of the authors of this chapter, however, indicates that many of the above-noted procedures are manipulated so that the desires of the person with disabilities are not considered.

Around the world, women whose rights have been violated in these ways are developing a shared voice. Hundreds of women with disabilities from over 30 nations joined women without disabilities in Beijing, China, for the UN 4th World Conference on Women, and addressed issues of particular concern to women with disabilities. Workable strategies continue to be enforced, but at last, the world is becoming aware of issues of need (United Nations Enable 2002b).

A question needs to be posed regarding whether people with intellectual disabilities are, in fact, 'in control of their own body' with respect to making decisions about birth control and contraceptive choices. It is suspect that parents, caregivers, and agencies continue to place doubt on the cognitive capacity of individuals with intellectual disabilities to be parents; often they will encourage medical professionals to prescribe contraceptives without the individual being fully informed. Brief explanations may be provided to these recipients, yet no follow-up is conducted to see whether, in fact, these women understand what medications they are taking and whether they are satisfied with their method of contraception (McCarthy 1998). Researchers have suggested that Depo-Provera injections and birth control pills are being dispensed with little or no explanation to women with intellectual disabilities (Christian, Stinson and Dotson 2001; McCarthy 1998).

In addition to contraception, researchers have consistently found that individuals with disabilities have poor knowledge of sex, pregnancy, childbirth, abortion, sexually transmitted infections (STIs), marriage, homosexuality, and sexual intimacy (Cheng and Udry 2003; McCabe and Cummins 1996; Szollos and McCabe 1995). Given this poor knowledge base, it is assumed that individuals with intellectual disabilities are not in a position to make informed decisions about contraceptive methods. Now, more than ever, the full movement of people with disabilities into community living makes it even more pertinent that individuals with intellectual disabilities receive adequate training on the different options they have regarding birth control. Such education is required if they are to make informed choices about their sexual behaviour (Szollos and McCabe 1995).

Marriage/cohabitation

According to Traustadottir (1990), people with intellectual disabilities are less likely to marry than those without disabilities – if they do marry, it typically happens later in life. Koller, Richardson and Katz (1988) examined the frequency of marriage for individuals with intellectual disabilities compared to individuals without disabilities. Marriage was found to be significantly lower for males and females in the former group; however, within-group comparisons showed that females with disabilities were marrying more than men. One's intelligence quotient (IQ) plays a large role in whether people married or not (Koller *et al.* 1988; May and Simpson 2003). In their study, May and Simpson (2003) found no individuals with an IQ below 50 were married or cohabitating. Thus, not only is there a small percentage of people with intellectual disabilities who marry, but it is a very specific group of people who are involved in marriage and/or cohabitation.

Lesseliers and Van Hove (2002) conducted one-on-one interviews with people who had an intellectual disability to explore how they perceived their relationships and sexuality, and to identify surrounding and important issues. They found that the participants who wanted to marry often lacked the support for that goal from staff and family members. Some explained that they needed permission from family members or care providers, while others stated that they were not allowed to be away from home; still others felt that it would cost too much money to get married. Denying the prospect of marriage to people with intellectual disabilities was standard practice when individuals with disabilities were typically confined to institutions. As we move toward more integrated and inclusive community living for people with intellectual disabilities (May and Simpson 2003), marriage and cohabitation issues should be less of a challenge and more easily accepted.

Given the lack of sex education, and typically inadequate policies and procedures to support sexual rights and opportunities for individuals to engage in healthy sexual relationships, it is not surprising that the prevalence of marriage is low in this population. Typically, organizational structures are not set up for married couples, and are ill-equipped to encourage marriage among this population. If agency policies and practices adopt the position that all people are to be provided education and should be free from obstacles surrounding healthy and intimate relationships, the notion of marriage would automatically be put into the equation as often as it is for people without disabilities.

Parenting

The repressive laws that prohibit marriage are largely based on the debunked eugenics principles. Eugenics is driven by a fear that people with an intellectual disability would: (i) give birth to children with disabilities; (ii) be incapable of adequately parenting their children regardless of supports provided; (iii) be incapable of understanding the legal implications of marriage and parenthood; and (iv) be unable to bond with their children (Aunos and Feldman 2007a; Dickson and Beyer, cited in Rowe and Savage 1987). However, the same concerns are true for persons without disabilities, and as such, do not stand up under scrutiny (Rowe and Savage 1987).

Until recently, society sanctioned involuntary sterilization or birth control for individuals living in institutions and community settings in order to prevent procreation (Rowe and Savage 1987). For those who do become parents, their children are often removed at birth without any evidence of child maltreatment (Booth, Booth and McConnell 2005; Hayman 1990; Llewellyn, McConnell and Ferronato 2003a; Tymchuk and Feldman 1991). Parents with intellectual disabilities are over-represented in child custody decisions with up to 80 per cent losing their children, often facilitated by discriminatory and invalid parenting assessments (Aunos and Feldman 2007a).

However, the picture is not entirely bleak for these families. Over the last 20 years, an evidence-based intervention technology has been developed to teach parenting skills to parents with intellectual disabilities (Aunos and Feldman 2007b). Using behavioural instructional strategies, these parents have learned a variety of skills including: basic newborn, infant and child care; nutrition; health and safety; and positive interactions, often in only a few training sessions (Feldman 1994, 1998; Llewellyn et al. 2003b). When measured, their children's health and development benefit from parent training (e.g. Feldman, Garrick and Case 1997; Feldman, Sparks and Case 1993), and family preservation increased (Feldman, Case and Sparks 1992; Feldman et al. 1993). Recently, self-directed learning tools have been designed to allow parents to acquire child-care skills on their own, and the results have been impressive (Feldman 2004). Clearly, evidence is accumulating to show that, with appropriate supports (including evidence-based parent education), many of these parents are able to provide a nurturing, healthy, and safe home environment for their children. Nonetheless, negative attitudes towards parenting by persons with intellectual disabilities still prevail (Aunos and Feldman 2002), but progress is being made to reduce the number of children who are removed from the home simply because their parent has an intellectual disability (Aunos and Feldman 2007a).

Sexual orientation

Typically, it is assumed that individuals who have an intellectual disability are heterosexual (Corbett, Shurberg Klein and Bregante 1987). Hingsburger (1993) discussed the added problems faced by individuals who have an intellectual disability who are homosexual, referring to this population as 'a minority within a minority' (p.19). It is important to note, however, that regardless of age and setting, men with disabilities are significantly more likely to have had sex with another man than with a woman (McCarthy 1996; Thompson 1994). Gebherd (1973) found homosexual behaviour incidence figures reaching 100 per cent for older men in institutions. In a poignant study, Thompson (1994) discusses interviews with men with disabilities who have had sex with other men. Thompson states that it is important to be aware of the filters that may stand in the way of the discussion of their sexual experience. For example, it is quite taboo for men to have sex with other men and, therefore, if a man with disabilities states that he has not had sex with other men, he should not be thought of as lying if he has actually had this experience. More accurately, the social context of this denial should be understood. Furthermore, when men do discuss their sexual experiences with other men, there is a lack of mutuality between partners; many men report painful experiences of sex, and for many of the men in Thompson's (1994) study, the sexual contact was not welcomed.

The situation is not the same for women; when women with disabilities were interviewed, McCarthy (1996) found that 97 per cent reported they had never had sex with another woman. Walmsley (1993) asserts that it is 'exceptionally difficult for women with learning difficulties to recognize themselves as lesbians' (p.94). McCarthy (1999) speculates that this is because of the lack of lesbian role models women with disabilities are exposed to. Further, McCarthy (1999) asserts that many women with disabilities learn what sex is about through abuse perpetrated by men, but since they are rarely abused by women, they do not learn what sex between women is.

Same-sex relationships have been ignored, marginalized, or pathologized in the early sexuality literature (McCarthy 1999). When it has been discussed, the concept of institutional homosexuality, wherein all same-sex relationships are explained by the argument that people had no other choice and their natural heterosexual instincts were distorted by their living arrangement, was very prevalent (McCarthy 1999; Thompson 1994). This notion is now challenged because it implies that same-sex relationships are second best to opposite-sex ones (McCarthy and Thompson 1998; Thompson 1994).

Nonetheless, in the 1990s, some sex education materials were produced that presented relationships and sex between women and between men as positive and valued (McCarthy and Thompson 1998). However, even today, sex education materials are still created in a way that marginalizes same-sex relationships, perpetuating an essentially homophobic view (McCarthy 1999) and assuming a heterosexual perspective (Whitehouse and McCabe 1997).

Negative perceptions of homosexuality have been reported by individuals with disabilities (McCabe 1999; Timmers, Du Charme and Jacob 1981). However, Garwood and McCabe (2000) discuss the fact that people with intellectual disabilities tend to have low levels of knowledge regarding homosexuality thus it is difficult to determine their feelings toward this topic in an accurate and comprehensive manner. Staff members certainly have an influence on the negative attitudes that have been reported, since many of them report discouraging same-sex affectionate behaviour (Thompson 1994). It must also be recognized that men with disabilities would not be easily accepted into the gay community because they do not belong to the privileged social classes that typify it (Connell *et al.* 1991), and would likely experience rejection similar to that from other parts of society.

Competency/consent to sexual relations

According to Sheehan (2002), the fundamental principle of human dignity in individual autonomy over sexual relations has formed the definition of consent. Moreover, for people to have the capacity for sexual relations they must have the ability to appreciate the nature of the sexual activity along with its risks and methods of reducing these risks. In other words, people are required to comprehend that there is always the option to refuse to engage in a sexual activity including the ability to exercise that choice at any time for a variety of personal and legal reasons. The notion of competency has created much debate among professionals, often questioning whether people with intellectual disabilities have the capacity to consent to sexual activity. According to Ames and Samowitz (1995), having 'protectors' will reduce the sexual rights of people with intellectual disabilities as a safety measure. This belief has provided a justification that this group is unable to give informed consent. This in itself confuses caregivers and support staff with respect to balancing the issues of sexual rights versus protection against sexual victimization.

Rowe and Savage (1987) suggest that 'it is extremely common in both institutional and community service systems to treat clients as sexually incompetent' (p.138). There is an assumption that persons with intellectual disabilities are incapable of such relationships and act irresponsibly with sexual knowledge. However, persons without disabilities who are incapable of solid relationships or irresponsible with their sexual and parenting knowledge are not equally discriminated against by educational or experiential sanctions (Rowe and Savage 1987).

While understanding the rationale and principles that guide the overall positions of consent to engage in sexual relations, it is curious as to the level of consenting power that individuals with intellectual disabilities have been granted. For instance, how can people consent to something about which they have no information? The capability to give free and voluntary consent for sexual activity assumes that the consenter has the knowledge and intelligence to judge the appropriateness of the activity for him or herself (Ames and Samowitz 1995; Sheehan 2002). In a review of past practices for people with intellectual disabilities, there is evidence to suggest that knowledge is limited because they have not been provided with adequate educational training and supports. As well, while cognitive functioning is compromised, systems need to include adaptive functioning as a factor in determining consenting ability. People's opportunity to give consent to a relationship they want is often tainted by the increased vulnerabilities to sexual abuse. Caregivers are often left in the 'protector' role and, therefore, unlikely to favour any sexual relationships. Consent to sexual relations has and remains an intimate topic for individuals with disabilities. Service providers and families often struggle to find the precise solution in supporting individuals in their quests for sexual relations. Providing individuals with sexuality training will increase their knowledge, and enable and guide their decisions based on informed consent (Watson *et al.* 2002).

Sexual activity and the law of consent is a major topic for discussion in the United States. It can be difficult to strike a balance between the rights to sexual self-expression and the need to protect persons with disabilities from harm. The onus remains on treatment professionals and other staff members both to protect and to support the rights of people with disabilities. In the United States three bodies of law apply to sexuality: the Constitution, the civil law, and the criminal law.

- *Constitutional law* – maintains protection from harm, promotion of well-being, individual autonomy, freedom of choice, protection of marriage, family procreation, child rearing

- *civil law* – (parens patriae), state acting as a protective and nurturing parent, and

- *criminal law* – police power.

All three legal foci require the presence of knowledge, intelligence, and voluntariness. Therefore in the United States, all the laws rest largely on the question of whether a person has the capacity or competence to consent. Relevant professional standards largely determine issues of competence and capacity to consent and although this approach is utilized to protect individuals with disabilities from harm and ensure rights, it has both crippled and enhanced issues of consent in America's litigious society (Stavis 1991).

Privacy

Privacy is a fundamental right. Unfortunately, the right to privacy is one of the least respected privileges among service providers for persons with intellectual disabilities (Rowe and Savage 1987). Violating privacy is, to some degree, the result of group living or congregated living, which often times does not afford individuals with personal living spaces. Such restricted living quarters are often determined justifiable because of financial restrictions. According to Hingsburger (1993), a lack of privacy can lead to inappropriate sexual expression, such as public masturbation. Such acts may lead to punishment by a caregiver and may even have legal repercussions.

Lesseliers and Van Hove (2002) state that if we believe in and respect the sexual rights of people with intellectual disabilities, then there are changes that can and must take place in the systems of care that are provided for people with intellectual disabilities. Support services must establish policies and procedures that insure the provision of private space and a supportive social environment to promote the enactment of people's sexuality rights. Additionally, staff and parents need training that addresses attitudes and perceptions as well as respect for individual privacy. If such matters are put into place, there is greater potential for individuals with intellectual disabilities to have sexual relationships via appropriate sexual expression.

Often, medical professionals are unfamiliar about how to explain medical issues and concepts to women with intellectual disabilities in a manner that is easy to understand, and that will adequately address questions and provide information to parents or caregivers (Christian *et al.* 2001). This can be problematic if the patient wishes to discuss confidential issues surrounding possible options for contraception use or pregnancy prevention, for example, while a support person or family member is present. The onus is on medical professionals and service providers to ensure that people with intellectual disabilities feel comfortable communicating their medical needs. Essentially, there is a need for practical training for people with intellectual disabilities that specifies their right to privacy and autonomy. This is important so they understand that doctors do not have the right to discuss their medical concerns and treatments with other people without their consent, even if they believe they are acting in the individual's best interest.

ATTITUDES TOWARD SEXUALITY AND THE IMPACT ON RIGHTS INFRINGEMENTS

The attitudes, beliefs, and opinions held by others can have a powerful effect on the sexual lives of persons with intellectual disabilities. People with disabilities depend on a system that necessitates positive supports and services provided by agencies and caregivers who have an invested interest in their lives. Hingsburger and Tough (2002) propose four components of a healthy service system, which include comprehensible policies with respect to sexuality expression and staff responses; active participation by families and staff in sexuality awareness training; self-advocacy; and relationship training. Nestled within any one system, prejudice and negative beliefs must be addressed, whilst positive attitudes are cultivated.

Unfavourable attitudes toward the sexuality of people with intellectual disabilities at the societal and individual level can be destructive and damaging to their personal sense of sexual self (Di Giulio 2003). Society's perceptions act as a powerful barrier that may prevent the likelihood that these individuals will ever completely achieve the fundamental human and sexuality rights they deserve (Lumley and Scotti 2001). The responsibility lies particularly with the cyclical perceptions and beliefs held by informants who have a hand in the sexual adjustment, self-perception (Szollos and McCabe 1995), self-development, and quality of life of people with intellectual disabilities. Namely, these individuals include general practitioners, gynecologists, psychologists, counsellors and therapists, residential and community support workers, educators, and families/carers.

According to Trudel and Desjardins (1992), 'staff's attitudes often reflect the reactions society has toward people living in institutions' (p.178). Negative attitudes perpetuated at the individual level by family members or support staff can literally destroy a person's sense of self, make him or her feel constant fear and anxiety about sexuality, perpetuate unhealthy sexual behaviour (Hingsburger and Tough 2002), and hinder his or her chances of developing healthy intimate relations. To prevent the internalizing of these demeaning attitudes is a difficult task, but necessary to avoid a devaluation of the self (Milligan and Neufeldt 2001).

Attitudes of personnel/staff

There are many ways that attitudes can become barriers and end up hindering the sexual development of people with intellectual disabilities. Examples include actions on the part of staff members, including: limiting clients' access to sexuality education (Christian et al. 2001; Stinson et al. 2002); the deliberate provision of misinformation about sexuality (Hingsburger and Tough 2002); infringement on reproductive rights such as lack of choice of contraception use, inadequate gynecological and breast health care, high rates of sexual abuse and exploitation (Stinson et al. 2002); denial of privacy (Di Giulio 2003; Hingsburger and Tough 2002); and finally, restriction of contact with sexual partners (Di Giulio 2003).

Fortunately, there has been a gradual shift in acceptance and understanding of sexuality for adults with intellectual disabilities, with a resulting shift away from conservatism and taboo attitudes (Griffiths and Lunsky 2000; Murray and Minnes 1994). Such attitude shifts are evident in the improvements made to the design, implementation, and evaluation of sex education programs, as well as in the increased provision of care in sexual health services. According to McCarthy (1999), care staff are slowly moving toward accepting their clients as sexual beings. While attitude change does not necessarily manifest in behavioural change (Van Hove 2000), this is still a considerable progress. Considerable variability in attitude still exists among direct care staff, educators, and parents. Furthermore, the rigid disapproval that existed in earlier years has now given way to indecision (Griffiths and Lunsky 2000).

Numerous researchers have explored the attitudes toward the sexuality, sexual practices, and sexual relationships of people with intellectual disabilities (e.g. Szollos and McCabe 1995; Trudel and Desjardins 1992; Wolfe 1997). A host of studies was conducted in the mid- to late 1970s and throughout the 1980s sparked by the normalization movement conceptualized by Bank-Mikkelsen in the 1950s, studied by Nirje in the 1960s, and further pioneered in North America in the 1970s by Wolfensberger (Trudel and Desjardins 1992). In their review of studies, Trudel and Desjardins (1992) found that attitudes vary in relation to the type of institution in which the studies were conducted and based on the professional status of informants. For example, nurses who work in close contact with individuals with intellectual disabilities tend to be the least tolerant of all health-care employees. This finding was repeated by Plaute, Westling and Cizek (2002), who found that gynecologists were less liberal in their thinking than educators and residential workers. Attitudes also tend to diverge according to the sexual behaviours engaged in by clients. Thus, sexual behaviours conducted in private are considered more acceptable than those conducted in public. Trudel and Desjardins (1992) also suggest that staff hold varied beliefs about the sexual orientation of their clients. Consistent with previous research, homosexual behaviour is less accepted than heterosexual behaviour.

Christian et al. (2001) found that despite low levels of staff training in sexuality for women with intellectual disabilities (only 7.1%), the majority felt comfortable and positive supporting their clients in sexual expression (76.7%), offering sex education (61.9%), supporting reproductive rights (90.6%) and helping acquire gynecological care (86%). Over 90 per cent of respondents agreed that women's issues with respect to freedom of sexual expression, motherhood, and reproductive rights/health issues were relevant to their well-being. Still, 44.2 per cent believed that there were more important issues to focus on than sexuality (Christian et al. 2001), highlighting the disregard for sexuality in the lives of people with disabilities.

The degree of disability has also been shown to affect the level of acceptance of sexuality for persons with intellectual disabilities. Wolfe (1997) found that based on the level of disability, special education administrators and teachers held different attitudes about sexuality expression, types of relationships seen as acceptable, and the right to bear children. Specifically, respondents' attitudes were more liberal and accepting concerning sexual behaviour for students with *moderate* disabilities (IQs between 40 and 55), than for students with *severe* disabilities (IQs between 0 and 40). Similarly, Owen *et al.* (2000) state that as the degree of intimacy and sexual behaviour of people with intellectual disabilities increases, the degree of acceptance by staff decreases.

Recently, Yool, Langdon and Garner (2003) examined medium-security staff attitudes toward the sexuality of individuals with intellectual disabilities. Staff members held liberal attitudes about sexuality and masturbation and less liberal attitudes when topics involved sexual intercourse, homosexual relations, and client freedom concerning decision-making about their sexuality (Yool *et al.* 2003). In general, staff felt that sexual relations amongst clients should be prohibited. Similar to the proposition made by Hingsburger and Tough (2002), Yool *et al.* (2003) conclude that sexuality training for staff with more negative-held beliefs may be a viable solution to changing attitudes.

Only a few researchers have assessed the public's view on the sexuality of adults with intellectual disabilities (e.g. Cuskelly and Bryde 2004). One study conducted by Karellou (2003) looked at Greek laypeople's attitudes. Consistent with previous research, age had a significant effect on people's attitudes (Cuskelly and Bryde 2004; Oliver *et al.* 2002; Plaute *et al.* 2002) in that younger respondents had more liberal attitudes than older respondents. Persons over 60 years of age held the most conservative attitudes (Cuskelly and Bryde 2004; Oliver *et al.* 2002).

Researchers also suggest that respondents with higher levels of education have more liberal viewpoints than those with lower levels (Karellou 2003; Plaute *et al.* 2002). Plaute *et al.* (2002) found that educators with higher education, living in urban areas were the most liberal, while educators who had a strong belief in God and who were older were the least liberal. In general, Karellou (2003) found that older and less educated individuals held the most conservative and traditional attitudes towards issues on homosexuality and human sexuality, and were less accepting and more discriminative. A more positive attitude was found in a community sample in Australia with regards to sexuality toward people with intellectual disability (Cuskelly and Bryde 2004). Studies have found that community people tend to hold more conservative attitudes towards marriage and parenthood for persons with intellectual disabilities than for those without disabilities (Oliver *et al.* 2002). These attitudes offer insight into how people with intellectual disabilities are acknowledged, accepted, and included in their communities.

Attitudes of people with intellectual disabilities

For people with intellectual disabilities to lead sexually healthy lives, a strong sense of self-advocacy and personal voice needs to be encouraged by families and support staff. Hingsburger and Tough (2002) state 'self-advocacy…holds much promise as a means of developing pride, enhancing relationships, and developing skills' (p.15). Lindon (cited in Hingsburger and Tough 2002) says, 'people with disabilities need to find their own voice in order to speak about the lives they want to live' (p.11). All too often, however, people with intellectual disabilities live and work in a system that does not always nurture their sexual selves and where negative, indifferent, and repressive attitudes about sexuality prevail. DeLoach (1994) contends that negative attitudes work to isolate and marginalize people with intellectual disabilities. Such perceptions can damage individuals' personal beliefs about themselves as sexual beings. Milligan and Neufeldt (2001) add that by internalizing the negative feelings, people with intellectual disabilities set in motion a kind of recoiling from healthy sexual experiences in love and intimacy. In the past, the feelings, attitudes, opinions, and experiences of persons with intellectual disability concerning their own sexuality have been completely neglected and ignored. Recently, however, professionals have come to acknowledge that for these individuals to enjoy sexually healthy lives, their personal attitudes and perspectives matter significantly.

Consistently, it has been found that people with intellectual disabilities tend to hold more conservative and negative feelings toward sexuality (Lunsky and Konstantareas 1998; Owen et al. 2000; Siebelink et al. 2006). Edmonson and Wish (1975) assessed the sexual attitudes of men with moderate intellectual disabilities and found that individuals saw masturbation as wrong (37%); heterosexual intercourse as wrong (31%); and homosexual behavior as wrong (86%). More recently, it was revealed that adults with intellectual disabilities did not approve of sexual relationships regardless of the partner (Owen et al. 2000). Furthermore, when comparisons were made to a group of first-year university students, McCabe and Cummins (1996) found that people with mild intellectual disabilities had more negative attitudes because of their sexual experiences towards dating, use of condoms, sexual intercourse, oral sex, masturbation, and homosexuality; these same individuals had less negative feelings about sexual abuse and promiscuous behaviour. Individuals in this study also had negative opinions about marriage and having a family (McCabe and Cummins 1996).

Lunsky and Konstantareas (1998) found that participants with intellectual disabilities disapproved of more than half (12/20) of the sociosexual situations presented to them (e.g. masturbating, petting, and homosexuality) and were less accepting than individuals without disabilities. Participants with intellectual disabilities were, in turn, far less accepting of the sociosexual situations than were individuals with autism. Similar findings were found by McCabe (1999) who suggests that, in general, people with mild intellectual disabilities had negative feelings towards sexuality when compared to people without disabilities. Clearly, their lack of knowledge and negative attitudes dictates that their needs are nowhere near being met, and that sexuality needs to be more integrated into their everyday lives through sex education and opportunities for sexual expression (McCabe 1999). Consistent with McCabe and Cummins' (1996) findings, Garwood and McCabe (2000) found that people with intellectual disabilities developed more negative feelings toward getting married, pregnancy, and giving birth after sex education. In general, negative feelings of some participants were still apparent after sex education towards girlfriends, masturbation, oral-genital sex, and sexual intercourse. Findings from the Plaute *et al.* (2002) study, however, revealed that the majority of individuals with intellectual disabilities felt sexuality was an important topic (90%) and that they should be allowed to have a baby (60%). Nevertheless, 50 per cent disapproved of masturbation.

A recent study by Lesseliers and Van Hove (2002) explored the way persons with intellectual disabilities perceived their own sexuality and personal relationships to provide a voice for their sexual needs and concerns. Forty-six adults with intellectual disabilities from residential programs in Belgium were interviewed about being in love, dating, getting married, having children, and being sexually active. Several general ideas emerged. For example, respondents stated that they often have very few opportunities to discuss their personal love relationships openly with others; feel that the 'middle field' (e.g. kissing, petting) of sexual contact is acceptable and appropriate, but that exploring more than the 'middle field' would be cause for punishment by parents or staff; are rarely offered opportunities for privacy in the context of their living situations; fear staff disapproval if they approach the topic of sexuality; feel that their experiences of intimacy are not satisfactory and thus are indifferent or pessimistic about having intercourse; experience sadness and despair about their communal living arrangements and have little say in this matter; feel challenged when faced with resolving conflicts and do not feel supported by staff to do so; feel guilty about masturbation; experience painful sexual acts and feel suppressed in their opportunities to talk about their abuse; and finally, feel positive about getting married and having children but at the same time sense a lack of support in doing so.

Women with intellectual disabilities also face their own unique sexual issues. According to Stinson *et al.* (2002), 'negative stereotypes not only impact the way society views women with intellectual disabilities, but may also impact the way women view themselves' (p.22). For example, because of the normalization movement's push to be more 'normal', women with intellectual disabilities may feel inadequate next to the bombardment of unrealistic mass media images portraying perfect body images (Milligan and Neufeldt 2001). Olney and Kuper (1998) state that the risk of feeling helpless and dependent is high for women, as is their risk of suffering from negative self-worth.

Attitudes of parents

Often with good intentions, parents of children with intellectual disabilities suppress their child's attitudes toward sexuality and sexual expression because of personal fears. Although rightfully natural for parents, fears of abuse, pregnancy, rape, personal misconduct, and sexual vulnerability (Hingsburger and Tough 2002; Löfgren-Mårtenson 2004; Rousso 1993; Szollos and McCabe 1995) only perpetuate and stimulate personal vulnerability and thus susceptibility to exploitative situations (Lesseliers and Van Hove 2002). Cuskelly and Bryde (2004) found that parents and staff held different viewpoints about sexuality for people with intellectual disabilities, with parents holding attitudes that are more conservative. Parents were older than staff in this study, which in the past has been linked to a more conservative viewpoint regarding sexuality (Karellou 2003). Löfgren-Mårtenson (2004) explored the possibilities and hindrances for sexuality and love of youth with intellectual disabilities. Findings revealed that staff and families expressed feelings of ambivalence with respect to the sexuality of their loved one or client. Although they realized the need to provide autonomy and opportunities for sexual expression to these individuals, this was overcome by even greater fear of unwanted pregnancy, sexual abuse, or loss of sexual control. Families had reservations and restrictive feelings toward specific issues regarding their adolescent children, namely having sexual intercourse and raising children (Löfgren-Mårtenson 2004).

Attitudes summary

In general, people with intellectual disabilities hold negative attitudes about their own sexuality, and are particularly uneasy about sexual intercourse, masturbation, and homosexuality (Garwood and McCabe 2000; Lunsky and Konstantareas 1998; McCabe 1999; McCabe and Cummins 1996; Owen et al. 2000; Siebelink et al. 2006). Some studies, however, have shown that some men and women have positive attitudes about marriage and raising a family (Brantlinger 1985; Lesseliers and Van Hove 2002; Löfgren-Mårtenson 2004; Szollos and McCabe 1995). Between 60 and 90 per cent of people with disabilities look forward to these events (Brantlinger 1985). Parents, on the other hand, tend to fear their child being abused and exploited, becoming pregnant or raped, and as a result, are resistant to change (Hingsburger and Tough 2002; Löfgren-Mårtenson 2004). Parents tend to avoid discussions about sexuality because they are uncomfortable with the subject matter (Brantlinger 1985; Lesseliers 1996; Lesseliers and Van Hove 2002) when in fact sex education has been shown to be critical to successful sexual health.

Ambivalent and negative attitudes are still prevalent amongst direct-care workers, professionals, and educators (Aunos and Feldman 2002) despite the recent trend toward inclusive communities (Cuskelly and Bryde 2004). Unfavourable attitudes dictate much of the sexual lives that people with intellectual disabilities will (or will not) have. These attitudes are 'most likely influenced by cultural images and ideologies, personal values, and direct personal experience with persons with disabilities' (Milligan and Neufeldt 2001, p.105). In the end, the onus is on society as a whole to acknowledge that attitudes dictate, to a great extent, whether individuals with intellectual disabilities experience a healthy and safe sexual life, or one of shame, fear, and anxiety.

FRAMEWORK FOR CHANGE

Debunking the myths

The sexuality of persons with intellectual disabilities has historically been grounded in myth. Therefore, it is instrumental to create systems change that eliminates the stereotypes that promote this atmosphere. Importantly, there are two prevailing and yet contradictory myths.

Myth # 1. All individuals with disabilities are promiscuous and impulsive, and you need to watch your children around them (Griffiths 2003). The reality is that individuals with intellectual disabilities do not show any more inappropriate sexual expression than would be present in individuals without disabilities, if provided appropriate and normative learning opportunities regarding their sexuality.

Myth # 2. Society continues to hold the image that people with intellectual disabilities are 'eternal children'. Because of this myth, people with disabilities are denied sexual education and the typical experiences that might afford. The basis for this belief is the misunderstood concept of mental age as a predictor of all aspects of the person's life rather than a description of functioning on a test of cognitive abilities (Griffiths and Fedoroff, in press). This misapplication of the concept of mental age results in people with disabilities being viewed as sexually immature and disinterested, and as such, their sexuality is ignored. The outcome of this misapplication is a lack of normative learning and a failure to educate regarding potential risks (e.g. abuse, disease, unwanted pregnancy).

Key sexuality myths of persons with disabilities have been challenged by numerous authors (Kempton 1993; Griffiths 2003). Griffiths (2003) noted people with intellectual disabilities, except those with certain genetic or endocrine abnormalities, follow a similar developmental trajectory regarding their secondary sexual characteristics. For the most part, they experience sexual feelings and respond sexually to the same sexual stimuli as persons without disabilities. The caveat is that persons with intellectual disabilities are rarely provided normalized habilitative environments to learn personal, moral, social, and legal responsibility regarding sexuality, nor formal educational opportunities to learn sex education.

Researchers have shown that individuals with disabilities benefit from formal sociosexual education designed to provide knowledge and guidance necessary to learn responsibility about one's sexuality, to learn appropriate rather than inappropriate sexual expression, and to increase awareness and protective strategies for abuse (e.g. Griffiths 2007; Hard 1986). The development of sexually inappropriate behaviour in persons with intellectual disabilities can be affected by many factors, including a lack of sexual education; deprivation of peer group interactions; family restrictions on activities; lack of social exposure; and even lack of motor coordination. When people with intellectual disabilities act inappropriately in a sexual way, their offences are often less serious than those committed by persons without disabilities, and sexual paraphilia is considered common in this population (Day 1994).

The historical concern regarding the procreation of future generations of persons with intellectual disabilities is also flawed (Griffiths 2003). Persons with intellectual disabilities typically have fewer children, if any; there are a number of genetic syndromes associated with intellectual disabilities that have high rates of infertility (Griffiths *et al.* 2002). Additionally, because many causes of intellectual disability have no genetic cause, there would be no genetic reason to assume that offspring would automatically inherit a disability. However, even when genetic causes are present, they are not always passed on to the child because of the limited probability factors related to genetic sharing. Social factors play a critical role in the development of most disabilities (Feldman 2002); 90 per cent of infant disability is related to social factors, and 85 per cent of adult disability is caused after the age of 13 (Rioux 1996).

Policies and guidelines

Public policy affects the equal rights to sexual health of persons with intellectual disabilities in myriad ways. These include denial of access to information and education, unreasonable restrictions on relationships and marriage, lack of treatment for sexual dysfunction, gender identity issues or paraphilia, control of reproductive decisions, inadequate protection against sexual abuse, or support for abuse victims therapeutically or in assertion of their rights to have their perpetrators prosecuted (Griffiths and Lunsky 2000).

Policies such as the sexuality policy statement adopted by the American Association on Mental Retardation in 2002 need to be established and implemented to address the sexual needs of people in such a way that provides opportunity to engage in sexual/intimate relationships (Siebelink *et al.* 2006). Repeating the words of the research by McConkey and Ryan (2001), until staff training and policy guidelines are established, 'sexuality will remain an issue to which staff respond on their initiative with all the consequent dangers and inadequacies of idiosyncratic responses' (p.87). McConkey and Ryan (2001) stress the powerful role of staff members in the lives of people with intellectual disabilities, and support this notion by stating that sexual attitudes vary among staff. Further, people with intellectual disabilities may find themselves constantly adjusting to these differences, thereby creating additional confusion in an already complex situation. As service providers, it is essential that people's needs are being listened to, addressed, and followed through on. It is imperative that opportunities and choices are being made available upon the request of individuals. It is also important that the appropriate skills and education are being taught to create personal successes in the intimate and sexual lives of people, and that policies and procedures are created to insure that this occurs.

Löfgren-Mårtenson (2004) emphasizes that the lack of clear guidelines or regulations for the ways in which staff members should deal with sexuality often leads to a larger dilemma; staff members differ in their beliefs and therefore, in the absence of clear policies, consumers of an agency may be afforded divergent, conflicting, and inconsistent messages that could potentially be counterproductive to promoting healthy and positive sexuality (Griffiths *et al.* 2002).

Policies can help to protect the rights of people living within the guidelines of a service system and can relieve staff members of the responsibility to make decisions spontaneously as situations arise. Issues related to consent to sexual relations are extremely complex in nature; however, this must not impede the process of developing and implementing clear policies to provide a principled and consistent framework to guide caregivers, and most importantly, to ensure that individual sexual rights are respected (Sheehan 2002).

Lesseliers and Van Hove (2002) state that, if we believe and agree that respecting the sexual rights of people with intellectual disabilities is important, then there are changes that *can* and *must* take place. In the absence of supportive environments around people having intimate and sexual relationships, there needs to be space created and this needs to be written in policy and practices in order to consistently preserve human rights. Additionally, staff and parents need training that addresses attitudes and perceptions as well as respect for the privacy of people with intellectual disabilities. If such matters are put into place, there is greater potential for individuals with intellectual disabilities to have sexual relationships via appropriate sexual expression.

In the past few years, there has been a growing awareness of the need for community agencies and other organizations to develop sociosexual policies to ensure that the rights of people with intellectual disabilities are respected. Policies are vital to ensure that a consistent and responsible atmosphere exists to facilitate learning about culturally appropriate sociosexual interactions. Unless there is a clear direction for staff in a school or community agency to provide direction on sociosexual issues, each staff member may create his or her individual approach. This would lead to great inconsistency in what is being taught. Sometimes, certain behaviours might be accepted and at other times they may be punished depending on which staff member is on duty. This type of inconsistent treatment creates an environment in which it is difficult for people to learn to take responsibility for their own behaviour. Policy is the only means by which agencies can ensure that the sexuality of persons with intellectual disabilities will be responsibly, consistently and proactively addressed.

Rights training for people with intellectual disabilities and support staff

The importance of staff training needs to be recognized, particularly with respect to implementing information about policies and procedures designed to support people in their sexual relationships. Through training and education, paid support providers should feel empowered in their positions to encourage positive healthy sexual relationships for the individuals they are supporting. Notwithstanding the long history of exclusion from equality, there is an increasing trend toward the creation of stronger resources for respecting and protecting basic freedoms and human rights (Owen *et al.* 2000). As an illustration, Wolfensberger's normalization movement in the 1970s revealed signs of progress when groups advocated for individual choices that created movement towards independent and community living to enable people with intellectual disabilities to lead as 'normal' a life as possible (Wolfensberger 1972). The goal of the normalization movement was to maximize individual decision-making by people with intellectual disabilities to facilitate their independent living. From an agency standpoint, this focus on independent decision-making needs to continue, wherein individuals with disabilities are informed of their rights and provided opportunities to make choices about their own sexuality.

Systems change

Identifying the systemic obstructions and realizing that service providers have an obligation to respect the rights of people receiving service is one of the first steps to creating human equality that accommodates differences (Quinn and Degener 2002). Discerning staff members' attitudes and beliefs can provide an understanding of the climate in which services are provided, and ensuring that policies and procedures training is made available to staff is essential. Service providers need to commit to examining and reviewing staff's attitudes and evaluating policies, procedures, and training. Foremost, people with intellectual disabilities must be respected as sexual beings, and recognized as being capable of making decisions and choices in terms of their sexuality. Through action and advocacy, agencies and support staff, significant changes can transpire in removing the multiple barriers that impede sexual expression (Christian *et al.* 2001).

It is essential that systems be set up in such a way to create respect and responsibility for the sexuality of persons with intellectual disabilities (Griffiths *et al.* 2003; Owen *et al.* 2000). Disability is not the cause of abuse of persons with intellectual disabilities; however, the social conditions and systems in which persons with intellectual disabilities typically interact by virtue of their disability create the increased risk (Griffiths *et al.* 1996; The Roeher Institute 1988; Sobsey 1994). Persons with intellectual disabilities experience far more social isolation and economic disadvantage, restriction on their personal life, and are denied self-determination when compared with individuals without disability. They are often socialized to be compliant to those in power and to tolerate breaches in sociosexual boundaries. Furthermore, they are typically provided minimal opportunity for normative sociosexual experiences (Watson *et al.* 2002).

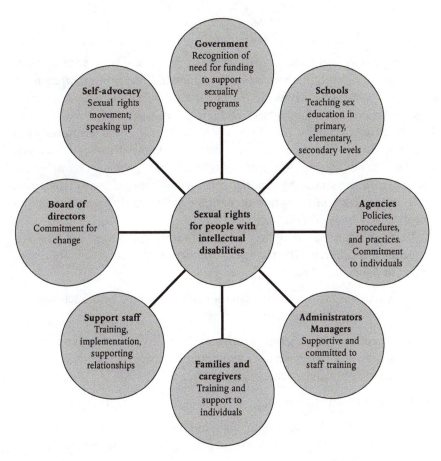

Figure 7.1 Multifaceted systems approach

There are apparent risk factors for abuse associated with the service delivery system and social attitudes related to people with disabilities (Sobsey and Doe 1991). These include the isolation of individuals within service environments, the lack of screening of staff and of policy enforcement, the devaluing of people with disabilities, and power inequalities, which leaves them desiring acceptance, their training in compliance, limitations in their verbal communication skills, and the use of psychotropic medication (Cox-Lindenbaum and Watson 2002; Sobsey and Doe 1991).

Figure 7.1 represents a holistic approach in which all systems and supports work cohesively, simultaneously, seamlessly, and in harmony to ensure that persons with developmental disability achieve equality in sexual rights. Such a model sees these individual units working together to support the individual with disability and takes a positive approach to ensuring that their sexual rights and needs are met.

SUMMARY OF CHANGE

According to Griffiths (2003), social service agencies have imposed restrictions on the human rights of individuals being supported because of the structure of the support systems, which would indicate that organizations need to be challenged to examine current practices, and implement a person-centred approach through strategic planning. As Sobsey (1994) states, people who have intellectual disabilities cannot exercise their rights until they know that they have them. While he stresses the importance of rights training for people with intellectual disabilities, Sobsey argues the importance lies within the environmental support, where individuals can learn that their rights are more than empty talk and actually have a basis in reality.

To create a positive atmosphere in which to teach appropriate and responsible sociosexual behaviour, it is recommended that a school or community agency commit in policy to:

- a statement that recognizes the sexuality of people with intellectual disabilities and their related rights

- an educational program, which ensures staff members respond to sociosexual issues, whether appropriate or inappropriate, in a consistent manner across staff and over time

- opportunities to learn appropriate sociosexual behaviour

- access to medical and counselling intervention, as needed, for sexual issues, including abuse counselling and treatment for inappropriate sexual behaviour

- a clear policy and set of procedures to prevent abuse, and procedures to follow should there be suspicion of abuse.

Sexual abuse prevention programs have been developed to address the risk factors individuals face through a lack of knowledge about sexuality as well as overcoming learned compliance and communication difficulties that render them particularly vulnerable to abuse (Collins, Schuster and Nelson 1992; Haseltine and Miltenberger 1990; Lumley *et al.* 1998).

CONCLUSION

Sexuality remains a complex and unresolved issue due to the imposition of a social construct and the continued pathologizing of the disability itself. Attitudes are a social construct, learned and culturally bound in time and place, which can change over time and space. We see evidence of altered and sometimes positive attitudes in our culture over time, intervals, and events, although this has not occurred without struggle. In accordance with that framework, attitudes towards individuals with intellectual disabilities have changed over time. At a broad level, Quinn and Degener (2002) contend that the core problem related to rights for people with disabilities is based on the invisibility of disability in the system of basic freedoms – that provisions 'are either not applied or are applied with much less rigour in the case of persons with disabilities' (p.15). The work of Wolfensberger influenced the reconstruction of services for people with intellectual disabilities, and progress has been made towards increased provision of choice and autonomy, community presence and integration. However, only recently have researchers investigated the relevance of this reconstruction in relation to people's sexuality (Withers *et al.* 2001). Researchers need to continue so that the rights of individuals with intellectual disabilities are valued and honoured.

There is evidence of progress since the days of Buck v. Bell, yet there continue to be barriers and obstacles in the sexual lives of people with intellectual disabilities. Organizational systems, families, disability advocates, community, and all those who know or work with people with intellectual disabilities should provide effective sex and relationship education, and ample opportunities for individual sexual expression.

The implementation of sociosexual education, staff training, parent training, attitude evaluation, policy statements, and counselling, will remain ineffective unless all those involved in supporting people with intellectual disabilities believe that all people are sexual and equal. Traustadottir (1990) articulates that people with disabilities rarely have the same options and access to traditional roles as people without disabilities. This is clearly a failure in providing the most basic of rights – love and intimacy.

Last, whether or not there is recognition of the infringement of rights, the fact remains that rights violations do exist for people with intellectual disabilities with regard to their sexuality. While being cognizant of this reality, it should be acknowledged that progress is being made in service systems. As they move toward a more person-centred planning approach to the evaluation of human rights, the protection of those rights will become embedded in the culture of individualized support (Griffiths 2003).

REFERENCES

Advocacy, Incorporated (2000) *CS5 – Guardianship for Texans With Disabilities.* Eleventh Edition, October.

Ames, T. R. H. and Samowitz, P. (1995) 'Inclusionary standard for determining sexual consent for individuals with developmental disabilities.' *Mental Retardation, 33*, 4, 264–268.

Aunos, M. and Feldman, M. A. (2002) 'Attitudes toward sexuality, sterilisation, and parenting rights of persons with intellectual disabilities.' *Journal of Applied Research in Intellectual Disability, 15*, 3, 285–296.

Aunos, M. and Feldman, M. (2007a) 'Parenting by people with intellectual disabilities.' In I. Brown and M. Percy (eds) *A Comprehensive Guide to Intellectual & Developmental Disabilities.* Baltimore, MD: Paul H. Brookes Publishing Co.

Aunos, M. and Feldman, M. (2007b) 'Assessing parenting capacity in parents with intellectual disabilities.' In C. Chamberland, S. Léveillé and N. Trocmé (eds) *Des enfants à protéger, des adultes à aider: Deux univers à rapprocher.* Québec City: Presses de l'université du Québec.

Blatt, E. R. and Brown, S. W. (1986) 'Environmental influences on incidents of alleged child abuse and neglect in New York state psychiatric facilities: Towards an etiology of institutional child maltreatment.' *Child Abuse and Neglect, 10*, 2, 171–180.

Booth, T., Booth, W. and McConnell, D. (2005) 'The prevalence and outcomes of care proceedings involving parents with learning difficulties in the family courts.' *Journal of Applied Research in Intellectual Disabilities, 18*, 1, 7–17.

Brantlinger, E. A. (1985) 'Mildly mentally retarded secondary students' information about sexual and attitudes toward sexuality and sexuality education.' *Education and Training of the Mentally Retarded, 20*, 2, 99–108.

Buck v. Bell, 274 U.S. (1927).

Cheng, M. M. and Udry, J. R. (2003) 'How much do mentally disabled adolescents know about sex and birth control?' *Adolescent and Family Health, 3*, 1, 28–38.

Christian, L. Stinson, J. and Dotson, L. A. (2001) 'Staff values regarding the sexual expression of women with developmental disabilities.' *Sexuality and Disability, 19*, 4, 283–291.

Cole, S. S. and Cole, T. M. (1993) 'Sexuality, disability, and reproductive issues through the life-span.' *Sexuality and Disability, 11*, 3, 189–205.

Collins, B. C., Schuster, J. W. and Nelson, C. M. (1992) 'Teaching a generalized response to the lures of strangers to adults with severe handicaps.' *Exceptionality, 3*, 2, 67–80.

Connell, R., Dowset, G., Rodden, P. and Davis, M. (1991) 'Social class, gay men and AIDS prevention.' *Australian Journal of Public Health, 15*, 2, 178–189.

Corbett, K., Shurberg Klein, S. and Bregante, J. L. (1987) 'The role of sexuality and sex equity in the education of disabled women.' *Peabody Journal of Education, 64*, 4, 198–212.

Cox-Lindenbaum, D. and Watson, S. L. (2002) 'Sexual assault against individuals who have a developmental disability.' In D. Griffiths, D. Richards, P. Federoff and S. Watson (eds) *Ethical Dilemmas: Sexuality and Developmental Disability.* Kingston, NY: NADD Press.

Cuskelly, M. and Bryde, R. (2004) 'Attitudes towards the sexuality of adults with an intellectual disability: Parents, support staff, and a community sample.' *Journal of Intellectual and Developmental Disability, 29,* 3, 255–264.

Day, K. (1994) 'Male mentally handicapped sex offenders.' *British Journal of Psychiatry, 165,* 5, 630–639.

DeLoach, C. P. (1994) 'Attitudes toward disability: Impact on sexual development and forging of intimate relationships.' *Journal of Applied Rehabilitation Counseling, 25,* 1, 18–25.

Department of Justice Canada (1982) *Canadian Charter of Rights and Freedoms.* Ottawa: Department of Justice Canada.

Di Giulio, G. (2003) 'Sexuality and people living with physical or developmental disabilities: A review of key issues.' *The Canadian Journal of Human Sexuality, 12,* 1, 53–68.

Doucette, J. (1986) *The Future Is Now: Networking for Change.* Report from the DisAbled Women's Network Ontario Networking Conference. Toronto: DAWN.

Edmonson, B. and Wish, J. (1975) 'Sexual knowledge and attitudes of moderately retarded males.' *American Journal of Mental Deficiency, 80,* 2, 172–179.

Feldman, M. A. (1994) 'Parenting education for parents with intellectual disabilities: A review of outcome studies.' *Research in Developmental Disabilities, 15,* 4, 299–332.

Feldman, M. A. (1998) 'Preventing child neglect: Child-care training for parents with intellectual disabilities.' *Infants and Young Children, 11,* 1–11.

Feldman, M. (2002) 'Parents with intellectual disabilities: Impediments and supports.' In D. M. Griffiths, D. Richards, P. Fedoroff and S. L. Watson (eds) *Ethical Dilemmas: Sexuality and Developmental Disabilities.* Kingston, NY: NADD Press.

Feldman, M. A. (2004) 'Self-directed learning of child-care skills by parents with intellectual disabilities.' *Infants and Young Children, 17,* 17–31.

Feldman, M. A., Case, L. and Sparks, B. (1992) 'Effectiveness of a child-care training program for parents at-risk for child neglect.' *Canadian Journal of Behavioural Science, 24,* 1, 14–28.

Feldman, M. A., Garrick, M. and Case, L. (1997) 'The effects of parent training on weight gain of nonorganic-failure-to-thrive children of parents with intellectual disabilities.' *Journal on Developmental Disabilities, 5,* 1, 47–61.

Feldman, M. A., Sparks, B. and Case, L. (1993) 'Effectiveness of home-based early intervention on the language development of children of parents with mental retardation.' *Research in Developmental Disabilities, 14,* 5, 387–408.

Field, S., Martin, J., Miller, R., Ward, M. and Wehmeyer, M. (1998) *A Practical Guide for Teaching Self-determination.* Reston, VA: Council for Exceptional Children.

Frazier v. Levi 440 SW 2nd 293, Texas Civil Appeals, Houston (1969).

Garwood, M. and McCabe, M. P. (2000) 'Impact of sex education programs on sexual knowledge and feelings of men with a mild intellectual disability.' *Education and Training in Mental Retardation and Developmental Disabilities, 35,* 3, 269–283.

Gebhard, P. M. (1973) 'Sexual behaviour of the mentally retarded.' In F. F. De La Cruz and G. D. La Veck (eds) *Human Sexuality and the Mentally Retarded.* London: Butterworth.

Gillies, P. and McEwen, J. (1981) 'The sexual knowledge of the "normal" and mildly subnormal adolescent.' *The Health Education Journal, 40,* 4, 120–124.

Griffiths, D. (2003) 'Sexuality and people with developmental disabilities: From myth to emerging practices.' In I. Brown and M. Percy (eds) *Developmental Disabilities in Ontario.* Toronto: Ontario Association on Developmental Disabilities.

Griffiths, D. (2007) 'Sexuality and people who have intellectual disabilities.' In I. Brown and M. Percy (eds) *A Comprehensive Guide to Intellectual and Developmental Disabilities*. Baltimore, MD: Paul H. Brookes Publishing Co.

Griffiths, D. and Fedoroff, P. (in press) 'Persons with intellectual disabilities who sexually offend.' In F. M. Saleh, A. J. Grodzinskas Jr., D. Brodsky and J. M. Bradford (eds) *Sex Offenders: Identification, Risk, Assessment, Treatment, and Legal Issues*. New York: Oxford University Press.

Griffiths, D. M. and Lunsky, Y. (2000) 'Changing attitudes towards the nature of socio-sexual assessment and education for persons with developmental disabilities: A twenty year comparison.' *Journal on Developmental Disabilities, 7*, 1, 16–33.

Griffiths, D., Baxter, J., Haslam, T., Richards, D., Stranges, S. and Vyrostko, B. (1996, November) 'Building healthy boundaries: Considerations for reducing sexual abuse.' *National Association for Dual Diagnosis Annual Conference Proceedings*, pp.143–148. New York, NY: National Association for Dual Diagnosis.

Griffiths, D., Owen, F., Gosse, L., Stoner, K. *et al*. (2003) 'Human rights and persons with intellectual disabilities: An action-research approach for community-based organizational self-evaluation.' *Journal on Developmental Disabilities, 10*, 2, 25–42.

Griffiths, D., Richards, D., Fedoroff, P. and Watson, S. (2002) 'Sexuality and mental health in persons with developmental disabilities.' In D. Griffiths, C. Stavrakaki and J. Summers (eds) *An Introduction to the Mental Health Needs of Persons with Developmental Disabilities*. Sudbury, ON: Habilitative Mental Health Resource Network.

Guidry Tyiska, C. (2001) *Working with Victims of Crime with Disabilities*. Washington, DC: Office for Victims of Crime, Department of Justice. Retrieved from www.ojp.usdoj.gov/ovc/publications/factshts/disable.htm on May 11, 2007.

Gust, D. A., Wang, S. A., Grot, J., Ransom, R. and Levine, W. C. (2002) 'National survey of sexual behavior and sexual behavior policies in facilities for individuals with mental retardation/developmental disabilities.' *Mental Retardation, 41*, 5, 365–373.

Hard, S. (1986) *Sexual Abuse of the Developmentally Disabled: A Case Study*. Paper presented at the National Conference of Executives of Associations for Retarded Citizens, Omaha, NE.

Haseltine, B. and Miltenberger, R. G. (1990) 'Teaching self-protection skills to persons with mental retardation.' *American Journal of Mental Retardation, 95*, 2, 188–197.

Hayman, R. L. (1990) 'Presumptions of justice: Law, politics, and the mentally retarded parent.' *Harvard Law Review, 103*, 6, 1201–1271.

Heshusius, L. (1982) 'Sexuality, intimacy and persons we label mentally retarded: What they think – what we think.' *Mental Retardation, 20*, 4, 164–168.

Hingsburger, D. (1993) 'Staff attitudes, homosexuality, and developmental disability: A minority within a minority.' *The Canadian Journal of Human Sexuality, 2*, 1, 19–21.

Hingsburger, D. and Tough, S. (2002) 'Healthy sexuality: Attitudes, systems, and policies.' *Research and Practice for Persons with Severe Disabilities, 27*, 1, 8–17.

Horgos, J. (1998) *Sexuality Education for Young People with Disabilities: An Introduction for Service Providers*. Vancouver: Children's & Women's Health Centre of British Columbia.

Instituto de Sexologia Y Psicoterapia Espill (1997) *Valencia Declaration on Sexual Rights*. Valencia, Spain: Institute de Sexologia Psicoterapia Espill.

Irvine, A. C. (1988) 'Balancing the right of the mentally retarded to obtain a therapeutic sterilization against the potential for abuse.' *Law and Psychology Review, 12*, 95–122.

Jacobson, A. (1989) 'Physical and sexual assault histories among psychiatric outpatients.' *American Journal of Psychiatry, 146*, 6, 755–758.

Karellou, J. (2003) 'Laypeople's attitudes toward the sexuality of people with learning disabilities in Greece.' *Sexuality and Disability, 21*, 1, 65–84.

Kempton, W. (1993) *Socialization and Sexuality: A Comprehensive Training Guide for Professionals Helping People with Disabilities that Hinder Learning.* Haverford, PA: Winifred Kempton.

King, R. and Richards, D. (2002) 'Sterilization and birth control.' In D. Griffiths, D. Richards, P. Fedoroff and S. L. Watson (eds) *Ethical Dilemmas: Sexuality and Developmental Disability.* Kingston, NY: NADD Press.

Kohan, M., Pothier, P. and Norbeck, J. (1987) 'Hospitalized children with history of sexual abuse: Incidence and care issues.' *American Journal of Orthopsychiatry, 57,* 2, 258–264.

Koller, H., Richardson, S. A. and Katz, M. (1988) 'Marriage in a young adult mentally retarded population.' *Journal of Mental Deficiency Research, 32,* 2, 93–102.

Lesseliers, J. (1996) 'Seks, anticonceptie, huwelijk, ouderschap van Personen met een matig mentale handicap. Standpunten van ouders, professionelen en derden terzake nader onderzocht.' *Echo's Uit de Gehandicaptenzorg, 17,* 1, 21–26.

Lesseliers, J. and Van Hove, G. (2002) 'Barriers to the development of intimate relationships and the expression of sexuality among people with developmental disabilities: Their perceptions.' *Research and Practice for Persons with Severe Disabilities, 27,* 1, 69–81.

Llewellyn, G., McConnell, D. and Ferronato, L. (2003a) 'Prevalence and outcomes for parents with disabilities and their children in an Australian court sample.' *Child Abuse and Neglect, 27,* 3, 235–251.

Llewellyn, G., McConnell, D., Honey, A., Mayes, R. and Russo, D. (2003b) 'Promoting health and home safety for children of parents with intellectual disability: A randomized controlled trial.' *Research in Developmental Disabilities, 24,* 6, 405–431.

Löfgren-Mårtenson, L. (2004) '"May I?" About sexuality and love in the new generation with intellectual disabilities.' *Sexuality and Disability, 22,* 3, 197–207.

Lumley, V. A., Miltenberger, R. G., Long, E. S., Rapp, J. T. and Roberts, J. (1998) 'Evaluation of a sexual abuse prevention program for adults with mental retardation.' *Journal of Applied Behavior Analysis, 31,* 1, 91–101.

Lumley, V. A. and Scotti, J. R. (2001) 'Supporting the sexuality of adults with mental retardation: Current status and future directions.' *Journal of Positive Behavior Interventions, 3,* 2, 109–119.

Lunsky, Y. and Konstantareas, M. M. (1998) 'The attitudes of individuals with autism and mental retardation towards sexuality.' *Education and Training in Mental Retardation and Developmental Disabilities, 33,* 1, 24–33.

Mansell, S., Sobsey, D. and Calder, P. (1992) 'Sexual abuse treatment for persons with disabilities.' *Professional Psychology: Research and Practice, 23,* 5, 404–409.

May, D. and Simpson, M. K. (2003) 'The parent trap: Marriage, parenthood and adulthood for people with intellectual disabilities.' *Critical Social Policy, 23,* 1, 25–43.

McCabe, M. P. (1993) 'Sex education programs for people with mental retardation.' *Mental Retardation, 31,* 6, 377–387.

McCabe, M. P. (1999) 'Sexual knowledge, experience, and feelings among people with disabilities.' *Sexuality and Disability, 17,* 2, 157–170.

McCabe, M. P. and Cummins, R. A. (1996) 'The sexual knowledge, experience, feelings, and needs of people with mild intellectual disability.' *Education and Training in Mental Retardation and Developmental Disabilities, 31,* 1, 13–21.

McCabe, M. P. and Schreck, A. (1992) 'Before sex education: An evaluation of the sexual knowledge, experience, feelings, and needs of people with mild intellectual disabilities.' *Australia and New Zealand Journal of Developmental Disabilities, 18,* 2, 75–82.

McCarthy, M. (1996) 'The sexual support needs of people with learning disabilities: A profile of those referred for sex education.' *Sexuality and Disability, 14,* 4, 265–279.

McCarthy, M. (1998) 'Whose body is it anyway? Pressures and control for women with learning disabilities.' *Disability and Society, 13*, 4, 557–574.

McCarthy, M. (1999) *Sexuality and Women with Learning Disabilities.* London: Jessica Kingsley Publishers.

McCarthy, M. and Thompson, D. (1998) *Sex and the 3 Rs: A Guide to Sex Education Work with People with Learning Disabilities* (2nd edn). Brighton: Pavilion.

McConkey, R. and Ryan, D. (2001) 'Experiences of staff in dealing with client sexuality in services for teenagers and adults with intellectual disability.' *Journal of Intellectual Disability, 45*, 1, 83–87.

Medlar, T. (1998) 'The manual of policies and procedures of the SHIP sexuality education program.' *Sexuality and Disability, 16*, 1, 21–42.

Milligan, M. S. and Neufeldt, A. H. (2001) 'The myth of asexuality: A survey of social and empirical evidence.' *Sexuality and Disability, 19*, 2, 91–109.

Murphy, N. A. and Elias, E. R. (2006) 'Sexuality of children and adolescents with developmental disabilities.' *Pediatrics, 118*, 1, 398–403.

Murray, J. L. and Minnes, P. M. (1994) 'Staff attitudes towards the sexuality of persons with intellectual disability.' *Australia and New Zealand Journal of Developmental Disabilities, 19*, 1, 45–52.

Oliver, M. N., Anthony, A., Leimkuhl, T. T. and Skillman, G. D. (2002) 'Attitudes toward acceptable socio-sexual behaviors for persons with mental retardation: Implications for normalization and community integration.' *Education and Training in Mental Retardation and Developmental Disabilities, 37*, 2, 193–201.

Olney, M. F. and Kuper, E. V. (1998) 'The situation of women with developmental disabilities: Implications for practitioners in supported employment.' *Journal of Applied Rehabilitation Counseling, 29*, 2, 3–11.

Owen, F. A., Griffiths, D. M., Feldman, M. A., Sales, C. and Richards, D. A. (2000) 'Perceptions of acceptable boundaries of persons with developmental disabilities and their careproviders.' *Journal on Developmental Disabilities, 7*, 1, 34–49.

Plaute, W., Westling, D. L. and Cizek, B. (2002) 'Sexuality education for adults with cognitive disabilities in Austria: Surveys of attitudes and the development of a model program.' *Research and Practice for Persons with Severe Disabilities, 27*, 1, 58–68.

Price, D. P. (1990) 'Comparative approaches to the non-consensual sterilization of the mentally retarded.' *Medicine and Law, 9*, 3, 940–949.

Quinn, G. and Degener, T. (2002) 'The moral authority for change: Human rights values and the worldwide process of disability reform.' In G. Quinn and T. Degener (eds) *Human Rights and Disability: The Current Use and Future Potential of United Nations Human Rights Instruments in the Context of Disability.* New York: United Nations.

Rehabilitation Act of 1973. Office of the Law Revision Counsel, US House of Representatives Pub. L. No. 93–112, 87 Stat. 394 (Sept. 26, 1973).

Ridington, J. (1989) *Beating the 'Odds': Violence and Women with Disabilities* (Position Paper 2). Vancouver: DisAbled Women's Network: Canada.

Rioux, M. (1996) 'Reproductive technology: A rights issue.' *Entourage,* Summer, 5–7.

Rioux, M. H. and Prince, M. J. (2002) 'The Canadian political landscape of disability: Policy, perspectives, social status, interest groups and the right movement.' In A. Puttee (ed.) *Federalism, Democracy and Disability Policy in Canada.* Montreal: McGill-Queen's University Press.

Rioux, M. and Yarmol, K. (1987) 'The right to control your own body: A look at the "Eve" decision.' *Entourage, 2*, 1, 26–31.

Roets, G., Adams, M. and Van Hove, G. (2006) 'Challenging the monologue about silent sterilization: Implications for self-advocacy.' *British Journal of Learning Disabilities, 34*, 3, 167–174.

Rousso, H. (1993) 'Special considerations in counseling clients with cerebral palsy.' *Sexuality and Disability, 11*, 1, 99–103.

Rowe, W. S. and Savage, S. (1987) *Sexuality and the Developmentally Handicapped.* Queenston, ON: Edwin Mellen Press.

Servais, L., Jacques, D., Leach, R., Cood, L. *et al.* (2002) 'Contraception of women with intellectual disability: Prevalence and determinants.' *Journal of Intellectual Disability Research, 46*, 2, 108–119.

Sheehan, S. (2002) 'Consent for sexual relations.' In D. Griffiths, D. Richards, P. Fedoroff and S. L. Watson (eds) *Ethical Dilemmas: Sexuality and Developmental Disability.* Kingston, NY: NADD Press.

Siebelink, E. M., de Jong, M. D. T., Taal, E. and Roelvink, L. (2006) 'Sexuality and people with intellectual disabilities: Assessment of knowledge, attitudes, experiences, and needs.' *Mental Retardation, 44*, 4, 283–294.

Sobsey, D. (1994) 'Sexual abuse of individuals with intellectual disability.' In A. Craft (ed) *Practice Issues in Sexuality and Learning Disabilities.* London: Routledge.

Sobsey, D. and Doe, T. (1991) 'Patterns of sexual abuse and assault.' *Sexuality and Disability, 9*, 3, 243–259.

Sobsey, D., Gray, S., Wells, D., Pyper, D. and Reimer-Heck, B. (1991) *Disability, Sexuality, and Abuse: An Annotated Bibliography.* Baltimore, MD: Paul H. Brookes Publishing Co.

Stavis, P. F. (1991) 'Sexual activity and the law of consent.' *Quality of Care Newsletter, 50; November–December.* New York State Commission on Quality of Care and Advocacy for Persons with Disabilities.

Stimpson, L. and Best, M. (1991) *Courage Above All: Sexual Assault Against Women with Disabilities.* Toronto: Disabled Women's Network Canada (DAWN).

Stinson, J. Christian, L. and Dotson, L. A. (2002) 'Overcoming barriers to the sexual expression of women with developmental disabilities.' *Research and Practice for Persons with Severe Disabilities, 27*, 1, 18–26.

Szollos, A. A. and McCabe, M. P. (1995) 'The sexuality of people with mild intellectual disability: Perceptions of clients and caregivers.' *Australia and New Zealand Journal of Developmental Disabilities, 20*, 3, 205–222.

The Roeher Institute (1988) *Vulnerable: Sexual Abuse and People with an Intellectual Handicap.* North York, ON: The Roeher Institute.

The Roeher Institute (1994) *Harm's Way: The Many Faces of Violence and Abuse Against People with Disabilities in Canada.* North York, ON: The Roeher Institute.

Thompson, D. (1994) 'Sexual experience and sexual identity for men with learning disabilities who have sex with men.' *Changes, 12*, 254–263.

Ticoll, M. (1994) *Violence and People with Disabilities: A Review of the Literature.* Family Violence Prevention Unit Health Canada. L'Institut Roeher Institute.

Ticoll, M. and Panitch, M. (1993) 'Opening the doors: Addressing the sexual abuse of women with an intellectual disability.' *Canadian Woman Studies, 13*, 2, 84–87.

Timmers, R. L., Du Charme, P. and Jacob, G. (1981) 'Sexual knowledge, attitudes and behavior of developmentally disabled adults living in a normalized apartment setting.' *Sexuality and Disability, 4*, 1, 27–39.

Traustadottir, R. (1990) 'Women, disability and caring.' *TASH Newsletter, 16*, 6–7.

Trudel, G. and Desjardins, G. (1992) 'Staff reactions towards the sexual behaviours of people living in institutional settings.' *Sexuality and Disability, 10*, 3, 173–188.

Tymchuk, A. J. and Feldman, M. A. (1991) 'Parents with mental retardation and their children: Review of research relevant to professional practice.' *Canadian Psychology/Psychologie Canadienne, 32*, 3, 486–496.

United Nations Enable (2002a) 'International norms and standards relating to disability, Part V rights of women with disabilities.' Retrieved from www.un.org/esa/socdev/enable/comp504.htm on January 13, 2008.

United Nations Enable (2002b) 'Compilation of international norms and standards relating to disability.' Retrieved from www.un.org/esa/socdev/enable/discom00.htm on May 14, 2007.

Van Hove, G. (2000) 'Mensen met een verstandelijke beperking: Van defecte zorgobjecten tot mensen met rechten. In E. De Belie., C. Ivens, J. Lesseliers and G. Van Hove (eds) *Seksueel Misbruik bij Personen met een Versstandelijke Handicap. Handicap Preventie en Hulpverlening.* Leuven/Leusden, Belgium: Uitgeverij Acco.

Walmsley, J. (1993) 'Women first: Lessons in participation.' *Critical Social Policy, 13*, 1, 6–99.

Ward, M. J. and Meyer, R. N. (1999) 'Self-determination for people with developmental disabilities and autism: Two self-advocates' perspectives.' *Focus on Autism and Other Developmental Disabilities, 14*, 3, 133–140.

Watson, S., Venema, T., Molloy, W. and Reich, M. (2002) 'Sexual rights and individuals who have a developmental disability.' In D. Griffiths, D. Richards, P. Fedoroff and S. L. Watson (eds) *Ethical Dilemmas: Sexuality and Developmental Disability.* Kingston, NY: NADD Press.

Whitehouse, M. A. and McCabe, M. P. (1997) 'Sex education programs for people with intellectual disability: How effective are they?' *Education and Training in Mental Retardation and Developmental Disabilities, 32*, 3, 229–240.

World Health Organization (WHO) (1975) *Education and Treatment in Human Sexuality: The Training of Health Professionals.* Technical Report Series Nr. 572. Geneva, Switzerland: WHO.

Withers, P., Ensum, I., Howarth, D., Krall, P. *et al.* (2001) 'A psychoeducational group for men with intellectual disabilities who have sex with men.' *Journal of Applied Research in Intellectual Disabilities, 14*, 4, 327–339.

Wolfe, P. S. (1997) 'The influence of personal values on issues of sexuality and disability.' *Sexuality and Disability, 15*, 2, 69–90.

Wolfensberger, W. (1972) *The Principle of Normalization in Human Services.* Toronto: National Institute on Mental Retardation.

Wolfensberger, W. (1983) 'Social role valorization: A proposed new term for the principle of normalization.' *Mental Retardation, 21*, 6, 234–239.

Yool, L., Langdon, P. E. and Garner, K. (2003) 'The attitudes of medium-secure unit staff toward the sexuality of adults with learning disabilities.' *Sexuality and Disability, 21*, 2, 137–150.

8

Right to Evidence-Based Treatment for Individuals with Developmental Disabilities: Issues of the Use of Therapeutic Punishment

Tricia Vause, Kaleigh Regehr, Maurice Feldman, Dorothy Griffiths and Frances Owen

INTRODUCTION

At a recent conference, in a panel discussion on 'Ethical Issues in Punishment', the first author observed an audience member raising her hand and asking the group of expert panel members the following question, 'Can punishment be avoided in a just world?' The first author's recollection of the situation was that a few panel members immediately shook their heads, and one member spoke up. In his response, he alluded to the fact that we encounter punishment in our everyday lives, and that it is, in fact, unavoidable. Speaking from the standpoint of a behaviour analyst, a *punisher* is 'an event that, when presented immediately following the behaviour, causes the behaviour to decrease in frequency' (Martin and Pear 2007, p.151). As an example, for a young infant or child, the immediate consequence of touching a hot stove or putting a finger too close to a candle flame teaches him or her to never engage in that behaviour again. As we grow up, we encounter stimuli in our environment that act as punishers, and in many instances, a stimulus that is a punisher for one individual may not be a punisher for another. For example, in a classroom, a student may raise his or her hand and provide an answer to a question. Let's suppose that the response from the classroom teacher is an immediate frown; this consequence would only be a punisher if the student became less likely to raise his/her hand in a similar situation in the future. For another student, if the teacher praises him/her for answering a question, and the student decreases answering questions, then in this case, praise also acted as a punisher.

Thus far, we have discussed some everyday experiences, and natural consequences that control our behaviour. However, let's consider the deliberate use of punishment, as a treatment strategy (which we will refer to as 'therapeutic punishment'), for individuals with severe behavioural challenges. Although there are many different definitions of what constitutes challenging behaviour, we will use the definition offered by the National Institutes of Health Consensus Panel (1991) that challenging behaviour consists of self-injury, aggression, and property destruction. Within the field of developmental disabilities, the use of therapeutic punishment is an issue that has raised many moral, ethical, and political issues. Further, we have seen many advances towards protecting the rights of individuals with developmental disabilities. Nevertheless, controversial issues still exist among researchers and practitioners pertaining to individuals' right to treatment and, more specifically, the inclusion of punishment procedures in a treatment program.

In this chapter, we will first provide a historical view on the use of punishment with individuals with developmental disabilities from the 1930s to the 1970s. Second, we will address the emergence, in the latter part of the 20th century, of established policies to protect individuals' rights, and emerging controversies among practitioners, researchers, and advocates concerning the use of aversive procedures. In a chapter written by Feldman (1990), the third author of this paper, he juxtaposes two positions: (i) the 'Right to Effective Treatment' position where advocates argue that clients should have the right to the most effective treatment, although it may not be the least intrusive; and (ii) the 'Freedom From Harm' position, in which advocates believe that the use of therapeutic punishment procedures is unjustifiable and unnecessary. The current perspectives of these two positions will be discussed.

Third, Feldman (1990) proposed a model in which he attempted to balance these two positions. A review of Feldman's model will be provided, in conjunction with the extent to which his recommendations, throughout the past 15 years, have been addressed. As part of this discussion, this chapter tracks the frequency and type of punishment procedures used with individuals with developmental disabilities (including autism) in research studies from 1985 through 2005, published in the state-of-the-art behavioural journal, the *Journal of Applied Behaviour Analysis* (JABA). Implications of this data (accompanied by other literature reviews) regarding individuals' right to treatment will be discussed.

PUNISHMENT IN THE EARLY YEARS (1930S TO 1970S)

1930s through 1950s

From the 1930s through the 1950s, only one research journal, the *American Journal of Mental Deficiency* (later renamed the *American Journal on Mental Retardation*) existed that was dedicated to research and treatment for individuals with developmental disabilities. During the latter part of this time period, several papers showed simple demonstrations of the effects of the application of behavioural principles (e.g. reinforcement, extinction, punishment) to produce behaviour change. For example, Allyon and Michael (1959) demonstrated, in a psychiatric institution, that social attention by staff members following the occurrence of appropriate social interaction among residents resulted in an increase in this behaviour; in contrast, withholding staff attention contingent upon delusional self-talk resulted in aberrant behaviour decreasing. However, studies manipulating environmental variables to reduce problem behaviour in persons with developmental disabilities were rare; from 1930 to 1959, most behaviour change studies evaluated (newly invented) psychotropic medications and tranquilizers such as Reserpine and Chlorpromazine. Craft (1959) noted several design and methodological limitations in these drug studies. Further, results on the use of tranquilizers indicated no significant improvement in problem behaviour in persons with developmental disabilities.

1960s and 1970s

In the 1960s, research expanded the range of treatments for decreasing problem behaviour, as well as increasing adaptive behaviours (e.g. daily living skills). During this time period, two relevant journals were established including *Behaviour Research and Therapy* in 1963, and *Journal of Applied Behaviour Analysis* (JABA) in 1968. Moreover, numerous aversive treatments were documented to be successful in decreasing problem behaviour (e.g. physical punishment, contingent electric shock, time-out, response-cost procedures; for a more detailed description of these procedures, see operational definitions in Appendix A). For example, in 1966, Marshall attempted to decrease soiling in an eight-year-old boy who lived in an institutionalized setting. This author described success using physical punishment which included 11 instances of slapping, contingent upon soiling, over a 30-day period. As another example, Burchard and Tyler (1965) used time-out (placement in a 'quiet room') to decrease challenging behaviour in a 13-year-old boy who was institutionalized.

During the 1960s and 1970s, punishment was used frequently in published studies on decreasing problem behaviour in institutionalized persons with developmental disabilities, although non-punitive methods were also utilized (e.g. extinction, positive reinforcement). Interestingly, no mention is made of the treatment of problem behaviours exhibited by persons with developmental disabilities in the 115 pages of 'Standards for State Residential Institutions for the Mentally Retarded' published in the *American Journal on Mental Deficiency* in 1964.

In the 1970s, we began to see the emergence of behaviour modification as a *formalized treatment approach*. Behaviour modification involves the systematic application of (primarily operant) learning principles to increase adaptive behaviour and decrease maladaptive behaviour, with the overall goal of improvement in quality of life (Martin and Pear 2007). It does not include electroconvulsive therapy, psychosurgery, or psychotropic drugs. The majority of behaviour modification studies with persons who had developmental disabilities focused on teaching adaptive skills (e.g. Bondy and Erickson 1976; Carr *et al.* 1978; Handleman 1979; Reid and Hurlbut 1977). In addition, behaviour modification was the most common nonmedical treatment to decrease problem behaviour (Birnbrauer 1976; Gardner 1971). Therapeutic punishment grew in prominence as an efficacious treatment for severe self-injury, such as headbanging, eye gouging, biting and slapping. Aversive treatments included physical restraint (e.g. Favell, McGimsey and Jones 1978), aromatic ammonia (e.g. Tanner and Zeiler 1975), and contingent electric shock (e.g. Linscheid and Cunningham 1977). For instance, Tanner and Zeiler (1975) used aromatic ammonia to treat self-slapping in a 20-year-old woman with autism. Prior to implementing ammonia, contingent electric shock had been successful in suppressing the slapping behaviour, but it reemerged upon removal of the shock stimulator. During the initial observation periods of this study, the participant was given psychotropic drugs, including chlorpromazine hydrochloride, which failed to reduce the self-slapping. An A-B-A-B withdrawal design was used to evaluate the effects of aromatic ammonia on self-slapping. The treatment consisted of 'a capsule of ammonia [being] crushed and thrust under the subject's nose when she slapped herself, and withdrawn when she stopped' (Tanner and Zeiler 1975, p.55). The withdrawal design indicated that ammonia was an effective punisher in eliminating self-injurious behaviour. Although positive reinforcement for appropriate behaviour often accompanied therapeutic punishment, as seen in the Tanner and Zeiler study, little attention was paid in these punishment studies to the motivation or function of behaviour, and the role of environmental stimuli in instigating or controlling behaviour. In the late 1970s, ethical standards of behaviour change programs emerged (American Association for the Advancement of Behavior Therapy 1977).

In summary, from the 1930s to the 1970s, numerous advances occurred within the field of behaviour modification including: (i) the emergence of a treatment technology for persons with developmental disabilities based on the principles of operant learning; (ii) increasing empirical validity for behaviour modification as a treatment for challenging behaviours; (iii) an increase in the number of journals and books that published these findings; and (iv) an emerging recognition for the need to develop and publish ethical standards in using behaviour modification techniques.

1980s and 1990s: reaction and controversy

The latter part of the 20th century led to many advances in the field of behaviour modification. First, there was an increased emphasis on functional assessment of problem behaviour and the importance of identifying its causes (Didden, Duker and Korzilius 1997). In 1982, a groundbreaking paper was published by Iwata *et al.* that introduced functional analysis methodology, and the systematic manipulation of variables in an attempt to identify the specific causes of problem behaviour. In the 1980s, numerous papers included a functional assessment of problem behaviours exhibited by individuals with developmental disabilities, and how these findings were used to inform (nonaversive) treatment. A meta-analysis conducted by Didden *et al.* (1997) that evaluated treatment effectiveness of 482 studies involving treating problem behaviour in individuals with an intellectual disability showed that treatments based in functional assessment were more effective than those that were not. Ellingson, Miltenberger and Long's (1999) review indicated that staff in agencies were making use of a range of functional assessment strategies.

One may ask, how does the development of functional assessment procedures tie into human rights, and, specifically, the right to evidence-based treatment? Before the 1980s, assessment typically was not tied into behavioural treatment. Therapeutic punishment was usually effective in reducing problem behaviour, so why not just use it? With the advent of functional assessment, many effective nonaversive interventions emerged, such as Functional Communication Training (FCT) wherein the person is taught a simple communicative response (e.g. ringing a bell) that is effective in obtaining the same reinforcer (e.g. caregiver attention) as the self-injurious behaviour (Carr and Durand 1985). Increasingly, researchers and practitioners advocated the least restrictive/intrusive model (Feldman 1990) – there were now 'alternatives to punishment' (LaVigna and Donnellan 1986). Some advocates went so far as to argue that with functional assessment and the nonpunitive interventions derived from them, punishment was no longer necessary, even for the treatment of severely challenging behaviour (LaVigna and Donnellan 1986). Of course, not everyone agreed (Van Houten *et al.* 1988); the field became polarized, and two opposing positions emerged: 'Right to Behavioural Treatment' and the 'Freedom From Harm,' as discussed by Feldman (1990).

INTRODUCTION TO THE TWO POSITIONS

'Right to Effective Treatment' position

In 1988, an article was published in *JABA* entitled 'The right to effective behavioral treatment' (Van Houten *et al.*). In this article, Van Houten and colleagues discussed several rights that recipients of behavioural treatment are entitled to, and the importance of honouring these rights to ensure the ethical application of behavioural treatment procedures. More specifically, Van Houten *et al.* focus on: (i) the *right to a therapeutic environment* whereby an individual is treated in a safe and humane manner, and the treatment provided is individualized to his or her needs; (ii) the *right to services that emphasize personal welfare*, such that, when considering a treatment program, both short- and long-term welfare are considered by involving the client and/or a substitute decision-maker and appropriate committees are consulted when treatments may involve potential risk; (iii) *right to a competent behaviour analyst* to ensure proper assessment, treatment, and follow-up, as well as treatment integrity on the part of the staff delivering the treatment; (iv) right to programs that attempt to alleviate problem behaviour, as well as *teach functional skills*; (v) *right to a behavioural assessment* in order to identify potential variables that are maintaining a behaviour, and ongoing evaluation of the behaviour through data collection in order to determine whether a particular treatment is beneficial; and, most controversially, (vi) *right to the least restrictive but most effective treatment*, whereby the benefits of implementing the treatment outweigh the potential risks.

Emphasis on right to 'most effective and least restrictive' treatment

Building on point (vi) in the previous section, proponents of the 'Right to Treatment Approach' argue that individuals have the right to the *least restrictive* as well as the *most effective* treatment available. To clarify further, as clinicians and researchers, we must ensure that the chosen treatment is safe for the individual, is likely to result in a clinically significant change, and an equally effective less restrictive intervention is not available. This approach to treatment is congruent with the medical model. Specifically, a continuum of empirically validated treatments is attempted, beginning with treatments that have been documented to be the safest, have the least number of side effects, and create the least amount of discomfort for the individual (Van Houten *et al.* 1988). Following this model, several studies have shown that nonaversive treatments (e.g. FCT) may not always be sufficient in reducing behaviour to levels that are clinically acceptable unless therapeutic punishment is added (Grace, Kahng and Fisher 1994; Lerman and Vorndran 2002).

To illustrate, Hagopian *et al.* (1998) examined the efficacy of FCT for treating challenging behaviour in 21 inpatient cases, with individuals ranging from 2 to 16 years of age. Across the 21 cases, using punishment procedures (including room/chair time-outs, basket holds, hands down, facial screen, and contingent demands) along with FCT resulted in at least a 90 per cent reduction in problem behaviour in all cases to which it was applied; inclusion of other behaviour analytic principles and procedures such as extinction, demand fading, and delay-to-reinforcement fading resulted in a lesser reduction in challenging behaviour. These authors demonstrated and advocated the need to publish both positive and negative findings concerning the implementation of various treatment components, in order to obtain a better understanding of the effectiveness of different treatment procedures for challenging behaviour.

Related to the findings of Hagopian *et al.* (1998), consider a study conducted by Grace *et al.* (1994) that involved an 11-year-old boy with a severe intellectual ability who engaged in aggression and destruction of property, as well as less severe behaviours (e.g. banging objects). A functional analysis indicated that the challenging behaviour was maintained by escape from demands. Out of a number of procedures, FCT (i.e. teaching the participant that he could take a break when signing 'finish') proved to be most effective; however, the challenging behaviour was still occurring at unacceptable rates (i.e. over 3.5 to 9 instances per minute). Adding verbal reprimands and a three-minute basket hold contingent on challenging behaviour resulted in reductions to near-zero levels. However, due to the wishes of school administrators, a condition was attempted where the less severe behaviour was initially ignored. In the absence of the aversive component for less severe behaviour, the treatment proved to be less effective and resulted in an increased use of intrusive procedures for both severe and less severe behaviours. When these results were shared with school administrators, an exception to the school policy was made, and the aversive procedure (i.e. basket hold and verbal reprimands) was added to existing procedures for both severe and less severe behaviours; near-zero levels of problem behaviour were maintained during follow-up. This case study demonstrates the use of the least intrusive, most effective approach as advocated by the Right to Treatment group. Note that an attempt to minimize the use of punishment for mild problems ironically resulted in an increase in the use of aversives.

Interestingly, in 1999, Pelios *et al.* conducted an extensive literature review (1963 through 1997) of a series of journals that contained a large number of published papers on the treatment of self-injurious behaviour and aggression in individuals with developmental disabilities and autism. In particular, these authors were interested in the use of reinforcement-based versus punishment-based procedures, with and without a functional analysis. Overall, results indicated an upward trend in the use of reinforcement-based procedures since the late 1980s, and when researchers conducted a functional analysis, there was an increased tendency to use reinforcement-based as opposed to punishment-based procedures. Also, they noted that, over the years, the proportion of articles using punishment procedures decreased.

However, consider other situations where functional analyses do not reveal the maintaining variables of the behaviour, where the variables cannot be controlled, or when competing reinforcers are not available. Further, consider an individual who, in the absence of a punishment procedure, is at risk of or engaging in serious physical self-harm. In these cases, it is argued that punishment procedures may also be needed (Dura 1991; Lerman and Vorndran 2002; Lerman *et al.* 1997). However, although punishment procedures have proven effective, the issue of practicality is often brought into question. As Lerman *et al.* (1997) point out, several studies have shown that participants often require rich schedules of punishment in order to suppress behaviour, and for some individuals, the thinning of reinforcement has been shown to result in an increase in challenging behaviour. Besides the challenge of successfully fading aspects of treatment, researchers acknowledge many unwanted effects of punishment such as emotional side effects and poor short-term as well as long-term generalization and maintenance (Foxx and Livesay 1984; Lerman and Vorndran 2002; Newsom, Favell and Rincover 1983). Furthermore, there may be a risk of desensitization to the use of punishment procedures on the part of those administering treatment (Turnbull *et al.* 1986). Given these unwanted side effects as well as others, it is suggested that continued work needs to be conducted on the use of nonaversive function based treatments, punishment procedures should be replaced with nonaversive treatment as quickly as possible, and detailed plans should be laid out regarding how to deal with potential side effects of punishment procedures (Feldman 1990; Lerman and Vorndran 2002).

'Freedom From Harm' position

Proponents of this position believe that antecedent-focused and reinforcement-based procedures are sufficient in treating challenging behaviour, and that punishment procedures are unnecessary (Carr *et al.* 1999, 2002; LaVigna and Donnellan 1986). Advocates of the Freedom From Harm position outlined several factors that they believe to have influenced certain researchers and practitioners that 'punishment is necessary' (Donnellan and LaVigna 1990, p.35). These factors include: (i) a predisposition to engage in punishment when an offence occurs; (ii) an individual's social learning history; and (iii) the overt clinical use and publication of punishment procedures. To emphasize a few key points concerning rights, Donnellan and LaVigna (1990) stated that focusing on the right to the 'least intrusive intervention' as discussed by the proponents of the other position (e.g. Van Houten *et al.* 1988) is inherently problematic. Specifically, they argue that the notion of attempting a least-to-most intrusive procedure to treat a challenging behaviour implies that 'the power is in the aversives' (p.41). Building on this argument and speaking of the notion of 'power', it is stated that because of the concern to protect the rights of the individual, certain practitioners learn how to use punishment procedures very thoroughly, but limited attention is dedicated to training in nonaversive procedures. Yet, controlled studies using nonaversive procedures have proven successful in treating very difficult problems (see review by Carr *et al.* 1999). Last, as emphasized earlier, Donnellan and LaVigna emphasize the need to publish treatment failures; they believe the failure to do so contributes to the notion that punishment is necessary. Publishing of positive and negative findings is a common thread across both positions; it is recognized that this is necessary in order to determine the efficacy and effectiveness of treatment.

Besides LaVigna and Donnellan (1986), in the 1980s, there were several other researchers (e.g. Guess *et al.* 1987; McGee, *et al.* 1987; Turnbull *et al.* 1986) as well as groups/organizations (e.g. American Association on Intellectual and Developmental Disabilities, Canadian Association for Community Living, The Association for Persons with Severe Handicaps) in favour of the use of nonaversive treatment procedures to deal with challenging behaviour exhibited by persons with disabilities. There was further development of this movement when *positive behaviour support* (PBS) gained momentum in the 1990s (Carr *et al.* 1999).

Emergence of positive behaviour support

As stated in a synthesis of research literature conducted by Carr *et al.* (1999), the goal of positive behaviour support (PBS) is to 'apply behavioural principles in the community in order to reduce problem behaviours and build appropriate behaviours that result in durable change and a rich lifestyle' (p.3). Similar to proponents of the 'Right to Effective Treatment' position, there is an emphasis on the need to conduct a thorough functional assessment in an attempt to identify maintaining variables of challenging behaviour (e.g. O'Neill *et al.* 1997). However, proponents of PBS assert that, instead of a reliance on 'reactive' procedures that are often aversive in nature, a strong emphasis should be placed in contextually based interventions which emphasize a focus on antecedent stimuli such as choice-making, teaching strategies, daily routines, as well as other variables that are both proximal and distal in nature. Also, it is emphasized that PBS explores variables that are unique to the individual, focuses on person-centred values, and attempts to show meaningful outcomes with the use of both comprehensive assessment techniques and multifaceted intervention strategies (Anderson and Freeman 2000). Specifically, besides the emphasis on function-based assessment, proactive strategies, and person-centred values, proponents of PBS (similar to many applied behaviour analysts) focus on parents taking an active role in assessment and treatment, social validity, ecological validity, a need for broad systemic change, generalization and maintenance of treatment effects, and improvements in overall quality of life. In recent years, we have seen the emergence of the *Journal of Positive Behaviour Interventions,* publication of various PBS textbooks (e.g. Bambara and Kern 2005; Carr *et al.* 1999; Crone and Horner 2003), an organization and annual conference, the development of a PBS technical assistance centre (funded by the US Government) and the rise in publications focusing on PBS. Given these accomplishments, Carr and Sidener (2002) asserted that proponents of PBS should be commended for their work in dissemination of the application of behaviour analytic principles and procedures in the treatment of challenging behaviour. Note that it is a common misconception that PBS researchers and practitioners will never use therapeutic punishment. Using the least restrictive/intrusive model, and basing treatment decisions on individual time series behavioural data, may lead to the recommendation that, in some cases, punishment is needed to reduce challenging behaviour significantly (Feldman *et al.* 2002). Often the aversive stimuli used are relatively mild and socially acceptable (e.g. brief hand restraint, removal of privileges), especially compared to the aversive consequences (e.g. contingent electric shock, overcorrection) used in the early behaviour modification literature.

Criticisms by nonproponents of PBS include the notion that use of nonaversive procedures may not always lead to better generalization and maintenance (Matson and Taras 1989). Also, Foxx (2005) asserted that studies claiming to focus on severe behaviours may not necessarily be that severe when examining the frequency (e.g. exhibiting less than two episodes of aggression per week) and/or quality (e.g. spitting, smearing saliva, and less than two episodes of aggression per week) of the behaviour. Also, he contends that what is considered 'aversive' is typically judged by proponents of the nonaversive movement; this may be indirectly connected to the undocumented use of aversive treatments that, at times, appears in published literature (Santarcangelo, Dyer and Luce 1987).

A FURTHER ANALYSIS OF BOTH POSITIONS AND INDIVIDUALS' RIGHT TO BEHAVIOURAL TREATMENT BY FELDMAN (1990)

Feldman (1990) proposed a model that attempted to strike a balance between 'Right to Effective Treatment' and 'Freedom From Harm.' He emphasizes that both positions 'garner moral, clinical, and scientific arguments in defense of their positions' (p.10). Further, he argues that it is not a matter of reinforcement (good) versus punishment (bad), but rather taking a closer look at the particular individual(s) being treated, the individual behaviour problem(s) at hand, what treatment components may work for an individual based on a functional assessment, as well as potential setting events for problem behaviour. It was acknowledged by Feldman that many practitioners, when working with individual clients, likely try to balance recommendations made by proponents of the two positions, and, undoubtedly, try to look at both the relative strengths and weaknesses of both models when designing a particular intervention. Therefore, in an attempt to balance both positions, Feldman's model maintained the emphasis of both positions on choosing the least restrictive/intrusive alternative, and the development of a program that utilizes nonaversive antecedent and consequent manipulations (e.g. stimulus control, differential reinforcement, extinction, and FCT; for formal definitions, see Martin and Pear 2007). Also, he acknowledges that, in the case of an individual for whom nonaversive strategies are not sufficient in reducing behaviour to acceptable levels, there may be a need to incorporate a punishment procedure. However, before doing so, there needs to be an appropriate ethical review of procedures by trained professionals, with appropriate consents, safeguards, and written procedures concerning variables mentioned earlier such as monitoring of side effects, how to deal with emotional responses of family members, strategies to aid in the generalization/maintenance of behaviour, and an emphasis on functional skill development.

Last, given the differing positions regarding use of punishment in treating challenging behaviour in individuals with developmental disabilities and autism, Feldman states that 'more research and development is needed in the areas of prevention, behavioural assessment, prognosis, diagnosis-treatment interactions, and positive-based interventions' (p.13). Also, there is a need to partial out what works best for certain individuals, for what types of behaviour problems, and results in the least number of side effects (Kazdin and Wilson 1978 as cited in Feldman 1990). To accomplish this, it was suggested that following alongside medical studies, methodologically sound randomized clinical trials (with sufficient power) need to be conducted.

Have the model and suggestions proposed by Feldman (1990) been implemented?

In order to address this question, we are going to draw on the results of our review of research studies (1985 through 2005) published in the *Journal of Applied Behaviour Analysis* (JABA) that provide information concerning the frequency and types of punishment procedures used to treat challenging behaviours of individuals with developmental disabilities and autism. A discussion follows that further reflects on Feldman's suggestions, as well as the many advances made in our field over the past 15 years. Future directions concerning research and practice will be discussed.

TRACKING OF THE FREQUENCY OF PUNISHMENT IN *JABA* FROM 1985 TO 2005

Rationale for selection of *JABA*

We chose to track the frequency of therapeutic punishment in JABA for several reasons. First, this journal is considered rigorous and cutting edge within the field of applied behaviour analysis. Second, even though other populations are represented, it focuses largely on the assessment and treatment of problem behaviour and skill development for individuals with developmental disabilities and autism. Third, *JABA* articles are invariably included in meta-analyses of treatments for persons with developmental disabilities (e.g. Didden *et al.* 2006). Last, it represents work published by researchers from both positions discussed above.

Hypotheses concerning data collection

Given the focus of many researchers in behaviour modification on stimulus control and antecedent manipulations (e.g. Pelios *et al.* 1999), we hypothesized that, over the 20 years of tracking, we would see a decrease in the use of punishment procedures when dealing with challenging behaviour exhibited by persons with developmental disabilities and autism. Also, concerning the use of therapeutic punishment, we hypothesized that there would be more emphasis on the use of less versus more restrictive procedures.

Method

Participants

Participants in reviewed studies were those individuals with a developmental disability (DD), a pervasive developmental disorder (PDD), or individuals with a dual diagnosis of DD and PDD.

Definition of challenging behaviour

Our definition of challenging behaviour will conform with the NIH Consensus Panel (1991) definition of destructive behaviour cited earlier in this chapter, which included self-injury, aggression, and property destruction.

Punishment treatments

See Appendix A for a list of treatment procedures and their respective operational definitions. These definitions were borrowed, with permission, from Feldman *et al.* (2004). They derived this list based on research team members' experience as well as relevant references.

Procedure

The second author (who has an M.A. in Child and Youth Studies, with a strong emphasis in Applied Behaviour Analysis and eight years of research and clinical experience working in individuals with developmental disabilities and autism) tracked the use of therapeutic punishment in *JABA* by randomly selecting two out of the four journals per year from 1985 to 2005, and reviewing all articles within selected journals. Additionally, all journals from 1985, 1992, and 2000 were reviewed in the beginning stages of data collection as the authors were deciding how to review the appropriate number of years and journals for an accurate representation of the type and frequency and punishment procedures. Specifically, we identified publications that included the use of punishment procedures, using the operational definitions specified in Appendix A. Note that we only included studies where punishment was used as an intervention; we did not include punishment procedures used as part of a functional assessment. Also, there were some studies that may have included instances of 'hidden punishment'; the textual information appeared to describe the use of a punishment procedure but it was not mentioned as part of the treatment package. Given the difficulty in confirming whether the authors did or did not use punishment, these observations were excluded.

Results

Refer to Figure 8.1 for the frequency of punishment procedures, using the operational definitions that are provided in Appendix A, that are documented in *JABA* articles from 1985 through 2005. The plotted linear line indicates a relative stability in the use of punishment procedures over the years, with an approximate mean of 3.95 (range = 0 to 10) punishment procedures implemented in any given year.

Figure 8.2 indicates the use of individual punishment procedures for each year over the targeted 20 years. As can be observed from the data, blocking and time-out were the most frequently used punishment procedures, with calculated frequencies over a 20-year time period of 24 and 20, respectively. Considerably more intrusive procedures such as electric shock and mechanical restraint were observed to have occurred on an infrequent basis, with frequencies of 9 and 1, respectively. Note that this number may be attenuated given the tracking of two out of four journals per year.

Discussion

As indicated from the data, our first hypothesis regarding a predicted decrease in the general use of punishment procedures was not confirmed; instead of an observed downward trend, we see stability in the use of punishment procedures published in *JABA* from 1985 to 2005. Our review also shows that seemingly less intrusive procedures (e.g. response blocking and time-out) were utilized to a greater extent than seemingly more intrusive procedures (e.g. contingent electric shock). It is important to point out, however, that the tracking in two out of four journals per year indicated that punishment procedures were used fairly infrequently, with an approximate mean of 3.95 punishment procedures documented in a given year.

Pelios *et al.* (1999) tracked published aversive (punishment-based) and nonaversive (reinforcement-based) treatments from 1963 through 1997 in JABA as well as five other journals that publish largely on the treatment of self-injury and aggressive behaviour. They found the proportion of articles reporting the use of punishment-based procedures decreased over that time period. Our review suggests that the frequency of punishment studies published may now be in a period of stability. However, the decline seen in Pelios *et al.* (1999) may be related to the punishment controversy of the late 1980s, when there was an increased emphasis on the use of functional assessment and nonpunitive interventions. More recently, however, it has been recognized that not all individuals show significant decreases in challenging behaviour when given functionally-based nonpunitive interventions alone, but do improve when punishment is added (e.g. Hagopian *et al.* 1998). This trend was predicted by Feldman (1990) who said that while preventative and nonaversive strategies should be used as much as possible, there may be individual cases where punishment procedures are needed.

Taking into account both literature reviews as well as reviews of a number of individual cases (e.g. Hagopian *et al.* 1998), it appears that Feldman's proposal of a 'balance' between the two differing viewpoints (i.e. Right to Effective Behavioural Treatment and Freedom From Harm) is occurring. As illustrated by various sources, since the late 1980s, there has been an increased interest in exploring and improving nonaversive function-based treatment for challenging behaviour, a tendency to attempt nonaversive treatments before aversive treatments (e.g. Hagopian *et al.* 1998; Pelios *et al.* 1999), a recognition that, in documented individual cases, punishment (in combination with nonaversive treatments) is superior to nonaversive treatment only (e.g. Hagopian *et al.* 1998; Hanley *et al.* 2005), and, as indicated in our literature review, when punishment procedures are used, there is an increased tendency to choose less versus more intrusive treatments.

As stated earlier, Feldman asserted that more research needs to be conducted on behavioural assessment techniques, prevention, use of nonaversive and aversive strategies, prognosis, and pretreatment variables such as type of diagnosis. Also, he argued that in order to explore what treatment(s) work best based on individual variables, between-group studies with sufficient power are needed. In response to Feldman's statements, the above findings indicate that we are making some headway in many of these areas using single-subject design methodology, but fall short regarding his latter suggestion of randomized clinical trials. Unfortunately, thus far, between-group studies designed to explore the above variables have not been attempted. Indeed, the most recent meta-analysis of behavioural treatments for persons with (mild) intellectual disabilities relied on an analysis of single-case experimental designs (Didden *et al.* 2006), presumably because of the dearth of between-group treatment evaluations. There continues to be a need for increased collaboration among researchers, and the establishment of multi-site studies to increase sample sizes. The absence of these studies may likely be a result of lack of funding, as well as ethical issues concerning assignment of individuals with severe challenging behaviours to control groups. However, Feldman (1990) pointed out that wait-list control groups may be defensible and feasible, when considering that most treatment centres are unable to treat individuals on an immediate basis (e.g. Feldman and Werner 2002).

With regard to clinical treatment, Axelrod (1990) emphasizes that if caregivers are not trained in ethical and effective techniques to deal with challenging behaviours, they may find alternative ways for dealing with the problem at hand. In a similar vein, Feldman *et al.* (2004) conducted a study involving 96 agencies across Ontario where they interviewed staff concerning their use of formal versus informal (undocumented) interventions in dealing with challenging behaviour in persons with developmental disabilities. They concluded that low levels of training, supervision, and accountability seen in the majority of interventions surveyed may place clients at increased risk of the use of ineffective and aversive interventions, as well as physical abuse. Recent meta-analyses have shown that programs based on functional assessment are more effective than those that are not, and the preponderance of behavioural treatment studies do not use punishment procedures (Didden *et al.* 1997, 2006). We need to continue to encourage the use of evidence-based nonpunitive interventions based on functional assessment. In addition, there still is a lack of research on predictors of success with different types of interventions. Such information would allow for faster identification and tailoring of treatments, to reduce the prolonged exposure of certain individuals to therapies that are likely to be ineffective for them. As discussed earlier, the publication of both positive and negative treatment findings, coupled with detailed descriptions of client and setting characteristics, would help both clinicians and researchers to sort out the types of treatment that may be best for individual clients.

The focus on setting characteristics has gained ascendancy with emergence of person-centred planning (see Chapter 4 of this book). In this context, questions have been raised about the relative effect of individualized planning on behavioural treatment plans. Person-centred planning involves developing a personally designed support or treatment plan that is based on learning about the life the person would like to live and developing a plan to work towards the achievement of that life (Kincaid and Fox 1992). Although many terms exist to describe similar individualized goal setting processes, such as personal futures planning (Mount and Zwernike 1988) and essential lifestyle planning (Smull and Burke Harrison 1992), the most common term used currently is person-centred planning. Kincaid and Fox (1992) suggest that the person-centred planning approaches, consistent with the self-determination and self-advocacy movement, emphasize empowerment, personal preferences and choice, and learning and growth. The emphasis of the person-centred approaches is not rehabilitation, but one of habilitation, which focuses on the building of strengths and competencies. Person-centred planning builds services and supports around the person rather than fitting the person into available services. In such a planning approach, the power is shifted from the professional services to the individual and his or her support circle. Kincaid and Fox (1992, p.44) suggest that 'person-centered planning offers a framework for achieving the essential elements of PBS...advocating for the marriage of PBS methods and person-centered planning'.

This chapter has provided a historical overview on the use of punishment and other behavioural procedures over the past 20 years. We have discussed advancements in functional assessment based interventions for treating challenging behaviour in persons with developmental disabilities and autism, and the rise of a more holistic approach to planning. Compared to the contentious climate of the 1980s and 1990s concerning the use of therapeutic punishment, currently the field appears to be in a relatively stable state. To the extent to which publications mirror clinical practice, for the most part, punishment procedures are rarely being used, as a nonpunitive intervention technology is proving effective in most cases in the context of an increasingly participatory and holistic planning approach. However, when these techniques are warranted in individual cases, mild, socially acceptable forms of punishment appear to augment the efficacy of the nonpunitive interventions. In closing, we return back to the question quoted at the beginning of the paper that was asked of a member on an expert panel discussing 'Ethical Issues in Punishment' – 'Can punishment be avoided in a just world?' As addressed above, the current answer appears to be 'not entirely', but it may be that with continued improvement in individualized nonaversive function-based treatment(s), it will be avoided to an even greater extent in the future.

REFERENCES

Allyon, T. and Michael, J. (1959) 'The psychiatric nurse as a behavioral engineer.' *Journal of the Experimental Analysis of Behaviour, 2*, 2, 323–334.

American Association for the Advancement of Behaviour Therapy (1997) *Ethical Issues for Human Services.* Printed in the Membership Directory of the Association.

Anderson, C. M. and Freeman, K. A. (2000) 'Positive behaviour support: Expanding the application of applied behaviour analysis.' *The Behavior Analyst, 23*, 1, 85–94.

Axelrod, S. (1990) 'Myths that (mis)guide our profession.' In A. C. Repp and N. N. Singh (eds) *Perspectives on the Use of Nonaversive and Aversive Interventions for Persons with Developmental Disabilities.* Pacific Grove, CA: Brooks/Cole Publishing.

Bambara, L. M. and Kern, L. (2005) *Individualized Supports for Students with Problem Behaviors: Designing Positive Behavior Plans.* New York, NY: Guilford Press.

Birnbrauer, J. S. (1976) 'Mental retardation.' In H. Leitenburg (ed.) *Handbook of Behaviour Modification and Behavior Therapy.* Englewood Cliffs, NJ: Prentice-Hall.

Bondy, A. and Erickson, M. T. (1976) 'Comparison of modeling and reinforcement procedures in increasing question-asking of mildly retarded children.' *Journal of Applied Behavior Analysis, 9*, 1, 108.

Burchard, J. and Tyler, V. Jr., (1965) 'The modification of delinquent behaviour through operant conditioning.' *Behavior Research and Therapy, 2*, 2–4, 245–250.

Carr, E. G., Binkoff, J. A., Kologinsky, E. and Eddy, M. (1978) 'Acquisition of sign language by autistic children. 1: Expressive labeling.' *Journal of Applied Behavior Analysis, 11*, 4, 489–501.

Carr, E. G., Dunlap, G., Horner, R. H., Koegel, R. L. *et al.* (2002) 'Positive behavior support: Evolution of an applied science.' *Journal of Positive Behavior Interventions, 4*, 1, 4.16, 20.

Carr, E. G. and Durand, V. M. (1985) 'Reducing behavior problems through functional communication training.' *Journal of Applied Behavior Analysis, 18*, 2, 111–126.

Carr, E. G., Horner, R. H., Turnbull, A. P., Marquis, J. G. *et al.* (1999) *Positive Behavior Support for People with Developmental Disabilities: A Research Synthesis.* Washington, DC: AAMR.

Carr, J. E. and Sidener, T. M. (2002) 'In response: On the relation between applied behavior analysis and positive behavior support.' *The Behavior Analyst, 25*, 1, 245–253.

Craft, M. (1959) 'Mental disorder in the defective: The use of tranquilizers.' *American Journal on Mental Deficiency, 64*, 1, 63–71.

Crone, D. A. and Horner, R. H. (2003) *Building Positive Behavior Support Systems in Schools: Functional Behavioral Assessment.* New York, NY: Guilford Press.

Didden, R., Duker, P. C. and Korzilius, H. (1997) 'Meta-analytic study on treatment effectiveness for problem behaviors with individuals who have mental retardation.' *American Journal on Mental Retardation, 10*, 4, 387–399.

Didden, R., Korzilius, H., van Oorsouw, W. and Sturmey, P. (2006) 'Behavioral treatment of challenging behaviours in individuals with mild mental retardation: Meta-analysis of single-subject research.' *American Journal on Mental Retardation, 111*, 4, 290–298.

Donnellan, A. M. and LaVigna, G. W. (1990) 'Myths about punishment.' In A. M. Donnellan and G. W. LaVigna (eds) *Perspectives on the Use of Nonaversive and Aversive Interventions for Persons with Developmental Disabilities.* Pacific Grove, CA: Syracuse Press.

Dura, J. R. (1991) 'Controlling extremely dangerous aggressive outbursts when functional analysis fails.' *Psychological Reports, 69*, 451–459.

Ellingson, S. A., Miltenberger, R. G. and Long, E. S. (1999) 'A survey of the use of functional assessment procedures in agencies serving individuals with developmental disabilities.' *Behavioral Interventions, 14*, 4, 187–198.

Favell, J. E., McGimsey, J. F. and Jones, M. L. (1978) 'The use of physical restraint in the treatment of self-injury and as positive reinforcement.' *Journal of Applied Behaviour Analysis, 1*, 2, 225–241.

Feldman, M. A. (1990) 'Balancing freedom from harm and right to treatment in persons with developmental disabilities.' In A. Repp and N. Singh (eds) *Current Perspectives in the Use of Nonaversive and Aversive Interventions with Developmentally Disabled Persons.* Sycamore, IL: Sycamore Press.

Feldman. M. A., Atkinson, L., Foti-Gervais, L. and Condillac, R. (2004) 'Formal versus informal interventions for challenging behavior in persons with intellectual disabilities.' *Journal of Intellectual Disability Research, 48*, 1, 60–68.

Feldman, M. A., Condillac, R. A., Tough, S., Hunt, S. and Griffiths, D. (2002) 'Effectiveness of community positive behavioral intervention for persons with developmental disabilities and severe behavior disorders.' *Behavior Therapy, 3*, 3, 377–398.

Feldman, M. A. and Werner, S. E. (2002) 'Collateral effects of behavioral parent training on families of children with developmental disabilities and severe behavior disorders.' *Behavioral Interventions, 17*, 1, 75–83.

Foxx, R. M. (2005) 'Severe aggressive and self-destructive behavior: The myth of the nonaversive treatment of severe behavior.' In J. W. Jacobson, R. M. Foxx and J. A. Mulick (eds) *Controversial Therapies for Developmental Disabilities: Fad, Fashion, and Science in Professional Practice.* Mahwah, NJ: Lawrence Erlbaum Associates.

Foxx, R. M. and Livesay, J. (1984) 'Maintenance of response suppression following overcorrection: A 10-year retrospective examination of eight cases.' *Analysis and Intervention in Developmental Disabilities, 4*, 1, 65–79.

Gardner, J. M. (1971) 'Behavior modification in mental institutions: A review of research and analysis of trends.' In R. O. Rubin and C. M. Franks (eds) *Advances in Behavior Therapy – Proceedings.* Osh Kosh, WI: Academic Press.

Grace, N. C., Kahng, S. and Fisher, W. W. (1994) 'Balancing social acceptability with treatment effectiveness of an intrusive procedure: A case report.' *Journal of Applied Behaviour Analysis, 27*, 1, 171–172.

Guess, D., Helmstetter, E., Turnbull, H. R. and Knowlton, S. (1987) *Use of Aversive Procedures with Persons Who Are Disabled: A Historical Review and Critical Analysis.* [Monograph] Seattle, WA: The Association for Persons with Severe Handicaps.

Hagopian, L. P., Fisher, W. W., Thibault Sullivan, M., Acquisto, J. and Leblanc, L. A. (1998) 'Effectiveness of functional communication training with and without extinction and punishment: A summary of 21 inpatient cases.' *Journal of Applied Behavior Analysis, 31*, 2, 211–235.

Handleman, J. S. (1979) 'Generalization by autistic-type children of verbal responses across settings.' *Journal of Applied Behaviour Analysis, 12*, 2, 273–282.

Hanley, G. P., Piazza, C. C., Fisher, W. W. and Maglieri, K. A. (2005) 'On the effectiveness of and preference for punishment and extinction components of function-based interventions.' *Journal of Applied Behavior Analysis, 38*, 1, 51–65.

Iwata, B. A., Dorsey, M. F., Slifer, K. J., Bauman, K. E. and Richman, G. S. (1982/1994) 'Toward a functional analysis of self-injury.' *Journal of Applied Behavior Analysis, 27*, 2, 197–209.

Kazdin, A. E. and Wilson, G. T. (1978) *Evaluation of Behavior Therapy: Issues, Evidence, and Research Strategies.* Cambridge, MA: Ballinger.

Kincaid, D. and Fox, L. (1992) 'Person-centered planning and PBS.' In S. Holburn and P. M. Vietze (eds) *Person-centered Planning: Research, Practice and Future Directions.* Baltimore, MD: Paul H. Brookes Publishing Co.

LaVigna, G. W. and Donnellan, A. M. (1986) *Alternatives to Punishment: Solving Behavior Problems with Nonaversive Strategies.* New York, NY: Irvington.

Lerman, D. C. and Vorndran, C. M. (2002) 'On the status of knowledge for using punishment: Implications for treating behavior disorders.' *Journal of Applied Behavior Analysis, 35*, 4, 431–464.

Lerman, D. C., Iwata, B. A., Shore, B. A. and DeLeon, I. G. (1997) 'Effects of intermittent punishment on self-injurious behavior: An evaluation of schedule thinning.' *Journal of Applied Behavior Analysis, 30*, 2, 187–201.

Linscheid, T. R. and Cunningham, C. E. (1977) 'A controlled demonstration of the effectiveness of electric shock in the elimination of chronic infant rumination.' *Journal of Applied Behavior Analysis, 10*, 3, 500.

Marshall, H. H. (1966) 'The effect of punishment on children: A review of the literature and a suggested hypothesis.' *The Journal of Genetic Psychology, 106*, 23–33.

Martin, G. L. and Pear, J. J. (2007) *Behavior Modification: What It Is and How to Do It* (8th edn). Upper Saddle River, NJ: Prentice Hall.

Matson, J. L. and Taras, M. E. (1989) 'A 20 year review of punishment and alternative methods to treat problem behaviors in developmentally delayed persons.' *Research in Developmental Disabilities, 10*, 1, 85–104.

Mount, B. and Zwernik, K. (1988) *It's Never Too Late: A Booklet About Personal Futures Planning.* (Publication No. 421–88–109.) St. Paul, MN: Metropolitan Council.

McGee, J. J., Menolascino, F. J., Hobbs, D. C. and Menousek, P. E. (1987) *Gentle Teaching: A Nonaversive Approach to Helping Persons with Mental Retardation.* New York: Human Sciences Press.

National Institutes of Health (NIH) Consensus Panel (1991) *Consensus Development Conference Statement on Treatment of Destructive Behaviors in Persons with Developmental Disabilities.* Bethesda, MD: NIH.

Newsom, C., Favell, J. E. and Rincover, A. (1983) 'The multiple effects of punishment.' In J. Apsche and S. Axelrod (eds) *Punishment: Its Effects on Human Behavior.* New York: Plenum Press.

O'Neill, R. E., Horner, R. H., Albin, R. W., Sprague, J. R., Storey, K. and Newton, J. S. (1997) *Functional Assessment and Program Development for Problem Behavior: A Practical Handbook* (2nd edn). Pacific Grove, CA: Brooks/Cole Publishing Company.

Pelios, L., Morren, J., Tesch, D. and Axelrod, S. (1999) 'The impact of functional analysis methodology on treatment choice for self-injurious and aggressive behavior.' *Journal of Applied Behavior Analysis, 32*, 2, 185–195.

Reid, D. H. and Hurlbut, B. (1977) 'Teaching nonvocal communication skills to multihandicapped retarded adults.' *Journal of Applied Behavior Analysis, 10*, 4, 591–603.

Santarcangelo, S., Dyer, K. and Luce, S. (1987) 'Generalized reduction in disruptive behavior in unsupervised settings through specific toy play.' *Journal of the Association of Persons with Severe Handicaps, 12*, 38–44.

Smull, M. E. and Burke Harrison, S. (1992) *Supporting People with Severe Reputations in the Community.* Alexandria, VA: National Association of State Mental Retardation Programme Directors.

Tanner, B. A. and Zeiler, M. (1975) 'Punishment of self-injurious behavior using aromatic ammonia as the aversive stimulus.' *Journal of Applied Behavior Analysis, 8*, 1, 53–57.

Turnbull, H. R., Guess, D., Backus, L., Barber, P. A. *et al.* (1986) 'A model for analyzing the moral aspects of special education and behavioral interventions: The moral aspects of aversive procedures.' In P. R. Dokecki and R. M. Zaner (eds) *Ethics of Dealing with Persons with Severe Handicaps.* Baltimore, MD: Paul Brookes Publishing Co.

Van Houten, R., Axelrod, S., Bailey, J. S., Favell, J. E. *et al.* (1988) 'The right to effective behavioral treatment.' *Journal of Applied Behavior Analysis, 21*, 4, 381–384.

APPENDIX A

Operational definitions of punishment procedures from Feldman *et al.* (2004)

1. Contingent electric shock: is a punishment procedure in which an aversive electrical stimulus is briefly applied (e.g. to the bare skin of the leg or forearm for a one-second duration) immediately following the occurrence of a pre-defined response, with the goal of decreasing the future probability of that response.

2. Time-out: includes both confinement and non-confinement time-out:

    (a) Non-confinement time-out: is any procedure used to withhold reinforcement from an individual for a brief and limited period of time and does involve confinement in a lock area or in a room with the door closed.

    (b) Confinement time-out: is a procedure whereby the individual is placed briefly in an enclosed area that is devoid of reinforcing stimuli and from which escape is not permitted.

3. Blocking: the use of the arms of upper body or soft, flexible objects to interrupt a response.

4. Physical restraint: is any physical manipulation of a client using strength, weight, or any combination of these and/or techniques that are designed to immobilize an individual in a crisis situation.

5. Contingent exercise: is the repeated practice of physical activities or exercises contingent on the occurrence of a targeted maladaptive behaviour.

6. Mechanical restraint: is any device or equipment which reduces freedom of movement or exposure to stimulation (e.g. restraint jackets, straps, nets, mitts, helmet, blindfolds).

7. Contingent restraint: is any procedure by which an individual's motor activity is reduced contingent upon the occurrence of a targeted maladaptive behaviour.

8. Response cost: is a procedure in which the individual or group loses a positive reinforcer contingent upon a specified behaviour.

9. Overcorrection: is a procedure in which the individual is required to overcorrect the environmental effects of his/her misbehaviour and/or to practise appropriate forms of behaviour in those situations in which the misbehaviour commonly occurs.

10. Positive practice: is a procedure in which the individual is required to repeatedly practice an appropriate alternative response to the maladaptive behaviour.

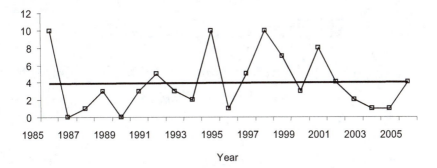

Figure 8.1 Frequency of all punishment procedures used in JABA treatment studies from 1985 through 2005.

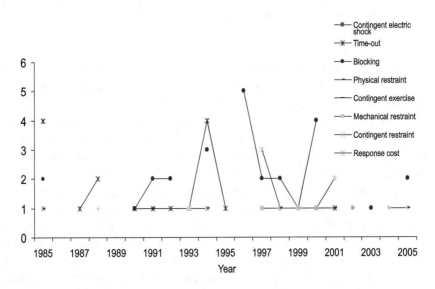

Figure 8.2 Frequency of individual punishment procedures used in JABA treatment studies from 1985 through 2005.

9

Rights and Education

Christine Y. Tardif-Williams, Marion Trent-Kratz
and Krystine Donato

Despite the barriers I have faced, being part of an inclusive educational environment has allowed me to achieve my academic goals. It is my hope that future generations of students with disabilities will have the same inclusive educational opportunities, but will encounter fewer barriers.

(Krystine Donato, 2007)

A wealth of research and literature has focused on education for persons with intellectual disabilities, and progress has been made both ideologically and in the implementation of special educational services for these persons. Nevertheless, persons with intellectual disabilities continue to be denied educational opportunities equal to those of their peers without intellectual disabilities. This chapter will begin by reviewing historical and current perspectives in theory and practice associated with education for persons with intellectual disabilities. As outlined in various legislations and charters, educational access and inclusion is a basic right for persons with intellectual disabilities and in this chapter the extant empirical data that highlights the academic, social and emotional benefits of more inclusive educational settings for these persons is briefly reviewed. Consideration is then given to some of the actual and perceived challenges that continue to be associated with the successful implementation of more inclusive educational practices within both North American and international contexts. In this chapter the global fragmentation that exists in the way that inclusive education is currently theorized and practised is also highlighted and suggestions for future research in the field of inclusive education are offered. In conclusion, it is suggested that a *social philosophy of interdependence* that fosters community collaboration and reciprocity by educating administrators, teachers, caregivers and all persons about the educational rights of persons with disabilities is essential in resolving some of the challenges often associated with inclusive education (Anderson 2006; Bach 2002; Frazee 2003; Sapon-Shevin 2003). This latter approach can go a long way toward the goal of achieving synchrony in the field of inclusive education theory and practice.

HISTORICAL AND CURRENT PERSPECTIVES IN SPECIAL EDUCATION THEORY AND PRACTICE FOR PERSONS WITH INTELLECTUAL DISABILITIES

The controversy over the degree to which special education placement has an impact on the academic, social and emotional adjustment of persons with disabilities remains unresolved, despite 30 years of legislation and practice supporting more inclusive education. Concern centres specifically on the most appropriate placement setting in which to provide special education to persons with disabilities (Chesley and Calaluce 1997; Freeman and Alkin 2000; Fuchs and Fuchs 1994; Gartner and Lipsky 1987; Kauffman 1993; Wang, Reynolds and Walberg 1994; Williamson *et al.* 2006). This latter concern is intensified as an estimated 300 million persons worldwide have disabilities, one third of which are children and youth (United Nations Educational, Scientific and Cultural Organization, UNESCO 2007). Also, the number of young people receiving special education services continues to increase worldwide. In Canada, for example, 15.5 per cent of the school-age population was classified as exceptional in 1983, and within Ontario (the highest populated Canadian province) the percentage of young people receiving special education increased from 6.5 per cent in 1986 to 12.8 per cent in 2002 (Weber and Bennett 2004). Increases in the numbers of persons receiving special education services likely result from higher survival rates at birth, improved identification procedures, and the expansion of special education services in areas where such services were unavailable (Weber and Bennett 2004).

As early as 30 years ago, special education for persons with disabilities within North America (and around most of the world) was characterized by a *social philosophy of difference*; these persons were thought to differ from other members of the community in almost every respect. Accordingly, persons with disabilities were educated mainly in institutional settings (e.g. residential or training schools) that were separated from the general educational system (Weber and Bennett 2004; Winzer 2005), and their access to an inclusive education was denied and/or severely limited. The eugenics movement, a popular philosophy among intellectuals during the first part of the 20th century, resulted in the segregation and total social isolation of persons with disabilities, as followers of the movement sought to protect society from *genetic contamination* and argued that these persons should be protected in institutions (Galton 1869; Sobsey 1994; Stratford 1991; Weber and Bennett 2004). The eugenics movement ended in the early

1940s when an estimated 300,000 people with various disabilities were involuntarily euthanized in Nazi Germany (Wolfensberger 1984).

Concern for the rights of all persons grew rapidly during the 1960s and this fuelled both North American and international governments to protect those rights. During this time, special education for persons with disabilities was characterized by a *social philosophy of normalization*, whereby it was argued that persons with disabilities should be viewed more in terms of the characteristics on which they are similar to, versus different from, others (Weber and Bennett 2004). The main goal of the normalization movement was to promote full integration of all persons with disabilities into the mainstream of everyday life (Wolfensberger 1972). At the local, national, and international levels, the growth of the Community Living movement represented a step towards deinstitutionalization and the integration of persons with disabilities into as many aspects of the *mainstream of normal* life as possible. Similarly, the emergence of self-advocacy groups, such as People First, highlighted the rights of persons with disabilities (Radford and Park 1999; Sobsey 1994; Wolfensberger 1972). The *social philosophy of normalization* was an important precursor to the inclusion movement in both the United Kingdom and North America, and was accompanied by legislation that changed the face of special education services for persons with disabilities.

For example, in 1975 the Education for All Handicapped Children Act (P.L. 94–142), which legislated certain basic educational rights for all children, was passed in the United States. The Education for All Handicapped Children Act of 1975 was further clarified through the Individuals with Disabilities Education Act (IDEA) passed in 1990, and renewed in 1997 and 2004, which required that all children be given *free and appropriate* educational opportunities in the *least restrictive environment* (LRE) (see Epps and Tindall 1987). Prior to P.L. 94–142 the majority of persons with disabilities received their education in specialized settings such as self-contained classrooms. In the United Kingdom, the 1978 Warnock Report, followed by the 1981 Education Act, introduced the idea of *special educational needs (SEN)* assessments and a more inclusive philosophy of education (Frederickson and Cline 2002). Today, in the United Kingdom, when a child or young adult is experiencing significant difficulty with learning, due to a physical, sensory, communication, cognitive or behavioural difficulty a statutory assessment is conducted by a Local Authority and a statement of SEN is issued. The goal of SEN statements is to specify the resources that are required to help a child or young person succeed educationally within his/her mainstream school setting. In Canada, the provision of special education services has tended to follow the model adopted by the United States (Winzer 2005). Today, the Education Act of each Canadian province and territory ensures that all learners receive a free and appropriate education. However, there is still much variation in how this latter service is delivered across Canada, since provincial policy and individual school districts ultimately guide decisions about inclusive practices within the classroom.

Discontent soon followed with the mainstreaming approach to the delivery of special education services within North American schools, as some people believed that the movement toward *normalization* fell short of its aim and an increasing number of caregivers, educators and policymakers questioned the appropriateness of educating persons with disabilities in settings separate from the general education classroom (see, for a review, Fuchs and Fuchs 1994; Kauffman 1993). While the original impetus for the mainstreaming movement was to ensure equal access for all persons regardless of disability, it was often the case that, without the full supports for ensuring the success of inclusive education, persons with disabilities were required to *fit into the educational system*. In this way, many schools hosted two parallel groups of persons, a regular group and a group who had disabilities trying to make their way into the regular classroom ('Exceptional students were *in* the neighbourhood school but not really *of* it', Weber and Bennett 2004, p.14).

Around this time, general discontent spurred two separate education initiatives: the Regular Education Initiative (REI) and the Inclusive Schools Movement (ISM). Both initiatives suggested that, whenever possible, persons with disabilities should be integrated within the general education classroom. The REI, which emerged in the mid-1980s, focused on persons with mild to moderate disabilities and recommended placement of these persons in the least restrictive environment (Fuchs and Fuchs 1994; Gartner and Lipsky 1987; Stainback and Stainback 1992). The REI does not advocate an end to special education altogether. Rather, proponents of the REI question whether full inclusion in the general education classroom is always the most appropriate placement for all persons with disabilities, as individualized instruction does not always occur or may not always be feasible (Baker and Zigmond 1990; McIntosh *et al.* 1993). Accordingly, the initiative highlights the importance of maintaining a continuum of educational settings for persons with disabilities (e.g. resource withdrawal, in-class support, self-contained classrooms), as it is argued that the individual instructional and social needs of each person must be considered first (e.g. Kauffman 1993; Vaughn and Schumm 1995). Conversely, the ISM (an offshoot of the REI) represents a more radical perspective that focuses on students with severe disabilities and calls for the inclusion of all persons with disabilities (Fuchs and Fuchs 1994; Gartner and Lipsky 1987; Stainback and Stainback 1992; Wang *et al.* 1994). This initiative clearly advocates the elimination of the entire continuum of special educational services (e.g. resource rooms, self-contained special education classes). Moreover, in contrast with the REI, the ISM places greater emphasis on the social, versus the academic, benefits thought to be associated with full inclusion in the regular education classroom (see, for a review, Gartner and Lipsky 1989; Stainback and Stainback 1996).

It is clear that advocacy for inclusive education has firm philosophical foundations and is based on a critical analysis of the role of segregationist approaches to special education and on issues such as equity, justice, and cohesion among community members; inclusive education is considered as morally superior and as a basic human right. As such, for many proponents of inclusive education, the efficacy question about the influence of integration to promote academic, social, and emotional gains holds less value, since the fundamental concern is that inclusive education is a basic right for all persons with disabilities (Kavale and Forness 1999; Nakken and Pijl 2002). However, caution should be exercised in adopting a radical stance toward inclusive education as outlined by the ISM because it might not be in the *best interests* of most persons to eliminate the continuum of special education services in favour of full inclusion given the many practical challenges that continue to characterize the successful realization of inclusive education (as discussed later).

Rather, it is important to consider carefully how inclusionary practices sometimes work to provide persons with equal opportunities that are associated with unsuccessful inclusive experiences for persons with disabilities (Bach 2002; Culham and Nind 2003; Sapon-Shevin 2003; Weber and Bennett 2004). Equality of opportunity is based on the idea that everyone will be provided the same experiences, and this in turn can work to support homogeny rather than diversity (Anderson 2006; Bach 2002). Social justice should be about doing what is fair so that everyone is provided what he or she needs to be successful (Anderson 2006; Bach 2002). Classroom interdependence and fairness work to support diversity, while simultaneously encouraging all persons to develop an understanding of the social harm caused by oppression and discrimination (Sapon-Shevin 2003). Practically, this latter approach translates into persons (with disabilities) who are engaged in the classroom curriculum in alternative ways, rather than striving to meet some normative or standard outcome (Kluth, Villa and Thousand 2001). A *social philosophy of interdependence* is a necessary precursor to effecting real systemic social and institutional change which eliminates systemic barriers for persons with intellectual disabilities, as advocated by adherents of the social model of disability (Corker 2000; Hahn 1988; Jung 2002).

EDUCATIONAL ACCESS AND INCLUSION AS A BASIC RIGHT OF PERSONS WITH INTELLECTUAL DISABILITIES

The meaning of social inclusion has evolved to refer to the rights of all persons to be fully included within a community. Hence, social inclusion is not only about persons' intellectual and developmental disabilities, but refers to the deeper moral imperative that all members of a community must embrace to ensure that each of its members experiences a sense of community belonging and acceptance (Bach 2002; Blanchet 1999; Department of Justice Canada 2006; Frazee 2003; Poirier and Goguen 1986; Sapon-Shevin 2003; Thomas and Wolfensberger 1999). Inclusive education is both a philosophy and a practice (Winzer 2005). From a philosophical standpoint, it represents a conceptual shift in the way that persons with disabilities are perceived and in the way that members of their community value their educational rights. Practically, inclusive education necessitates the restructuring and transformation of classrooms. According to UNESCO (2003, p.7), 'Rather than being a marginal theme on how some learners can be integrated in the mainstream education, inclusive education is an approach that looks into how to transform education systems in order to respond to the diversity of learners.'

Advancements in rights for persons with disabilities have been a major catalyst behind the push towards educational access and inclusion as the socially just response (Weber and Bennett 2004; United Nations Convention on the Rights of Children 1989; United Nations Convention on the Rights of Persons with Disabilities 2006; United Nations Declaration on the Rights of Mentally Retarded Persons 1971). Legislation and charters that affirm the educational rights of persons within countries, such as Canada, the United States, and Britain, serve to protect and support the importance of establishing and maintaining a sense of community belonging for all members, and they have provided a framework for inclusion that ensures no person experiences oppression (Sapon-Shevin 2003). The United Nations Declaration on the Rights of Disabled Persons (DRDP 1975), the United Nations Convention on the Rights of Children (UNCRC Convention on the Rights of Children 1989), and the United Nations Convention on the Rights of Persons with Disabilities (UNCRPD Convention on the Rights of Persons with Disabilities 2006) all affirm the right to education for children, youth, and adults with disabilities. The DRDP, made on December 9, 1975, represents a framework that can be used to guide the formation of international and domestic law, and consists of 13 clauses that broadly promote the rights of persons with disabilities. Clause six asserts that:

> Disabled persons have the right to medical, psychological and functional treatment, including prosthetic and orthetic appliances, to medical and social rehabilitation, education, vocational training and rehabilitation, aid, counselling, placement services and other services which will enable them to develop their capabilities and skills to the maximum and will hasten the processes of their social integration or reintegration. (Para. 13)

Article 28 of the UNCRC recognizes the right of all children to receive basic education and Article 29 highlights the objectives of this education, including the development of the child's personality, talents and mental and physical abilities to their fullest, and the preparation of the child for responsible life in a free society.

In addition, Article 24 (sections 1 and 2) of the UNCRPD (2006) further recognizes the special needs and care of persons with disabilities, including educational access and inclusion:

> States Parties recognize the right of persons with disabilities to education. With a view to realizing this right without discrimination and on the basis of equal opportunity, States Parties shall ensure an inclusive education system at all levels (section 1) (p.16)

Further, section 2 states that:

> In realizing this right, States Parties shall ensure that:
>
> (a) Persons with disabilities are not excluded from the general education system on the basis of disability, and that children with disabilities are not excluded from free and compulsory primary education, or from secondary education, on the basis of disability;
>
> (b) Persons with disabilities can access an inclusive, quality and free primary education and secondary education on an equal basis with others in the communities in which they live;
>
> (c) Reasonable accommodation of the individual's requirements is provided;
>
> (d) Persons with disabilities receive the support required, within the general education system, to facilitate their effective education;
>
> (e) Effective individualized support measures are provided in environments that maximize academic and social development, consistent with the goal of full inclusion. (p.17)

Dividing persons with intellectual disabilities as a group to be educated in segregated environments can be regarded as a form of exclusion and discrimination as they are denied the social and emotional developmental opportunities that are afforded other persons who do not have intellectual disabilities (Anderson 2006; Frazee 2003; Hertzman 2002). Further, the act of segregating persons with intellectual disabilities implicitly devalues their worth through the process of identification and placement, which works to establish a hierarchy of intelligence which does not recognize the common human value of all persons (Anderson 2006; Frazee 2003). In fact, educators are creating *artificial classrooms* when group membership is excluded to only those persons who do not have intellectual disabilities (Anderson 2006, p.50). It is socially unjust to all persons when they are not provided the benefits of an education within a context that can better prepare them for the diversity that exists in our increasingly global communities (Anderson 2006; Bach 2002; Frazee 2003; Sapon-Shevin 2003). All persons are at risk of being marginalized and isolated when exclusion is perceived as a reasonable and acceptable practice, rather than as a diametrically opposing force against the democratic process and basic rights to which all community members are entitled (Bach 2002; Frazee 2003; Sapon-Shevin 2003). Inclusion offers all persons their legal entitlement to equal citizenry (Frazee 2003).

The social justice movement has come a long way toward eliminating barriers in accessing inclusive education for persons with intellectual disabilities (Anderson 2006; Bach 2002; Frazee 2003). Meaningful inclusion, however, is not only about accessing physical space in the regular classroom; rather it is also a way of being that fosters a sense of community belonging and acceptance (Anderson 2006; Frazee 2003). Anderson (2006) proposes that social justice should be about the human need for interdependence rather than about equality of opportunities. Community interdependence fosters a sense of belonging and highlights that 'what we do affects the lives of others and the earth itself' (Black 1996, p.47). Community interdependence would provide a cultural shift away from the concepts of independence and self-reliance which typify Western culture (Anderson 2006), in favour of the belief that all members are essential to the community. By fostering interdependence and highlighting the value of relationships based on reciprocity, all persons within a community are recognized as having needs that require support; in this way, persons with intellectual disabilities are perceived as *part of*, rather than as disabled and *dependent upon*, the community.

Despite much legislative advancement, social justice often fails to support inclusive education for persons with disabilities. For instance, wording exists within both the UNCRC and the UNCRPD that provides those in authority or caregivers with the power to decide what is in a child's *best interest*, which in turn can create situations where what is in the *best interest* of the child might infringe upon his/her rights (Grover 2002; UNCRC 1989; UNCRPD 2006). An example is the case of Eaton vs. the Brant County Board of Education, Ontario, Canada (see Grover 2002). The Supreme Court of Canada decided that it would be in Emily's *best interest* to be placed in a segregated classroom, away from her peers with whom she had spent the three previous years. At the time, Emily was 12 years old, used a wheelchair, communicated using technological devices, and required visual supports. While it was Emily's right to receive an education alongside her peers, the Board of Education and the Supreme Court of Canada circumvented this right in consideration of her special needs. In this case, the Board of Education and the Supreme Court of Canada made the grievous mistake of assuming that Emily's disabilities would make her *dependent upon, rather than an equal part of,* her classroom; thus also failing to recognize how this decision would contribute to the creation of an *artificial* classroom community that could not optimally prepare Emily and her peers for the diversity they will encounter in the *real world* (Anderson 2006; Bach 2002; Frazee 2003; Sapon-Shevin 2003).

ACADEMIC, SOCIAL AND EMOTIONAL BENEFITS OF MORE INCLUSIVE EDUCATIONAL PRACTICES FOR PERSONS WITH INTELLECTUAL DISABILITIES

Proponents of full inclusion argue that persons with disabilities can benefit academically, socially, and emotionally (e.g. feel less stigmatized, be better liked and accepted, have more friends, and positive self-perceptions) from more inclusive education placements because of the opportunities to make friends with persons without disabilities (see, for a review, Gartner and Lipsky 1989; Leondari 1993; Stainback and Stainback 1996). Proponents of inclusion have also noted that instruction in more inclusive contexts can help foster equity in achievement levels among all learners (Cohen *et al.* 1998; Yell and Shriner 1997). Finally, proponents of inclusion have pointed out that inclusive education has many potential benefits not only for persons with disabilities, but also for their peers who do not have disabilities by providing opportunities for extended contact and by creating more positive attitudes towards persons with intellectual disabilities (Allan 1997; Copeland *et al.* 2004; Fisher 1999; Helmstetter, Peck and Giangreco 1994; Kishi and Meyer 1994; McDonnell *et al.* 2003; Peck, Donaldson and Pezzoli 1990; Rillotta and Nettlebeck 2007; Roeyers 1996; Shevlin and Mona O'Moore 2000).

More importantly, perhaps, proponents of inclusion have argued that it is essential that students with disabilities be given opportunities to interact with students without disabilities in regular education settings, if educators are to successfully prepare all children and youth, regardless of disability, for the *real world* in which they will live (O'Neill 1996). The regular education classroom in which the child with disabilities is integrated is said to build a sense of classroom community and interdependence, and to provide a frame of reference for more normative and successful friendships and interactions with a heterogeneous group of peers. In a classroom where a sense of community and interdependence is fostered, the actions of each community member have a direct and meaningful impact on the experiences of others within the community. Inclusive education should be offered to all learners regardless of disability; as all learners have a right to receive an education that will best prepare them to confidently and successfully navigate the real, rather than artificial, social and interdependent contexts in which they will live (Anderson 2006; Bach 2002; Frazee 2003; Sapon-Shevin 2003).

Efficacy of inclusive education for children and youth with intellectual disabilities

Unfortunately, disagreement and debate continues among parents, educators, researchers, and policymakers regarding the most appropriate educational placement setting for persons with intellectual disabilities (Chesley and Calaluce 1997; Fuchs and Fuchs 1994; Gartner and Lipsky 1987; Kauffman 1993). This debate continues despite the recognition of inclusive education as a basic right for all learners and despite research findings highlighting the academic (e.g. higher achievement levels), social (e.g. sense of belonging and richness of friendship) and emotional (e.g. lower levels of loneliness and depression) benefits of this type of education for all learners (Baker, Wang and Walberg 1995; Carlberg and Kavale 1980; Fisher and Meyer 2002; Frazee 2003; McDonnell *et al.* 2003; Peetsma *et al.* 2001; Stainback and Stainback 1996; Wang and Baker 1985–1986; Wiener and Tardif 2004). On this latter point, some researchers have noted that the observed academic and social benefits of inclusive education do not appear to hold for all learners, regardless of type of disability (e.g. specific learning versus intellectual disabilities), and that the research findings in this regard are at best equivocal (see Carlberg and Kavale 1980; Freeman and Alkin 2000; Kavale and Forness 1999; Klingner *et al.* 1998; Nakken and Pijl 2002; Wang and Baker 1985–1986; Zigmond and Baker 1995). Therefore, the critical question remains: do persons with intellectual disabilities fare better when placed within more inclusive versus special educational placements? Indeed, the data in favour of the academic and social benefits of inclusive education are fairly robust, and arguably most pronounced, when considering persons with intellectual disabilities. For example, in an early meta-analysis (Carlberg and Kavale 1980), including 50 studies with multiple outcome measures (i.e. achievement, behaviour, social), learners who had been identified as having intellectual, versus specific learning or behavioural/emotional, disabilities were the group most disadvantaged by placement within a special versus regular classroom. Similarly, in another meta-analysis in which most of the sample (53%) was identified as having an intellectual disability (Wang and Baker 1985–1986), mainstreamed students were found to make greater gains on achievement and self-concept measures as compared with their counterparts in self-contained settings.

In a more recent comprehensive review of the research, Freeman and Alkin (2000) concluded that more inclusive educational placements yield positive academic and social benefits for children and youth with mild intellectual disabilities. Academic gains were found when children with mild intellectual disabilities were more fully integrated into the general education classroom (this positive finding did not apply to children and youth who had moderate or severe intellectual disabilities). Further, children who had both mild and severe intellectual disabilities were more socially competent (e.g. level of engagement, interaction, adjustment) when they were fully included within the general class-room, as compared with their peers who were included only part-time or were segregated (this positive finding did not extend to reports of higher social accep-tance or sociometric status by peers). Other recent studies also document the academic (Peetsma *et al.* 2001) and social (e.g. peer acceptance and inclusion; Abbott and McConkey 2006; Carter *et al.* 2005; Cutts and Sigafoos 2001; Fisher 1999; Mu, Siegel and Allinder 2000) benefits of inclusive education for persons with intellectual disabilities.

At least two important reasons exist to support continued efforts toward fos-tering more inclusive educational environments for persons with intellectual disabilities. First, one must consider the philosophical argument that all learners regardless of disability have a basic right to receive a truly inclusive education to prepare them for the diversity they will encounter in their social communities (Anderson 2006; Bach 2002; Frazee 2003; Sapon-Shevin 2003). Second, one must consider the empirical argument and refer to the data reviewed earlier in this section which overwhelmingly supports the academic, social, and emotional ben-efits of more inclusive education for all learners, as evidenced through the use of both objective measures (e.g. teacher reports, observations) and subjective reports. The goal of creating truly inclusive education is a reciprocal responsibil-ity shared among all learners and depends on mutual respect and collaboration, and it is one which can yield many important practical (e.g. academic and social) benefits for all learners of an educational community. While great strides have been made over the past 30 years toward more inclusive education, policy and practice are not always neatly aligned and some crucial problems remain in the implementation of inclusive education both nationally and internationally (Winzer 2005). The equality status of persons with intellectual disabilities as it pertains to educational access and inclusion continues to be jeopardized world-wide by deeply entrenched patterns of social exclusion, hierarchical differences, and unequal treatment through the denial of educational opportunities (Frazee 2003).

CHALLENGES ASSOCIATED WITH THE SUCCESSFUL IMPLEMENTATION OF INCLUSIVE EDUCATIONAL PRACTICES WITHIN NORTH AMERICA AND INTERNATIONAL EDUCATIONAL CONTEXTS

In 2002 the World Education Forum reported that almost one-third of the world's population resides in countries where *Education For All (EFA)* is 'a dream rather than a realistic proposition' (UNESCO 2002, p.6). The goal of EFA is to obtain universal access to education for all children; however, according to a recent UNESCO (2003) report at least 113 million elementary aged children did not attend school and 90 per cent of these children lived in countries with poor economic conditions. Recently, UNESCO (2007) reported on the continuing efforts of countries to halt the educational exclusion of marginalized people (e.g. girls, persons with disabilities). Currently, approximately 80 per cent of persons with disabilities are from developing countries in which participation in school is typically very low; in Africa participation in school is at less than 10 per cent (Balescut and Eklindh 2006). South and West Asia, sub-Saharan Africa, the Arab States and North Africa have been identified as countries unable to achieve the goal of EFA (UNESCO 2002). Further, whereas East Asia and the Pacific have been identified as countries that are continuing to make progress toward the goal of EFA, Central and Eastern Europe have been identified as falling behind in their efforts toward this goal. Further, Kristensen *et al.* (2006) reported that in Uganda only 25 persons are integrated into regular schools out of the more than 1000 learners with special needs. Typically, the G-10 countries, such as Canada, United States, United Kingdom, Switzerland, and France, have been the leaders in adopting inclusive practices (Organization for Economic Co-operation and Development 2002). However, even these more developed countries continue to face significant challenges in inclusive educational practices. Fragmentation still characterizes inclusive educational practices, both globally and locally within North America, as many challenges impede progress toward a model of inclusive education based on a *social philosophy of interdependence.*

Legislation and policy on inclusive education: national and international fragmentation

UNESCO reported in 2007 that 'forty-three countries still have no constitutional guarantee of free and compulsory basic education, while thirty-seven countries limit education to citizens and legal residents' (p.69). Forty-five countries reported that they have legislation that ensures the right of persons with disabilities to access educational services (Schindlmayr 2006). UNESCO (2007) points out, however, that basic access to educational services does not ensure that persons will receive the highest quality education. Schindlmayr (2006) foresees the UNCRPD (2006) as a major vehicle towards the global adoption of EFA, thus ensuring the highest quality of education for persons with disabilities. Notwithstanding these legislative developments, a great deal of variation still exists in the way that inclusive education is practised both locally and globally. In this regard, practices and research within the inclusion movement are characterized by a variety of discourses. For instance, definitions of inclusion can range from part- or full-time placement in a general education classroom to the complete transformation of a school philosophy; thus resulting in multiple and competing discourses both nationally and internationally.

It is interesting that in countries defined by traditional cultural values and strong political conservatism there is often greater exclusion of persons with disabilities; this latter observation is especially surprising since many countries sharing these characteristics have also been characterized as more collectivist in social orientation (Crabtree 2007; Kuwon 2005). For instance, although legislation exists in South Korea to ensure the legal rights of all persons to an education, this legislation has been associated with a dramatic increase in separate, special schools for children with disabilities from one school in 1935 to 137 schools in 2003 (Kuwon 2005). Further, while formal legislation for inclusive education also exists in the United Arab Emirates, conservative religious beliefs are often perceived as grounds for excluding families and their children with disabilities (Crabtree 2007).

As was discussed earlier, legislation in both the United Kingdom and North America is progressive in promoting the need to include all individuals, stressing the importance of using various teaching methods to suit individual needs (e.g. United Kingdom procedure of conducting SEN assessments), and requiring that persons with disabilities receive an education in the LRE (Frederickson and Cline 2002; Rueda, Gallego and Moll 2000). At first glance it appears that countries in which democracy is valued and political liberalism is strongly felt tend to more readily embrace the importance of social inclusion. These countries, nevertheless, continue to struggle with the successful application of inclusive educational practices (Connor and Ferri 2007; Forlin 2006; Wasburn-Moses 2006). Australia and Canada, for instance, struggle with the implementation of inclusive practices and this is likely a reflection of differences in state or provincial philosophies toward inclusive education. Forlin (2006) points out how each state and territory in Australia is responsible for establishing its own Education Act which has resulted in a multitude of approaches toward inclusive educational practice. The same is true within Canada as education is a provincial or territorial responsibility and inclusive practices vary across provinces and school boards (Weber and Bennett 2004). Further, a close examination of special education placement rates in North America suggests that just as many children with intellectual disabilities are likely to be segregated from the regular classroom as compared with their peers in South Korea, a country defined by traditional cultural values and strong political conservatism (Weber and Bennett 2004).

Inadequate economic resources to support inclusive education

Countries that suffer from poor economic conditions such as Africa rely strongly on external funding for education (UNESCO 2003, 2007). In developing countries such as Uganda, residential institutions comprise the majority of educational systems (Kristensen *et al.* 2006) and these educational environments are often described as inadequate, unhealthy, and overcrowded. It is the case that in all countries economic investments are essential to eradicate the exclusion and marginalization of persons with disabilities (Anderson, Klassen and Georgiou 2007; Cheuk and Hatch 2007; Crabtree 2007; Forlin 2006; Kristensen *et al.* 2006). Inclusive education is often very costly, and this can limit the number of persons who can access this type of education. For instance, in the United Arab Emirates inclusion is limited to private schools that are expensive and accessed by few persons (Crabtree 2007). However, even in more developed and affluent countries with public education, such as Canada and the United States, inclusion is often perceived as the first place to save costs when education is under-funded (Anderson *et al.* 2007).

Inadequate professional development and training, shortage of educational resources and monetary investment, and lack of support from administrators and governments are often cited by educators as major challenges to successful inclusion (Anderson *et al.* 2007; Cheuk and Hatch 2007; Crabtree 2007; Kuwon 2005). Generally, most educators adopt an inclusive pedagogy and recognize that it is developmentally healthy for all persons (see previous section). However, financial shortages often limit educators' access to the additional professional training they require to engage confidently in meaningful inclusion, which can in turn translate into frustration and poor attitudes toward persons with disabilities and inclusive education among educators (Allan 2006; Anderson *et al.* 2007; Cheuk and Hatch 2007; Connor and Ferri 2007; Crabtree 2007; Forlin 2006; Kuwon 2005). For instance, a lack of investment in inclusive education in South Korea and Hong Kong has been associated with educators' perceptions of segregated schools as being less harmful for children with disabilities than regular schools (Cheuk and Hatch 2007; Kuwon 2005).

Internationally, there is great variation in educators' professional development in special education and the value associated with this type of specialized training (Anderson *et al.* 2007; Fisher 1999; Rainforth 2000; Weber and Bennett 2004). In some countries, special education is not mandatory and ongoing professional development is not provided or not required (Forlin 2006; Weber and Bennett 2004). In the United States, 11 per cent (of 387 surveyed) reported that they were not sufficiently trained to meet the needs of children with severe or disruptive behaviours and they felt these children were not appropriate candidates for inclusion (Connor and Ferri 2007). The Australian government has made efforts towards investing in the *Quality Teacher Program* which offers educators inclusive workshops, and in the *Index for Inclusion* which assists schools in determining how inclusion practices can improve (Forlin 2006). While having an educational assistant (EA) was cited as the most important support for successful inclusion (Idol 2006) in both Western Australia and North America, EAs are not a regulated profession in these countries and access to EAs is limited due to a lack of financial resources.

Social philosophy of difference and disabling attitudes

The belief that persons with intellectual disabilities are *uneducable* still exists in some countries, despite a body of research indicating that they are capable of learning and that inclusive education enhances their cognitive development (Cheuk and Hatch 2007; Kristensen *et al.* 2006; Kuwon 2005; UNESCO 2003). Many countries continue to rely on an assessment-based medical or deficit model for determining educational placement services for persons with intellectual disabilities, and it is interesting that these countries are often characterized by more traditional values and political conservativism (Cheuk and Hatch 2007; Crabtree 2007; Kristensen *et al.* 2006; Kuwon 2005). For instance, in the United Arab Emirates patriarchal social conditions and political indifference towards families caring for children with disabilities is likely responsible for the paucity of educational services offered to children with disabilities (Crabtree 2007). In Canada, the United States, and South Korea, assessments are still used to determine where persons with intellectual disabilities should be placed along a continuum of educational services (Allan 2006; Anderson *et al.* 2007; Forlin 2006; Weber and Bennett 2004).

Although educators generally support the move towards inclusive education, Forlin (2006) found that teachers' attitudes in Australia were less favourable towards the inclusion of persons with high needs or severe behavioural issues, and similar findings have been noted towards persons with intellectual disabilities in Hong Kong and South Korea (Anderson *et al.* 2007; Cheuk and Hatch 2007; Kuwon 2005). While some teachers continue to resist the increased responsibility associated with teaching children with disabilities, still others express concern with their own competence to meet the needs of these children (Allan 2006). Interestingly, in both North American and international research inclusive education has been linked to more favourable attitudes towards persons with disabilities by their peers who do not have disabilities (Maron, Cohen and Naon 2007; Rillotta and Nettlebeck 2007).

Movement towards inclusion has been met with mixed responses from caregivers (Allan 2006; Crabtree 2007; Weber and Bennett 2004). A small majority of caregivers simply do not want their children (who do and do not have disabilities) to receive an inclusive education (Duhaney and Salend 2000; Fisher 1999; Palmer, Borthwick-Duffy and Widaman 1998; Palmer *et al.* 2001; Soodak and Erwin 2000). However, it is often the case that caregivers' attitudes toward inclusion are mitigated by fear of social rejection, teachers' abilities, and expressed support for inclusion by educators and other caregivers (Leyser and Kirk 2004). In countries such as Hong Kong, the United Arab Emirates and South Korea, caregivers are likely to reject the idea of inclusive education because they fear their families will face discrimination (Cheuk and Hatch 2007; Crabtree 2007; Kuwon 2005). Allan (2006) noted that in Scotland, caregivers of children with special needs were nervous about new legislation that promoted inclusive educational practices because they were uncertain what kinds of services would be available to their children. Caregivers in North America have expressed similar concerns about the quality of education their children will receive if special education is eliminated in favour of more inclusive educational practices (Weber and Bennett 2004). Maron *et al.* (2007) found that parents of children who did and did not have disabilities generally had positive attitudes towards inclusive education only after their children had successful experiences with inclusion. Finally, many caregivers may not even know about or how to advocate for their children's educational rights, and even when they do advocate for their children's educational rights they often face many barriers. While there have been a number of educational options developed to support caregivers and advocates of children with disabilities, these people still face considerable challenges in advocating for children's educational rights. The Canadian documentary *My Different Life* (O'Donnell 2007) offers an intimate example of a Canadian mother's struggle to advocate for the educational rights of her two children with disabilities.

Global competitiveness

In increasingly global and competitive economies, individualism and competition are highly valued and this likely impacts strongly on the struggle to engage in inclusive education (Cheuk and Hatch 2007; UNESCO 2007). Neo-conservatives argue that educational systems are producers of human capital and that in an era of increasing global competition and unprecedented economic progress, the goal of these systems must be aligned with the needs of the economy, and must therefore produce skilled and competitive persons ready to enter the labour force (Apple 1996). From this perspective, intolerance and hostility towards families and their children with disabilities can arise when they are perceived as threatening the success of their peers or their country's economic position (Cheuk and Hatch 2007; Crabtree 2007; Kuwon 2005). In Hong Kong, for example, there are strong expectations for academic excellence and fierce competitiveness and rigid structures may undermine inclusive education. In fact, Hong Kong teachers report that children with disabilities are an extra burden and that their work-related stress is diminished when these children are excluded from the regular classroom (Cheuk and Hatch 2007). A similar pattern has been noted in North American educational practices since the mid-1990s with a greater emphasis on standardized testing and academic literacy and numeracy, thus diverting attention away from inclusive educational practices (Bernard *et al.* 2005; Weber and Bennett 2004). In an educational environment focused on academic excellence, it is contingent upon the individual who has an intellectual disability to reach standard academic outcomes; access to an inclusive education is considered an individual responsibility, rather than a shared responsibility among administrators, educators, caregivers, and peers (Cheuk and Hatch 2007; Crabtree 2007; Kuwon 2005).

THE IMPACT OF A SOCIAL PHILOSOPHY OF INTERDEPENDENCE FOR INCLUSIVE EDUCATION: FINAL REFLECTIONS

Clearly, efforts toward the successful inclusion of all learners continue to be hampered by many practical challenges, and theory and practice within the field of inclusive education is characterized by a great deal of fragmentation both nationally and internationally. By definition, the *right to education* for persons with disabilities requires that these persons receive an education within the most inclusive (and least restrictive) setting. The *right to education* also signifies that persons with disabilities are entitled to engage as equal, active and full participants in all aspects of their educational experiences. It is important to reiterate here that a paradigm shift in philosophical beliefs is required to underscore the *right to education* as defined above and to make inclusive education a truly meaningful and successful experience for persons with disabilities. Specifically, it is necessary to adopt a *social philosophy of interdependence*, whereby the value of relationships and collaboration among all persons within a community is highlighted (Anderson 2006). The core belief that all humans have value and that all humans share an equal role in shaping communities that will prepare persons to live in diverse and accepting communities represents a starting point toward a *social philosophy of interdependence* in the field of inclusive education. This latter philosophy can, to some extent, overcome many of the practical challenges associated with inclusion (e.g. lack of economic resources, disabling attitudes) and can contribute to the goal of achieving synchrony in the field of inclusive education theory and practice. The question follows: 'What meaningful steps can be taken toward the goal of translating a *social philosophy of interdependence* into practice to establish and support optimally inclusive classrooms?'

This chapter concludes with an example of our work which represents one step toward this latter goal. Currently, our 3Rs (Rights, Respect and Responsibility) multidisciplinary research team is exploring the impact of various methodologies (e.g. role-playing, drama, interactive technology) in educating Canadian persons with intellectual disabilities and their caregivers (e.g. family members and support staff) about their human rights (including educational rights) in the context of respect for and responsibility to both oneself and others. A preliminary evaluation of our training materials in agencies supporting persons with intellectual disabilities has been encouraging and several elements of our work reflect a *social philosophy of interdependence* and are fundamental to the goal of supporting optimally inclusive classrooms. (For a comprehensive review of the development and evaluation of our training materials please refer to Owen *et al.* 2003; Stoner *et al.* 2002a, 2002b; Tardif-Williams *et al.* 2007.) First, our work focuses directly on educating persons with intellectual disabilities about human rights issues, including a focus on educational rights, which constitutes complex subject matter not before tackled in previous studies. Second, our work adopts a truly systemic approach toward effecting change with the goal of increasing capacity for the development of promising, new, community-wide, systemic programs and approaches to teach human rights to persons with intellectual disabilities, their caregivers (i.e. family member, support staff) and other support services (e.g. teachers, health-care professionals, classroom peers, law enforcement officers). Caregivers are often key advocates for the persons they support; therefore, by also empowering caregivers the way can be paved for self-advocacy among persons with intellectual disabilities. Third, the integrity of our work rests on the full membership and meaningful collaboration of persons with intellectual disabilities; they continue to be equal partners at all levels of the research process.

Scholars have suggested that the paradigm shift from exclusion to inclusion within education is one that involves the active membership and participation of all persons with differing abilities (Schwartz 2000; Thousand *et al.* 1997). Our perspective is consistent with post-modern approaches which argue that inclusion is an ethical project (Allan 2006, p.128), one in which persons with intellectual disabilities can be repositioned as active agents, or as participants rather than subjects, in the inclusion debate (Snelgrove 2005). In this way, an important step is taken toward creating a new discursive space for persons with intellectual disabilities, one in which they can actively contribute to theory and practice in inclusive education.

REFERENCES

Abbott, S. and McConkey, R. (2006) 'The barriers to social inclusion as perceived by people with intellectual disabilities.' *Journal of Intellectual Disabilities, 10,* 4, 275–287.

Allan, J. (1997) 'With a little help from my friends: Integration and the role of mainstream pupils.' *Children and Society, 11,* 3, 183–193.

Allan, J. (2006) 'The repetition of exclusion.' *International Journal of Inclusive Education, 10,* 2, 121–133.

Anderson, C., Klassen, R. and Georgiou, G. (2007) 'Inclusion in Australia: What teachers say they need and what school psychologists can offer.' *School Psychology International, 28,* 2, 131–147.

Anderson, D. (2006) 'Inclusion and interdependence: Students with special needs in the regular classroom.' *Journal of Education and Christian Belief, 10,* 2, 43–59.

Apple, M. W. (1996) *Cultural Politics and Education.* New York: Teachers College Press.

Bach, M. (2002, June) *Social Inclusion as Solidarity: Rethinking the Child Rights Agenda.* Toronto: Laidlaw Foundation.

Baker, E. T., Wang, M. C. and Walberg, H. J. (1995) 'The effects of inclusion on learning.' *Educational Leadership, 52,* 1, 33–35.

Baker, J. M. and Zigmond, N. (1990) 'Are regular education classes equipped to accommodate students with learning disabilities?' *Exceptional Children, 56,* 6, 515–526.

Balescut, J. and Eklindh, K. (2006) 'Historical perspective on education for persons with disabilities.' Background paper for *EFA Global Monitoring Report.*

Bernard, J., Wade-Woolley, L., Barnes, M., Godbout Beitel, M. *et al.* (2005) *Education For All: The Report of the Expert Panel on Literacy and Numeracy Instruction for Students with Special Education Needs, Kindergarten to Grade 6.* Toronto: Ontario Ministry of Education.

Black, K. (1996) *A Healing Homiletic: Preaching and Disability.* Nashville, TN: Abingdon.

Blanchet, A. (1999) 'The impact of normalization and social role valorization in Canada.' In R. Flynn and R. Lemay (eds) *A Quarter-century of Normalization and Social Role Valorization: Evolution and Impact.* Ottawa: University of Ottawa Press.

Carlberg, C. and Kavale, K. (1980) 'The efficacy of special versus regular class placement for exceptional children: A meta-analysis.' *The Journal of Special Education, 14,* 3, 295–309.

Carter, E., Cushing, L., Clark, N. and Kennedy, C. (2005) 'Effects of peer support interventions on students' access to the general curriculum and social interactions.' *Research and Practice for Persons with Severe Disabilities, 30,* 1, 15–258.

Chesley, G. M. and Calaluce, P. D. Jr. (1997) 'The deception of inclusion.' *Mental Retardation, 35,* 6, 488–490.

Cheuk, J. and Hatch, J. A. (2007) 'Teachers' perceptions of integrated kindergarten programs in Hong Kong.' *Early Child Development and Care, 177,* 4, 417–432.

Cohen, P., Forgan, J. W., Klinger, J. K., Schumm, J. S. and Vaughn, S. (1998) 'Inclusion or pull-out: Which do students prefer?' *Journal of Learning Disabilities, 31,* 1, 29–38.

Connor, D. and Ferri, B. (2007) 'The conflict within: Resistance to inclusion and other paradoxes in special education.' *Disability and Society, 22,* 1, 63–77.

Copeland, S., Hughes, C., Carter, E., Guth, C. *et al.* (2004) 'Increasing access to general education: Perspectives of participants in a high school peer support program.' *Remedial and Special Education, 25,* 6, 342–352.

Corker, M. (2000) 'Disability politics, language planning and inclusive social policy.' *Disability and Society, 15,* 3, 445–461.

Crabtree, S. A. (2007) 'Family responses to the social inclusion of children with developmental disabilities in the United Arab Emirates.' *Disability and Society, 22,* 1, 4–62.

Culham, A. and Nind, M. (2003) 'Deconstructing normalization: Clearing the way for inclusion.' *Journal of Intellectual and Developmental Disability, 28,* 1, 65–78.

Cutts, S. and Sigafoos, J. (2001) 'Social competence and peer interactions of students with intellectual disability in an inclusive high school.' *Journal of Intellectual and Developmental Disability, 26,* 2, 127–141.

Department of Justice Canada (2006) *Canadian Charter of Rights and Freedoms.* Retrieved from www.laws.justice.gc.ca on September 10, 2005.

Duhaney, L. G. and Salend, S. J. (2000) 'Parental perceptions of inclusive education placements.' *Remedial and Special Education, 21,* 2, 121–128.

Epps, S. and Tindall, G. (1987) 'The effectiveness of differential programming in serving students with mild handicaps: Placement options and instructional programming.' In M. C. Wang, M. C. Reynolds and H. J. Walberg (eds) *Handbook of Special Education: Research and Practice Vol. 1: Learner Characteristics and Adaptive Education.* Oxford: Pergamon Press.

Fisher, D. (1999) 'According to their peers: Inclusion as high school students see it.' *Mental Retardation, 37,* 6, 458–467.

Fisher, M. and Meyer, L. (2002) 'Development and social competence after two years for students enrolled in inclusive and self-contained educational programs.' *Research and Practice for Persons with Severe Disabilities, 27,* 3, 165–174.

Forlin, C. (2006) 'Inclusive education in Australia ten years after Salamanca.' *European Journal of Psychology of Education, 21*, 3, 265–277.

Frazee, C. (2003, January) *Thumbs Up! Inclusion, Rights and Equality as Experienced by Youth with Disabilities.* Toronto: Laidlaw Foundation.

Frederickson, N. and Cline, T. (2002) *Special Educational Needs Inclusion and Diversity: A Textbook.* Buckingham: Open University Press.

Freeman, S. E. N. and Alkin, M. C. (2000) 'Academic and social attainments of children with mental retardation in general and special education settings.' *Remedial and Special Education, 21*, 1, 2–18.

Fuchs, D. and Fuchs, L. S. (1994) 'Inclusive schools movement and the radicalization of special education reform.' *Exceptional Children, 60*, 4, 294–309.

Galton, F. (1869) *Hereditary Genius.* New York: The World Publishing Company. Garrick.

Gartner, A. and Lipsky, D. (1987) 'Beyond special education: Toward a quality system for all students.' *Harvard Education Review, 57*, 4, 367–395.

Gartner, A. and Lipsky, D. (1989) *The Yoke of Special Education: How to Break It. Working Paper.* Rochester, NY: National Centre on Education and the Economy. (ERIC Document Reproduction Service No. ED307792.)

Grover, S. (2002) 'Whatever happened to Canadian children's equality rights? A reconsideration of the Eaton special education case.' *Education and the Law, 14*, 4, 253–263.

Hahn, H. (1988) 'The politics of physical differences: Disability and discrimination.' *Journal of Social Issues, 44*, 1, 39–47.

Helmstetter, E., Peck, C. A. and Giangreco, M. F. (1994) 'Outcomes of interactions with peers with moderate or severe abilities.' *Journal of the Association for Persons with Severe Handicaps, 10*, 2, 263–276.

Hertzman, C. (2002, May) *Leave No Child Behind! Social Exclusion and Child Development.* Toronto: Laidlaw Foundation.

Idol, L. (2006) 'Towards inclusion of special education students in general education.' *Remedial and Special Education, 27*, 2, 77–94.

Jung, K. E. (2002) 'Chronic illness and educational equity: The politics of visibility.' *NWSA Journal, 14*, 3, 178–200.

Kauffman, J. M. (1993) 'How we might achieve the radical reform of special education.' *Exceptional Children, 60*, 1, 6–16.

Kavale, K. A. and Forness, S. R. (1999) 'Effectiveness of special education.' In C. Reynolds and T. Gutkin (eds) *Handbook of School Psychology.* New York: Wiley.

Kishi, G. S. and Meyer, L. H. (1994) 'What children report and remember: A six-year follow-up of the effects of social contact between peers with and without severe disabilities.' *Journal of the Association for Persons with Severe Handicaps, 19*, 2, 277–289.

Klinger, J. K., Vaughn, S., Schumm, J. S., Cohen, P. and Fargan, J. W. (1998) 'Inclusion or pull-out: Which do students prefer?' *Journal of Learning Disabilities, 31*, 2, 148–158.

Kluth, P., Villa, R. and Thousand, J. (2001) '"Our school doesn't offer inclusion" and other legal blunders.' *Educational Leadership, 69*, 4, 24–27.

Kristensen, K., Omagor-Loican, M., Onen, N. and Okot, D. (2006) 'Opportunities for inclusion? The education of learners with special educational needs and disabilities in special schools in Uganda.' *British Journal of Special Education, 33*, 3, 139–147.

Kuwon, H. (2005) 'Inclusion in South Korea: The current situation and future directions.' *International Journal of Disability, Development and Education, 52*, 1, 59–68.

Leondari, A. (1993) 'Comparability of self-concept among normal achievers, low achievers and children with learning difficulties.' *Educational Studies, 19*, 3, 357–371.

Leyser, Y. and Kirk, R. (2004) 'Evaluating inclusion: An examination of parent views and factors influencing their perspectives.' *International Journal of Disability, Development and Education, 51*, 3, 271– 285.

Maron, M., Cohen, D. and Naon, D. (2007) 'Changing disability-related attitudes and self-efficacy of Israeli children via the partners to inclusion programme.' *International Journal of Disability, Development and Education, 54*, 1, 113–127.

McDonnell, J., Thorson, N., Disher, S., Mathot-Buckner, C., Mendel, J. and Ray, L. (2003) 'The achievement of students with developmental disabilities and their peers without disabilities in inclusive settings: An exploratory study.' *Education and Treatment of Children, 26*, 3, 224–236.

McIntosh, R., Vaughn, S., Schumm, J. S., Haagar, D. and Lee, O. (1993) 'Observations of students with learning disabilities in general education classrooms.' *Exceptional Children, 60*, 3, 249–261.

Mu, K., Siegel, E. and Allinder, R. (2000) 'Peer interactions and sociometric status of high school students with moderate or severe disabilities in general education classrooms.' *Journal of the Association for Persons with Severe Handicaps, 25*, 3, 142–152.

Nakken, H. and Pijl, S. J. (2002) 'Getting along with classmates in regular schools: A review of the effects of integration on the development of social relationships.' *International Journal of Inclusive Education, 6*, 1, 47–61.

O'Donnell, K. (Director/Producer) (2007, May 16) *My Different Life* [Television Broadcast]. Toronto: Workshop Productions Inc.

O'Neill. O. (1996) 'Children's rights and children's lives.' In R. E. Ladd (ed.) *Children's Rights Re-visioned: Philosophical Readings.* Scarborough: Nelson Canada.

Organization for Economic Co-operation and Development (2002) *Glossary of Statistical Terms.* Retrieved from http://stats.oecd.org/glossary/detail.asp?ID=7022 on June 19, 2007.

Owen, F., Griffiths, D., Stoner, K., Gosse, L. *et al.* (2003) 'Multi-level human rights training: The first step to changing systems.' *Journal on Developmental Disabilities, 10*, 2, 43–64.

Palmer, D., Borthwick-Duffy, S. and Widaman, K. (1998) 'Parent perceptions of inclusive practices for their children with significant cognitive disabilities.' *Exceptional Children, 64*, 2, 271–282.

Palmer, D. S., Fuller, K., Arora, T. and Nelson, M. (2001) 'Taking sides: Parent views on inclusion for their children with severe disabilities.' *Exceptional Children, 67*, 4, 467–484.

Peck, C. A., Donaldson, J. and Pezzoli, M. (1990) 'Some benefits nonhandicapped adolescents perceive for themselves from their social relationships with peers who have severe handicaps.' *Journal of the Association for Persons with Severe Handicaps, 15*, 4, 241–249.

Peetsma, T., Verger, M., Roeleveld, J. and Karsten, S. (2001) 'Inclusion in education: Comparing pupils' development in special and regular education.' *Education Review, 53*, 2, 125–135.

Poirier, D. and Goguen, L. (1986) 'The Canadian Charter of Rights and the right to education for exceptional children.' *Canadian Journal of Education, 11*, 3, 231–244.

Radford, J. P. and Park, D. C. (1999) 'Historical overview of developmental disabilities in Ontario.' In I. Brown and M. Percy (eds) *Developmental Disabilities in Ontario.* Toronto: Ontario Association on Developmental Disabilities.

Rainforth, B. (2000) 'Preparing teachers to educate students with severe disabilities in inclusive settings despite contextual constraints.' *Journal of the Association for Persons with Severe Handicaps, 25*, 2, 83–91.

Rillotta, F. and Nettlebeck, T. (2007) 'Effects of an awareness program on attitudes of students without an intellectual disability towards persons with an intellectual disability.' *Journal of Intellectual and Developmental Disability, 32*, 1, 19–27.

Roeyers, H. (1996) 'The influence of nondisabled peers on the social interactions of children with a pervasive developmental disorder.' *Journal of Autism and Developmental Disorders, 26*, 3, 303–330.

Rueda, R., Gallego, M. and Moll, L. (2000) 'The least restrictive environment: A place or a context?' *Remedial and Special Education, 21*, 2, 70–78.

Sapon-Shevin, M. (2003) 'Inclusion: A matter of social justice.' *Educational Leadership, 61*, 1, 25–28.

Schindlmayr, T. (2006) 'We need a global treaty for the disabled.' *International Herald Tribune*, August 17.

Schwartz, I. (2000) 'Standing on the shoulders of giants: Looking ahead to facilitating membership and relationships for children with disabilities.' *Topics in Early Childhood Special Education, 20*, 2, 123–128.

Shevlin, M. and Mona O'Moore, A. (2000) 'Fostering positive attitudes: Reactions of mainstream pupils to contact with their counterparts who have severe/profound intellectual disabilities.' *European Journal of Special Needs Education, 15*, 2, 206–217.

Snelgrove, S. (2005) 'Bad, mad and sad: Developing a methodology of inclusion and a pedagogy for researching students with intellectual disabilities.' *International Journal of Inclusive Education, 9*, 3, 313–329.

Sobsey, D. (1994) *Violence and Abuse in the Lives of People with Disabilities: The End of Silent Acceptance*. Baltimore, MD: Paul H. Brookes Publishing Co.

Soodak, L. and Erwin, E. (2000) 'Valued member or tolerated participant: Parents' experiences in inclusive early childhood settings.' *Journal of the Association for Persons with Severe Handicaps, 25*, 1, 29–41.

Stainback, W. and Stainback, S. (1992) *Controversial Issues Confronting Special Education: Divergent Issues*. Needham Heights, MA: Allyn and Bacon.

Stainback, S. and Stainback, W. (1996) *Inclusion: A Guide for Educators*. Baltimore, MD: Paul H. Brookes Publishing Co.

Stoner, K., Gosse, L., Vyrostko, B., Griffiths, D., Owen, F. and Sales, C. (2002a) *3Rs (Rights, Respect and Responsibility): Training for Staff in Agencies Supporting Persons Who Have Intellectual Disabilities*. Welland, ON: Community Living~Welland/Pelham.

Stoner, K., Gosse, L., Vyrostko, B., Owen, F., Griffiths, D. and Sales, C. (2002b) *3Rs (Rights, Respect and Responsibility): Training for Individuals in Agencies Supporting Persons Who Have Intellectual Disabilities*. Welland, ON: Community Living~Welland/Pelham.

Stratford, B. (1991) 'Human rights and equal opportunities for people with mental handicap – with particular reference to Down Syndrome.' *International Journal of Disability, Developmental and Education, 38*, 1, 3–13.

Tardif-Williams, C. Y., Owen, F., Feldman, M., Tarulli, D. *et al.* (2007) 'Comparison of interactive computer-based and classroom training on human rights awareness in persons with intellectual disabilities.' *Education and Training in Developmental Disabilities, 42*, 1, 48–58.

Thomas, S. and Wolfensberger, W. (1999) 'An overview of social role valorization.' In R. Flynn and R. Lemay (eds) *A Quarter-century of Normalization and Social Role Valorization: Evolution and Impact*. Ottawa: University of Ottawa Press.

Thousand, J., Rosenberg, R.L., Bishop, K. D. and Villa, R. A. (1997) 'The evolution of secondary inclusion.' *Remedial and Special Education, 18*, 5, 270–284.

UNESCO (2002) *Education For All: Is the World on Track?* Paris: UNESCO.

UNESCO (2003) *Overcoming Exclusion through Inclusive Approaches in Education: A Challenge and a Vision – Conceptual Paper*. Paris: UNESCO.

UNESCO (2007) *EFA Global Monitoring Report: Strong Foundations: Early Childhood Care and Education*. Paris: UNESCO.

United Nations Convention of the Rights of the Child, Resolution 44/25, November 20, 1989.

United Nations Convention on the Rights of Persons with Disabilities, Final report of the Ad Hoc Committee on a Comprehensive and Integral International Convention on the Protection and Promotion of the Rights and Dignity of Persons with Disabilities resolution 60/232, December 6, 2006.

United Nations Declaration on the Rights of Disabled Persons, resolution 3447 (XXX), December 9, 1975.

United Nations Declaration on the Rights of Mentally Retarded Persons, resolution 2856 (XXVI), December 20, 1971.

Vaughn, S. and Schumm, J. S. (1995) 'Responsible inclusion for students with learning disabilities.' *Journal of Learning Disabilities, 28,* 5, 264–270.

Wang, M. C. and Baker, E. T. (1985–1986) 'Mainstreaming programs: Design features and effects.' *The Journal of Special Education, 19,* 4, 503–521.

Wang, M. C., Reynolds, M. C. and Walberg, H. J. (1994) 'What works and what doesn't work: The case for an inclusive system.' In K. K. Wong and M. C. Wang (eds) *Rethinking Policy for At-risk Students.* Berkeley, CA: McCutchan Publishing Corp.

Wasburn-Moses, L. (2006) 'Obstacles to program effectiveness in secondary special education.' *Preventing School Failure, 50,* 21–30.

Weber, K. and Bennett, S. (2004) *Special Education in Ontario,* 5th edn. Ontario: Highland Press.

Wiener, J. and Tardif, C. Y. (2004) 'Social and emotional functioning of children with learning disabilities: Does special education placement make a difference?' *Learning Disabilities Research and Practice, 19,* 1, 20–32.

Williamson, P., McLeskey, J., Hoppey, D. and Rentz, T. (2006) 'Educating students with mental retardation is special education.' *Exceptional Children, 72,* 3, 347–361.

Winzer, M. (2005) *Children with Exceptionalities in Canadian Classrooms,* 7th edn. Toronto: Pearson Prentice Hall.

Wolfensberger, W. (1972) *The Principle of Normalization in Human Services.* Toronto,: National Institute on Mental Retardation (The Roeher Institute).

Wolfensberger, W. (1984) 'Holocaust II?' *Journal of Learning Disabilities, 17,* 7, 439–440.

Yell, M. L. and Shriner, J. G. (1997) 'The IDEA amendments of 1997: Implications for special and general education teachers, administrators, and teacher trainers.' *Focus on Exceptional Children, 30,* 1, 19–25.

Zigmond, N. and Baker, J. M. (1995) 'Full inclusion for students with learning disabilities: Too much of a good thing?' *Theory into Practice, 35,* 1, 26–34.

10

Ensuring Rights: Systemic and Educational Approaches

Frances Owen, Mark Julien, Carol Sales,
Christine Y. Tardif-Williams, Barbara Vyrostko
and Karen Stoner

The role of the formal and informal organizational context is evident in all the topics included in this book. Whether it is the structure of institutions as they have evolved over centuries (Scheerenberger 1983; Trent 1994), the agencies and support services that have developed through the Community Living movement (Radford and Park 1999), or the many organizations of self-advocates (Dybwad 1996), all function as organizational systems, subject to the pressures of scarcity, changes in government policy and prevailing social attitudes toward people with disabilities. They are also accountable to various, sometimes conflicting, constituencies.

In Chapter 1, an argument was made for the central importance of organizational supports to ensure that manifesto rights, such as the newly endorsed United Nations Convention on the Rights of Persons with Disabilities (2006), as well as national rights policies and legislation, are realized in everyday practice. In this chapter, we will review literature on the nature of organizational systems and the central role they play in fostering human rights for people who have intellectual disabilities. As such, this chapter represents something of a departure in perspective from the other chapters in this book. While the other chapters are more issue focused, this chapter takes a primarily macro perspective examining the nature of an organization as a whole and how it operates in relation to all other organizations in its external environment, i.e. the bigger picture. Although the perspective changes in this chapter, the single-minded focus on the issue of rights promotion does not change. Our overarching purpose is to examine the organizational fabric of human services and how human rights for people with intellectual disabilities can be woven deeply into that fabric to ensure systemic rights support. We will focus, especially, on the critical importance of the development of learning organizations to provide an environment in which systems can develop powerful feedback mechanisms to respond effectively to rights concerns, on the nature of organizational change and the ways in which change can be managed effectively, and on the foundational importance of organizational culture that promotes human rights.

COMMONALITIES OF ALL ORGANIZATIONS IN THE BEGINNING OF THE 21ST CENTURY

All organizations, to a greater or lesser extent, are grappling with unprecedented change. Today's organizations are caught up in a whirlwind of new trends such as: increasing globalization and workforce diversity, downsizing and rightsizing, the rising tides of contingent workers and workers in high-tech and other knowledge-based industries, the ever-increasing focus on the management of quality, a scarcity of resources, and a more educated workforce. Organizational structures are changing to meet these environmental threats and opportunities head-on, e.g. flatter organizations and more flexible structures (Greenberg *et al.* 2000). In the midst of such an avalanche of change, the most effective and enlightened administrators and managers have come to realize that change is not just an isolated event but has now become a way of life in all contemporary organizations.

In an article written over a decade and a half ago describing one company's philosophy of management, Forward, Beach, Gray and Quick (as cited in Robey and Sales 1994) said:

> Most importantly, they [comparable companies in the same industry as the focal company] will be learning organizations which emphasize cognitive skill development. People will be viewed as human resources to be invested in and developed, not as labor costs to be consumed… The human mind, not the hand, is most important to the organization. (p.516)

The company described in the article was Chaparral, an innovative, steel mini-mill in the United States. There are lessons for all organizations, from manufacturing companies to human services organizations, to be learned from this company.

Leonard-Barton (as cited in Robey and Sales 1994) saw Chaparral as a 'learning laboratory' made up of 'complex organizational ecosystems that integrate problem solving, internal knowledge, innovation, and experimentation, and external information' (p.517). Leonard-Barton ventured that such learning could only have come from 'constant managerial attention to communicating the underlying values, checking the management's systems smallest details for consistency, and adapting any inharmonious elements' (p.517). The then CEO, Gordon Forward (as cited in Robey and Sales 1994), painted a vivid picture of

Chaparral's vigilant and constant response to its relentless bombardment of change: 'We constantly chip away the ground we stand on' (p.518).

Administrators in human service organizations committed to promoting human rights would also do well to view their organizations as learning laboratories in order to address the demands of the turbulent environments in which they function. Human service organizations have to respond to changes in legislative requirements, threats to their funding base and changes in community demand and expectations of the people they support to say nothing of the demands and expectations of their workforce. Change in response to demands from inside the organization and from the broader environment requires organizational structures and leadership that are flexible, open and responsive, characteristics that can help to support the implementation of a commitment to human rights.

ENVIRONMENTAL SUPPORT FOR HUMAN RIGHTS: HOW ORGANIZATIONS ARE RESPONDING

The increasing focus on human rights is, of course, not particular to organizations of, and for, people with intellectual disabilities. Many companies in various sectors have developed charters of rights designed to articulate the protections to which they have committed. For example, after being cited for health and safety violations in the past, US based Tyson Foods Inc. developed a 'Team Member Bill of Rights' for employees that includes protections for the rights to safety, freedom from discrimination, fair compensation, clarity in communication of information, choice to engage in collective bargaining and continuing training (Smith 2005).

Canadian injection modelling company, Lakeside Plastics, has an employee charter that includes items that focus on workplace health and safety and a commitment to 'fair and equal treatment'. Their Employee Bill of Rights assures employees' rights to 'consistent and supportive leadership,' to 'fair treatment, self expression, safety, recognition, freedom from harassment', learning to 'be proud of and responsible for [their] work', and the right to enjoy and do well at their job (Lakeside Plastics Limited Employee Charter).

The notion of integration of human rights principles into the foundation of an organization can apply not only in human services, business and industry, but also with children and adults in schools. An action research project in a school in the West Midlands of England centred on moving human rights away from the traditional legalistic focus and into education with the goal of improving relationships and managing conflict. The investigators, Charlotte Carter and Audrey Osler (2000), make the point that while human rights provide principles to guide life in all kinds of organizational settings, 'they cannot be entirely effective unless they are seen as of universal relevance to everyday life' (p.335). Carter and Osler's study was prompted by a desire to challenge the culture of the school, 'A human rights framework offers a set of principles by which schools can enable conflicts to be resolved peacefully and equitably and for young people to act in the holistic interests of the wider community' (p.338). Their work illustrated barriers facing teachers who were interested in promoting rights education including the difficulty associated with a lack of management support.

In her article, appropriately entitled 'Do the right thing', Laura Bogomolny (2004) discusses the emotional and financial impact on organizations when a human rights complaint is made, and she describes the emotional and legal costs of such complaints. In Canada, the nature of work-related rights complaints has shifted from the sexual harassment focus of the 1970s and 1980s to broader based cases. She quotes labour and employment lawyer Caroline Ursukal who identified the new focus on 'a poisoned work environment' (p.96).

Prevention of these concerns is, of course, the key. Bogomolny emphasizes the importance of organizations developing and applying a human rights policy, reminding staff of organizational conduct expectations and educating organization members about issues related to diversity and inclusion. However, when these preventive strategies fail, responsible, confidential, and thorough investigation must be undertaken. It must also provide feedback on outcomes to complainants who may otherwise be lost in the investigation process.

Establishing mechanisms to monitor such rights commitments requires the development of review and adjudication mechanisms such as the ones at Brock University in Canada. The university's Respectful Work and Learning Environment Policy is monitored by a small department, Human Rights and Equity Services and, further, the policy is protected in the faculty union contract. Human Rights and Equity Services provides training in the policy to all university faculty and staff in an effort to be proactive and to foster a climate of respect. It also investigates complaints concerning policy violations.

Rights statements and monitoring processes are important first steps to rights promotion. However, organizations cannot simply espouse a commitment to the preservation and fostering of the human rights. Promulgation of rights is not solely a matter of writing a policy.

HOW ARE HUMAN RIGHTS SUPPORTED IN ORGANIZATIONS?

Agencies and service organizations whose leaders and members wish to embrace a philosophy founded on human rights must be prepared to examine all facets of their operation. They must also be prepared to establish functional mechanisms that allow for constant transformative feedback based on identification of rights concerns by organization members and people who consume their services. The absence of such protections can result in abuse. Sobsey (1994) warns of the dire consequences of administrative processes that promote rather than prevent abuse. Based on Marx's work on nonenforcement, covert facilitation and escalation as administrative contributors to deviance, Sobsey cautions, 'Through non-enforcement, institutional administrators permit abuse and implicitly condone it' (p.104). Instead, administrators must be prepared to address issues openly and to use the information they learn to promote truly transformative organizational change to address the problems. In short, we would argue that to promote rights, human services need to become true learning organizations. In particular, organizations must develop skills in what Peter Senge, chair of the Society for Organizational Learning, calls the 'fifth discipline' of systems thinking (Senge 1994) and of putting that into practice in all aspects of the organization's policies and procedures.

UNDERSTANDING HUMAN SERVICES ORGANIZATIONS AS SYSTEMS

All organizations exist within their external environment which is made up of a number of inter-related, interconnected and complex systems and are, themselves, made up of inter-related, interconnected and complex systems. To grasp the concept of 'systems' one only has to think of the age-old idea of a large birthday box that is filled with endless numbers of smaller and smaller boxes. Hence, the whole organization is made up of a large number of smaller systems, e.g. a community organization may include residential services and vocational support services, services for children, youth and adults living at home, consultation services, training services, and research units that develop new programs. Each unit has its own function but may also cooperate in supporting any given person and may collaborate in developing new initiatives.

The more successful organizations are described as 'open systems', i.e. they constantly monitor and interact effectively with their external environment. In contrast, those organizations which attempt to operate as a 'closed system' and which essentially do not monitor and interact with their external environment simply doom themselves to ultimate failure. For example, those administrators of human service organizations who are open to their environments, i.e. who vigilantly monitor their external environments for changes in trends, resources, changing philosophies and techniques in services and education for consumers, new development approaches for staff, opportunities for partnerships with other organizations, are more likely to be able to take advantage of new funding opportunities and service knowledge to promote the development and success of their organizations. Such enlightened administrators serve their organizations and their service consumers especially well. Those administrators who prefer to 'do business as they always have' do a great disservice to their organization, staff, service consumers, funders and supporters, as is the case of the managers Sobsey identified who were nonenforcers of abuse protection. However, this cannot be accomplished simply by listing rules. It must become a philosophy that is enacted throughout the organization.

In his opening address to the 1995 Disability-Life-Dignity Conference held in Montreal, Quebec Ombudsman Daniel Jacoby discussed the disconnect between mandatory codes of ethics in institutions and their application. 'Our experience has shown that the employees governed by the codes have little stake in seeing them applied' (Disability-Life-Dignity 1997, p.23). He identified the structural barriers that prevented service users' committees and user board representatives from having a true voice in organizational management due to low numbers of board representatives and lack of access to powerful management committees. The inherent difficulty in organizational self-evaluation was also highlighted. 'Senior managers responsible for examining complaints in institutions are often placed in conflict of interest when they have to criticize the impact of policies they themselves voted for, or when they have to take positions on the unacceptable behaviour of employees reporting to their colleagues' (p.24). To be effective, such self-criticism requires a culture that supports organizational learning rather than self-protection and system self-perpetuation.

LEARNING ORGANIZATIONS ('CHIPPING THE GROUND WE WALK ON')

If the organization is the fabric we spoke of earlier, rights promoting culture, policies, practices and procedures are all threads that have to be woven deeply into this fabric. The process of doing this weaving can be troublesome given the natural human tendency to avoid change, even when it is ultimately positive. What holds the cloth together, ultimately, is an organization that is committed to ongoing learning through constant monitoring of its internal systems and external environment. That learning involves challenging the organization to face constant change, as illustrated in the example cited earlier of Chaparral Steel. The 'chipping away at the ground we walk on' philosophy of Chaparral's CEO, Gordon Forward, reflects the essential nature of the learning organization.

In his article, 'Creating communities' (2004), Peter Senge explains that learning organizations are 'grounded in a culture based on transcendent values of love, wonder, humility, and compassion; a set of practices for generative conversation and coordinated action; and a capacity to see and work with the flow of life as a system' (p.4). Promotion and protection of human rights demand the kind of 'generative conversation' that challenges organization members to be aware of and responsive to rights restrictions in the lives of people they serve, and surely 'coordinated action' is a natural outgrowth of this conversation.

Senge asserts that learning organizations are led by servant leaders whose approach is collective rather than hierarchical and who lead 'because they choose to serve one another and a higher purpose' (p.5). These leaders must be skilled systems thinkers who, among other abilities, are able to distinguish between 'espoused theory' and 'theory in use' (Senge 1999a, p.12) – that is, recognizing the level of congruence between articulated values and beliefs and the extent to which they are enacted in daily life. This is particularly important in the context of rights promotion. While it is likely that most human service providers would identify themselves as supporting the human rights of the people they serve, when faced with a difficult decision, how many would rationalize a rights restriction as providing protection for people they support in the moment without considering an innovative alternative? Further, how many would be supported in this decision by their managers and supervisors? It is likely that Senge would argue that working through this dilemma is an opportunity for learning.

Learning organizations must have a process for ensuring that such learning is systematically captured and put to use by developing a learning infrastructure that includes 'practical experimentation and testing, capacity building, and diffusion and standardization' (Senge 1999b, p.12). He sees the need to integrate learning and working in the context of a workplace that is high in trust and the empowerment of organization members. Clearly, this philosophy will be fostered more effectively in an open organizational culture and will, in turn, shape that culture. Such responsive learning organizations may also provide a counterbalance against service approaches that can evolve away from their original intention. For example, Emerson (1992) and Griffiths and Hingsburger (1985) discussed the evolution of the normalization movement from its original focus on rights promotion as a means to improve the quality of life for individual people with disabilities, to a theory focused on the social repositioning of people with disabilities as a devalued group. In the process of this change, concepts such as age-appropriateness became ends in themselves. Griffiths and Hingsburger (1985) and Emerson (1992) identified the violation of individuals' right to choice and even the use of coercion being justified in the pursuit of such restricted visions of normalization. Wolfensberger (2002), on the other hand, argues that the more ideologically based normalization approach did focus on rights to some extent but that the more empirically rooted social role valorization focuses instead on the occupation of valued social roles as a more effective way for people with disabilities 'to get the good things of life' (p.254) given what he sees as the danger of putting people in the position of making decisions without due attention paid to 'the relevance or legitimacy of competency in any such decisions' (p.255). The constant experimenting and testing suggested by Senge may provide the kind of learning infrastructure that would prompt reflection on the service shifts that are prompted by these differing perspectives.

ORGANIZATIONAL CULTURE AS KEY TO RIGHTS PROTECTION AND PROMOTION

Earlier, we indicated that our overarching purpose in this chapter is to examine the organizational fabric of human services and to weave human rights for people with intellectual disabilities deeply into that fabric to ensure systemic rights support. The nature and evolution of organizational culture is a key thread in this fabric.

The elements of organizational culture include: 'shared norms, values, and assumptions' (Schein 1996, p.229). Schein goes on to elaborate by saying 'I am defining culture as the set of shared, taken for granted implicit assumptions that a group holds and that determines how it perceives, thinks about, and reacts to its various environments' (p.336). Schein has pointed out that organization members may not be aware of the nature of their organizational culture until they encounter one that differs from it. This is important in the context of the promotion of human rights. Community organizations serving people with disabilities but without a clear cultural commitment to day-to-day respect for people's human rights may not be aware of an alternative cultural reality until they are presented with a compelling model.

This concept of organizational culture must also be seen in the context of larger cultural forces. In the case of services for people with disabilities, the historical culture of protectionism and paternalism may reflect broader environmental and cultural influences. Sobsey (1994) contextualized the social forces that contribute to abuse of people who have disabilities. His model is a variant of Bronfenbrenner's ecological model combined with influences from counter-control and social learning theory. Included in his dynamic interactive model is the impact of the larger social culture on individual social units. He explains that 'The more firmly an environment is embedded within a culture, the greater the power of the cultural beliefs and attitudes to influence behavior within that environment' (p.161). By way of illustration, Sobsey refers to a 1981 study by Ritchie and Ritchie that showed that Polynesian families embedded in their traditional culture showed low rates of abuse; however, those families who moved out of their traditional culture showed higher rates of abuse than did those in the traditional culture or in the new culture to which they were moving.

While Sobsey's model was developed to provide a contextual dialogue on abuse with the central focus being on the relationship between a potential victim and a potential offender, the model can reasonably inform our larger systemic analysis of the organizational contexts that may or may not support active respect for human rights. In particular, the model suggests two issues for consideration with regard to work groups. The first is the need to analyze the impact of the larger socio-cultural forces within which the organization functions to determine the degree to which individual human rights, especially for people with disabilities, are valued. The second is the importance of promoting individual and group buy-in to the culture of respect for individual human rights. If an organization is unable to achieve clear commitment by individuals and work groups to the new rights promoting culture, the results could be the kind of potentially dangerous between-cultures alienation that Sobsey describes.

The outcomes of various organizational cultures for both staff and people who use services can be profound. In a survey of staff in residential services for people with intellectual disabilities in the United Kingdom, Hatton *et al.* (1999) identified nine dimensions of organizational culture with respect to the staff experience. These include the extent to which the organization is tolerant and staff oriented; 'achievement oriented; innovative; analytical' (p.214); promoting of collegial social relationships; rewarding of staff; providing a stable work environment; demanding of its staff; and able to resolve conflicts. For each of these factors they evaluated the staff members' perceived distance between their real and ideal organizational cultures and found the greatest distances occurred on two factors: rewarding staff and managing conflict, with the staff reporting that their real organizational cultures were less than ideal in these areas. The smallest distances between real and ideal cultures were in the areas of being analytical and achievement-oriented. Interestingly, staff rated their real organizations as better than ideal on the dimension that focused on the level of demands placed on staff. While the nature of the organizational culture varied from one service to another, these authors found general agreement among staff within organizations about the nature of their culture. Based on these outcomes, the authors emphasize the applicability of organizational culture analysis in examining service values and suggest that 'Whilst individual staff may have sets of values, the impact of such values on service users is likely to be mediated bt the organizational cultures within which staff work' (p.215).

This link to performance and outcomes for people supported by service organizations has been further investigated by Gillett and Stenfert-Kroese (2003) who compared results on an organizational culture inventory from two residential programs for people with intellectual disabilities: one with high and the other with low scores on a quality of life measure for people supported in these demographically similar services in the UK. While the total number of respondents is low, with eight in one house and seven in the other, the outcome is of interest especially since the houses were identified as being similar on the other dimensions that previous studies had identified as contributing to quality of life. The Organizational Cultural Inventory used in this study yielded scores for three cultural styles: constructive, which included items identified as 'achievement, self-actualizing, humanistic-encouraging, affiliative' (p.282); passive-defensive, which included items identified as 'approval, conventional, dependent, avoidance' (p.282); and aggressive-defensive, which included items identified as 'oppositional, power, competitive, perfectionistic' (p.282). The high performing group had scores that were higher than or equal to the lower performing group in the constructive style and lower scores than the low performing group on the passive-defensive and aggressive-defensive styles. The authors emphasize the pilot nature of this study and the fact that while the results suggest an association between organizational culture and residential service outcomes, the nature of this association cannot be identified from these limited results. However, they also argue for the need to investigate the nature of organizational factors and their impact on service outcomes. 'A comprehensive understanding of organizational factors alongside clinical ones will ultimately contribute to the design of an environment that will support both staff and users living optimum quality lifestyles' (p.283).

With respect to the protection and promotion of human rights specifically, there are many aspects of both formal and informal culture that have a direct impact. White et al. (2003) identified 'seven aspects of environments and cultures associated with risk of abuse [in services for people with intellectual disabilities]: management; staff deployment and support; staff attitudes; behaviour and boundaries; training and competence; power, choice and organizational isolation; service conditions, design and placement planning' (p.1). These authors suggest that care systems seem to be better at responding to than preventing abuse. This suggests a systemic failure to protect people's right to freedom from abuse. They argue for a broader, systemic focus on the nature of abuse, away from the lone wolf acting alone philosophy and toward locating abuse in the organizational context with a particular focus on organizational culture. Included among the factors that they identify as key in addressing this issue are a culture of accountability which includes good managers who provide regular supervision; respect for the dignity of people who have disabilities and respect for appropriate professional, rather than self-serving, boundaries; and avoidance of disrespectful cultures in which abuse is normalized. White et al. (2003) argue for the importance of organizational culture and environment as factors that contribute to abuse rather than perpetuating the prevailing tendency to examine only the role of the individual perpetrator. As a corollary, an organizational culture that is open, includes a constant corrective feedback loop, a commitment to promoting human rights and structures to protect those rights, may help to prevent abuse. For organizations that have not established such an open culture, the prospect of initiating meaningful organizational change can be daunting.

THE ANATOMY OF CHANGE IN ORGANIZATIONS

Fear, inertia, and habit are all factors that may prevent individuals and organizations from undertaking change. Organization members may fear loss of power or social relationships, or just fear all the unknowns that may be associated with change. People may not see the need for change and therefore resist it, or the organization may have had past failed attempts at change that may result in their being less than enthusiastic about new initiatives (Greenberg *et al.* 2000). John Kotter (1995) describes eight steps to effecting organizational change:

1. Establishing a sense of urgency.

2. Forming a powerful guiding coalition.

3. Creating a vision.

4. Communicating the vision.

5. Empowering others to act on the vision.

6. Planning for and creating short-term wins.

7. Consolidating improvements and producing still more change.

8. Instituting new approaches. (Kotter 1995, p.61)

In services for people with disabilities, staff members who have seen service trends ebb and flow may scoff at new service models calling them the latest 'flavour of the month'. In Scoggins' (2006) review of change in an American health-care facility, he emphasizes the foundation of meaning arising from organization members' perceptions of reality and the schemas they generate from these perceptions. 'Organizational schemas operate as fundamental assumptions for why events happen as they do, what the events mean, and how individuals are to behave and act in response to the events' (p.86). From this perspective, managers wishing to initiate change must engage in a process of impacting on this social construction. To make major second order change in organizations, managers must 'alter organizational schemas to create perceptual and meaning congruence between top administration and organizational members' (p.88). Scoggins' ethnographic analysis of organizational change in this hospital suggested that a key intervention top management used to further strategic change was shifting the language from describing consumers of health services as 'patients' to 'customers'. This shift in discourse focus reflects the cornerstone of the hospital's perception that it had to compete for customers. In an effort to achieve congruence between management's customer orientation and the orientation held by staff, a variety of strategies was undertaken including reworking of the hospital's advertising to reflect the new vision and organization members' participation in various training initiatives including etiquette and appearance to support the hospital's new image. Scoggins' work suggests that 'managers can create realities that facilitate the implementation of strategy and strategic change at all levels of the organization by changing organizational members' schemas and cognitions through action, discourse, the creation of organizational artifacts and other methods' (p.100).

In the United Kingdom, the *Valuing People* initiative has precipitated a proactive focus on service change that 'was born from a genuine desire on the part of key stakeholders to promote positive change in the lives of people with learning disabilities' (Fyson and Simons 2003, p.153). Fyson and Simons signal this initiative as unusual in its focus on the involvement of all stakeholders in the policy's creation and implementation. These stakeholders are agency representatives as well as people who have intellectual disabilities and their care providers. The project focused on the development and implementation of Joint Investment [strategic] Plans for service improvement. They emphasize the need for the broad framework to be translated to match local needs if the national plan is to result in effective action. While the authors acknowledge that much remains to be accomplished, they also saw evidence that 'Joint Investment Plans suggest that some local authorities have the prerequisites in place to create cultural, organizational and outcome change within both specialist and mainstream services' (p.158). Changes of this magnitude, involving a wide range of stakeholders in a major organizational shift, take much time and effort, and require trust and shared commitment. Sternberg (2002) would suggest that for such a transformation to occur the organizations involved would have to first be 'modifiable'. He proposes a theory of organizational modifiability that focuses on three questions:

1. How much desire is there for actual change in this organizational culture as a whole?

2. How much desire is there for the appearance of change in the culture of the organization?

3. What is the perceived quality of the culture of the organization? (p.148)

Eight cultural modifiability types arise from the permutations of responses to these questions, but underlying these are two fundamental kinds of modifiability: 'surface structural or deep structural' modifiability (p.148). The former refers to change that builds on the organization's current culture while the latter reflects fundamental cultural change. Obviously there are points on the continuum between these extremes and modifiability may vary from one work unit to another within organizations. Sternberg describes eight mineralogical organizational types with respect to modifiability that range from Rust-Iron, in which the answer to all three key questions is no, and Granite, with high perceived cultural quality but no desire for change, to Lead, with a desire for real and apparent change but low cultural quality, and Diamond in the Rough with a desire for real and perceived change and high cultural quality.

This model is useful in considering organizational cultural factors that can moderate adoption of a truly rights-based approach to services for people with intellectual disabilities. Those organizations that desire no change or only the appearance of change will be less likely to truly weave a commitment to human rights into the fabric of their organizational culture and processes, especially considering the need for constant monitoring and deep structural change that facilitates responsivity to shifting needs that such a commitment demands. However, the picture is not entirely bleak. Sternberg suggests that modifiability can, itself, be a focus for change but the process involves a concerted effort that includes identification of the organization's cultural problems that stand in the way of change and then work toward addressing them.

TOOLS FOR CHANGE: THE 3RS PROJECT AS A RIGHTS LEARNING LAB

For those of us involved with the 3Rs: Rights, Respect and Responsibility project described in the Introduction to this book, one of the most compelling learning experiences has been the process of ongoing organizational change associated with an active and overt commitment to fostering human rights for people with intellectual disabilities. Implementation of a concerted focus on human rights education has required a commitment to systems thinking and to organizational learning. It has also required the courage to embark on a process of cultural change.

The process started with a commitment to adoption of a human rights statement by the organization's Board of Directors, a statement that would inspire staff and managers and would clarify the agency's philosophical stance. It was also designed to guide the organization's vision. Community Living Welland Pelham's statement consists of the tenets of the Canadian Charter of Rights and Freedoms:

1. Rights to equal treatment without discrimination because of race, ancestry, origin, colour, ethnicity, citizenship, creed, sex, sexual orientation, age, marital status, family status, disability, or other analogous ground.

2. Freedom of conscience and religion.

3. Freedom of opinion and expression.

4. Freedom of peaceful assembly and association.

5. Rights to vote.

6. Right to enter, remain in or leave Canada or any Province.

7. Right to life, liberty and security.

8. Right not to be deprived of one's life, liberty, or security except in accordance with the principles of fundamental justice.

9. Right not to be subjected to any cruel and/or unusual treatment or punishment.

10. Right to be secure against unreasonable search or seizure.

11. Right to equal protection and equal protection and equal benefit of the law. (Owen *et al.* 2003, pp.49–50)

The statement also includes an additional ten principles that address some issues of specific concern for people with disabilities:

1. Right to equal treatment under the law.

2. Right to participate in affirmative action progammes designed to ameliorate the conditions of individuals or groups who are disadvantaged.

3. Right to contract for, possess, and dispose of property.

4. Right to income support.

5. Right to an education.

6. Right to sexual expression, marriage, procreation, and the raising of children.

7. Rights to privacy.

8. Rights to adequate health care.

9. Right to equal employment opportunities.

10. Right to appropriate support services of the individual's own choosing. (Owen *et al.* 2003, pp.50–51)

However, had the process been left here, at what would have been a stage of functionally localized manifesto rights, the danger would have remained that little would change in the day-to-day experiences of people who have disabilities. As O'Neill (1996) has explained, rights commitments must be used to guide the building of organizational structures that translate rights into action. Key in the structure of rights support in the 3Rs model is the establishment of a Rights Facilitation Committee. This is a committee of the organization's Board of Directors with voting membership comprised of a member of the Board, a consumer of agency services, a family member, community specialists in various professions (e.g. behaviour analyst, psychologist, religious leader, pharmacist, lawyer, nurse, police officer, etc.) and nonvoting staff representatives elected by their peers. The role of this committee is to adjudicate rights concerns brought forward by people with intellectual disabilities, their staff, and agency managers. While the committee was concerned initially that it would be seen as the 'rights police', it has become clear that it serves a problem-solving and consultation function in an atmosphere of 'sober second thought'. It is this committee that provides the kind of structural support for practical translation of the rights statement that O'Neill suggested was necessary.

After the adoption of the rights statement and establishment of the Rights Facilitation Committee, the agency conducted an extensive survey to determine which of the rights to which it had committed itself were being restricted in the organization. This is a clear example of the kind of mechanism necessary to promote organizational learning. Feedback was solicited from people who used the organization's services, as well as part-time and full-time staff. Factor analysis of the results of the 80-item survey revealed rights restrictions that aggregated into four factors: (1) access and autonomy; (2) relationship and community support; (3) safety, security and privacy; and (4) control and decision-making (Griffiths *et al.* 2003).

Identification of these four factors and the commitment by the organization to full implementation of its rights statement inspired the subsequent development of a training program for staff and managers employed in the agency and, most importantly, for people with intellectual disabilities who were supported by the organization (Owen *et al.* 2003; Stoner *et al.* 2002a and b). Management and staff training always precedes training of people supported by the agency to ensure that staff are prepared to respond to expressed rights concerns in a manner that is consistent with agency policy and procedures. Matching training for people with intellectual disabilities has taken several andragogical forms but still focuses on education related to the agency's rights statement and the four factors that arose from the rights survey.

As illustrated in Owen *et al.* (2003), the organizational process of moving from a rights statement through training is by no means linear. As awareness of rights increases through training, the likelihood of identifying rights restrictions might increase. As these issues are brought to the Rights Facilitation Committee they will be adjudicated and remedial actions suggested which may include changes to organizational policies and procedures. Organizations undertaking a true commitment to human rights praxis must be prepared to engage in ongoing organizational learning, with all of the associated pressures for change.

As Robey and Sales (1994) have suggested, much of organizational strategic planning is emergent in nature and that accurately characterizes our working experience with the 3Rs project. Organizations undertaking a shift to a rights-based service system have to be prepared to be challenged constantly as new sources of rights restrictions come to light, both within their organizations and in the broader environment. These emerging issues demand organizations that are not locked into a rigid strategic plan. Structures and strategies that facilitate responsiveness to changing individual needs make it possible for organizations to weave rights into every aspect of their operation.

The 3Rs: Rights, Respect and Responsibility project continues to be a work in progress, as all efforts to promote human rights must be in a turbulent environment. However, the experience has suggested that in the presence of an open culture and with a commitment to organizational learning, it is possible to integrate human rights principles as foundational to service delivery.

REFERENCES

Bogomolny, L. (2004) 'Do the right thing.' *Canadian Business, 77*, 14/15, 96–97.

Carter, C. and Osler, A. (2000) 'Human rights, identities, and conflict management: A study of school culture as experienced through classroom relationships.' *Cambridge Journal of Education, 30*, 4, 335–356.

Disability-Life-Dignity (1997) *Speaking Out Against Abuse in Institutions: Advocating for the Rights of People with Disabilities.* North York: The Roeher Institute.

Dybwad, G. (1996) 'Setting the stage historically.' In G. Dybwad and H. Bersani (eds) *New Voices: Self-advocacy by People with Disabilities.* Cambridge, MA: Brookline Books.

Emerson, E. (1992) 'What is normalisation?' In H. Brown and H. Smith (eds) *Normalisation: A Reader for the Nineties.* London: Tavistock/Routledge.

Fyson, R. and Simons, K. (2003) 'Strategies for change: Making *Valuing People* a reality.' *Journal of Learning Disabilities, 31*, 3, 153–158.

Gillett, E. and Stenfert-Kroese, B. (2003) 'Investigating organizational culture: A comparison of a "high" – and a "low" – performing residential unit for people with intellectual disabilities.' *Journal of Applied Research in Intellectual Disabilities, 16*, 6, 279–284.

Greenberg, J., Baron, R. A., Sales, C. A. and Owen, F. A. (2000) *Behaviour in Organizations* (2nd Canadian edn). Scarborough: Prentice Hall Canada Inc.

Griffiths, D. and Hingsburger, D. (1985) 'Appropriately inappropriate.' *Journal of Practical Approach to Developmental Handicap, 9*, 2, 5–7.

Griffiths, D., Owen, F., Gosse, L., Stoner, K. *et al.* (2003) 'Human rights and persons with intellectual disabilities: An action-research approach for community-based organizational self-evaluation.' *Journal on Developmental Disabilities, 10*, 1, 25–42.

Hatton, C., Rivers, M., Mason, H., Mason, L. *et al.* (1999) 'Organizational culture and staff outcomes in services for people with intellectual disabilities.' *Journal of Intellectual Disability Research, 43*, 3, 206–218.

Kotter, J. P. (1995) 'Leading change: Why transformation efforts fail.' *Harvard Business Review,* March–April, 59–67.

Lakeside Plastics Limited Employee Charter Retrieved from www.Lakesideplastics.com/charter.htm on November 14, 2007.

O'Neill, O. (1996) 'Children's rights and children's lives.' In R. E. Ladd (ed) *Children's Rights Revisioned: Philosophical Readings.* Scarborough: Nelson, Canada.

Owen, F., Griffiths, D., Stoner, K., Gosse, L. *et al.* (2003) 'Multi-level human rights training in an Association for Community Living: First steps toward systemic change.' *Journal of Developmental Disabilities, 10*, 1, 43–64.

Radford, J. P. and Park, D. C. (1999) 'Historical overview of developmental disabilities in Ontario.' In I. Brown and M. Percy (eds) *Developmental Disabilities in Ontario.* Toronto: Front Porch Publishing.

Robey, D. and Sales, C. A. (1994) *Designing Organizations* (4th edn). Chicago, IL: Irwin.

Scheerenberger, R. C. (1983) *A History of Mental Retardation.* Baltimore, MD: Paul H. Brookes Publishing Co.

Schein, E. (1996) 'Culture: The missing concept in organization studies.' *Administrative Sciences Quarterly, 41,* 229–240.

Scoggins, W. A. (2006) 'Managing meaning for strategic change: The role of perception and meaning congruence.' *Journal of Health and Human Services Administration, 29,* 1, 83–102.

Senge, P. (1994) *The Fifth Discipline Fieldbook: Strategies and Tools for Building a Learning Organization.* New York: Currency Doubleday.

Senge, P. (1999a) 'Creative tension.' *Executive Excellence, 16,* 12 (2 pages).

Senge, P. (1999b) 'Learning leaders.' *Executive Excellence, 16,* 12 (2 pages).

Senge, P. (2004) 'Creating communities.' *Executive Excellence, 21,* 4 (2 pages).

Smith, S., (2005) *Tyson Introduces 'Employee Bill of Rights'.* www.occupationalhazards.com/News/Article/37409/Tyson_Introduces_Employee_Bill_of_Rights.aspx.

Sobsey, D. (1994) *Violence and Abuse in the Lives of People with Disabilities: The End of Silent Acceptance.* Baltimore, MD: Paul H. Brookes Publishing Co.

Sternberg, R. J. (2002) 'Effecting organizational change: A "mineralogical" theory of organizational modifiability.' *Consulting Psychology Journal: Practice and Research, 54,* 3, 147–156.

Stoner, K., Gosse, L., Vyrostko, B., Owen, F., Griffiths, D. and Sales, C. (2002a) *3Rs (Rights, Respect and Responsibility): Training for Individuals in Agencies Supporting Persons Who Have Intellectual Disabilities.* Welland, ON: Community Living Welland Pelham.

Stoner, K., Gosse, L., Vyrostko, B., Griffiths, D., Owen, F. and Sales, C. (2002b) *3Rs: (Rights, Respect and Responsibility): Training for Staff in Agencies Supporting Persons Who Have Intellectual Disabilities.* Welland, ON: Community Living Welland Pelham.

Trent, J. W. (1994) *Inventing the Feeble Mind: A History of Mental Retardation in the United States.* Berkeley: University of California Press.

United Nations Convention on the Rights of Persons with Disabilities, Final report of the Ad Hoc Committee on a Comprehensive and Integral International Convention on the Protection and Promotion of the Rights and Dignity of Persons with Disabilities, resolution 60/232, December 6, 2006.

White, C., Holland, E., Marsland, D. and Oakes, P. (2003) 'The identification of environments and cultures that promote the abuse of people with intellectual disabilities: A review of the literature.' *Journal of Applied Research in Intellectual Disabilities, 16,* 1, 1–9.

Wolfensberger, W. (2002) 'Social role valorization and, or versus, "empowerment".' *Mental Retardation, 40,* 3, 252–258.

Contributors

The authors of this book represent a wide diversity of professions, experience and theoretical perspectives. This international interdisciplinary perspective is necessary to provide the broadest possible exploration of a topic as evocative and complex as human rights.

Marjorie Aunos, Ph.D. is a psychologist and scientist-practitioner at the Lisette-Dupras and West Montreal Readaptation Centers and holds an adjunct appointment at the University of Quebec, Montreal, Quebec, Canada.

Diane Cox-Lindenbaum, M.S.W., L.C.S.W. is a clinician and private consultant in the state of Connecticut, USA.

Krystine Donato is an M.A. candidate in the Department of Child and Youth Studies, Brock University, St. Catharines, Ontario, Canada.

Paul Fedoroff, M.D. is an Associate Professor of Psychiatry and Director of the Forensic Research Unit of the Institute of Mental Health Research of the University of Ottawa, Co-Chair of the Research Ethics Board of the Royal Ottawa Hospital and Co-Director of the Sexual Behaviors Clinic of the Forensic Program of the Royal Ottawa Hospital, Ottawa, Ontario, Canada.

Beverly Fedoroff, R.N., B.Sc. (Hons) is a nurse with a special interest in forensic psychiatry and people with intellectual disabilities. She is affiliated with the Centre for Nursing and Health Studies at Athabasca University, Alberta, Canada.

Maurice Feldman, Ph.D, C. Psych. is a Professor in the Department of Child and Youth Studies and Chancellor's Research Chair, Faculty of Social Sciences, Brock University, St. Catharines, Ontario, Canada.

Leanne Gosse, B.A., M.A., is a Ph.D. Candidate in Psychology at Brock University, St. Catharines, Ontario, Canada.

Carolyn Gracey, M.Sc. is a Research Analyst for the Dual Diagnosis Program at the Centre for Addiction and Mental Health, Toronto, Ontario, Canada.

Dorothy Griffiths, Ph.D., O. Ont. is Profesor of Child and Youth Studies and Applied Disability Studies, and Associate Dean of Social Science at Brock University, St. Catherines, Ontario, Canada.

Susan Havercamp, Ph.D. is Assistant Professor in the Florida Center for Inclusive Communities, Center for Excellence on Developmental Disabilities Research, Education, and Service at the University of South Florida, Florida, USA.

Mark Julien, M.I.R., Ph.D. is Assistant Professor of Organizational Behaviour, Human Resources, Entrepreneurship and Ethics, at Brock University, St. Catharines, Ontario, Canada.

Kajsa Klassen, R.N., Bsc.N. is an M.A. candidate in Child and Youth Studies at Brock University, St. Catharines, Ontario, Canada.

Jocelin Lecomte, L.L.B. is the Information and Research Consultant at the West Montreal and Lisette-Dupras Readaptation Centers, Montreal, Quebec, Canada.

Nicholas Lennox, M.D. is Director of the Queensland Centre for Intellectual and Developmental Disability in the School of Medicine at The University of Queensland, Brisbane, Australia.

William Lindsay is Head of Clinical Psychology Services (Learning Disabilities) NHS Tayside, Consultant Psychologist, The State Hospital, Chair of Learning Disabilities and Forensic Psychology at the University Abertay, Dundee, Scotland.

Yona Lunsky, Ph.D. is an Assistant Professor at the University of Toronto in the Department of Psychiatry and a psychologist in the dual diagnosis program at the Centre for Addiction and Mental Health, Toronto, Ontario, Canada.

Voula Marinos, Ph.D. is an Assistant Professor in the Department of Child and Youth Studies at Brock University, St. Catharines, Ontario, Canada.

Céline Mercier, Ph.D. is a Professor at the Department of Preventive and Social Medicine, University of Montreal and Associate Professor in the Department of Psychiatry, McGill University, Director of the Research and Information Technologies Department at the Lisette-Dupras and West Montreal Rehabilitation Centers, Montreal, Quebec, Canada.

Nancy Miodrag, M.A. is a Ph.D. Candidate with specialization in Special Populations of Learners and Applied Developmental Psychology in the Department of Educational and Counselling Psychology at McGill University, Montreal, Quebec, Canada.

Jacqueline Murphy, Ed.D. is Associate Professor of Education at Niagara University, New York State, USA.

J. Gregory Olley is Interim Director, Psychologist, Clinical Professor, Department of Allied Health, University of North Carolina, North Carolina, USA.

Frances Owen, Ph.D., C. Psycho. is Associate Professor of Child and Youth Studies and Applied Disability Studies at Brock University, St. Catherines, Ontario, Canada.

Kaleigh Regehr, M.A. is a graduate of the Department of Child and Youth Studies at Brock University, St. Catharines, Ontario, Canada.

Deborah Richards, C.H.M.H., is the coordinator of the Sexuality Clinic at Community Living Welland Pelham, Welland, Ontario, Canada.

Jennifer Robinson, B.A., M.A. is a Ph.D. Candidate in the Department of Sociology, University of Waterloo, Ontario, Canada.

Carol Sales, Ph.D. is Professor of Organizational Behaviour and Human Resource Management in the Faculty of Business at Brock University, St. Catharines, Ontario, Canada.

Karen Stoner, B.A., M.A. Candidate (Brock University) is RCP Chapter Coordinator, Autism Ontario – Niagara Chapter, Ontario, Canada.

Christine Y. Tardif-Williams, Ph.D. is an Associate Professor in the Department of Child and Youth Studies at Brock University, St. Catharines, Ontario, Canada.

Donato Tarulli, Ph.D. is an Associate Professor in the Department of Child and Youth Studies at Brock University, St. Catharines, Ontario, Canada.

Marion Trent-Kratz, B.A. (McMaster University), B.A. (Hons), B.Ed., M.A. Candidate (Brock University) is a Researcher with the Understanding the Early Years Project hosted by Early Childhood Community Development Centre, St. Catharines, Ontario, Canada.

Tricia Vause, Ph.D. is an Associate Professor in the Department of Child and Youth Studies at Brock University, St. Catharines, Ontario, Canada.

Barbara Vyrostko, L.L.D. is the Executive Director of Community Living Welland Pelham, Welland, Ontario, Canada.

Shelley L. Watson, Ph.D. is an Assistant Professor in the Psychology Department at Laurentian University, Sudbury, Ontario, Canada.

Subject Index

Note: 3Rs (Rights, Respect, and Responsibility); Intellectual Disabilities (ID).

3Rs community-university research alliance 15
  goal of 3Rs education program 18
  group process skill development 38
  as learning lab 275–8
  rights restriction 277
  rights training 208
    institutional training 26
    for support staff 16, 208
    for persons with ID 16, 26, 208
3Rs educational package in three formats 17

'ableism,' definition of 35
adaptive behaviours 221
Americans with Disabilities Act 126
attitudes toward the sexuality of persons with ID 199
  attitudes of parents 204
  attitudes of personnel/staff 199–201
  attitudes of persons with ID 202–3
  attitudes summary 204–5
aversive interventions 19, 222
  aromatic ammonia 222

behaviour modification 222
  functional assessment of behaviour 223, 232
Bill of Rights (U.S.) 126

Canadian Charter of Rights and Freedoms 125–6, 275
Canadian Human Rights Act (1977) 33
Community Living movement, rise of 28, 242
  agency manifesto rights 18, 34, 263
  Community Living Welland Pelham 27–8

Constitution of the United States 126
criminal justice system see justice system
culture see organizational culture

deinstitutionalization 28, 32, 185, 242
desensitization, risk of 226
diagnostic overshadowing 171
'dignity of risk,' definition of 16
disability movement 103–8
  three waves of the disability movement 103–8
Down syndrome 84–85, 91, 127–8
'dual diagnosis,' definition of 135

education and rights see rights and education
Education For All (EFA) 250–1
  World Education Forum 250–1
English Direct Payments initiative 31
ensuring rights from an organizational perspective 263–278
eugenics 18-19, 24, 27–8, 32, 39, 76–7, 83–7, 194, 241–2
  'eugenics' definition of 77
  family eugenics 85
  genetic predisposition to disability 27, 39
  laissez-faire eugenics 85
  new Eugenics movement 80–1
  wrongful life and wrongful death lawsuits 81
European Convention on Human Rights (ECHR) 126–7
euthanasia 79, 90–1
  'death-making' definition of 90–1
  cold or passive euthanasia 90
  neglect 90
evidence-based treatment for persons with ID 219–34
exclusion 36, 244–7, 252
  artificial classrooms 246

fair trial, right to 33

fear for the public good 24
fragile X syndrome 84
Freedom from Harm position 226–8
Feldman balance model 228–9, 232

Genetic Interest Group (GIC) 83–84

health concerns of persons with ID 19, 159–64
  health disaparities 159–64
  participation in own health care 19
healthcare and environmental barriers 167–8
  physical constraints 167–8
healthcare and equity in access and utilization 164–176
  systemic barriers 164–7
    access to health promotion 164–6
    lack of coordination and collaboration between healthcare services 167
    reactive healthcare system 166
    time constraints 167
healthcare and role barriers 168–172
  role of caregiver/support person 169–70
  role of healthcare provider 170–172
  role of the individual 168–9
healthcare guidelines, need for 175–6
healthcare, roles in 165
heterosexuality and persons with ID 195
homosexuality and persons with ID 195–6
Human Genome project 80
human rights awareness 15–16, 17, 24
human rights legislation see also United Nations 24, 31, 33, 44–8
  legislative initiatives 24

legislative protections 31
human rights restrictions 24–32
  child workers with ID 25
  historical perspective of 24–32
  objects of perverse
    entertainment 25
human rights statements 16, 32,
  275–6
  Community Living Welland
    Pelham's human rights
    statement 275–6

inclusion 29, 32, 244–7
  social inclusion 244–7
inclusive education 19, 243–55
  benefits of 248–250
  challenges in implementation
    of 250–3, 255
  disabling attitudes 254–5
  legislation and policy
    approaches 19, 251–2
  review of historical approaches
    to 19
  review of theoretical
    approaches to 19
individual choice, centrality of 30
infanticide 18, 25, 87–90
informed consent 172–4
  participation in medical
    research and 173–4
international law, national
  application of 48–50

justice system and persons with ID
  18–19, 124, 130–1
  inaccessibility for persons with
    ID 18
  over-representation in the
    prison population 130–1

latent social biases 30
learning organization 19
leadership 19, 34
  leadership training 38
  managers 16
  servant leadership 269
  staff 16–17
    job responsibilities of 16
    perception of role as pro-
      tective 16
least restrictive environment (LRE)
  see rights and education
legal rights and persons with ID
  124–50, 148–9
  interviewing persons with ID
    and legal rights 148–9
legal system and persons with ID
  127–149
  competent to stand trial (CST)
    138–9
  courtroom challenges and
    accommodations
    131–149

persons with ID as accused
  persons 130–1
persons with ID as
  complainants/victims of
  crimes 129–30
persons with ID as litigants
  127–9
life narratives of and by persons
  with ID 24, 36–39

mainstreaming 242–3
medical interventions and rights of
  persons with ID 174–176
medical rights for persons with ID
  93–94, 155–176
  agency and health 158
  four fundamental principles of
    biomedical ethics 155–6
    application of the four
      principles to a clinical
      vignette 156–8
mental age 136–7
  definition of 137
Mental Disability Rights
  International (MDRI) 31
mental health problems and
  polypharmacy 162–3
mental health professionals and
  ID 135
mental illness and ID, a
  differentiation 25
Montreal Declaration on ID 18,
  50–63
  Montreal PAHO/WHO
    International Conference
    on ID 18
  content of 51–60
    principle of self-determina-
      tion 60–1
    principle of vulnerability
      and paternalism 61–2
    principle of consent 62–3
morbidity and common health
  problems 160–4
mortality and persons with ID 159
myths, debunking of 20–6
  eternal children 28, 205
  promiscuity and impulsivity
    205

nonaversive interventions 223
  Functional Communication
    Training (FCT) 223–5
  nonpunitive interventions 232
normalization 28–29, 185–6, 208,
  242–3, 269

organizational change 273–5
  eight steps to effecting 272
  theory of organizational
    modifiability 274
organizational commitment 19

organizational culture 266,
  268–272
  as key to protection and
    promotion of human
    rights 270–2
organizational learning 264, 267
  formal and informal
    organizational culture
    272
  learning organizations 268–70
organizational learning laboratory
  264
  3Rs project as rights learning
    lab 275–8
organizational self-evaluation 268
organizational strategic planning as
  emergent 277
organizational structures 276
organizational supports 19, 263
organizations and responses to the
  rights movement 265–8
  codes of ethics 268
  Employee Charter and Bill of
    Rights 265
  human rights framework 266
  human rights policy 266
  Respectful Work and Learning
    Environment Policy
    (RWLEP) 266
  Team Member Bill of Rights
    265
organizations as systems 267–8
  open systems

parenting rights 19, 194
parenting skills 194
pathology of disability 26
People First 38, 242
person-centered planning (PCP)
  112–21, 210–1, 234, 243
  defining features and
    assumptions 112–3
  individualized planning 234
  individualized instruction 243
  PCP and narratives and life
    histories 118–21
  PCP and self-determination
    113–8
  two conceptions of autonomy
    115–8
person-centered values 227
personal narratives see life narratives
physical safety, right to 33
positive behaviour support (PBS)
  227–8, 234
  PCP and PBS methods,
    marriage of 234
privacy, right to 198
protection under the law, right to
  23, 24
punishment, historical perspective
  221–3
  aversive treatment 221

notion of power in aversives
226
psychotropic medications and
tranquilizers 221
punishment, therapeutic 19
schedules of punishment 226
punishment, tracking of frequency
in JABA 230–4

questioning of persons with ID
145–9
questioning techniques 148–9
strengths and challenges 145

recommendations for school or
agency policy 210–1
reinforcement-based procedures
225
research methodology, Feldman's
suggestions for 232–3
retrieval process for persons with
ID, strategies for 148–9
Right to Effective Treatment 19,
223–8
Feldman balance model
228–9, 232
least restrictive treatment
224–6
right to life 18, 76–97
right not to have one's life
terminated at birth
87–90
right to be born 82–7
right to be conceived 80–1
right to choose life 94–6
right to nurturance and the
supports to sustain life
90–1
Rights Adjudication Committee 17
rights and education of persons
with ID 26, 240–57
Education for all Handicapped
Children Act 242
Inclusive Schools Movement
243
least restrictive environment
(LRE) 242
Regular Education Initiative
(REI) 243
special education, historical
perspective 241–4
special education needs (SEN)
assessments 242
rights culture in an agency 19
rights education 1–16, 35, 39
contextually grounded 16
curricula 15–16
local programs 15
socially contextualized 16
systemic approach to 16, 39
rights, ensuring of see ensuring
rights

Rights Facilitation Committee see
Community Living Welland
Pelham 18, 276–7
rights infringements 189–98
contraception/birth control
options 190–3
marriage/cohabitation 19,
193–4
parenting 33, 194
sex education and training
189–90
sexual orientation 195–6
rights, real versus assumed rights
186

safety and security of one's life,
right to 91–3
self-advocacy 18, 35, 37–9, 108,
242
self-determination 17–18, 24
agency or enacted
self-determination 158
and health 158
from a dialogical perspective
18, 102–112
self-injurious behaviour 222, 225
self-other or I-thou relationship
109–112
the other as object 109–10
the other as a form of
self-relatedness 110–11
the other as other 111–2
sexual abuse 187–9
sexual health and polices and
guidelines 206–8
sexual offenders 188–9
sexual relations and consent 196–7
sexual rights and systems change for
persons with ID 208–9
multifaceted systems approach
209
sexuality and rights for persons
with ID 19, 184–211
historical perspective 185–6
outcomes of denying one's
sexual rights 187
social control of persons with ID
27–8
social justice movement 247
social location of persons with ID
18, 23, 25–32
historical overview of 18,
23–32
different practices around the
world 23–32
Social Model of Disability 30
'social philosophy of difference
241, 254–5
'social philosophy of
interdependence' 244,
254–7
'social role valorization,' definition
30

sociosexual education and persons
with ID 206
sterilization 27, 37, 77, 127–8,
185
court cases and 128–9
special education see rights and
education
systemic context of support for
persons with ID 19

testifying in court and persons with
ID 139–142, 144–8
implications for the interaction
with the courts 144–148
learned compliance/deference
to authority figures
139–40
memory and intellectual ability
142–4
moral development level 141
preparation for the court
process 142
projection of false competence
and/or false feelings
140–1
stress and surrender of defences
141–2

United Nations and persons with ID
29
hard law 44–6
soft law 46–8
UNESCO (United Nations
Educational, Scientific and
Cultural Organization)
251
United Nations Universal
Declaration of Human
Rights (1948) 32, 76
United Nations Declaration on
the Rights of Disabled
Persons (1975) 33
United Nations Declaration on
the Rights of Mentally
Retarded Persons (1971)
33, 77
United Nations Convention on
the Rights of People with
Disabilities (2007) 32,
34, 63–67, 127
United Nations Convention on
the Rights of Persons
with Disabilities (2006)
263

Valencia Declaration of Sexual
Rights 189
voice, first-person of persons with
ID 37
'lost voices' 36
voiceless, experience of being
24
Valuing People white paper 31

Author
Index

Abbott, S. 250
Abel, G. G. 130
Adams, M. 190
Adler, P. 160
Ahern, L. 31–2
Aiken, L. R. 137
Alborz, A. 166–9
Albrecht, G. L. 97
Alkin, M. C. 241, 249
Allan, J. 248, 253–4, 257
Allinder, R. 250
Allyon, T. 221
Aman, M. G. 163, 173, 175
Ames, T. R. H. 196-7
Amnesty International 15
Anderson, C. M. 227, 253–4
Anderson, D. 240, 244, 246–8, 250, 256
Anteby, E. 84
Apple, M. W. 255
Arbour, L. 43
Armsrong, S. 175
Arnason, V. 109, 111
Aronow, H. U. 175
Arsott, K. 174
Asch, A. 80
Atkinson, D. 36–7
Atoni, R. 94
Aunos, M. 184, 194, 204
Axelrod, S. 233

Bach, M. 174, 240, 244–8, 250
Baker, W. 160, 243, 249
Bakhtin, M. M. 109–10, 120
Balescut, J. 251
Balogh, R. 161
Bambara, L. M. 228
Bank-Mikkelson, E. 28
Bannerman, D. J. 173
Barnes, C. 26
Barr, O. 159, 168
Baur, C. 172
Baxter, R. 32
Beadle-Brown, J. 113, 121
Beange, H. 158–62, 163–4, 167, 169

Beauchamp, T. L. 61, 155
Beecher, H. 172
Bennett, S. 241–5, 252–5
Berkobien, R. 108
Bernard, J. 255
Bernhardt, B. B. 82
Bersani, H. 32, 35, 37, 102–9, 112
Bertsch, J. M. 136
Binding, K. 88
Birnbrauer, J. S. 222
Bissonnette, G. 61
Black, E. 82
Black, K. 247
Blanchet, A. 93–5, 245
Blatt, E. R. 188
Boat, B. W. 147
Bobrow, M. 86
Bogdan, R. 24, 39
Bogomolny, L. 266
Bohmer, C. J. M. 161
Bomba, C. 144
Bond, L. 171
Bondy, A. 222
Booth, T. 37, 194
Booth, W. 37, 194
Boréus, K., 27
Borthwick-Duffy, S. 162, 254
Bouthilet, G. N. 124
Boyd, J. 19
Boxall, K. 30–1
Brabeck, M. M. 16
Bradley, E. 163, 175
Brantlinger, E. A. 204
Bredberg, E. 37
Bregante, J. L. 195
Brewer, N. 91, 129–30
Bright, C. 163
Brockley, J. 106
Brown, B. S. 130, 139
Brown, I. 28
Brown, R. I. 28
Brown, S. W. 188
Bruck, M. 142, 149
Bryde, R. 201, 204–5
Buckingham, J. 15
Burbridge, M. 171
Burchard, J. 221
Burd, L. 163

Burke Harrison, S. 234
Bying, S. 168

Calaluce, P. D. 241, 249
Calder, P. 188
Cameron, D. 160
Campbell, A. G. M. 89–90
Carlberg, C. 249
Carlson, L. 23, 24, 27–8
Carlson, T. 172
Carr, E. G. 222–3, 226–8
Carr, J. E. 228
Carson, I. 30–1
Carter, C. 265
Carter, E. 250
Case, L. 194
Cassidy, G. 160
Castles, K. 106–8
Cea, C. D. 62
Ceci, S. J. 142, 149
Centre, J. 162
Chadwick, R. 86
Chapman, E. 84
Chen, E. A. 82
Cheng, M. M. 192
Chesley, G. M. 241, 249
Cheuk, J. 253–5
Childress, J. F. 61, 155
Chong, I. 141
Chorlton. M. C. 171
Christian, L. 186, 192, 199–200, 209
Cizek, B. 200
Clarke, A. 82, 175
Cline, T. 242, 252
Cohen, D. 254
Cohen, P. 248
Cohen, W. 175
Cole, S. S. 189
Cole, T. M. 189
Coleman, E. M. 130
Collins, B. C. 211
Conley, R. W. 124–5, 131
Connell, R. 196
Connor, D. 252–3
Cooke, L. B. 164
Cooper, S. A. 163, 175
Cooper, V. G. 134

Copeland, S. 248
Corbett, K. 195
Corker, M. 244
Couch, M. A. 19
Cox-Lindenbaum, D. 184, 210
Crabtree, S. A. 252–5
Craft, M. 221
Crone, D. A. 235
Cross, P. K. 85
Crossley, R. 146
Courtless, R. F. 130, 139
Culham, A. 244
Cummella, S. 161
Cummins, R. A. 190, 192, 202–4
Cunningham, C. E. 222
Curran, J. 172
Cuskelly, M. 201, 204–5
Cutts, S. 250

Dagnan, D. 174
Dahlgren, G. 159
Dalton, A. 174
Daly, M. 88
David, E. 47
Davies, G. 138, 147
Davies, S. P. 28
Davis, R. 171
Day, K. 130–1, 206
Deb, S. 163, 175
Degener, T. 43–4, 184, 208, 211
DeLoach, C. P. 202
Denkowski, G. C. 130
Denkowski, K. M. 130
Department of Justice Canada 245
Desjardin, G. 199–200
Devlieger, P. J. 97
Didden, R. 223, 230, 233
Di Giulio, G. 185, 199
Diggens, J. 175
Dinerstein, R. D. 62
Disability Rights International 31
Doe, T. 129, 210
Dominello, A. 166
Donaldson, J. 248
Donato, K. 240

Donnellan, A. 78, 223, 226-7
Dormandy, E. 86
Dotson, L. A. 186, 192
Doucette, J. 187
Drake, H. 86
Drapeau, M. 52
Dresser, R. 174
Drouin, M. S. 61
Ducharme, P. 196
Duff, R. 89-90
Duhaney, L. G. 254
Duignan, A. 160
Duker, P. C. 222
Dunn, C. 134
Duplessis, I. 46
Dura, J. R. 226
Durand, V. M. 223
Durvasula, S. 164
Dybwad, G. 28-9, 33, 38-9, 263
Dye, L. 174
Dyer, K. 228

Eckstein, C. M. 92
Edgerton, R. B. 37-8, 140
Edwards, N. 158, 161, 167, 170-1
Eigner, W. 90
Eklindh, K. 251
Elias, E. R. 188
Ellingson, S. A. 223
Elwork, A. 136
Emerson, E. 29-30, 269
Ericson, K. I. 135, 138, 140, 144-5, 148
Erickson, M. T. 222
Erwin, E. 254
Esquirol, J. E. D. 25-6
Esses, V. M. 138, 145
Evenhuis, H. M. 160, 164, 169
Everington, C. T. 134-5
Everson, M. D. 147
Exworthy, T. 134, 136
Eyman, R. K. 159, 163

Favell, J. C. 226
Fedoroff, B. 155
Fedoroff, J. P. 131, 155-6, 205
Feldman, M. 94, 184, 194, 204, 206, 219-20, 223, 226, 228-30, 232-3, 238
Ferri, B. 252-3
Ferronato, L. 194
Field, S. 190
Fiolet, J. 162
Fisher, C. B. 62

Fisher, D. 248, 250, 253-4
Fitch, W. L. 137
Flegel, K. M. 87
Fletcher, A. 81, 89
Fletcher, R. 167
Flowers, N. 15, 18
Flynn, M. C. 36, 140
Flynn, R. 78
Forbat, L. 34
Forlin, C. 252-4
Forness, S. R. 244, 249
Forsgren, L. 159, 162
Fox, L. 119, 234
Foxx, R. M. 226, 228
Frazee, C. L. 33, 240, 245-8, 250
Frederickson, N. 242, 252
Freeman, K.A. 227
Freeman, S. E. N. 241, 249
Freire, P. 15
Friedman, J. M. 159
Fuchs, D. 241, 243, 249
Fuchs, L.S. 241, 243, 249
Fyson, R. 274

Gadamer, H. G. 102, 109-12, 118
Gagne, R. 104-5
Gallego, M. 252
Galton, F. 77, 241
Gambioli, N. 125, 129, 140
Garbarino, J. 140-1, 146
Gardner, J. M. 222
Garner, K. 201
Garrick, M. 194
Garth, B. 94
Gartner, A. 241, 243, 248-9
Garwood, M. 196, 203-4
Gaston, M. A. 38
Gebherd, P. M. 195
Gensburg, L. J. 85
Geogioou, G. 253
Giangreco, M. F. 248
Gill, C. 97
Gill, F. 171
Gillespie, C. 38
Gillett, E. 271
Gillies, P. 189
Gillman, M. 36, 118-9
Glasson, E. J. 84-5
Glover, N. M. 86
Glover, S. J. 86
Goddard, H. H. 19, 77
Goguen, L. 245
Goodey, C. F. 23, 32, 39
Goodley, D. 36

Gostin, L. O. 80
Grace, N. C. 225
Gracey, C. 155
Grant, G. 36
Gratsa, A. 176
Greenberg, J. 264, 273
Gregory, J. 130
Griffiths, D. 15, 16, 23, 80, 83, 94, 124, 132, 142-3, 184-5, 187, 199-200, 205-7, 209-10, 211, 219, 269
Grover, S. 247
Grunewald, K. 29
Gruskin, S. 55, 58
Guess, D. 227
Guidry Tyiska, C. 187
Gural, M. 132
Gust, D. A. 188

Hagopian, L. P. 224-5, 232
Hahn, J. E. 175, 244
Haire, A. 162
Hampton, S. J. 85
Hand, J. 171-2
Handleman, J. S. 222
Hanley, G. P. 232
Hanson, B. 60, 62
Hard, S. 206
Hare. D. 174
Harris, J. 81-2, 87
Haseltine, B. 211
Hatch, J. A. 254-5
Hatton, C. 138, 271
Havercamp, S. M. 155, 163
Hayes, S. 130-31, 133
Hayman, R. L. 194
Haynes, M. 130
Heller, T. 171
Helmstetter, E. 248
Hendy, S. 174
Herbers, S. 15
Herr, S. 50, 62, 76
Hertzman, C. 246
Heshusius, L. 190
Hewitt, H. L. 118
Heyman, B. 36, 118-9
Hingsburger, D. 20-2, 38, 195, 198-9, 204, 269
Hoche, A. 88
Hodgetts, A. 130
Holland, A. J. 171
Hollander, R. 78, 88-9, 90
Hollins, S. 163, 172
Holmes, O. W. 185
Horgos, J. 185
Horner, R. H. 228

Horwitz, S. M. 167
Hubbard, R. 82, 85
Hughes, J. P. 85
Hunt, P. 50
Hunter, D. 161
Hurlbut, B. 222
Hurley, A. D. 141, 171

Iacono, T. 19, 173
Idol, L. 253
Ignatieff, M. 60
Iredale, L. 84
Irvine, A. C. 167, 191
Irwin, A. 167
Irwin, E. 158
Isaacs, B. J. 135, 138, 145
Iwata, B. A. 223

Jacob, G. 196
Jacobson, A. 187
Jancar, J. 161
Jansen, D. E. M. C. 19, 168
Jobling, A. 164
Johnson, K. 36, 80
Johnson, S. D. 138
Jones, L. 174
Jones, R. 138
Julien, M. 263
Jung, K. E. 244

Kaplan, D. 83, 87, 234
Kavale, K. A. 244, 249
Karrelou, J. 185, 201, 204
Kauffman, J. M. 241, 243, 249
Kazdin, A. E. 229
Kebbell, M. 138, 147
Kempton, W. 205
Kern, L. 228
Kerr, A. M. 86, 163
Kerr, M. G. 136
Kerr, M. P. 19, 94, 163
Khouri, R. P. 62
Kincaid, D. 119
King, R. 185, 190
Kirk, R. 254
Kishi, G. S. 248
Kitcher, P. 85
Klassen, K. 155
Klassen, R. 253
Klingner, J. K. 249
Kluth, P. 244
Kohan, H. 187
Kohlberg, L. 141
Koller, H. 193
Konstantareas, M. M. 202, 204
Korzilius, H. 223
Kotter, J. P. 273
Kristensen, K. 251-4

Kuhse, H. 95
Kuper, E. V. 203
Kuwon, H. 252–5

Lachapelle, Y. 60
Langdon, P. E. 201
LaVigna, G. W. 223, 226–7
Law, J. 169, 171
Lazaroff, K. 28
Leeder, S. R. 166
Lecomte, J. 43, 50
Leenen, H. J. J. 89
Lemay, R. A. 78
Lennox, N. G. 19, 94, 155, 158, 161, 164, 166–7, 169, 171, 175
Lerman, D. C. 226
Leondari, A. 248
Lesseliers, J. 193, 198, 203–4, 207
Lester, S. 35
Levitan, G. W. 93
Lewis, M. A. 160, 163
Leyser, Y. 254
Linscheid, T. R. 222
Lippman, A. 84
Lipsky, D. 241, 243, 248–9
Liu, A. N. C. 80
Livesay, J. 226
Llewellyn, G. 194
Löfgren-Mårtenson, L. 204, 207
Loftus, E. F. 142–3
Long, E. S. 223
Lowe, C. 160
Lucardie, R. 129
Luce, S. 228
Luckasson, R. 62, 91, 124-5, 129, 134–5
Ludwig, S. 142
Lumley, V. 185, 199, 211
Lunsky, Y. 155, 163, 175, 185, 199–200, 202, 204, 206
Luther, M. 88
Lyle, C. 113

Maaskant, M. A. 160, 162
Mahr, J. 173
Malacrida, C. 37
Mansell, J. 113, 121, 129
Mansell, S. 188-9
Marini, Z. 124, 132, 142–3
Marks, B. A. 171
Marmot, M. 158
Maron, M. 254–5

Marshall, H. H. 221
Marteau, T. M. 86
Martens, M. 174
Martin, D. 160
Martin, G. L. 160, 219, 222, 229
Massé, R. 56, 60, 63
Matson, J.L. 228
May, D. 193
Mazzucchelli, T. G. 16, 24
McAffe, J. 132
McBrien, J. 130
McCabe, M. P. 189–90, 192–3, 196, 199–200, 202–3, 204
McCarthy, J. 19
McCarthy, M. 163, 192, 195–6, 200
McCauley, C. 142
McConkey, R. 187, 206–7, 250
McConnell, D. 194
McCulloch, D. L. 160
McDonnell, J. 248
McElduff, A. 160, 162
McEwen, J. 189
McGee, J. 130, 137, 140, 148, 227
McIlwain, D. 131
McIntosh, R. 243
McVilly, K. 174
Medlar, T. 186
Meininger, H. P. 116–8, 120
Melville, C. 171
Menolascino, F. J. 130, 137, 140, 148
Mental Disability Rights International (MDRI) 31–2
Mercier, C. 43, 50, 113
Meyer, L. H. 248
Meyer, R. N. 190
Michael, J. 221
Middlesex Community Living 15
Millar, L. 171
Milligan, M. S. 199, 202–3, 205
Miltenberger, R. G. 211, 223
Miodrag, N. 184
Minnes, P. M. 199
Mittler, P. 90
Moll, L. 252
Molyneux, P. 163
Mona O'Moore, A. 248
Morris, C. 173-4
Moschella, S. 130, 139
Mostert, M. P. 146

Mount, B. 112, 234
Mu, K. 250
Murphy, J. 23
Murphy, N. A. 188
Murphy, W. D. 130
Murray, J. L. 199

Nakken, H. 244, 249
Narveson, J. 78–9
Nason, D. 254
Neiderbuhl, J. 173
Nelson, C. M. 211
Nettlebeck, T. 248, 254
Neufeldt, A. H. 199, 202–3, 205
Neuman, E. 33
Newsom, C. 226
Nind, M. 244
Nirje, B. 28–9, 38, 200
Noble, J. H. 76, 89, 131
Norbeck, J. 187
Nussbaum, M. C. 55

O'Brien, C. L. 30, 112
O'Brien, J. 112–3, 119–20
O'Donnell, L. 255
O'Flaherty, M. 48
O'Kelly, C. M. E. 138
Oliver, M. J. 30
Oliver, M. N. 201
Olney, M. F. 203
Olsen, C. L. 85
O'Neill, O. 34, 62, 227, 248, 276–7
Osler, A. 265
O'Sullivan, J. 62, 171
Otto, R. K. 134
Ouellette-Kuntz, H. 159, 161, 167

Owen, F. A. 15, 17, 23, 94, 201–2, 204, 208–9, 219, 256, 263, 276–7
Ozdowski, S. 23–4

Palmer, D. 254
Panitch, M. 188
Park, D. C. 28, 242, 263
Parmenter, T. R. 158
Patja, K. 159
Pear, J. J. 219, 222, 229
Peck, C. A. 248
Pedlar, A. 38
Peetsma, T. 250
Pelios, L. 225, 230, 232
Penney, J. 56
Perlman, N. B. 135, 138, 144–5
Perske, R. 16, 17, 173

Petersilia, J. 124, 129–30
Pezzoli, M. 248
Pfohl, S. 128
Philips-Nootens, S. 62
Pijl, S. J. 244, 249
Pike, G. 15
Plaute, W. 200–1, 203
Poirier, D. 245
Polkinghorne, D. 120
Pothier, P. 187
Prem-Stein, J. 125, 129, 140
Prince, M. A. 186
Principe, G. F. 142
Pritchard, M. 81
Proulx, D. 54
Purdy, L. M. 81

Quinn, G. 43–4, 184, 208, 211

Race, D. G. 30–1
Radford, J. P. 28, 242, 263
Radouco-Thomas, M. 163
Rainforth, B. 258
Ramcharan, P. 36
Ramdas, L. 15
Ramsey, P. 89
Rasmussen, S. A. 159
Rawls, J. 56
Read, J. 24, 37
Reese, R. M. 163
Regehr, K. 219, 231
Reichard, A. 171
Reid, D. H. 222
Reiman, J. 124
Reindal, S. M. 97
Reiss, S. 93, 157, 162, 171, 174
Reynold, M. C. 241
Reynolds, D. 91–3
Richards, D. 184–5, 190
Richler, D. 135
Ridington, J. 187
Rillotta, F. 248, 254
Rincover, A. 226
Rioux, M. H. 33, 53, 78, 186, 190, 206
Robertson, J. 160, 163
Robey, D. 264, 277
Rock, M. 174
Roeher Institute, The 23, 26–8, 86, 141, 145, 187, 209
Roets, G. 190
Roeyers, H. 248
Rogers, L. 16, 164
Rose, J. 171
Rosenthal, E. 52, 54, 149
Rosentall, E. 31–2

Rouleau, J. 130
Rousso, H. 204
Rowe, W. S. 187, 190, 194, 196, 198
Rubin, S. S. 160
Rueda, R. 252
Russell, O. 77, 84
Rutherford-Turnbull, H. 171
Ryan, D. 187, 206–7
Ryan, R. 93,
Ryba, N. L. 134

Salend, S. 254
Sales, C. 102, 263–4
Samowitz, P. 196–7
Santamour, W. 130
Santarcangelo, S. 228
Sapon-Shevin, M. 240, 244–8, 250
Savage, S. 187, 190, 194, 196, 198
Schalock, R. L. 62
Scheerenberger, R. C. 24–6, 28, 76–7, 87, 127, 263
Schein, E. 270
Schiffman, J. F. 82
Schindlmayr, T. 251
Schneider, R. D. 130
Schreck, A. 190
Schumm, J. S. 243
Schuster, J. W. 210
Schwartz, I. 257
Schwartz, L. D. 137
Scoggins, W. A. 273
Scott, A. 161
Scotti, J. R. 185, 199
Séguin, E. 2–6, 104–5
Selby, D. 15
Senge, P. 267–9
Servais, L. 190
Shakespeare, T. 82–3, 86, 97
Sheehan, S. 196–7, 207
Shelp, E. E. 87
Shevlin, M. 248
Shogren, K. A. 158, 176
Shriner, J. G. 248
Shurberg Klein. S. 195
Sidener, T. M. 228
Siebelink, E. M. 202, 204, 206
Siegel, A. M. 136
Siegel, E. 250
Sigafoos, J. 250
Simons, K. 274
Simpson, M. K. 193
Singer, P. 89, 95
Siska, J. 31
Skoutajan, H. F. 92
Smith, J. D. 28, 38
Smith, S. A. 148, 265

Smull, M. E. 234
Snellgrove, S. 257
Sobsey, D. 16, 28, 7–9, 88, 90–3, 124, 129–30, 142, 188–9, 209–10, 241–2, 267, 270
Solar, O. 158, 167
Sommi, R. 163
Soodak, L. 254
Sovner, R. 141
Sparks, B. 194
Speller, C. J. 161
Sperber, R. 142
Spreewenberg, L. 89
Stavis, P. F. 186, 197
Stedman, R. L. 79
Stainback, S. 243, 248
Stainback, W. 243, 248
Stenfert-Kroese, B. 171, 174, 271–2
Sternberg, R. J. 274–5
Stiker, H. J. 97
Stimpson, L. 188
Stinson, J. 186, 192, 199, 203
Stoner, K. 23, 256, 263, 277
Stott, F. M. 140–1, 146
Straiko, A. 175
Stratford, B. 241
Sudre, F. 52
Sullivan, S. G. 158, 161, 175
Sutherland, G. 19
Suzuki, D. 97
Swain, J. 36, 118–9
Szollos, A. A. 189–90, 192–3, 199–200, 204
Szyszko, J. 93, 157, 162, 171

Tanner, B. A. 222
Taras, M.E. 228
Tardif-Williams, C. Y. 17, 240, 249, 256, 263
Tarulli, D. 17, 23, 94, 102
Taylor, S. J. 24, 39
Temple, V. 160
Thomas, M. 163
Thomas, S. 245
Thompson, D. 195–6
Thousand, J. 244, 257
Ticoll, M. 78, 188
Timchuk, A. J. 194
Timmers, R. L. 196
Tohill, C. 162
Tooley, M. 89
Tones, K. 164
Tough, S. 199, 201–2, 204

Traustadottir, R. 193, 211
Trent, J. W. 2–7, 23, 104–5, 263
Trent-Kratz, M. 240
Trudel, G. 199–200
Turnbull, D. 82–3, 86–7
Turnbull, H. R. 226–7
Tyler, V. Jr. 221

Udry, J. R. 192
UNESCO 251
United Nations Convention on the Rights of Persons with Disabilities (2006) 263
United Nations Convention on the Rights of People with Disabilities (2007) 32, 34, 63–7, 127
United Nations Declaration on the Rights of Mentally Retarded Persons (1971) 33, 77
United Nations Declaration on the Rights of Disabled Persons (1975) 33
United Nations Universal Declaration of Human Rights (1948) 32, 76
Unwin, G. 175
U.S. Dept. of Health and Human Services 19

Valencia Declaration of Sexual Rights 189
Valenti-Hein, D. C. 137
Van den Akker, M. 160, 162
Van der Gaag, A. 168
Van der Wal, G. 89
Van Eijk, J. T. 89
Van Houten, R 224
Van Hove, G. 190, 193, 198, 200, 203–4, 207
Van Schrojenstein Lantman-de Valk, H. M. J. 160, 162
Vann, B. H. 31
Varnhagen, C. 91, 129–30
Vaughn, S. 243
Vause, T. 219
Villa, R. 244
Volosinov, V. N. 120
Vorndran, C. M. 226

Vyrostko, B. 263

Wagmans, A. 162
Walberg, H. J. 241, 249
Walmsley, J. 24, 36–7, 195
Wang, M. C. 241, 243, 249
Ward, M. J. 190
Wasburn-Moses, L. 252
Watson, S. L. 76, 80, 83, 184, 197, 209
Web, O. J. 164
Weber, K. 241–5, 252–5
Wehmeyer, M. L. 60, 104–5, 107–8, 114–5, 117
Werner, S. E. 233
Westling, D. L. 200
Wessman, L. 29
West, B. 130
White, C. 272
White, M. R. 84
Whitehead, M. 159
Whitehouse, M. A. 189, 196
Widaman, K. 254
Wiener, J. 249
Wilbur, H. 105
Williamson, H. J. 241
Wilson, C. 91, 129–30
Wilson, D. N. 162
Wilson, G. T. 289
Wilson, M. 88
Winzer, M. 241–2, 245, 250
Wish, J. 202
Witcombe, D. 143
Withers, P. 211
Williamson, L. 87
Wolbring, G. 78
Wolfe, P. S. 200
Wolfensberger, W. 28–30, 90, 93–4, 97, 185, 200, 208, 242, 245, 269
Woodhouse, J. M. 160

Yagel, S. 84
Yang, Q. 159
Yarmol, K. 190
Yell, M. L. 248
Yool, L. 201
Younglove, J. A. 136

Zapf, P A. 134
Zieler, M. 222
Zigmond, N. 243
Ziviani, J. 164
Zwernik, K. 234